M000205381

TAILORED GARMENTS

ESSENTIALS OF TAILORING
TAILORED BUTTONHOLES, BUTTONS, AND TRIMMINGS
TAILORED POCKETS
TAILORED SEAMS AND PLACKETS
TAILORED SKIRTS
TAILORED BLOUSES AND FROCKS
TAILORED SUITS, COATS, AND CAPES
GARMENTS FOR MEN AND BOYS

1926

British Library Cataloguing-in-Publication Data
A catalogue record for this book is available from the
British Library

Dressmaking and Tailoring

Dressmaking and Tailoring broadly refers to those who make, repair or alter clothing for a profession. A dressmaker will traditionally make custom clothing for women, ranging from dresses and blouses to full evening gowns (also historically called a mantua-maker or a modiste). Whereas a tailor will do the same, but usually for men's clothing - especially suits. The terms essentially refer to a specific set of hand and machine sewing skills, as well as pressing techniques that are unique to the construction of traditional clothing. This is separate to 'made to measure', which uses a set of pre-existing patterns. Usually, a bespoke tailored suit or dress will be completely original and unique to the customer, and hence such items have been highly desirable since the trade first appeared in the thirteenth century. The Oxford English Dictionary states that the word 'tailor' first came into usage around the 1290s, and undoubtedly by this point, tailoring guilds, as well as those of cloth merchants and weavers were well established across Europe.

As the tailoring profession has evolved, so too have the methods of tailoring. There are a number of distinctive business models which modern tailors may practice, such as 'local tailoring' where the tailor is met locally, and the garment is produced locally too, 'distance tailoring', where a garment is ordered from an out-of-town tailor, enabling cheaper labour to be used - which, in practice can now be done on a global scale via e-commerce websites, and a 'travelling tailor', where the man or woman will travel between cities, usually stationing in a luxury hotel to provide the client the same tailoring services they would provide in their local store. These processes are the same for both women's and men's garment making.

Pattern making is a very important part of this profession; the construction of a paper or cardboard template from which the parts of a garment are traced onto fabric before cutting our and assembling. A custom dressmaker (or tailor) frequently employs one of three pattern creation methods; a 'flat-pattern method' which begins with the creation of a sloper or block (a basic pattern for a garment, made to the wearer's measurements), which can then be used to create patterns for many styles of garments, with varying necklines, sleeves, dart placements and so on. Although it is also used for womenswear, the 'drafting method' is more commonly employed in menswear and involves drafting a pattern directly onto pattern paper using a variety of straightedges and curves. Since menswear rarely involves draping, pattern-making is the primary preparation for creating a cut-and-sew woven garment. The third method, the 'pattern draping method' is used when the patternmaker's skill is not matched with the difficulty of the design. It involves creating a muslin mock-up pattern, by pinning fabric directly on a dress form, then transferring the muslin outline and markings onto a paper pattern or using the muslin as the pattern itself.

Dressmaking and tailoring has become a very well respected profession; dressmakers such as Pierre Balmain, Christian Dior, Cristóbal Balenciaga and Coco Chanel have gone on to achieve international acclaim and fashion notoriety. Balmain, known for sophistication and elegance, once said that 'dressmaking is the architecture of movement.' Whilst tailors, due to the nature of their profession - catering to men's fashions, have not garnered such levels of individual fame, areas such as 'Savile Row' in the United Kingdom are today seen as the heart of the trade.

PREFACE

Time was when the word *tailoring* called to mind heavy, woolen materials, and heavy-appearing seams and finishes. But today, silks, lawns, and dimities, and even voiles and Georgettes, have tailored seams and edges, so that tailoring, as it is known now, is one of the vital parts of dressmaking.

This book treats of the subject of tailoring in its broad, present-day meaning, one section dealing with buttonholes, buttons, and trimmings that are suitable for many materials and garments. The making of tailored buttonholes can become as significant a task as building a brick wall, or shingling a roof, or building a fortress. Each stitch, as with stones or shingles, is placed for permanent security. It has its definite place and must fit in against the others with ease and accuracy in order that a serviceable buttonhole may result.

A whole section devoted to skirt-making may seem inconsistent with the commonly recognized theory that skirts that give evidence or emphasize the waist line are incorrect in line. But the sports skirt and the tailored skirt as a part of a coat suit will always find a place in the well-dressed woman's wardrobe; so, to know how to make all kinds of skirts, full or narrow, straight or circular, plain or plaited, one-piece or many-gored, is essential to a complete sewing knowledge.

When a garment is ready for its inserted pocket, or pockets, it has arrived at the first door of destiny, for upon the success of the pockets depend the care and deliberate pains with which the remainder of the garment is completed. There is a feeling of responsibility when a pocket is to be made—to the skilled worker a delightful responsibility, to the less sure, an anxious one. But the moment the stitched slash is cut and the edges are turned, pride takes the place of concern; and from that stage to the last, the work will be interesting and painstakingly done. So skill should be at one's command at this vital moment.

Usually, a desire for tailored garments goes hand in hand with neatness, so that perfect harmony is naturally attained. Puckered ruffles are permissible, but tailored stitching must travel as straight as an arrow, as is reiterated many times in the pages of this book.

CONTENTS

v

CONTENTS

CHAPTER I

ESSENTIALS OF TAILORING

SCOPE OF TAILORING

1. What is Tailoring?—Tailoring is one of the foremost of the sewing arts, because more than two-thirds of the garments worn require some form of tailoring. It really is a recognized trade followed by many hundreds of people, men especially. Time, patience, and a knowledge of both garment construction and materials are essential in one's training for tailoring.

Until about a half century ago, many materials were of a very heavy quality, so that much care had to be given to their assembling, basting, steaming, and pressing to obtain good-looking results. Today, with the weaver's art so perfected that exquisite fabrics are offered on all sides, very inexpensively priced in proportion to quality, the responsibility is reversed. Now, one needs not so much to beautify the fabric by careful sewing as to do justice to its beauty by sewing it as perfectly as possible. When much sewing, basting, and pressing, especially machine sewing, must be done, the work properly comes under the head of tailoring—a word frequently misunderstood.

Many persons, in thinking of tailoring, think only of suits with padding and heavy seams, braid-trimmed skirts, and linings throughout. But today, one tailors a silk, machine-made blouse, a sports skirt, or a simple frock of linen or flannel. Sheer materials, fine silks, and laces must always be reserved for lingerie sewing or dressmaking, but all other moderately firm fabrics that require the friendship of sponge cloth and iron and that demand basting and straight, perfect stitching, may safely be classed with tailoring materials.

2. Necessity for Good Equipment.—Making tailored garments is often regarded a much more difficult task than making fluffy, frilly ones, but this is not necessarily the case.   True, tailoring is not of the sewing-basket variety.   One must spread all pieces out on a flat surface, cut all seam edges neatly, join all edges accurately, and baste with a definite precision.   But none of these is a difficult process nor requires any more effort than work on lingerie garments, particularly if the right sort of equipment is chosen.

In addition to the special equipment mentioned later, be sure to have a cutting board or table, on which both cutting and basting may be done; a firm, well-padded ironing board; shears that are sharp; and a machine that is well regulated as to stitch, an elastic, medium-long stitch proving best, because tailoring materials are usually fairly heavy and by their thickness shorten the stitch somewhat.   Also, have your brush (a substantial clothes brush is satisfactory, or a tailor's brush is even more desirable) washed and kept perfectly clean for lifting the nap on fabrics when, by accident, it is pressed too flat with too hot an iron.   Number 7 or 8 sewing needles are usually best for tailoring.   Silk thread should always be used, for it presses better and breaks less often than cotton thread.

3. Requisites of Good Tailoring.—In tailoring, very accurate patterns are almost a necessity, for in materials that are even slightly heavy, perfect seams are necessary.   Irregular seams might go unnoticed in a voile dress that is full and easy, but in a linen dress, because of its very plainness, a jagged or an uneven seam will spoil the whole appearance.

A good tailor always sponges and shrinks his material, so that the seams of the garment will not shrink unevenly in the process of making nor spot or shrink from dampness when it is worn.   Of course, all woolen materials are shrunk, or sponged, in the process of manufacture; nevertheless, in spite of the fact that merchants in some cases insist that certain materials do not have to be treated in this manner, it is advisable to do so, because materials that are kept in stock become relaxed and need to be responged to be in condition for cutting.   In the large cities, it is possible to have the cloth shrunk by the merchant from whom it is purchased, usually at a small additional cost per yard; but in the smaller cities and towns, the stores, as a rule, are not equipped to carry on such work, and it must of necessity be done at home.

4. With the material shrunk and the perfection of his pattern determined, a tailor marks each side exactly alike so that the pattern pieces will go together perfectly. Next, he bastes with as much care as though the garment were to be made by hand. Before he starts to stitch, he tries a scrap of two thicknesses of material under the presser foot to satisfy himself that the machine is free of dripping oil, that the stitch is easy and of the right length, that the tension is free enough, that the machine needle is smooth and perfect at its point, and that the needle itself is correctly set. With these precautions, neat satisfying work is sure to result and a pride be developed that will make tailoring a real joy and inspiration.

TAILORING EQUIPMENT

5. So that the best results may be obtained in the development of tailored garments, a certain amount of equipment is necessary. As many of these articles are in common use in the home, first see what equipment you have on hand that may be utilized, and then provide as much new equipment as you consider essential for your purpose. The various kinds of tailoring equipment are considered here, for even though some of these are not an actual necessity for home use, all are a decided convenience. Then, too, it is important that you gain a very clear understanding of their appearance and use so that if you are ever called upon to do such work you will be familiar with all the equipment.

6. Sponge and Press Cloths.—If you intend to do much pressing, you will find one sponge or, better still, a medium-size sponge and two press cloths, a convenience. These cloths should be used for no other purpose than sponging and pressing materials and garments in the making.

Firm, unbleached muslin or light-weight duck or drilling is suitable for *sponge cloths*, ¼ to ½ yard of this being sufficient for each one. Take the precaution not to have the *press cloths* linty nor too sheer. For each *press cloth*, provide about 1½ yards of unbleached muslin. It is not necessary to hem any of these pieces, but, if you wish, you may pink or overcast the raw edges to prevent them from raveling.

7. In order to remove the filling that is put in when the material is woven, boil the cloths before using them in fairly strong soapsuds to which a pinch of baking soda has been added. This precaution should always be taken, because new muslin scorches readily and because it is almost impossible for the new material to absorb sufficient water to be of any service in sponging if the filling is not removed.

8. Brushes.—In sponging and pressing materials, and especially in dampening the press cloths, to avoid making them too wet, you will find a *small brush* invaluable. This may be of the type commonly used for cleaning vegetables, one about 4 inches long and 2 inches wide, with strong bristles ½ to ¾ inch long and an unvarnished back that may be washed, being suitable. Such brushes are very inexpensive and will last indefinitely.

9. Another desirable article is a *tailor's brush,* which is a heavy brush with a long handle and a flat top. It is useful in both pressing and steaming garments, the back of it to beat down heavy seams or any thick places and the bristles to aid in sending steam through the material and keeping its nap up. Such brushes may be purchased in any tailors' supply house. The wooden part of the brush must be unfinished, or unvarnished, however; if it is varnished, there is always danger of ruining garments on which it is used because of the fact that the steam generated in pressing and steaming garments will soften the varnish.

10. An ordinary *whisk broom*, too, should be on hand for this work, as it is valuable for raising the nap of material when steaming garments if something stiffer than a brush is required. It is useful, also, in pressing materials that have a very long nap, as such nap must always be brushed straight before pressing.

11. Irons.—In order to obtain the best results in the pressing of woolen materials, a heavy iron is essential. As a rule, the *flat irons* used in the home come in sets of three; it is the heaviest of these three that is most suitable for such work. A medium-sized or large *electric iron,* the kind commonly in use in the home, because of its weight, is even better for tailoring than an ordinary flat iron.

12. An iron much heavier than an ordinary flat iron and known as a *tailor's goose* is considered a necessity in tailoring establishments. This may be had in weights ranging from 16 to 24 pounds.

13. Ironing Board.—For pressing and sponging, or shrinking, woolen materials, a smooth, well-padded *ironing board* of good size is an absolute necessity; that is, one at least 5 feet long and 12 to 14 inches wide, so that it will accommodate practically any skirt.

Many persons are of the opinion that an ironing board requires but little padding; such is not the case, however, for to get the best results sufficient padding should be used to give a firm, smooth surface. Light-colored, worn woolen blankets make the best padding for an ironing board, especially a board on which woolen materials are to be pressed, because the wool has a tendency to "give" under the material that is being pressed, thus making possible a softer, smoother-pressed finish than would otherwise be the case. If wool for padding is not procurable, a worn cotton blanket may be used, or, if desired, very heavy flannelette may be purchased for the purpose. The chief essential is to have each thickness of padding in one piece, so as to avoid seams or ridges on the padded board. As a rule, the padding should be from $\frac{1}{4}$ to $\frac{3}{8}$ inches thick.

The covering for an ironing board should be made of unbleached muslin of a medium quality. New muslin that has been washed is best, because it has very little lint. Old sheets make an excellent covering for an ironing board on which light-colored wash garments are to be ironed and pressed, but a covering with any sign of lint should always be avoided where dark materials, especially woolens, are to be pressed.

14. Small holders for stretching and keeping in place both the padding and the covering of an ironing board may be purchased in sets of four or six at a very low cost. These holders are excellent for stretching out every wrinkle and for holding the padding permanently in place. However, if they cannot be procured, the board may be padded and covered as follows:

Stretch both the padding and the covering over the board, one at a time, just as tight as possible, and tack them in place on the underneath side, placing a tack every 2 or 3 inches so as to make sure of holding the material in place. To get the best results in the covering of a board, the padding and the covering should be at least 2 or 3 inches larger in every way than the top of the ironing board. Begin by tacking the middle of the pieces of material to the middle of the board; that is, the center of each end and the center of each edge. Tack, first, one end; then draw the material across tight and tack the other end; next, tack one edge and then the other, drawing the covering and padding materials tight in each instance. Next, draw the corners of the material to their respective corners and tack them in place, stretching the materials well along the lines leading to the middle tacks. With this done, fasten the rest of the padding in place, putting tacks between those already in place. This method obviates the gathering of fulness at any point, which would result in wrinkles otherwise impossible to work out.

15. Sleeve Board.—After the seams of a sleeve of woolen or of silk material have been joined, it is difficult to press them open without considerable care and effort or to press the sleeve satisfactorily in its entirety without the use of a sleeve board.

A sleeve board should be padded and covered in practically the same manner as an ironing board. It should be slender and on a substantial stand, if possible.

16. Edge and Seam Pressers.—An *edge press block*, which consists of a piece of hard wood, ¾ to 1 inch in thickness, mounted edgewise on a stand and pointed at each end, is a great convenience for the pressing open of the seam that joins the facing to a coat. This board is used without padding. The pointed ends make it possible to push the board well up into the corners of the revers and thus permit a tailored effect that it is difficult to obtain otherwise.

For home tailoring, a thin piece of hard wood may be substituted for the edge press block. Cut this ¾ to 1 inch wide, point it at the ends, and sand paper it until it is perfectly smooth.

17. A *covered broom stick* may be used to excellent advantage in the pressing of seams, especially in materials that require unusual care in handling in order to prevent them from becoming shiny. With the seam laid over the curved surface of the broom stick, it is possible to press only the center of the seam and prevent the outer seam edges from forming a ridge or shiny line on the right side of the fabric.

To prepare a broom stick for a seam presser, pad it with a thin layer of cotton or wind it with soft rags, being careful to distribute the thickness very evenly; then cover the padding with muslin, stretching this as tight as possible, and whip one turned edge over the other edge so as to secure it.

18. A *velvet presser*, which is a device consisting of a board set with firm, fine, wire projections, or teeth, closely laid, makes it possible to press velvet or other napped fabrics without flattening the pile and makes unnecessary the steaming method that must otherwise be employed.

To use such a presser, place the fabric, face down, on the presser, so that the nap is downward on the teeth of the presser. Then put a slightly dampened cloth on the back of the fabric and press it with a medium-hot iron. This pressing will send the steam through the pile and raise it and, at the same time, remove any wrinkles in the velvet.

19. Ham Cushion.—For the pressing of curved seams, such as the bust and shoulder seams of coats and dresses and the hip seams of coats and skirts, there is perhaps no better device than what is commonly known by tailors as a *ham cushion;* in fact, no custom-tailoring establishment is complete without one. Such a cushion, which is illustrated in Fig. 1, consists simply of a covering of white tailors' felt carefully stuffed with rags. Ham cushions can be purchased in tailors' supply houses, but a cushion that will prove to be just as serviceable and much less expensive can be made in the home.

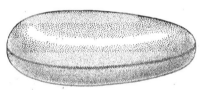

Fig. 1

20. For a ham cushion, purchase at a tailors' supply house ⅝ yard of 36-inch white tailors' felt. Such felt is very durable, and while it is firm it is not so compact as the felt used for upholstery or for shoes and hats. The small pieces of felt that remain after cutting out the covering need not be wasted, for they can be used to make a cushion one-fourth as large as the other, which will be found very useful as it can be used inside of sleeves, under the armhole seam, and in many places where the large one might be too large or too unhandy. In addition to the felt, provide sufficient heavy muslin or galatea for an interlining and enough clean, old woolen rags for stuffing. Rags from old woolen shirts, coats, or blankets are satisfactory, provided all hard spots are removed.

21. In order to cut out the covering and the interlining for a ham cushion, develop a pattern in the manner shown in Fig. 2, as follows: Fold lengthwise through the center a piece of paper that is 14 inches wide and 21 inches long, and, then, with the folded edge next to you, locate the necessary points for outlining the pattern. Locate point A 1 inch from the right edge of the paper; point B 19 inches to the left of A on the fold; point C 6 inches directly above B; and point D 6 inches directly above A. Then draw lines from A to D, from C to B, and from D to C. To locate points to be used as an aid in drawing the curves, place point B_2 1½ inches

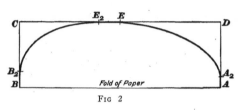

Fig 2

above B on line BC; point A_2 1 inch above A on line AD; point E midway between C and D; and point E_2 2 inches to the left of E. Then connect B_2 and E_2, as well as E and A_2, with a well-curved line, as shown in the illustration, being careful to avoid forming points at B_2, E_2, E, and A_2.

To form the pattern, which, when cut out, should be egg-shaped, cut through both thicknesses of paper, from B through B_2 to E_2, and from E_2 through E and A_2 to A.

22. When the pattern is cut out, place the lengthwise center on a double thickness of the felt folded to produce a true bias and cut out the cushion covering. Cutting the material on the true bias will enable you to shape the cushion more easily. Do not allow for seams, as the edges of the felt must be whipped together, as shown in Fig. 1. Also cut out the interlining, using the same pattern, but allowing ⅜-inch seams on all edges.

With the material cut out, the next process will be to seam the interlining together with the exception of a small opening to admit the filling, and then prepare the filling. To make the filling, tear and cut into small pieces old woolen rags that are free from hard seams, and dampen these bits of material a trifle so that they will pack very tight. Then proceed to stuff them into the interlining, being careful to pack the rags even and close, so that the outside will be smooth and firm. After making sure that the interlining is stuffed as full as possible and will keep its shape, close the opening of the interlining with diagonal basting and then overhand it closely.

With the interlining thus prepared, place the felt over it, and then, drawing the edges together, overhand them closely, keeping the surface absolutely smooth and as tight as possible. Put such a cushion, after making, in the sun, near the stove or on a radiator so that the rags that have been dampened may become thoroughly dry. Of course, if the cushion is put into use at once, the heat from the iron will dry it sufficiently.

23. Cheese Block.—When it is desired to press seams very flat and hard or to make them scarcely visible, it is well to use a press block, commonly called a *cheese block,* one style of which is shown in Fig. 3. Such a block consists of a piece of 3-inch oak that measures 18 inches on the straight side and 14 inches across,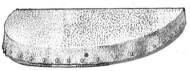

FIG. 3

and is covered with two thicknesses of tailors' felt stretched just as tight as possible and tacked in place on the block, as shown.

24. Tailors' Press Stand.—Another device used in pressing tailored work is the *tailors' press stand* shown in Fig. 4. Such a stand may be made to take the place of a ham cushion, and as it has a sleeve board attached, as at *a*, it has a double utility value. A tailors' press stand is usually 28 inches long, 7 inches high, and 10 inches wide. It is, however, much more difficult and expensive to make than a ham cushion, and, on account of its weight, it is much more difficult to handle.

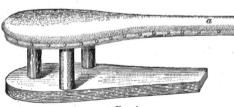

FIG. 4

25. Pinking Knife or Pinking Machine.—*Pinking,* which consists of a series of notches or small scallops in plain or fancy effects, is a finish sometimes used in place of hand notching for finishing seam edges. It may also be employed in place of picoting as a trimming or as a finish for ruffles or petticoat flounces that are made of sateen or firmly woven silk.

Pinking is done by means of a specially constructed knife or small hand machine. Machines with which to do pinking make a very valuable addition to a sewing or tailoring outfit; in fact, in shops where considerable work is done, a pinking machine is practically invaluable. It is usually provided with three blades, one for cutting a very small notch, one for cutting a medium-sized notch, and the other for cutting a fancy notch that may be used for trimming. The directions for operating such a machine are usually contained in the book of instructions that accompanies it. A pinking knife is rather tedious to use if very much pinking is done, for each scallop must be cut separately. However, with a pinking machine, a considerable amount of pinking can be done in a few minutes.

26. *To use a pinking knife,* first place the seam edge that is to be pinked on a block of *hard* wood. Begin at one end of the seam. Place the cutting end of the knife so that the extreme outer edge of the scalloped portion is at the outer edge of the seam. Strike the upper end of the knife with a small hammer, giving it a hard blow. If one blow is not sufficient to cut the seam edge, strike the knife again, taking care, however, that the position of the knife is not changed.

In this way, cut each scallop separately, placing the knife each time so that the scallops will be in an even, continuous line.

SHRINKING WOOLEN MATERIALS

27. Equipment for Shrinking.—To obtain the best results in the shrinking of woolen materials, a *board* or *roller* covered with muslin and a piece of *unbleached muslin* from which all the filling has been removed are required. In tailoring establishments, a roller is considered practically indispensable, but as such rollers are in some places difficult to procure or too expensive to be practical for the home dressmaker, the use of a board as a substitute for the roller is advisable.

The board should be thin, about 10 inches wide, and of a length equal to the width of the cloth, provided it is single-width, or to the width of the folded cloth, provided it is double-width. Also, it should have rounded edges to prevent the formation of creases in the material. The muslin must be about 1 yard longer than the cloth and a little wider than single-width cloth, or just a little greater in width than the distance from the fold to the selvage of double-width material.

Both single- and double-width materials are treated in the same manner, the double-width goods being left folded lengthwise through the center, just as it is when purchased.

28. Usual Method of Shrinking.—First of all, to prevent the selvages of the woolen material from drawing, clip them at intervals of 1 to 1¼ inches, or, better still, tear them off entirely. Then, wet the muslin thoroughly and wring it out enough to distribute the moisture evenly. An even distribution of moisture is very important in such work, for if the muslin is too wet in some places it will cause the formation of spots that are difficult to remove.) Next, spread the cloth that is to be shrunk across the top of a large table and place the wet muslin over it, smoothing out the wrinkles of each very carefully. Wrinkles must not be allowed to form in shrinking, because it is almost impossible to remove them. With the materials thus laid out, put the board on top of one end of the muslin, pin or hold the cloth and the muslin together along one side of the board, and be sure to have the weave in the cloth straight with the board. Then begin to roll them on the board, but not too tight, being sure to smooth out the wrinkles ahead of each turn, to keep the materials straight on the board, and to adjust the muslin at the ends so that it will come well over the cloth.

After the material is thus rolled, allow it to remain on the board for 4 to 6 hours. Then unroll it, remove the muslin, and spread the cloth out so that it may dry thoroughly. For drying, you may spread the cloth on a large table, or, if such a table is not available, hang it over the top of a door. If a door must be used for this purpose, put several thicknesses of newspaper across its top before hanging up the cloth, so as to cover the sharp corners. If they are not covered in this way, the corners will cause water marks to form on the cloth, and such marks are almost impossible to remove. It is also well to put paper on each side of the door, so as to prevent the cloth from touching it.

29. If care is taken in the placing of the material over the board and then in the drying of it, no pressing will be required. In case any creases, or wrinkles, are evident, remove these by laying a slightly dampened press cloth over them on the wrong side and then pressing lightly over the dampened cloth with a moderately hot iron. In pressing, work up and down, that is, with the warp threads of the fabric, so as to avoid drawing it out of shape; but keep the iron moving almost constantly in a slightly rotary motion. Also, lift some of the weight of the iron as you move it from one spot to another, in order to avoid forming ridges or lines on the surface of the fabric.

30. Shrinking Glossy-Surface Materials.—Although the method just given is suitable for shrinking all kinds of materials, there are some tailors who prefer the following method for the shrinking of fabrics that have a glossy surface, as in the case of broadcloth. Place the material, right side down, across the ironing board; lay over it a muslin press cloth which should first be dipped in water and then wrung out well; and then run a hot iron over the muslin several times. Remove the muslin from the cloth next, and press the material until the full length is sponged and pressed. When the shrinking, or sponging, is completed, go over all the material carefully with an iron to make sure that there are no wrinkles.

31. Shrinking Light-Weight Woolens.—It is very necessary to be careful in the sponging and pressing of light-weight woolen materials so as not to stretch the edges. These should be kept straight both in width and in length. If too hot an iron or too much water is used on very light woolens, such as challis or nun's veiling, the cloth will show a decided tendency to pucker. However, puckering must be avoided, because a smooth cloth is absolutely necessary for accurate cutting.

CHAPTER II

TAILORED BUTTONHOLES, BUTTONS, AND TRIMMINGS

TAILORED BUTTONHOLES

CHARACTERISTICS AND TYPES

1. A **buttonhole** is a slit in a garment made to receive a button. A tailored buttonhole, which is one that is used in tailored garments, differs from a plain buttonhole in several ways, although it is intended for the same simple purpose. / In the first place, it is generally larger, and as it is subject to greater strain it must be made firmer, thus calling for heavier thread. Such a buttonhole does not shape itself around the button when used as a fastening, so it must have an eyelet at the front end to provide a resting place for the shank of the button or for the thread that holds the button in place on the garment and to permit the buttonhole to come down smooth on the button, a really essential feature. In addition, the tailored buttonhole must almost invariably have a bar at the end opposite the eyelet to give it strength and to present a substantial appearance.)

2. Above all, tailored buttonholes must be neatly and correctly made. The tailored garment that is perfect in every other particular will have an amateurish appearance if its buttonholes are poorly cut and improperly worked. Tailors and other persons in the trade take great pride in the buttonholes they make, and many of them judge the skill of another by the buttonholes alone. One way, and sometimes the only way, of determining whether a suit is factory- or custom-made is by observing the manner in which the buttonholes are made, that is, whether they are hand-done. It should therefore be the aim of every woman who desires garments that

13

are above the ordinary, to give particular attention to the tailored buttonholes she works in them.

3. Position and Types of Buttonholes.—Tailored buttonholes are generally cut so as to be horizontal—that is, perpendicular to the edge of a garment—and in rare cases they are placed so as to be diagonal, or slanting. Seldom, if ever, are they made vertical, that is, parallel with the edge of a garment, because such buttonholes do not hold the buttons so well as do the others and they are not in harmony with the strictly tailored lines of a tailored garment.

Although there is only one true tailored buttonhole, namely, that which is worked with buttonhole twist and buttonhole-stitches, certain others are classed as tailored buttonholes, because they are often placed on tailored garments. These are known as the *simulated buttonhole,* which consists simply of stitches made on the material for trimming purposes in imitation of a buttonhole, no slit being used; the *material-bound buttonhole,* that is, the one that has the cut edges bound with material; and the *braid-bound buttonhole,* which has the cut edges bound with braid, usually military braid.

4. Making Perfect Buttonholes.—The making of perfect buttonholes demands practice and the use of proper tools and materials. The woman unaccustomed to making buttonholes will do well to practice until she is able to make perfectly uniform stitches, both as to depth and distance apart, and has mastered the art, for it is indeed an art, of cutting, basting, stitching, overcasting, stranding, and working a perfect buttonhole.

The tools and materials required for the making of buttonholes, as well as the various steps that are necessary for perfect workmanship, are taken up in detail in this Chapter. After the woman has had sufficient practice and has acquired a knowledge of the steps and tools and materials, she need have no hesitancy in undertaking the making of any tailored buttonhole. In fact, she will be inclined to look forward to the time of cutting and working buttonholes, as, for instance, in a coat that has been painstakingly done, as not only an important event, but one that will not be enjoyed unless full preparation has been made beforehand for every detail of the work and each step and tool is fully understood. But as hand-worked buttonholes take time, they should be used chiefly on good materials, concealed fasteners being employed on cheap materials.

BUTTONHOLE TOOLS AND MATERIALS

5. Buttonhole Cutters.—A pair of buttonhole cutters, an example of which is shown in Fig. 1, is an invaluable tool for cutting tailored buttonholes. Such a tool is constructed so as to cut slits and eyelets with one operation, as well as ordinary slits, such as are made with a pair of buttonhole scissors, thus insuring buttonholes that are absolutely uniform. The initial cost of such a tool is rather high, but in a shop or in other places where many tailored buttonholes must be made it works a great economy because it cuts buttonholes quickly and accurately.

At first glance, a buttonhole cutter may seem like a mysterious device for the cutting of so commonplace a thing as a buttonhole;

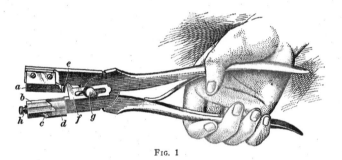

Fig. 1

but it is really very simple when all its parts are understood. As will be observed, there is on one side a knife, or cutting blade, *a,* directly behind which is an eyelet punch *e,* and on the other side a base *b,* against which the knife and punch are pressed in cutting. This base is cylindrical and is made so that it can be turned and fastened in place. This cylindrical base usually has ten irregular sections, as at *c* and *d,* and it is the length and the position of each of these sections that control the length of the buttonhole and permit buttonholes to be cut with or without eyelets. At *f* is a guide bar that serves to regulate the distance of the eyelet from the edge of the garment in cutting, a thumbscrew *g* being used to fasten this bar in place. At *h* is another thumbscrew, which fastens the base of the cutter in place when it is turned to a position that will give the length and kind of buttonhole desired.

In cutting a buttonhole with a tool of this kind, place the material over the cylindrical base and push the guide bar, properly adjusted, up against the edge of the garment; then bring the blade and punch down over the material resting on the base by pressing the handles of the cutter together. With a little experimenting, no difficulty will be encountered in adjusting and using the cutter for any length of buttonhole ranging from $\frac{1}{2}$ inch to $1\frac{1}{4}$ inches. Before using the cutter on a garment, it is advisable to prepare a strip of three thicknesses of material and cut a number of buttonholes, spacing them for a certain length and a certain distance apart and adjusting the cutter so as to cut both the eyelet and the straight buttonhole.

6.   Buttonhole Scissors and Punches.—Buttonhole scissors may be used for cutting tailored buttonholes, but they must be very sharp and, after making the slit, it is necessary to form the eyelet with a punch. An ordinary eyelet punch, or awl, such as is used by harnessmakers to punch holes in leather, is satisfactory for this purpose. In cutting a buttonhole with buttonhole scissors and an eyelet punch, take particular pains to have the eyelet directly in line with the buttonhole slit. If it is a fraction of an inch too high or too low, it will spoil the shape of the finished buttonhole.

7.   Buttonhole Gimp.—As tailored buttonholes are subject to considerable wear, they must necessarily be made durable. For this reason, as well as to give a firm finished edge to a buttonhole, the edge should be stranded with what is known as buttonhole gimp. Buttonhole gimp, which is made in black and white, consists of very firm, small cotton cord closely wound with silk thread, being similar in appearance to fine, silk-covered hat wire. It is a scant $\frac{1}{16}$ inch in diameter and very firm. It may be purchased at nearly all notion counters and tailors' supply houses.

8.   Stranding Thread.—If it is not convenient to use buttonhole gimp or if the material in which the buttonhole is to be worked is not very heavy, a stranding thread, which may be made of heavy linen thread, will serve the purpose very well; in fact, some persons consider it to be even better than gimp, because it is softer and thus prevents the working thread from wearing through readily.

9.   To make stranding thread, thread a needle with a convenient length of linen thread, say $1\frac{1}{2}$ to $1\frac{3}{4}$ yards, bringing the ends together just as if making ready to sew with a double thread. Then wax this thread with beeswax, which may be purchased at any notion counter, carrying the thread over the beeswax quickly and bringing it down carefully in order to wax the thread the full length and yet not have too much wax at any one place. The beeswax serves to hold the strands of the thread together and also to make it firmer, so that it will not press down too closely on the material when the working thread, or buttonhole twist, used in making the buttonhole is put over it.

After the thread is waxed, finish making the stranding thread by twisting the strands together in the following manner: Hold the needle in the left hand between the thumb and the forefinger, letting the thread fall at the lower edge of the inside of the hand. Then, with the inside of the right hand, roll the thread between the hands, bringing it around toward the thumb of the left hand. After the twisting is begun, run the hand down the thread over the wrist for 4 or 5 inches. Repeat this operation over the same length of thread two or three more times in order to twist and smooth the strands well.

Place the portion of the thread just twisted around the little finger of the left hand, bringing it up over the thumb and forefinger, and allow the loose end of the thread to take the same position over the lower part of the hand as at first. Then repeat the twisting operation; that is, twist another section of the thread by bringing the hand over it and rolling it between the hands. Do this two or three times to keep the thread smooth. Then bring the thread up around the little finger and then around the thumb, as before, forming a figure 8 out of it, and continue to roll and twist the strands of thread until the entire length is twisted.

By twisting the thread in this manner, an even twist is insured and the two threads will hold as one thread; whereas, if they are not rolled and twisted from the needle, kinks will come when the thread is in use, causing inconvenience and probably imperfect work. This amount of stranding thread is usually sufficient for several buttonholes, as each buttonhole requires about ⅛ yard. Also, by preparing it all at one time in this manner, a more even thread is secured and time is saved.

10. Buttonhole Thread.—Buttonhole thread, or twist, as it is generally called, is used for working tailored buttonholes, and to distinguish it from the stranding thread it is frequently referred to as the *working thread*. Buttonhole twist is usually purchased in

10-yard spools, but it is also sold in large spools at tailor shops or in tailors' supply houses. In the large spools, however, it may be had in only a few colors; namely, black, white, dark gray, and brown. For home use, it is advisable to buy the twist in small quantities; in fact, no one would be justified in buying large spools unless there is work to require a large amount of one color of twist. For shop work, however, it is much more economical and convenient to obtain the twist in large quantities.

11. The twist, sizes A to D, comes in black only, while in size D it may be had in a variety of colors. Size A twist is the finest, and size D, the heaviest and coarsest.

In purchasing buttonhole twist, it is advisable to lay the thread out on a sample of the material and then to make sure that it is two shades darker. Although sewing silk should be purchased one shade darker than the material with which it is to be used, buttonhole twist should be two shades darker because the stitches embed themselves in the material securely and they will not entirely conceal the interlining unless they are two shades darker. Some materials in the medium and darker shades, especially blue, will be found difficult to match, so buttonholes in them are worked in black.

12. As it is difficult to join the thread used in working buttonholes, the best plan is to use a length of thread that is sufficient to work the entire buttonhole. If this is done, the purl will be in no danger of appearing broken or irregular in any place. A small tailored buttonhole may be worked with ¾ yard of twist, but buttonholes of average size take a full yard length. If a thread breaks and a new thread must be used in the process of making the buttonhole, fasten off the first thread well and secure the new one, beginning a stitch back of the first thread and bringing the stitch of the second thread up through the last purl of the first thread, so as to make the joining as nearly invisible as possible.

13. Thimble.—In making tailored buttonholes, the thimble finger and the forefinger come very close to the buttonhole and the thread. Therefore, as the thread is of silk, it is very essential to have a thimble that is smooth, that is, without any rough places. If the thread catches on the thimble even once, it will become rough and possibly spoil the effect of the buttonhole.

14. Needles.—Needles of the best quality should be used in buttonhole work. A medium-heavy needle is necessary for the stranding thread, and one that has an eye just large enough to carry the working thread should be used for it. A needle that is too large makes a close placing of the stitches difficult and also weakens the edges. As a general rule, a No. 6 short needle is the proper size for correct working, the term *short* meaning a needle about $1\frac{1}{2}$ inches long. Such a needle permits all the thread to be used and also facilitates the looping of the thread around the needle.

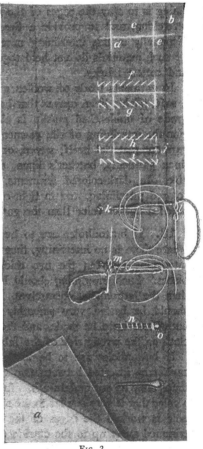

Fig. 2

15. Stiletto.—For shaping the eyelet after a buttonhole is worked, a stiletto is a very satisfactory tool. Men tailors generally prefer the awl previously mentioned, possibly because they are accustomed to using it. However, the stiletto from the embroidery basket will answer very well.

MAKING A TAILORED
BUTTONHOLE

16. In Fig. 2 is shown in detail the making of a tailored buttonhole, including each step and the operation in the development — the marking, basting, stitching, c u t t i n g, stranding, working, and final basting and shaping—as well as the position of the buttonhole from the edge, and the interlining, which serves as a foundation. This illustration should be studied in connection with the following directions so that a correct knowledge of how to make tailored buttonholes may be obtained.

17. Foundation for Tailored Buttonholes.—Tailored button-holes are almost invariably worked through three thicknesses of material, two of them consisting of the material of which the garment is made and the other of the interlining between the two thicknesses, as is indicated at *a*, Fig. 2. (The purpose of the interlining is to stay the edges of the garment and thus prevent it from stretching, and to provide a firm foundation for the buttonholes. Especially is this interlining necessary in woolens, as the threads of such materials do not hold together so well as do those of linen and cotton fabrics.)

In garments made of woolen materials, the interlining should be a soft, pliable linen canvas that has been carefully shrunk. A firm grade of unbleached muslin is also desirable for such a purpose. For the interlining of silk garments, silk of lighter weight than the garment material itself, sateen, or soft cambric is suitable, and for linen garments, butcher's linen, soft cambric, or muslin is desirable. In dark-colored garments, it is advisable to use a dark-colored interlining, and in light-colored ones the interlining should be of a lighter color than the garment material.

18. If buttonholes are to be worked in places on a garment where there is no interlining, then it is necessary to baste a piece of interlining between the two thicknesses of the material at these places. Such interlining should be 1 inch wide and ¼ inch longer than the buttonholes themselves. All three thicknesses of material should be basted very smoothly together at each place where a buttonhole is to be made, and then carefully pressed with a damp cloth on the wrong side of the fabric.

If buttonholes are to be worked in places where an interlining cannot be inserted between two thicknesses of material, a piece of lining may be put underneath. In such a case, the lining must be of a color that is very similar to the material itself, and after the buttonhole is worked the edges of the lining material must be carefully trimmed away up to the outside edge of the buttonhole-stitches.

19. For practice in the making of tailored buttonholes, it will be necessary to prepare a strip on which to work the buttonholes, using for this purpose a piece of woolen material, 8 inches long and 8 or 10 inches wide, and a piece of canvas or firm muslin, as shown at *a*, of the same length as the woolen piece and half as wide. So that this practice strip will be the same as the edge of a garment, fold it lengthwise through the center and place the canvas between the two thicknesses. Then baste the outer edge carefully and stitch ⅜ inch from the edge, as shown at *b*. With such a strip made, the marking and making of tailored buttonholes may be begun.

20. Position and Size of Buttonholes.—As buttonholes must be properly spaced and marked before they are cut, locating their position and determining their size are the first points to consider after the outside edge of the garment is stitched or basted, as at *b*. Tailored buttonholes should be spaced uniform distances apart, and the distance between the eye of each one and the finished edge of the garment must not vary in the least. When used as a closing, the buttonholes should be at least ⅛ inch from the stitching.

Just how far apart the buttonholes should be depends on the fashions of the day, for they regulate the size and number of buttons to be used, and these, in turn, regulate the buttonholes. Sometimes buttons are placed very close together almost the entire length of the coat front, and at other times only one, two, or possibly three are used. When the size and the number of buttons are determined, the positions for the top and bottom buttonholes must be marked accordingly, and then the distance between these two points equally divided into the required number of spaces. As a rule, the larger the buttons, the fewer of them will be used and the greater will be the space between them, the buttonholes, of course, being spaced to correspond. The size of the buttonhole is likewise governed by the size and the thickness of the buttons. The length of the buttonhole should be equal to the diameter of the button, plus ⅛ to ⅜ inch, depending on its thickness.

If buttonholes must be placed so as to be diagonal with the edge of the garment, they should be carefully stayed in order to give them the required strength. Such buttonholes must be so marked that all will be in a true line and each one will be parallel with the other.

21. Marking Buttonholes.—After deciding on the size and position of the buttonholes and the number there are to be, the next step consists in marking them on the material, as is shown at *c*, Fig. 2. The marking should be done with tailors' chalk having a sharp edge, so as to make distinct lines, and a perfectly straight edge should be used as a guide in marking. In marking for buttonholes, make the horizontal lines first, and in order to space them accurately, procure a piece of cardboard equal in width to the distance they are to be apart. Place this cardboard so that the first two buttonholes can be marked by running the chalk along the top and the bottom edge; then place the cardboard so that its top edge is along the second buttonhole mark, and mark for the third one. Continue the work in this way until all the buttonholes are made.

After the horizontal lines are drawn, make the vertical lines that indicate the width that each buttonhole is to be, as at d and e. To aid in this work, use a piece, or strip, of cardboard that is exactly as wide as each buttonhole is to be. Place this cardboard parallel with the edge of the garment or with the warp threads of the material and make a chalk mark on each side, thus insuring uniformity. The lines for the buttonholes should be of about the same proportion as those shown in the illustration.

22. Basting Preparatory to Stitching.—The next step in making a tailored buttonhole is to baste around the chalk lines in the manner shown at f and g; that is, with bastings that are a scant $\frac{1}{4}$ inch long and are placed diagonally with the chalk marks that indicate the width that the buttonholes are to be. The purpose of such basting-stitches is to hold the material so that it will not pull or slip out of place.

23. Outlining Buttonholes.—After the marking and the diagonal basting have been completed, stitch through all thicknesses of the material with the sewing machine $\frac{1}{16}$ inch on each side of the horizontal chalk line, as shown at h and i, and around the outside end of the line in the form of a circle, as at j. This stitching serves to outline the buttonhole, to secure the material so that the edges of the three thicknesses will remain together firmly after the buttonhole slit is cut, and to prevent the fabric from slipping when the buttonholes are being worked. Care should be taken to form the circle over the chalk marks as indicated, so that the center of the eyelet, when the buttonhole is cut and worked, will be in exact line with the finished buttonhole. Begin the stitching and end it at the back, or inside, end of the buttonhole, and after it is completed bring the thread ends through to the wrong side, thread a sewing needle with them, and take a couple of back-stitches to make sure that they will hold securely. Then cut away the surplus thread up close to the machine stitches.

24. Cutting Buttonholes.—After the machine stitching has been done on all the buttonholes that are to be made, they are ready to be cut.   It is not advisable to cut all the buttonholes before beginning to work them; rather, the best plan is to cut one and work it and then proceed with the next, and so on.   In this way, the danger of their fraying out while one is being worked will be overcome. If the buttonhole cutter is to be used for this work, place the punch of the cutter directly in the center of the stitched circle prepared for the eyelet, and the blade in line with the mark; also, be sure that the cutter is adjusted for the correct width of buttonhole.   If buttonhole scissors are to be used, place the notch of the scissors just inside the stitched circle and cut on the marked line.

In the absence of both buttonhole cutter and buttonhole scissors, a pair of ordinary scissors may be used.   With such scissors, first cut a slit by inserting the point of one blade in the center of the circle and then cut through all thicknesses exactly on the mark, or midway between the stitching.   The scissors used for cutting should be sharp, so that the buttonhole slit may be cut with one movement of them.

After the slit is cut with either buttonhole or ordinary scissors, the eyelet must be formed.   This may be done with an eyelet punch; but if there is none at hand punch a hole in the space provided with a stiletto or an awl, putting it in from the right side and then from the wrong side.   Then trim away the surplus material up to within the same distance of the stitched edge of the eyelet space as the buttonhole slit is from the edges of the rows of stitching.

25. Securing the Edges of Buttonhole Slits.—The next step, after cutting the buttonhole slit, is to secure the edges so as to keep them from raveling and to make them very firm.   This may be done by overcasting them with very close, uniform stitches, taking them back almost to the machine stitching and overcasting with strong cotton thread.   In some custom-tailor shops, in addition to overcasting, the trimmed edges are secured by waxing.   On gray or novelty goods, beeswax is used, and on dark-blue or black materials, harnessmakers' wax is employed.   To apply either wax, heat the blade of an ordinary steel kitchen knife and rub it over the wax; then quickly insert it in the buttonhole slit and rub it back and forth a few times so that part of the wax will adhere to the slit edges.   The wax keeps these edges from raveling and also holds the material together, making it possible to work the buttonholes more rapidly than if the edges are just overcast.

26. Stranding Buttonholes.—After a buttonhole is cut and before it is worked, it must be stranded with gimp or with stranding thread, as has already been mentioned. The method of stranding is the same, whether gimp or stranding thread is used, but whether one or the other should be used depends somewhat on the material, gimp being more suitable for heavy materials and stranding thread, for light-weight fabrics. Stranding should be done in the following manner:

Thread a needle with a length of the gimp or the stranding thread and tie a knot in one end of it. Then, at a point about ¼ inch beyond the back end of the buttonhole and in a direct line with the upper edge of the buttonhole slit, insert the needle through the three thicknesses of the material from the right side, pulling it through so that the knot will come as at *k*, Fig. 2. With the finished edge of the garment—that is, the eyelet of the buttonhole—toward you, bring the thread out at the left end of the buttonhole, just below the stitching, and carry it across to the eyelet end. Then secure it in this position until half the buttonhole is worked, pushing the needle firmly into the material and wrapping the gimp or the stranding thread around it, as at *l*. When the upper half of the buttonhole is worked, bring the gimp or the stranding thread along the lower half and fasten it in the same way at the back end of the buttonhole, as shown at *m*. After the buttonhole is completed, bring the gimp or stranding thread straight through the material precisely at the back end of the buttonhole and to the under side; then cut it off close to the material. Likewise, cut off the knotted end and pull the gimp or the stranding thread away from the right side.

In very firm materials, where the hole made by putting the needle in, as at *k*, might show in the material, it is better to pin the gimp or stranding thread right at the end of the buttonhole, rather than to take a stitch. In this way, no marks will show, as those made by the pin will be concealed by the buttonhole-stitches when the buttonhole is finished.

27. Working Buttonholes.—After a buttonhole is stranded, it is ready to be worked. Thread a needle with a strand of buttonhole twist, or working thread, of the proper length and color. Pull it lightly over beeswax and then over the edge of a warm iron, so as to distribute the wax evenly. Then, holding the garment so that the outer edge is at the left, fasten the thread at the end, on the left side and up very close to the end of the buttonhole slit, with a tiny back-stitch. Hold the buttonhole in this position over the fore-finger of the left hand, and bring the fastened end of the thread toward the inside of the buttonhole. Insert the needle through the slit and bring it up just outside of the machine stitching; then bring the two threads as they come from the needle around the point under the needle, and draw up the thread firm and close to form the stitch. Then insert the needle again and continue working to the opposite end of the buttonhole, keeping the nail of the left thumb just back of the stitching as a guide in taking the stitches, so as not to make them too deep in any place.

28. When the eyelet is reached in working the buttonhole, release the strand of gimp or stranding thread at the front end and hold it in position around the eyelet while the buttonhole-stitches are taken over it. Arrange the stitches at the beginning and ending of the eyelet so as to form corners; that is, so that the circle of the eyelet will be as nearly perfect as possible. Turn the work grad-ually and change the direction of each stitch slightly while working the eyelet, so that the stitches will radiate from the center. To do this, the purl must be crowded and the other end of the stitches placed a trifle farther apart and more slanting than they are at the sides of the buttonhole. After the eyelet is completed, pull up the stranding thread under the working thread, so as to take out any slack that may be in it and to insure a true, uniform eyelet edge, securing the stranding thread at the back end of the buttonhole, as at *m*.

29. Next, turn the work so that the other side of the button-hole will be toward you and proceed to work this half of the button-hole. Just before the end is reached, remove the stranding needle at *m* from the cloth and take the stranding thread down through the cloth, precisely at the end of the buttonhole, to the wrong side; then twist it around the end of the finger and hold it tight until the last buttonhole-stitch is finished.

30. When the buttonhole-stitches are completed, a bar may be worked at the end, if desired. To make such a bar, turn the work so that the back end of the buttonhole will be next to you. Then take two or three bar-stitches across the end with the working thread, keeping them very close to this end of the buttonhole, and cover these stitches with tiny over-and-over stitches. Make the little over-and-over stitches directly alongside of each other, so that a neat, narrow bar will be the result. By putting the eye of the needle instead of the point under the bar threads, the work may be done more quickly, as the eye of the needle will not catch the thread. When the over-and-over stitches are completed, fasten the working thread securely on the inside of the material and cut off the stranding thread.

31. Pressing and Finishing.—When a buttonhole is worked, it is advisable to overcast it with basting thread, as at *n*, Fig. 2, and to press it well on the wrong side, using a press cloth, so that the edge will be smooth and the ends of the buttonholes properly shaped. The overcasting-stitches should be left in until the garment is entirely completed. In pressing, the eyelet of the buttonhole should be rounded out into a perfect circle, as at *o*, by means of a stiletto.

32. Commercial Buttonhole Making.—The person who acquires skill in the making of buttonholes may feel that she possesses an accomplishment of which she may well be proud—one that will mean the saving of money or possibly place her in a position to earn money by making tailored buttonholes for others. In the large custom-tailoring establishments are employed buttonhole makers, that is, persons who make nothing but buttonholes. These persons take a garment, for example a coat, that is finished with the exception of the lining, and then stitch, overcast, strand, work, and press the buttonholes. The price they receive depends on the quality of material used in the garment and also on the standing of the tailor shop. In estimating charges, the length of the buttonhole is measured.

SIMULATED BUTTONHOLES

33. The **simulated buttonhole,** or *blind buttonhole,* as it is sometimes called, is merely an imitation buttonhole. As will be observed from Fig. 3, it resembles a tailored buttonhole, yet it has no eyelet nor opening. It consists merely of single-purl buttonhole-stitches made in two rows and placed in position as a trimming where no fastener is needed. Chain-stitches, knot-stitches, as well as stem-stitches may be used to work simulated buttonholes, but then only one row of stitches placed very close together is worked. The advantage of this buttonhole is that it may be quickly worked, and, as the material in which it is worked is not cut, no interlining is required, nor does it have to be stayed. As this kind of button-hole is used as trimming, colored thread that contrasts with the material is often used in working it.

34. The way in which a simulated buttonhole is worked with the single-purl buttonhole-stitch is clearly indicated in Fig. 3, the various steps being as follows: First mark the position of the buttonhole with tailors' chalk in the manner explained for a tailored buttonhole. Then pro-ceed to strand or outline the buttonhole with s t r a n d i n g thread or gimp. Thread a needle w i t h t h e stranding thread, tie a knot in the end of the thread, and then insert the needle from the right side of the material, so that the knot will be placed as at *a*. Then bring the needle up through the material as at *b*, put it in as at *c*, and out as at *d*, and then bring it over to *e*, here taking a stitch through the material and then pulling the stranding thread through to the wrong side. With the stranding thread thus placed, proceed with the mak-ing of the buttonhole-stitches. Begin at the left side of the

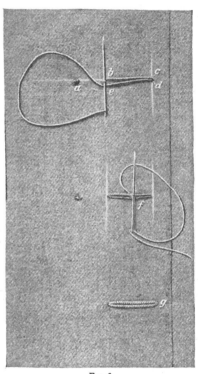

Fig. 3

buttonhole and work over the upper thread and through the material, as at *f*. When this edge of the buttonhole is completed, turn the work and make the stitches over the other stranding thread, taking the stitches through the material, as before, and keeping the purl very close to the adjoining side. When this side is worked, fasten the threads on the wrong side as for a tailored buttonhole, trim them off, and press the buttonhole carefully from the wrong side, when it will appear as at *g*.

35. Buttonholes may be bound with the material of which a garment is made or with braid. The material-bound buttonholes, however, are the more important of the two, because braid button-holes are used only when a garment has braid applied elsewhere as a trimming. The bound buttonhole, like the tailored buttonhole, must be made larger than the plain buttonhole. Seldom, if ever, is it made smaller than 1 inch, and to accommodate large buttons it is often made 2 to $2\frac{1}{2}$ inches wide.

36. Material-Bound Buttonhole.—At a, Fig. 4, is shown a buttonhole bound with the material of which the garment is made, although for this kind of buttonhole heavy silk or satin may also be used as binding. Before applying the binding in making a material-bound button-hole, an interlining may be placed between the two

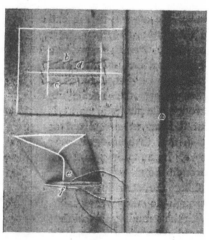

FIG. 4   FIG. 5

thicknesses of material, as in the tailored buttonhole. The under thickness, or inside facing, of the material, however, must be turned back out of the way, as at a, Fig. 5, until the buttonhole binding is applied. For each buttonhole there must also be provided a piece of binding material that is $2\frac{1}{2}$ inches wide and of a length that will permit it to extend $\frac{3}{4}$ inch on each end of the buttonhole opening. This binding may be cut from a straight or a bias piece of material. The bias piece is usually preferred, as it is easier to apply. The procedure in making a material-bound buttonhole is as follows:

37. First, as directed for marking the position of tailored buttonholes, mark the position of the bound buttonholes, and at the same time mark the position of the buttonhole on each binding piece, placing the mark so that there will be ¾ inch of material on each side of it and 1¼ inches above and below it. Next, baste a binding piece to the upper, or outside, thickness of the garment material and the interlining, placing it so that the mark for the buttonhole is exactly over the buttonhole mark on the material. Use diagonal basting all over the buttonhole mark, placing it about ¼ inch from this mark, as at *b* and *c*, Fig. 5, so as to hold the thicknesses of material perfectly smooth. With this done, machine stitch ⅛ inch on each side of the chalk mark, as shown at *d,* and straight across the end marks, pulling the ends of the machine stitches through and tying them securely at the under side.

Fig. 6

After stitching in this manner, remove the basting thread and cut the slit with a pair of sharp scissors. Cut through both the material and the binding on the chalk mark between the rows of stitching, beginning ¼ inch from one end and continuing to within ⅛ inch of the other end, and then, from each end of the slit, make a diagonal cut to the corners. With the opening thus cut, turn the binding piece through to the wrong side, as at *e,* and with the fingers press the seam edges at the sides and ends of the slit back from the opening, or allow one of the seam edges to extend out into the welt if the firmness this affords seems necessary. Trim the edges slightly to fit the welt and roll the binding out ⅛ inch from the machine stitching, as in a welt pocket, so that it will fill up half of the opening and form little plaits underneath at the ends on the wrong side, as at *c,* Fig. 6, and then baste close to the stitching, as at *f,* Fig. 5. Next, baste across the opposite side and the ends in the same way, and the buttonhole will appear as at *a,* Fig. 6. After basting in this manner, trim away the surplus material on the under side to within ½ inch of both sides and both ends of the opening and then overcast the edges of the binding piece to the interlining, as shown at *b*.

Next, remove the basting around the buttonhole, bring the under thickness of the material *a*, Fig. 5, back into position, as in Fig. 7,

which shows the under side of the garment, and then baste all thicknesses together around the buttonhole, as at *a*. With this done, cut carefully from the right side through the under thickness of material between the buttonhole edges, as at *b*, beginning ⅛ inch from one end and continuing to within ⅛ inch of the other; then turn to the wrong side and at each end of the opening just cut make a short, diagonal cut to the ends of the buttonholes, as at *c*. Turn the *raw* edges of the underneath material under ⅛ inch at the sides, as at *d*, and the ends, and whip the turned edges, as at *e*. Then remove the basting, and the buttonhole on the under side will appear as at *f*.

Fig. 7

When the buttonhole is finished on the under side, overcast its edges from the right side, as at *b*, Fig. 4. Then press the buttonhole under a cloth, remove the overcasting-stitches, and the completed buttonhole will appear on the right side as at *a*, Fig. 4.

38.   Braid-Bound Buttonhole.—In Fig. 8 is shown a buttonhole bound with braid.   For buttonholes like this, use silk braid ¾ inch wide, the grade known as military braid being best.   Although black braid may be used on materials of dark color, the braid should preferably be of a color that matches the material of which the garment is made, and for stitching sewing silk of a color that exactly matches the color of the braid should be employed.

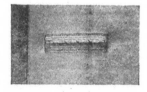

Fig. 8

As in the material-bound buttonhole just described, there should be an interlining between the two thicknesses in which braid-bound buttonholes are to be made.   The procedure in making a braid-bound buttonhole is similar to that for a material-bound buttonhole, and is as follows:

39. To begin, mark the position and length of the buttonholes on the garment, and then, to serve as a guide in basting on the braid, make another chalk mark ¼ inch above and another ¼ inch below each horizontal buttonhole mark. Next, turn back the underneath thickness of the material, so that it will not be caught in stitching. With the material thus made ready for the buttonholes, cut two pieces of braid for one buttonhole, cutting each piece 1 inch longer than the buttonhole is to be. It is advisable to cut only enough braid at a time for one buttonhole, so that the ends of the cut pieces will not become frayed. Baste one edge of each piece close along the chalk mark at each side of the center mark, beginning at one end mark of the buttonhole, continuing to the other, and letting ½ inch of the braid extend beyond each end. Next, stitch the braid close along its edges with the sewing machine from one end of the buttonhole to the other, as it was basted, as shown at *a*, Fig. 9, and when the stitching is done pull the ends of the thread through and tie them securely on the under side.

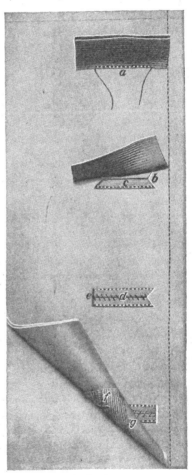

Fig. 9

With the braid stitched in place, remove the basting and proceed to cut the opening. Cut along the chalk mark, between the braid, to within ⅛ inch of the ends, and then cut diagonally to the corners, as indicated at *b*. Next, turn one piece of the braid over the edge of the buttonhole slit, as at *c*, working it back well over the edge. Then baste it firmly to the interlining on the under side, just outside the machine stitching. Next, bring the other piece of braid through in the same manner and baste it in place. With this done, overcast the edges of the braid together, as at *d*. Next, turn the material back at the ends of the buttonhole, as at *e*, and, from underneath, back-stitch straight across these ends, fastening them securely to the braid; also, whip together the edges of the braid that extend beyond the ends of the buttonhole, as at *f*. Next, whip the sides and ends of the braid to the interlining, as indicated at *g*, and then carefully press the buttonhole from the right side under a cloth.

From this stage on, the work is practically the same as that for the material-bound buttonhole. Bring the under thickness of material back into position and baste all thicknesses together, close around the buttonhole. Turn the work to the right side, remove the over-casting, and cut between the edges of the buttonhole through the under thickness of material, beginning $\frac{1}{8}$ inch from one end and extending to within $\frac{1}{8}$ inch of the other; then turn to the wrong side and from each end of the opening make a diagonal cut to the corners. When the cutting of the opening is completed, turn under the triangular points at the ends the same as for the right side, whip along the turned edges, and then remove the basting. Finish the buttonhole by pressing carefully.

BUTTONS AND OTHER TRIMMINGS

BUTTONS FOR STRICTLY TAILORED GARMENTS

40. Buttons for strictly tailored garments are of two kinds; those made of vegetable ivory, bone, and various compositions, and those covered with material, which may be plain or decorated. Many persons fail to appreciate the value of suitable buttons, looking at them simply as necessities. Nevertheless, it is a fact that the kind of button often proclaims the class to which a suit or a coat belongs, because a person who knows the value of buttons that are in good taste almost invariably knows to the fullest extent the value of good material and correct lines and is sure to combine them. As a strictly tailored garment should be dignified in line and of excellent workmanship, a knowledge of the right kind of button to use will be of great assistance in giving to it just the right finishing touch. The original cost of good buttons, that is, those which are not covered, is sometimes considerable, but neat dark or light buttons can be used repeatedly on tailored garments of dark or light colors, because they seldom break, do not wear out, and are almost always in vogue on tailored garments.

41. Types of Buttons.—In Fig. 10 are shown two styles of buttons in different sizes.

The style of button shown in (a) is known as a *four-hole button* and is used on men's garments to give them the tailored look. Such buttons may also be had with two holes and in innumerable designs. In choosing buttons of this kind, it is well to remember that the design must be neat and plain to be in keeping with strictly tailored garments.

The style of button shown in (b) is a *shank button,* called, also, by some the *women's tailored button,* because it was designed originally for women's garments. This kind of button is to be had in as many sizes and designs as the hole buttons, and while either kind is in good taste, the two- and four-hole but-

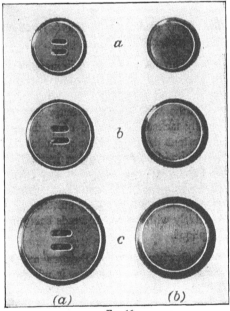

Fig. 10

tons seem to have preference even for women's garments.

Of the three sizes of buttons shown in full size in Fig. 10, that at *a* is used for trimming cuffs and belts; that at *b*, when buttons are to be placed close together on the front of a coat or a skirt; and that at *c*, when three to five buttons are to be used for the front of a coat or a skirt.

42. Decorative Self-Covered Buttons.—If a garment is to be trimmed with braid or if it is desired to use a button that is a little more decorative than a plain self-covered button, braid or thread may be used to relieve the plainness, as in the buttons shown in Fig. 11. In (a) is shown a covered button that is decorated with strands of thread arranged in hexagonal design and knotted in the center; in (b) is shown the spider-stitch worked over the covered

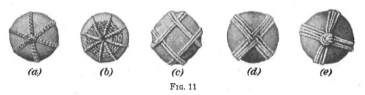

(a)   (b)   (c)   (d)   (e)

Fɪɢ. 11

button; and in (c), (d), and (e) are shown simple cross-applications of soutache braid.

43. The main point to remember in covering buttons is to secure the thread or the braid on the underneath side where it crosses. Thread used for ornamenting the buttons should be caught through the material at the center of the mold, and braid should be carefully tacked. The kind of material to use for decorating covered buttons depends on the individual requirements, the width and color of braid or thread giving inspiration for designs that are suitable for the purpose. Almost any of the embroidery-stitches—the basket-stitch, the brickwork-stitch, French knots, and many others—may be used in ornamenting buttons. Buttons may also be covered attractively with beads, the beads being applied to the covered button in appliqué.

44. Sewing Covered Buttons on Garments.—In sewing self-covered buttons on garments, it will be well to bear in mind that flat buttons are more attractive if sewed close to the garment, instead of being allowed to hang loose. Ball-shaped buttons, however, appear better if they are allowed to hang loose. Sometimes they are allowed to hang from a tiny cord made of buttonhole twist as for the overcast bar, the length of the cord varying according to the position of the button. This cord must be neatly made and of a color to match the garment.

In sewing on any type of button, take care not to draw the material with the sewing-stitches.

45. Crowfeet, arrowheads, and bow-tacks are ornamental stitches used extensively by tailors to give a finish and a suggestion of hand-work to a tailored garment, the arrowheads and bow-tacks being simpler to make than the crowfeet. They are placed at the corners of coat collars, pockets, and pocket laps, as well as at the termination of seams, tucks, and plaits, at the end of machine stitching, and at a given point on tucks or plaits. Aside from the buttons of a tailored garment, these ornamental stitches, or figures, as they may well be called, sometimes form the entire ornament or trimming, and they add greatly to the finish of a tailored garment if they are well made. In fact, they may be used in many ways and with more satisfaction as a simple ornamentation, but they are not attractive if they are not perfectly made. If it is desired to use these stitches, a good plan is to practice making them in various sizes until proficiency is attained. Once the methods are understood and skill is acquired, they will prove to be very simple.

46. Crowfeet.—In Fig. 12 (*a*) is shown an example of a crowfoot, which, as will be observed, has three points and a raised triangular center, all of which are formed in making the stitches. The

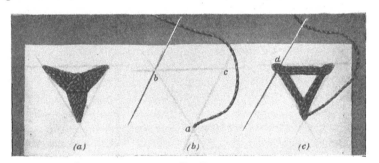

FIG. 12

size of crowfeet is governed by their location on a garment, as well as by a person's taste, one having triangular sides ¾ inch long being used perhaps the most. They are made larger than this, but seldom smaller. In working crowfeet, colored thread may be used, silk thread always being preferred for woolen materials and mercerized thread for cotton materials. The rule that governs the color of thread for working tailored buttonholes applies also to crowfeet.

47. Making Crowfeet.—To make a crowfoot, first, as shown in (b), outline a triangle with equal sides at the place where the crowfoot is to appear, using tailors' chalk that is well sharpened, so as to make distinct marks, especially at the corners. Begin the stitches by bringing the needle up just at the right of the triangle point marked a, in view (b). Then turn the work so that line ac of the triangle will be next to you and take a stitch as small as possible across point b. Turn the work to the left, so that line ab will be next to you, and take a similar stitch across point c. Again turn the work so that line bc is toward you and take a stitch across point a, bringing it up just below and close to the first stitch made at a. Continue to work in this manner, making stitches across the points and each one a little nearer the center, as shown at d, view (c), until the entire pattern is filled in. By working in this way, the crowfoot will work itself out in the center, as shown in (a), without any change in the way in which the stitch is taken.

(a)   (b)   (c)

FIG. 13

In working crowfeet, take stitches as close together as possible without overlapping, thus rendering a compact, even surface, and increase the length of the stitches very gradually, so that the outline will be perfectly smooth. If the thickness of the material in which the crowfeet are to be worked will not admit of stitches being taken across the points in the manner directed, then, to keep a perfect pattern on both edges, two separate stitches must be made; that is, the needle must be inserted at one edge of the outline, the thread pulled through to the wrong side, and the needle then brought out at the opposite side.

48. As an aid to the beginner in making crowfeet, it may be well to outline the shape of the crowfoot in the triangle used as a guide in placing the stitches. To do this, it will be necessary to use a cardboard pattern, which may be made as follows: Draw a triangle of the correct size on a piece of cardboard and locate a point at the center of each of its equal sides, as in Fig. 13 (a). With these three points as a guide, outline the shape of the crowfoot, as shown by the dotted lines in (b). Then cut on these dotted lines to form the pattern, which is shown in (c). To use a pattern of this kind, place it in the triangle marked on the goods in which the crowfoot is to be worked, and then outline it with tailors' chalk.

49. Arrowheads.—In Fig. 14 is shown how arrowheads may be used as trimming on a slot seam or an inverted plait. Such figures are so worked as to retain the straight sides of a triangle and are generally made smaller than crowfeet, being from ½ to ¾ inch long on a side. They are used more freely for garment decoration, too, because they are suitable for use in more places on tailored garments. Arrowheads are made in much the same manner as crowfeet; in fact, the difference lies in the stitch, as the marking of the triangular outline is the same, as is shown at b.

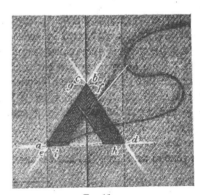

F ɪ ɢ. 14   F ɪ ɢ. 15

50. Making Arrowheads.—In making an arrowhead, refer to Fig. 15, which shows clearly the position of the thread and the way the stitches cross one another to form the points. With the arrow point of the triangle uppermost, bring the needle up as at a, in as at b, out as at c, in as at d, out as at e, in as at f, out as at g, in as at h, and out as at i, continuing in and out in this manner until the triangular outline is filled in and the arrowhead, when completed, appears as at *a*, Fig. 14. The necessity of a perfect outline will be fully realized by a close study of the finished arrowhead.

51. Bow-Tacks.—In Fig. 16 is shown an example of a bow-tack, which is a form of trimming for tailored garments used for

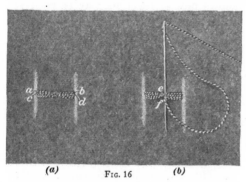

(*a*)   Fig. 16   (*b*)

the same purpose as crowfeet and arrow-h e a d s. Bow-tacks, w h i c h vary in size from ⅜ to ¾ inch, depending on their position on a garment, are very simple of construction, but they require accurate stitching in order to obtain attractive results.

52. Making Bow-Tacks.—To make a bow-tack, mark the position of the bow-tack by means of two vertical lines spaced the desired length of the bow-tack, using for this purpose a piece of well-sharpened tailors' chalk. Bring the needle up as at *a* view (*a*), in as at *b*, up as at *c*, and in as at *d*, continuing in this way and placing the stitches very close together until a sufficient number of stitches have been placed to make the bow-tack the desired width. After the last stitch is taken, bring the needle up midway between the two chalk lines, as at *e*, view (*b*), and then insert it, as at *f*, to make the cross-threads, making four or five of these through the material. In making the cross-threads, place them closer together than the width of the bow-tack in order to draw in the threads first placed and give the appearance of a bow.

TAILORS' STRAPS

53. During some seasons, straps made of the material and then applied by means of slip-stitching or machine stitching, prove very popular as trimming on tailored garments. Such straps vary in width from ⅜ to 1 inch and they may be used to cover seams or to form designs on a garment.

54. Making Tailors' Straps.—The material of which tailors' straps are made may be cut on a straight or bias grain, as desired,

but it should be twice the width of the desired strap and should be
cut very accurately. If bias pieces must be joined, be sure to join
them on a lengthwise thread
and then press the seams
open. To make the straps,
fold the strips through the
middle lengthwise and over-

Fig. 17

cast the raw edges with fairly loose stitches, as at a, Fig. 17.
Then lay the strips flat and press them so that the overcast edges
are in the middle of the strap, as at c, Fig. 18.

55. *To turn the edges of bias pieces,* pin one end of the piece
right side down, to the right end of the ironing board, placing the pin

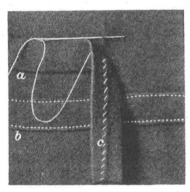

Fig. 18

where you wish the turn
made. With the left thumb
and forefinger, hold the strip
up a trifle from the ironing
board and keep it just tight
enough to cause the top edge
to turn over toward you; press
this turned edge with a warm
iron, taking care to keep the
turn the same width for the
entire length of the piece. When
one edge is completed, reverse
the strip and repeat the process
on the opposite side, bringing the
turned edges together but not overlapping them.

In silk and woolen materials, the edges should be held in place with
a diagonal basting-stitch, as shown in Fig. 19. In very thin materials,

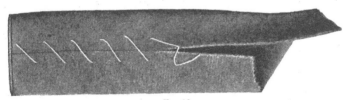

Fig. 19

which stretch easily, it is best to turn by hand and baste the edges,
as basting thread stays the edges, keeping them from stretching.

56. Applying Tailors' Straps.—Carefully mark with chalk where the straps are to be applied, and place the prepared strap on the marked line, holding it easy to avoid stretching. Then baste it care-- fully and slip-stitch it in place, as shown at *a,* Fig. 18. Or, if it is desired to have outside stitching, apply the straps as shown at *b.*

KNOTS FOR FROGS AND OTHER FANCY TRIMMINGS

57. To meet with fashion's requirements, it is often necessary to use frogs and similar devices as trimmings for garments. Such things can be purchased already made up, but usually they are expensive and not always procurable in a weight and color that will harmonize perfectly with the material of which a garment is made. So it is advisable to know how to make ornaments of this kind, for they will effect a great saving and make possible the matching of colors and fabrics. Such work is very simple, it often being possible to make a piece of covered cord or braid appear very attractive by simply twisting and arranging it carefully. The instruction given here on the development of certain knots and trimmings, besides teaching how these particular ones are made, may be used as a basis or may form a suggestion for working out more elaborate ones or ornaments suitable for some particular purpose.

58. Quality and Size of Braid or Cord.—In the making of cord and braid ornaments, the quality and size of the cord are impor- tant matters, as it is on them that successful results depend. If the cord is to be covered at home, the work should be done very care- fully, so that it will appear neat and the seam required in making the covering will be as inconspicuous as possible. If the braid or cord is purchased, it should be of as good a quality as the purse will permit, and of a color that is reasonably subdued, so that it will not appear to stand apart from the garment itself. The size of the cord or braid will depend on the garment itself and the material used in its construction, heavy materials and loose-fitting garments permitting of the use of heavier cord or braid than light-weight fabrics and tight-fitting garments.

59. Covering Cord for Frogs and Other Ornaments.—The way in which to cover cord that is to be used in making frogs and similar ornaments is illustrated in Fig. 20. The cord to be used for such work may be of very soft cotton or wool, cotton being preferred, but it should not be hard-twisted, because such cord causes ridges that will show through the covering material. Such cord, in black and white, can be obtained in different sizes, from ⅛ to ¼ inch in diameter. It comes in balls, although it may be purchased by the yard. The material to be used in covering should, as a rule, be soft and clingy, such as soft or light-weight velvet, and of the same color as the material of the garment or a harmonizing shade.

60. To cover the cord, secure one end of it to the eye of a bodkin that is blunt at one end, as shown at *a*, Fig. 20. Then prepare the material to be used for the covering. This material must be cut on the true bias, so that it will turn easily in covering the

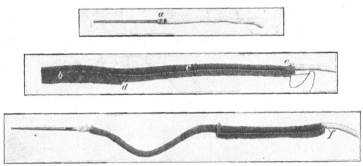

FIG. 20

cord and not form little plaits in making the ornament. Determine the width to which this material must be cut by placing it over the cord that is to be covered and pinning it so that it will fit close. Then cut it from ½ to 1 inch larger than the size called for by the measurement just made and, as mentioned, on the true bias. With the material cut, fold it through the center so that it is wrong side out and the edges are together and baste it in the manner shown at *b*, so that the slot formed will be just the right size to accommodate the cord. After basting it the entire length, stitch it with the sewing machine in a true, even line, as shown at *c*, and leave a good length of machine thread at the end. Then trim the edges of the covering along the seam thus made, as at *d*, leaving a space of about ¼ inch so as to prevent fraying in covering the cord. With the covering and the bodkin and cord thus prepared, insert the bodkin into the end of the covering and sew the covering securely to the cord with a needle threaded with the ends left in the stitching, as shown at *e*. Then proceed to slip the bodkin through the covering in the manner shown at *f*, being careful to do this work neatly. After the bodkin and cord are drawn through the entire length of covering, the seam will be on the inside, for the cord will pull the covering right side out. Finally, cut off the end of the cord secured to the bodkin, and the cord will be covered and ready for use.

61. Chinese Knots.—In Fig. 21 is shown a knot, known as the Chinese knot, made of one cord. Such knots may be made of any number of cords from one to five, depending on the size of the cord and the purpose for which the ornament thus made is desired. They may be adjusted, also, so as to form a flat knot with either one or two projecting looped ends or a flat knot with symmetrical loops that appear to be intertwined. In each of the finished Chinese

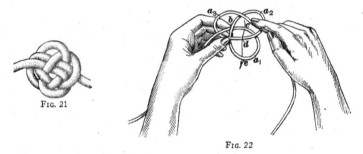

Fig. 21

Fig. 22

knots here illustrated, the ends of the cord used in making them are left free, so that a good idea may be formed of where these ends will come in tying.

62. To make the Chinese knot shown in Fig. 21, proceed to form loops in the manner shown in Fig. 22. Form loop a_1 by holding the cord of which the knot is to be formed in the left hand between the thumb and the fingers; then draw the cord around so as to form another loop a_2, letting it cross loop a_1 at *b*; and then bring it around under the first end to form still another loop a_3. Next, bring the end of the cord held in the right hand under loop a_1 at point *c*, over loop a_2 at point *d*, and again under loop a_1 at point *e*, as indicated by the arrow. Then, as shown in Fig. 23, bring the cord around so as to form a fourth loop a_4, bringing the end under loop a_2 at point *b*, over loop a_3 at point *c*, and again under loop a_2 at point *d*. If only one cord is to be used in making a knot of this kind, as in this case, pull both ends of the cord, and the knot, after a little adjusting, will appear as in Fig. 21. Then trim off the projecting ends and fasten them underneath with a needle and thread.

63. In Fig. 24 is shown a Chinese knot of three cords with symmetrical loops that are intertwined. In making this style of knot, proceed as in making the knot just explained, but do not draw

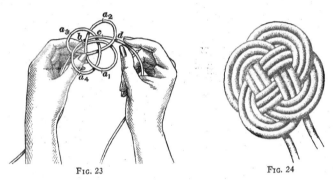

Fig. 23   Fig. 24

up the ends when loop a_4, Fig. 23, is finished. Instead, continue to form and weave the loops in the same way until the three cords are looped and woven alongside of one another, as shown, taking care to place the cords even in forming each loop and to draw them under and place them over the loops at the proper places, as directed in making the knot with only one cord. When the knot is tied, shape the loops well with the fingers, and then clip off the ends and fasten them so that the fastenings will not be visible.

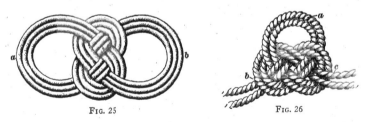

Fig. 25   Fig. 26

64. The style of Chinese knot shown in Fig. 25 has the loops at the sides pulled out in the form of circles. To form this knot, proceed in the manner directed for tying the knot shown in Fig. 24, and when it is tied draw out the two loops, as shown at a and b, Fig. 25, so as to make the center part tight and permit the side loops to be circular. In forming this style of Chinese knot, take pains to draw the cords evenly so that they will set smoothly. Finish the knot by cutting off the ends and fastening them in place.

65. Still another style of the Chinese knot is shown in Fig. 26. It is tied in practically the same way as the one described in Art. **62**, but instead of one cord, two cords are used at the same time. In this knot, only one loop, as *a*, is pulled away to form a circle. The ends *b* and *c* of this knot are, of course, cut off and fastened under as in finishing the other Chinese knots mentioned. Knots that are to show more than two cords side by side are made, preferably, in the manner directed for the knots shown in Figs. 24 and 25, but

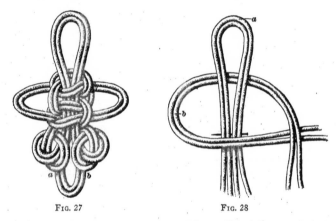

FIG. 27   FIG. 28

two cords may be used to make striking effects in much quicker time than is required to weave knots that have three or more cords.

66. Lovers' Knot.—In Fig. 27 is shown a knot commonly referred to by the name *lovers' knot*. It consists of a series of intertwining loops and can be tied with ease. A double cord is generally used in tying this kind of knot, although if a smaller ornament is desired a single cord may be used, and, likewise, if a larger knot is wanted three or more cords may be employed. However, it is generally difficult to handle more than two cords in tying this kind of knot.

67. The first step in tying the lovers' knot is shown in Fig. 28. With a double cord that is about 14 inches long, form a loop, as at *a*, fastening the cords together where they meet with a pin, as shown, or with stitches, and allowing the free ends to hang down until the

knot is to be finished. Then, with a double cord about 20 inches
long, form a loop, as at *b,* bringing it over and under the cords used
to form loop *a* in the manner shown. Next, bring the upper ends
of loop *b* under in the manner
shown at *a,* Fig. 29, and over,
as at *b,* remove the pin, and draw
up both ends so as to form the
knot shown at *c.* With this knot
tied, tie another in the manner
shown in Fig. 30; that is, form
two loops by bringing the free
ends *a* over the free ends that
hang down, and the other free
ends *b* over the ends *a* and under
the ends that hang down, and
then make the second knot by
drawing these ends *a* and *b*

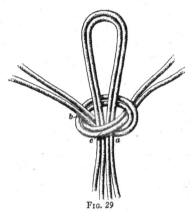

Fig. 29

together. Next, tie a third knot in the same manner as the first.
When the three knots are tied over the free ends of the loop, they
will appear as at *a,* Fig. 31. Next, form a loop out of the free
ends of the cords used in tying the three knots and fasten it under
the knots, as at *b*; also, form a loop out of the other free ends and

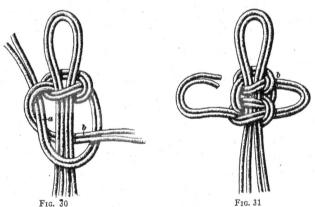

Fig. 30   Fig. 31

fasten it under the knots, as at *a,* Fig. 22. There now remain to be
disposed of the two free ends of the first loop made. Tie a knot
in one of these, as at *b,* and fasten the ends under the other knots,
as at *c.* Then tie a similar knot, but in the opposite direction, in

the other free ends and fasten it under, as at *a*, Fig. 33, which shows the lovers' knot complete, except for the loop that hangs down at the bottom. To form this loop, use an extra piece of the double cord, fastening the ends under the small knots formed out of the free ends of the 14-inch piece, as indicated at *a* and *b* in the completed lovers' knot, Fig. 27.

68. **Tassels.**—Garments very often call for the use of tassels, and as ornaments for hats they are very convenient and attractive. Tassels may be made out of wool, silk, or mercerized yarn or thread, silk being preferred, in either large or small size, to suit the purpose

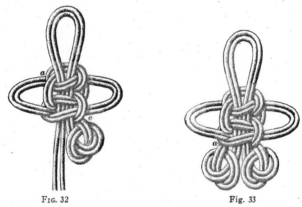

Fig. 32   Fig. 33

for which they are to be used. The color of a tassel, which likewise depends on its purpose, may harmonize or contrast with the material of the garment on which it is to be used, the color very often harmonizing with the other trimmings employed.

69. In Fig. 34 is shown a completed tassel and the various steps in its making. To make a tassel like that shown in view (*a*), make a double cardboard gauge, as shown in view (*b*), of a size that will give the desired length to the tassel and having its upper corners cut off as shown so that they will not interfere with the wrapping of the thread and will permit the loops of thread to be removed easily. Wrap the thread or yarn to be used around the cardboard gauge in the manner shown in view (*b*), leaving one end to project from 4 to 6 inches, as at *a*, to be used in finishing the upper part of the tassel, and tying the thread at the top with the other end in a loop knot, as at *b*, to hold the loops together after they are slipped off the cardboard. The number of times to wrap the thread will depend on the number of threads that are wanted in the tassel. After the thread is wrapped and secured, draw the knot *b,* view (*b*), down to the point where the tassel is to be wound, letting the free end hang down to form part of the tassel threads. Then thread an embroidery needle with the thread end *a,* remove all the wrapped thread from the cardboard gauge, and, holding it together at the center, wind the thread that is in the needle around the bunch of thread several times, as at *a,* view (*c*). Next, insert the needle, as at *b,* and bring it out, as at *c,* taking it through the thread so as to hold it in place. Then bring it around, as in view (*d*), to form a loop *a,*

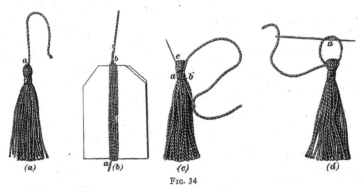

(a) (b) (c) (d)

Fig. 34

inserting the needle on the side opposite *c,* view (*c*). With this done, put the needle in the loop and draw this thread up so that it will hold the threads close together, as at *a,* view (*a*). With the upper part thus wrapped and fastened, slip the scissors inside the looped threads and clip the lower end of the tassel straight across, so that all the threads will be uniform in length.

70. Fringe.—Garments and certain accessories are often trimmed with fringe, a form of ornament consisting of threads, cords, or tassels from 1 to 40 inches deep, allowed to hang straight or knotted in various ways. The simplest form of fringe is that in which the edge of a loosely woven material is frayed out. The other form is the tied, or knotted, variety, made of wool, silk, or cotton threads attached to material or to a braid or binding.

71. *To make frayed fringe,* machine-stitch the material to be frayed, the number of inches from the raw edge that you wish the fringe to be in width, following a thread of the material, as at *a,*

Fig. 35.   Then, begin at the edge and pull out the threads up to the machine-stitching.   This method will prevent further fraying.

72.   *For tied, or knotted, fringe,* choose smoothly twisted thread that has enough weight to hang evenly.   To compute the amount required, determine what is needed for just one knot and then approximate the entire amount by multiplying this by the number of knots.

To cut the threads accurately, prepare a strip of cardboard as long as your fringe is to be, wind the thread on this, and then cut through the threads along one edge.

Supply a needle with a large eye, one that will accommodate from 3 to 4 strands of the thread, and thread this, the number of strands depending on the weight of the thread and the thickness of the fringe; then pull it through the

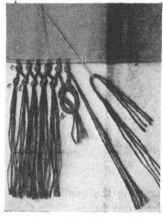

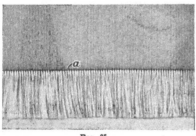

Fig. 35   Fig. 36

finished edge of your material, as at *a*, Fig. 36.   Adjust the threads so that they are even and, holding them all together, tie in a plain knot close to the edge of the fabric.   The knot in the process of tying will appear as shown at *b*, and the completed knot, as at *c*.

Now draw in a second group of threads, ½ inch or farther from the first, and tie these in the same manner as the first group. Proceed in this way across the entire edge.

To form the second row of knots, take one-half the threads from one group and one-half from the next and, drawing them together, knot them, as shown at *b*, the completed knots appearing as at *d*. Complete the fringe by knotting the threads at the beginning and the end, as at *e*.

CHAPTER III

TAILORED POCKETS

TYPES AND ESSENTIALS

1. By **tailored pockets** are meant all pockets used in tailored garments, with the exception of those in coat linings, regardless of their style or position. The pockets used in linings, properly termed *lining pockets*, will prove very simple in construction after a knowledge of tailored pockets is gained. There are only five distinct standard types of tailored pockets, namely, the *stand pocket*, the *flap pocket*, the *welt*, or *slit*, *pocket*, the *patch pocket*, and the *bound pocket*. Each type, however, is subject to many modifications in shape, some pockets assuming an entirely different appearance from the original of its type. It is well to remember, though, that the details of finishing pockets that vary from the original types will not be difficult, for the principle of making them always remains practically the same.

2. In considering the style, shape, position, and size of tailored pockets, it is important to know that they are governed more or less by prevailing styles at the time they are made, by the style of the garment in which they are to be placed, by the taste of the person that is to use them, and by their purpose. Such pockets are employed in both long and short coats, in skirts, and in wide belts. If a pocket is to be used on the breast of a coat, it is generally put on the left side, but there are cases where a breast pocket is placed on each side. If two pockets are used in this way, however, they are generally made smaller than if only one is used, as they are intended more for ornament than for service. The stand and the welt type of pocket are used most frequently in such places, although the flap and patch types are sometimes employed.

3. The all-important considerations in the making of tailored pockets are accuracy and neatness, for to have a perfect pocket the material must always match, whether it is the design or the grain. To beginners, such tailoring work may seem difficult, yet by studying each type of pocket diligently and doing the actual construction on each so as to come to know every little detail, no tailored pocket will be too hard to make. Really, the first step to success in work of this kind is a full appreciation of how much neatly made pockets add to tailored garments from the standpoint of both utility and ornament, and the next step is to be willing to spare no effort in the careful working out of every detail.

STAND POCKET

4. The first of the tailored pockets to be considered is the **stand pocket,** an example of which is shown in Fig. 1. This type of

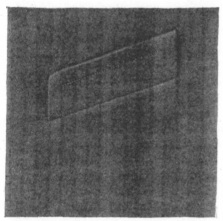

FIG. 1

pocket really consists of two parts—the *stand*, or part that serves as a finish for the opening, and is the only part visible, and the *pocket proper*, or *pouch*, which is inside the garment, that is, between the outside material and the lining. The stand pocket is very effective on garments of firm material that have wide stitching, as it imparts to them the smart look so much sought by wearers of tailored garments. As a rule, the stand pocket is used simply as a breast pocket, but sometimes it is placed below the waist line at the sides of garments; also, it is used in skirts and in belts. The pocket here shown is for the left breast, and its lines are diagonal. Of course, as such pockets may be placed in other positions and, as is explained later, the lines may assume various shapes, it is well in making them to be careful to have the lines run in the directions that will harmonize with the other lines of a garment.

So that a good knowledge of the way in which to make a stand pocket may be gained, the construction of the pocket illustrated in Fig. 1 is taken up in detail. To get the best results, the actual work should be done, but not before each step has been carefully studied and is clearly understood.

5. Size and Position of Pocket.—When the stand pocket is used as a breast pocket, the stand is generally made $3\frac{1}{2}$ to 5 inches wide and about 1 inch deep, and the pocket proper, or part that forms the pouch, about $3\frac{1}{2}$ to 5 inches wide and of the same depth. As mentioned before, however, the size of pockets varies and may be made to meet requirements.

The position of the pocket is usually marked in the first fitting of the garment in which it is to be used, especially if it is to serve as the breast pocket in a coat. After marking the pocket, observe its general effect in comparison with the coat design in order to insure correct size and shaping.

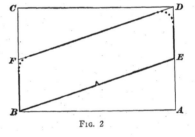

Fig. 2

6. Preparing the Stand Pattern.—The first step in the making of a stand pocket is to make a pattern for the stand, no pattern being necessary for the other part of the pocket. To make such a pattern for the pocket shown in Fig. 1, proceed as follows, using Fig. 2 as a guide:

On a piece of paper of suitable size, using a ruler or a square, draw first a rectangle, each side of which is $3\frac{1}{2}$ inches and each end of which is $2\frac{1}{4}$ inches, lettering the corners A, B, C, and D, as shown. Next, locate point E $1\frac{1}{8}$ inches below D on line AD, and point F $1\frac{1}{8}$ inches above B on line BC. Then connect B and E as well as F and D, with diagonal lines, as shown. If desired, the upper corners may be rounded off a trifle, as indicated by the dotted lines.

With the outline thus completed, form the pattern by cutting from B to E, from E to D, from D to F, and from F to B; if rounded corners are wanted, cut on the dotted lines. At the same time, also, so that there will be no danger of mistaking the top of the pattern for the bottom when using it as a guide in cutting out materials, cut a small notch in the pattern on the bottom line, as indicated in the illustration.

7. Marking the Garment Material for Matching.—Having prepared the pattern as directed, proceed next to locate the position of the stand on the garment material, so as to assist in matching the material of the stand and the garment. Good judgment must be exercised in doing this work, because it is imperative that the weave and the design of both materials match perfectly at the place where the pocket is to appear. It is necessary, also, to take into consideration the side of the garment on which the pocket is to come, as well as the direction in which it is to slant.

In this case, as the pocket is for the left side of the coat, pin the pattern on as shown in Fig. 3; that is, so that its ends are parallel with the lengthwise stripes or grain of the cloth and the highest part of the pattern when in this position will come at the left when the garment is on the wearer.

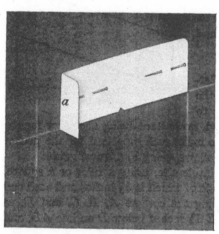

In placing the pattern, it is well to bear in mind that best results will be obtained by having its ends come between the stripes instead of directly on them; and, in order to make certain that the pattern edges are parallel with the stripes, crease the pattern at the exact edge of one of the prominent stripes, as shown at *a*.

Fig. 3

This crease in the pattern is valuable later in cutting out the stand material, for by placing it on the same stripe as in the garment material accuracy will be assured.

With the pattern correctly placed, outline its sides and its lower edge on the garment material with tailors' white chalk, as shown; tailors' colored chalk should always be avoided in such work, as it is next to impossible to remove it from some materials.

8. When striped material is used for a garment and there is a seam down its front, as in the semifitted coat, it is often difficult to match all the stripes. In a case of this kind, therefore, the best plan is to match only the stripes in the front section, rather than those in the side section. Otherwise, the procedure is the same.as that just mentioned.

9. Cutting Out the Stand.—After determining just where the stand is to come on the garment, the cutting out of the stand material so that it will match that of the garment is simple. To do this work properly, proceed as shown in Fig. 4.

Place the stand pattern on a piece of the material in exactly the same way as directed for marking the position of the stand on the garment. Make sure to have the pattern slant the same and to have the

Fig. 4

ends come on the same stripes of the cloth; also, turn back the pattern on the creased line to see that the crease comes along the edge of the same stripe as in the garment material. Then pin the pattern securely in place and cut out the stand, allowing $\frac{1}{2}$ inch all around the pattern for the finish and turnover. To insure accuracy, this allowance may be marked with chalk.

Before removing the pattern from the material thus cut out, run a basting thread all around the pattern or mark the material with tailors' chalk, so that the true outline of the stand will be known in making the pocket. Basting is the more satisfactory, as the chalk lines are so easily rubbed off and losing the pattern lines would cause trouble in the matching of the design or the weave of the materials.

10. Cutting Out the Canvas Interlining.—In order to prevent the stand of the pocket from sagging when it is on the garment, an interlining of canvas is generally inserted between the stand material and its lining. To cut out this interlining, proceed as shown in Fig. 5, using a piece of lengthwise canvas that has been shrunk. After pinning the pattern in place, as shown, cut the canvas exactly the same size as the pattern at the sides and the top, but at the bottom allow $\frac{1}{2}$ inch for a seam and cut a notch in it, as shown in Fig. 6.

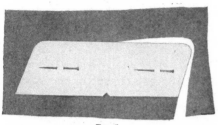

FIG. 5

11. Putting the Stand Together.—With the material and the interlining for the stand cut out, you are ready to put them together. Pin the canvas to the wrong side of the material and baste them together, basting from the right side of the material. With the right side of the material still up, turn all edges except the lower edge over on the canvas, being sure to follow the marked pattern lines carefully, and then baste them as shown in Fig. 6, always basting from the right side in such cases. These edges must be turned absolutely true, so that the lines of the finished pocket will be as perfect as possible.

Next, miter the corners as at *a*, first trimming the corners as at *b* and then whipping them as at *c*. If the corners are rounded, take care to bring them down well when whipping the material edges, so that a graceful, curved line will be obtained.

Now press the stand from the wrong side, and then stitch it. The stitching should be the same in width as the outside stitching

FIG. 6

on the seams of the garment, which usually varies from $\frac{3}{8}$ to $\frac{5}{8}$ inch from the edge. If the corners of the stand are round or if sufficient practice has not been had in turning accurate corners, it is advisable to outline the position of the machine stitching with basting threads. If the stitching is not outlined in this way, then the gauge of the sewing machine must be used because the stitching on the stand portion must be accurate.

When the stitching is done, remove all basting except that which marks the depth of the stand, and then press the stand again, this time, however, from the right side and with a damp cloth laid over the material. The stand is now ready for the lining.

12. Pocket Linings.—Before taking up the lining of the stand, it may be well to consider the material to be used in lining pockets. For the stand or the flap of a pocket, a very good quality of satin or silk is most suitable, and for the pouch part, especially if a durable pocket is desired, sateen of close weave is very satisfactory. Because of the fact that a pocket flap or a pocket stand comes on the outside of a garment, the lining material for it should harmonize in color.

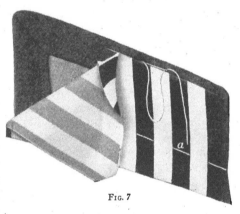

13. Lining the Stand. To line the stand, it is necessary to use a piece of lining of exactly the same size as the stand material, for when the seam edges of the lining are turned down they will come well inside the stand portion and will not show on the right

FIG. 7

side. Therefore, lay the stand pattern on a piece of the lining material, taking care to have the weave of the lining run the same as that of the stand material, and cut the lining. Then place the wrong side of the lining to the wrong side of the stand and proceed to whip the lining to the stand, as shown in Fig. 7, using small stitches. Next, press the stand again, and it will be ready to be applied to the garment.

At this time, also, to serve as a guide in stitching the stand to the garment, run a basting thread from the right side, as shown at *a*, through the lining in the mark-stitching.

14. Placing the Reinforcing Strip.—To strengthen the finished pocket, it is necessary to place underneath the opening a strip of lining, usually silesia or cambric, that is 3 inches in depth and 2 inches wider than the stand portion. This strip must be cut so that its *lengthwise threads* will run parallel with the opening and the lower edge of the stand,

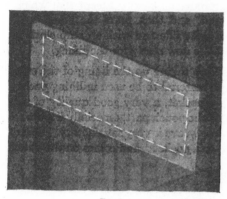

for it must neither give nor pull out of shape. In placing this strip, put it on the wrong side of the material, allowing two-thirds of it to extend above the mark for the pocket opening. Then turn over the material with the strip pinned to it and baste the strip on, as shown in Fig. 8, basting from the right side

Fig. 8

of the garment material in order to have it perfectly smooth.)

15. Placing and Basting the Stand in Position.—When the reinforcing strip is in position, it is next in order to place the stand in its proper place and baste it. Therefore, to be absolutely sure that the stripes of the stand and the garment materials match exactly, pin the stand on as illustrated in Fig. 9; that is, so that the basting in the stand is directly over the diagonal chalk mark on the garment and its ends come at the vertical chalk marks. If it differs even a trifle when placed according to the original marks,

Fig. 9

remove the stand and again mark along each end of the stand, as at *a* and *b*, for it is imperative that the matching be accurate.

Having matched the material correctly, remove the pin, turn the stand so that its top will be downwards, and then place it so that its right side will be to the right side of the garment, its basting directly over the diagonal chalk mark, and its ends on points *a* and *b*. Then, after pinning it in this position, baste it in place, basting through all thicknesses and lifting the ends of the stand so as to make certain that it is straight and that the stripes match exactly.

FIG. 10

16. Preparing the Material for the Pouch.—To prepare the lining material that is to form the pocket portion, or pouch, first,

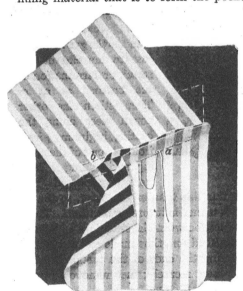

FIG. 11

cut out two pieces of lining, making each about 5 inches square, and then pin them so that their right sides are together, as in Fig. 10. Next, to give the top of the pocket portion exactly the same slant as the stand and thus permit it to hang straight across the bottom, as it should, draw a diagonal line from a point 1⅛ inches below the upper left-hand corner of the lining material, as at *a*, on the lengthwise edge, to the upper right-hand corner and cut along this line. At this time, also, round off the lower corners, in the manner shown in the illustration.

17. Joining the Stand and the Pouch.—Unpin the two pouch pieces and baste them in place, as shown in Fig. 11. Baste one piece over the pocket stand so that the stitches will come exactly in line with the basting on the stand, as at *a*, and the other piece as at *b*, leaving a space of just ½ inch between the basting of the pieces and *taking care not to catch the raw edges of the stand portion.* Keep a true basting line in each case and extend it exactly to the ends of the stand portion and no farther.

As will be observed, the seam edges of the pouch material overlap a trifle; this, however, is as it should be, because an ample seam allowance is required to prevent the pocket from pulling out when in use.

Fig. 12

With the basting done, stitch the pouch pieces in the manner shown in Fig. 12. First, stitch the piece over the stand, stitching through the basting that holds the stand to the garment and just to the end of the stand, or termination of the basting, as at *a*. Then stitch the other pouch piece along the basting, beginning ¼ inch from one end of the basting and ending ¼ inch from the other end. The stitching must be shorter on this side than on the other, so that it will not show when the stand is turned in its proper position. Then, too, sufficient space must be left between the stitchings to permit the ends of the pocket to be finished and thus made secure. When the stitching is completed, bring the ends of the thread through to the wrong side and fasten them securely; then remove all bastings that have been replaced with stitching.

18. Cutting the Pocket Opening.—So that the opening for the pocket may be cut, turn the seam allowance back, as shown at *b*.

and c, Fig. 12. Then, with a pair of very sharp-pointed scissors, cut the opening, inserting the point of the scissors at the center, as at d, and cutting from the center to within ¼ inch of each end of the stand stitching, as indicated at e. Next, cut precisely to each corner of this stitching in a diagonal line, exercising the greatest care, for the clipping should not extend so far as to weaken the ends of the pocket. By cutting the corners in this manner, there remains at each end a triangular piece that must be secured to the lining later.

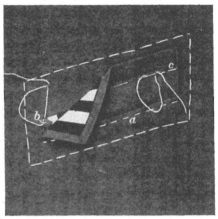

Fig. 13

19. Completing the Pocket.

—With the opening thus made, turn the pocket pieces to the wrong side by slipping them through the opening, when the outside of the pocket will appear as shown in Fig. 13.

Next, baste the lower edge of the stand, as at a, slipping two fingers of the left hand underneath the stand and in the opening, so that the underneath portion of the pocket will not be caught. Next, secure the triangular piece at each end of the opening to the under pouch part, as at b. Then, so as to make sure that the pocket will "set" perfectly, and, if of striped material, that the stripes will match exactly, baste the upper edge of the stand to the garment, as at c.

Fig. 14

With the stand thus basted and the triangular portions secured, turn the garment over so that the wrong side of the pocket is up,

4 W I—5

as in Fig. 14, and fasten the ends of the stand from the wrong side with buttonhole twist, as at *a* and *b*. In doing this, begin at the bottom of the stand and take short, diagonal stitches to the top of the pocket; then, reversing the direction of the stitch, work down to the starting point, crossing the stitches that are put in from the bottom and the top of the stand, as shown.

Next, baste the pouch portions together, trim them off evenly, and stitch them, as at *c*, being careful to catch the reinforcing strip. If the lining is likely to fray, overcast the edges, as at *d*.

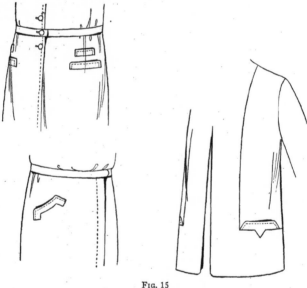

Fig. 15

Finally, remove all basting, and press the pocket thoroughly. When thus completed, the stand pocket will appear on the right side as in Fig. 1 and on the wrong side as in Fig. 14.

20. Stand-Pocket Variations.—As has been mentioned, each type of pocket is subject to many modifications in shape. To form a definite idea of some of the variations of the stand pocket, note the examples given in Fig. 15. These pockets differ only so far as shape is concerned, and no difficulty will be encountered in making them or other styles, or even in creating different shapes, provided the construction and finishing of the stand pocket just discussed are thoroughly understood.

FLAP POCKET

21. The next type of tailored pocket to be considered is the **flap pocket,** one style of which is illustrated in Fig. 16. This pocket also consists of two parts—the *flap,* which serves both as a finish for the pocket opening and as protection for the pocket itself, and the *pouch,* which is similar to that of the stand pocket. The flap pocket is a very desirable one, as it is adaptable to nearly all tailored fabrics and its size, shape, and position can be varied to give pleasing effects on many kinds of garments.

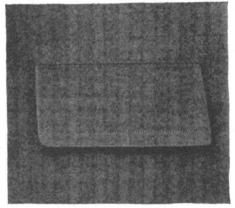

The materials re-.quired for the flap pocket—that is, for the lining and the reinforcement—are practically the same as those for the stand pocket, and, in fact, the making of this type of pocket differs very little from the making of the other type, it being necessary also to match the material very accurately.

Fɪɢ. 16.

As will be observed, the flap of this type of pocket resembles the stand of the other, its chief difference being that it is placed in the reverse position.

22. Determining the Position.—Flap pockets are generally placed at the sides of garments, and as a rule two pockets are made at the same time, one for each side. In such a case, therefore, so that the pockets will be exactly the same in size and shape when finished, mark-stitching must be used to mark the pattern lines of the flap, as well as the position of the pocket on the garment.

The position and the width of the flap pocket should be decided in the first fitting. The exact place where the pocket is to come should be determined when the garment is on, the location usually being governed by Dame Fashion, who calls for different positions, sizes, and shapes each season. The procedure, when these points are decided, is to mark with tailors' chalk the exact position and approximate size, remove the garment, pin it together carefully so that the seams or pattern edges on each side will correspond exactly, lay the garment out on a flat surface, and carefully mark-stitch on the chalk line through both thicknesses of the garment so that the pocket will come exactly in the same position on each side.

23. Preparing the Flap Pattern.—The only pattern required for the flap pocket is that for the flap. To get the dimensions required for the pattern in the actual making of flap pockets in garments, it is necessary to measure the chalked outline. To make a pattern for the pocket shown in Fig. 16, which is of average size, proceed as shown in Fig. 17, using a piece of paper of suitable size.

First, draw a rectangle, each of whose sides is $4\frac{1}{2}$ inches and each

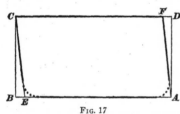

Fig. 17

of whose ends is $2\frac{1}{4}$ inches, lettering the corners A, B, C, and D, as shown. Next, locate point E $\frac{1}{4}$ inch to the right of B on line AB and point F $\frac{1}{4}$ inch to the left of D on line CD. Then connect points A and F, as well as C and E, with diagonal lines. If slightly rounded corners are desired at the lower edge of the flap, the pattern may be so marked, as indicated by the dotted lines.

With the drafting thus completed, form the pattern by cutting from A to F, from F to C, from C to E, and from E to A. For round corners, cut on the dotted lines.

24. Cutting Out the Flap.—With the pattern thus prepared, proceed to cut out the material required for the flaps. Pin the flap pattern on a double thickness of the garment material, placing it so that the stripe, or at least the weave, of the flap material will match that along the pocket mark of the garment material; in other words, match the material in the manner explained for the stand pocket.

If the material is dark, outline the pattern edges with tailors' white chalk; then cut all the way around the pattern, allowing $\frac{3}{8}$ inch for seams, and, after removing the pattern, mark-stitch all the chalk lines. If the material is of the kind on which tailors' white chalk will not show, cut the material in the manner directed, but mark-stitch around the pattern before removing it. With the material cut out, cut the pieces of lining required for the flaps, making them the same in size as the pieces of material for the flaps.

25. Making the Flap.—Next, proceed with the making of each flap. To do this work correctly, place the right side of the lining to the right side of the material and baste them together from the cloth side, beginning at the top of one end and continuing around to the top of the other, but not across the top. In basting, hold the flap material a trifle full in order that the lining will be a little smaller; then, when the flap is stitched, the lining will not show along the edges.

Fig. 18

With the basting done, stitch just outside of the mark-stitching where it is basted, as shown at *a*, Fig. 18, continuing to the edge, as at *b* and *c*. Do not stitch the upper edge of the flap, as it must be left open to permit the flap to be turned right side out.

Next, remove all basting and mark-stitching threads except the mark-stitching at *d*, which indicates the top of the flap, and trim the seam edges in the manner shown at *e*, trimming, in firm material, to within ⅛ inch of the stitching.

Now, turn the flap right side out and baste it a scant ¼ inch from the edge, taking care that the seam is rolled out to the edge. Then baste another row about ½ inch from the first row, using a short basting-stitch to hold the edge firm. When the basting is completed, press the flap thoroughly, and, after adjusting the gauge of the sewing machine, stitch the bottom and ends of the flap the same distance from the edge as the seams of the garment are stitched, usually ⅜ to ⅝ inch. If no stitching appears as a seam trimming on the right side of a garment, then the flap should be carefully pressed and applied without stitching on the outer edge.

Next, remove all the basting at the edge, and then run a basting through the lining along the upper edge at the mark-stitching. This marking is done so that it will show on the lining side, and also so that the mark-stitching can be taken out at this time in order to avoid catching it when stitching the flap in position with the sewing machine.

26. Applying the Reinforcing Strip and Flap.—Having made the flap in the manner directed, it is next in order to secure it

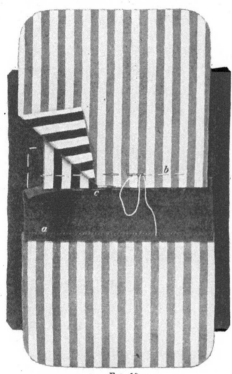

to the garment, to make the opening, and to apply the pouch part of the pocket. As in making the stand pocket, it is first advisable to place a reinforcing, or stay, strip in position. Therefore, pin to the wrong side of the garment material a lengthwise stay strip of cambric or silesia that is 2 inches deep and 1½ inches longer than the width of the pocket, placing it so that its lengthwise center is directly under the chalk marks on the material, and then baste it in position.

Next, baste the flap to the material in the manner shown in Fig. 19; that is, with its right side to the right side of the material and its basting line directly on the chalk mark on the garment material.

Fig. 19

27. Applying the Pouch Portion.—As in making the stand pocket, cut out the lining material for the two pieces that form the pouch. Cut each of these pieces 1½ inches wider than the flap or the pocket opening, but make the depth of only one equal to the desired depth of the pocket; for the other, make the depth 2 inches less than the pocket depth, but to this piece, as shown at a, stitch a lengthwise strip of the garment material that is 2 inches in depth and of a width equal to the width of the piece.

Baste the full-sized piece over the flap, as shown at *b*; that is, with its right side down and so that the basting will be on top of the basting with which the flap was basted on. Baste on the piece with the garment material attached, or the lower part of the pocket, as at *c*, also with its right side down. This strip of garment material on the pouch part must be used, in order to prevent the lining from showing on the right side of the garment when the flap of the finished pocket is lifted.

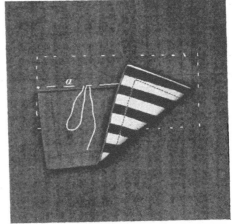

Fig. 20

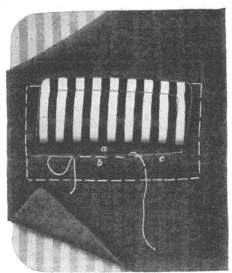

Fig. 21

28. Completing the Pocket.—With the pouch pieces thus basted in place, stitch both the flap and the lower part to the garment material, leaving a space of ½ inch between these stitchings. Having finished this stitching, remove all the basting and fasten the thread ends on the wrong side.

Then, holding the seam edges apart, cut the pocket opening, following the directions given in connection with the stand pocket; that is, cutting to within $\frac{1}{2}$ inch of each end and then diagonally to the end of the flap, as well as to the end of the stitching of the lower part of the pocket.

Fig. 22

29. After cutting the opening for the pocket, slip the lower portion through the opening, turn the flap down from the right side of the garment, and baste in the manner shown at a, Fig. 20.

Next, as in Fig. 21, bring the lower portion up, allowing the material to extend up far enough to fill the space between the stitching of the flap and that of the bottom, as shown at a, thus forming a welt, which aids in concealing the lining when the flap is lifted. Then turn the seam down and baste, as shown at b, slipping the fingers inside the pocket opening so as to prevent the stitches from catching the material underneath. Next, stitch along the lower edge, as at c, and bring the other pocket portion down into position, as in Fig. 22. Now turn under the triangular pieces to the wrong side and fasten them through both thick-

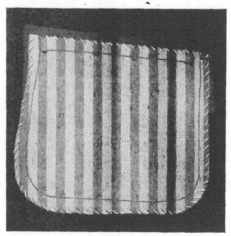

Fig. 23

nesses, as shown at a; also, to strengthen the pocket, finish the ends of the pocket opening with the overcast bar, as shown at b.

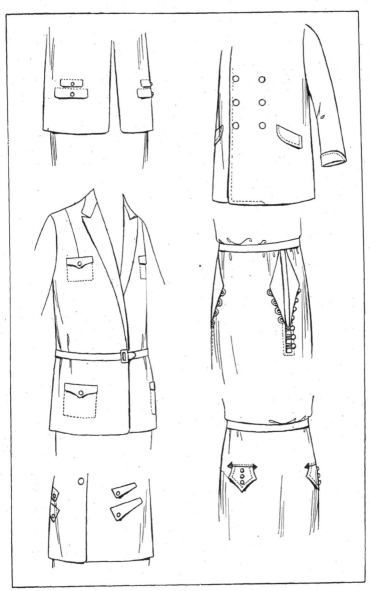

Fig. 24

Next, baste and stitch the pouch portions together, as at c, and then overcast the edges, as shown. With all the stitching done, remove all the bastings and press the pocket thoroughly from the right side. The flap pocket should now appear on the right side as in Fig. 16, and on the wrong side, as in Fig. 23.

30. Flap-Pocket Variations.—Several variations of the flap pocket are illustrated in Fig. 24. These pockets should serve to make clear the way in which flap pockets of different shapes may be applied, and to provide suggestions for developing other pockets. As will be observed, the flaps may be circular, triangular, rectangular, and so on, and may have square or round corners; also, buttons and buttonholes and other trimming may be added to create the right effect. In every case, however, the shape of the flap, the stitching, and the trimming are in harmony with the garment on which they are used, a point that should always be borne in mind in connection with garment making.

_____

WELT, OR SLIT, POCKET

31. The third type of pocket, namely, the **welt, or slit, pocket,** is illustrated in Fig. 25. This type of pocket has neither a stand nor a flap, simply a slit, or opening, secured with welt edges, and a pouch. Although the opening of the pocket shown here is in the

form of a reversed curve, or "line of beauty," as it is sometimes called, openings in the form of other curves, as well as straight and diagonal lines, may be used effectively, as is pointed out later.

The welt, or slit, pocket is used as a breast pocket; at the sides of a garment, below the waist line, as a pocket for a handkerchief, car fare, or any

FIG. 25

small article; and sometimes simply to create an ornamental effect on a garment. (If it is to be used as a breast pocket, as in this case, the opening should never be more than $3\frac{1}{4}$ or $3\frac{5}{8}$ inches wide, but if it is to be used in the lower part of a coat or a skirt it may be from 1 to $1\frac{1}{2}$ inches wider.)

No difficulty should be met in constructing the welt, or slit, pocket; for, with a good idea of how the stand and the flap pocket are made, the making of this pocket should be comparatively easy.

32. Preparing the Pattern for the Curved Opening.—The curved opening for the pocket shown in Fig. 25 may be drawn freehand or with the aid of any circular article, such as a drinking glass. But no matter what method is followed, it is necessary that you get the correct slant to the reversed curve, so that when it is transferred to the material in which the pocket is to be made it will assume a good line and appear well-balanced.

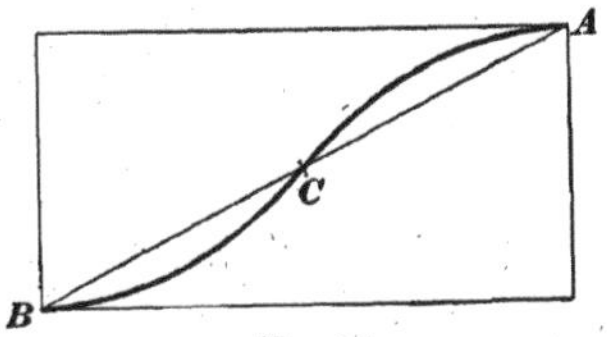

FIG. 26

For the pocket here shown, the opening of the original of which is practically $3\frac{1}{2}$ inches wide, it will perhaps be best to make a pattern in the manner shown in Fig. 26. Therefore, on a piece of paper of suitable size, draw first a rectangle whose top and bottom lines are each 3 inches and whose sides, or ends, are each $1\frac{1}{2}$ inches, and then, as shown, letter the upper right-hand corner A and the lower left-hand corner B. Then connect A and B with a diagonal line and mark the center of this line C.

With this done, proceed to draw the curve, extending it from B, below the diagonal line up to C, and from C above the diagonal line to A. Exercise great care to shape the curves attractively, being guided by the shaping shown in Fig. 26 and blending the curves together at point C with a free-hand line if you use some circular object for outlining the reversed curves below and above the diagonal line. With the curve outlined, cut it from A, through C, to B; then cut from A along the upper line of the rectangle, and from the upper left-hand corner to B. The pattern, which consists of the part above the curve, will then be ready for outlining the opening on the material.

33. As has been stated, the curved edge of any circular article may be used in drawing the curved line, or it may be drawn freehand. In either case, however, it is advisable to draw a rectangle first and then, so as to be sure of the proper slant for the curve, to connect two of its corners with a diagonal line, the direction, or slant, of which will depend on which side of the garment the pocket is to appear.

Of course, pockets of different size and curves of different curvature will require rectangles of different sizes, and just what the size ought to be must be determined by experiment. A good plan is first to decide on what the width and the slant of the pocket openings are to be and then, by actual measurement, determine what the length of the top, bottom, and side lines of the rectangle must be to accommodate the opening. The value of such a pattern lies in the fact that it insures accuracy, for its side or its top may be placed on a stripe or the grain of the garment material; whereas, if no such plan were followed, there would be danger of having the curved opening appear crooked on the garment and thus detract from its appearance.

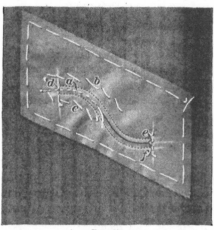

FIG. 27

34. Preparing the Material for the Pocket. With the pattern made ready, lay it on the garment at the place where the pocket opening is to appear, being careful to have it straight, and then outline the opening by drawing a chalk line along the curved edge of the pattern.

Next, on the wrong side of the material, baste a lengthwise piece of silesia or cambric 2½ inches deep and 5 inches wide, with the ends shaped as in Fig. 27, directly under the mark made on the right side for the pocket opening. Then, from the right side, run a basting thread along the mark and through the basted reinforcing strip, as at *a*, so as to outline the pocket opening on the wrong side, using very short stitches and following the curve exactly.

35. Securing the Pocket Material to the Garment.—Next, as shown in Fig. 28, pin to the garment material, over the marked pocket opening, a piece of material cut about 3½ inches by 5 inches, placing it right side down and taking care to match the stripes of the material if there are any. If there are no stripes in the material used, at least the weave of the materials must be matched;

that is, the lengthwise threads of each must run in exactly the same direction.

When this piece is properly matched and pinned in position, secure it in place from the wrong side by basting ½ inch from the marked threads, as shown at *b* and *c*, Fig. 27. Then, with the sewing machine, stitch it and the reinforcing strip in place, stitching from the wrong side and within ⅛ inch of each side of the marked thread, as well as across each end, as at *d*. Extreme care must be exercised in doing this stitch-

Fig. 28

ing, for to have the pocket opening correct, the lines must conform to its outline and the space between the stitching must be exactly the same for the entire length of the curve. Now remove the basting between the rows of stitching, as well as the diagonal basting just outside of the stitching.

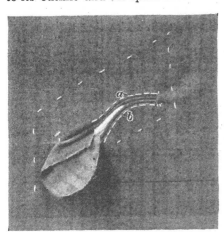

Fig. 29

36. Cutting the Pocket Opening.—The next step is to cut the opening for the pocket. Therefore, with a pair of sharp-pointed scissors, cut from the center to within ¼ inch of each end of the curved opening and then in a diagonal line to each corner, as at *e* and *f*, Fig. 27, and also as in Fig. 28. In cutting this opening, it is well to keep in mind the importance of exercising care when the seam allowance is so narrow, as well as the necessity of keeping the cutting line an even distance from the stitching.

37. Finishing the Pocket Opening.—With the pocket opening cut, slip the material through the slit in the manner indicated

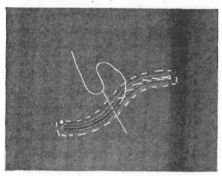

in Fig. 29, smoothing it back carefully at the ends. Then baste, as at *a* and *b*, holding the seam back from underneath with the forefinger of the left hand and along the top with the thumb, so that it cannot be caught in with the welt edges. Have the welts fill the entire space between the stitching and make them of the same

FIG. 30

width on each side of the opening of the pocket.

At this time, also form into plaits on the wrong side the material at the ends of the pocket. In some materials, these plaits may be shrunk out by pressing with a very hot iron and wet cloth. Before starting the basting, it is well to test the width that the welt will have to be to accomplish this, then begin to baste very close to the edge, as shown.

After this basting is done, baste the welts together with diagonal basting, as shown in Fig. 30, so as to make sure that their edges are true, and then, placing a press cloth over the wrong side of the material, press the pocket thoroughly.

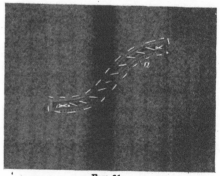

FIG. 31

With the pressing done, stitch the lower edge of the pocket $\frac{1}{16}$ inch from the edge, as at *a*, Fig. 31, and fasten the thread ends securely on the wrong side.

38. Making the Pouch Portion.—For the pouch portion, cut two pieces of silk lining, each 5 inches wide and 3½ inches long, and shape them as shown in Fig. 32. To one piece of lining, stitch a strip of the garment material 2½ inches wide on the lengthwise and 4½ inches on the crosswise, placing the right side of the strip to the right side of the pouch material, as shown at a, Fig. 33. Then stitch the other pouch piece to the lower edge of the pocket, as shown in Fig. 32. Now place the piece of pouch material to which the strip of material is sewed, directly over the pocket, having the right side next to the pocket and the edges even. Then baste and stitch the upper edge of

FIG. 32

the pocket opening the same width as directed for the lower edge, stitching through all thicknesses and fastening the ends of the stitching threads on the wrong side.

Next, baste and stitch the pouch portions together, and, if necessary, trim and overcast the edges. In stitching the pouch portions together, take care to catch the reinforcing strip, as in Fig. 34, so that it will be held to the pocket itself.

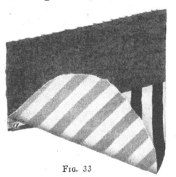

FIG. 33

39. Finishing the Pocket. Next, finish each end of the opening either with an arrowhead, as shown in Fig. 25, or with the overcast bar.

Finally, remove all basting, except the center diagonal basting, which must be left until the garment is finished, and press the pocket

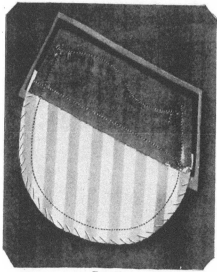

thoroughly. If the material is heavy, trim away the surplus material on the back of the pocket so that not all the edges will come at the same place, as they are likely to form a ridge when pressed. When completed, the pocket should appear on the right side as in Fig. 25 and on the wrong side as in Fig. 34.

40. Slit-Pocket Variations.—A few variations of the slit pocket are illustrated in Fig. 35. As will be observed, the slit may be made to assume various shapes and the pocket itself be placed in different positions; but, of course, the construction of the pocket is

FIG. 34

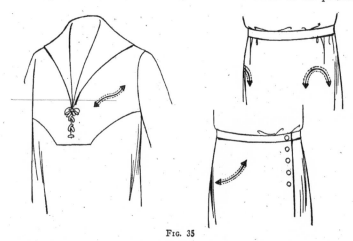

FIG. 35

always the same. Many decidedly pleasing effects can be secured by using just the correct position and shape of slit to harmonize 'with the garment on which the pocket is to be used. In placing pockets on a garment, as well as all other trimmings, due regard should always be given to the style of the garment itself and to current fashions.

SIMPLICITY WELT POCKETS

41. **Simplicity welt pockets** are shown in Fig. 36, the one at (a) being a pocket made on the straight of the material and the one at (b) being a curved pocket. These pockets may be quickly

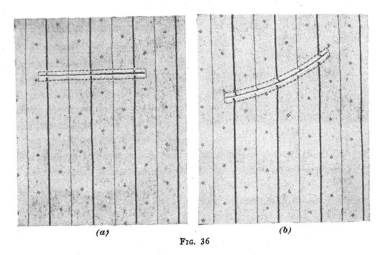

(a)   (b)

Fig. 36

made and are similar in effect to the strictly tailored welt pocket; consequently, this method may be applied to pockets made in woolen as well as cotton garments. They are especially suitable for wool dresses and semitailored jackets.

42. **Making the Simplicity Welt Pocket.**—To make a simplicity welt pocket, cut two pieces of material ⅝ inch larger on all sides than the pocket itself is to be. Place the right side of one of these pieces to the right side of the garment, as at a, Fig. 37, and stitch, as at b, across from one end of the pocket to the other. Slash in the center of the stitching, as at c, and then turn the piece to the wrong side of the material, bringing the material up and forming a welt to the right side as in the welt pocket; then fold it in shape on the wrong side, at the ends, as at a, Fig. 38, and stitch the lower

4 W I—6

edge of the opening, as at *b*. With this done, place the other pocket piece directly over the first one, and, turning the pocket right side

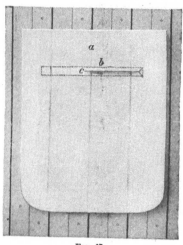

Fɪɢ. 37

up, stitch across the top and the ends so that it will appear on the wrong side, as at *c*, placing the row of stitching the same distance from the welt as the lower stitching is. Then turn in the edges, as at *d*, and stitch all around them, as at *e*. Finish the pocket by tying all the thread ends and pressing it neatly.

43. Choosing Material for the Pouch Portion.—The simplicity welt pocket here shown is of striped material. If the stripe of the material used for such a pocket is very prominent, then the pocket portions, or pouch pieces, should be made of material that is white or of a plain color that harmonizes with the color of the garment, for, as will be observed, the stripes will run irregularly and will not appear so attractive as would plain material in the pocket opening; also, they might show through from the right side.

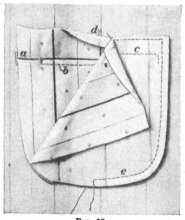

Fɪɢ. 38

PATCH POCKETS

NATURE OF PATCH POCKETS

44. A **patch pocket** is merely a piece of properly shaped material stitched to the outside of a garment in a manner not unlike that of a plain-apron pocket. To take away the severe plainness of a pocket in the form of a simple patch, it is common to resort to trimming and plaits; nevertheless, a pocket applied in the manner stated, whether trimmed, plaited, or plain, does not lose its identity. In making patch pockets, the chief essential is neatness. Especially is it necessary to turn the corners evenly and to use care in placing the pocket in position in order not to have it appear drawn or too full over the material. After having made the pockets thus far discussed, little difficulty will be experienced in making the patch pocket, as it is the most simple.

PLAIN PATCH POCKET

45. The first pocket to be considered is the plain patch pocket, which, owing to its simplicity, is not illustrated. To make such a pocket, first cut out the material, shaping it to suit the style of the garment. As a finish, place a $1\frac{1}{4}$- or $1\frac{3}{4}$-inch hem across the top; then turn the outer edges to the wrong side, baste it to the garment, and stitch it in place. With the stitching done and the thread ends secured neatly on the wrong side, remove the bastings and thoroughly press the pocket from the wrong side.

PATCH POCKET WITH STRAP AND FLAP

46. In Fig. 39 is shown a patch pocket with trimming in the form of a strap and a flap. This style of patch pocket is neat, attractive, and suitable for many styles of tailored coats and skirts, especially unlined coats, sport coats, and little boys' coats to which it is desired to give a mannish effect. It is cut a trifle narrower at the top than at the bottom, so that it will balance well with the garment and impart a trim appearance. This difference between the width at the top and the bottom of the pocket, however, must be so slight as to be scarcely noticeable—just enough to give a neater line than if the top and the bottom were the same in width.

A piece of material $4\frac{1}{2}$ to $5\frac{1}{2}$ inches square is required for this pocket, the size for a garment, of course, depending on the kind, style, and position of the pocket itself. To insure accuracy, however, it is advisable to prepare a paper pattern that is exactly the shape and size of the pocket desired.

47. Cutting the Pocket.—To prepare the pattern, use in this case a piece of paper that is $4\frac{1}{2}$ to $5\frac{1}{2}$ inches square or a little larger than the desired pocket. Trim off the sides a little at the top, so as to make it narrower there than at the bottom; then round off the corners at the lower edge with graceful curves, as the pocket in Fig. 39 shows. In some instances the corners of such pockets are left square, but they are a little more difficult to keep true than are the round corners; also, it is harder to get one side of a pocket with square corners to correspond with the other, especially when stitching is added.

When the pattern is made and in position on the material, the pocket may be cut out and mark-stitched and basted on the pattern lines so as to keep the edges even.

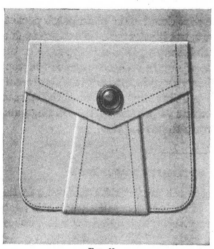

Fig. 39

48. Cutting the Strap. When the pocket material is cut out, cut the strap for the center trimming, shaping it as shown in Fig. 40, this illustration, in addition to giving the details of the work, showing the pocket with strap and flap attached, secured to the garment material w i t h the final stitching. Make the lower, or wider, end of the flap about one-half as wide as the bottom of the pocket and its top about one-third as wide as the top of the pocket; also, make it a generous inch longer than the pocket itself. After the strap material is cut out, line it with light-weight silk of a harmonizing color; or if the garment on which the pocket is to appear is trimmed in another color or with plaid, line the strap with it.

49. Making the Strap.—To make the strap, place the right sides of the material and the lining together and stitch along each side, using a $\frac{1}{4}$-inch seam and stitching outside the pattern line of the strap, so that when it is turned it will not appear narrower than the width originally intended. Stitch the sides only, leaving the ends open so that the strap can be turned right side out. When the stitched strap is turned, press it carefully from the wrong side.

In lining the strap, make sure that the lining is a trifle narrower than the strap material; that is, do not allow the edge of the lining to extend beyond the material. When the strap is finished and the stitching is added to the right side, it should appear as at *a*, Fig. 40.

50. Making the Over-lap.—With the strap thus prepared, proceed to make the overlap, as at *b*, Fig. 40. Cut the material for the overlap one-half as long as the pocket and the same in width. Line it with the same material as the strap is lined, and finish it in much the same manner as the flap of a flap pocket is finished. Stitch carefully all around the edges, making a narrow seam; then turn the flap right side out and stitch it, as at *c*. One or two rows of stitching may be used, depending on the stitching of the garment with which it is used.

FIG. 40

51. Putting the Pocket Pieces Together.—With this done, place the right side of the flap to the wrong side of the pocket, and stitch a good $\frac{1}{4}$ inch from the edge, as at *d*. Then turn the seam of the flap down on the pocket and stitch, as at *e*. Next, overcast the edge, as at *f*, and be very careful that the ends *g* and *h* do not extend beyond the pocket portion.

Now pin the strap to the lower side of the pocket, so that it can be stitched in position in the manner shown in Fig. 40.

52. Applying the Pocket.—Baste the pocket in position on the garment and stitch all around its outer edges, using stitching that comes close to the edge or corresponds with the stitching on the garment.   If the stitching comes very close to the edge, be extremely careful not to let it run off the edge.   Particular pains must be taken when stitching very close to the edge of a thick surface, because the presser foot of the sewing machine in such cases has a tendency to drop off, especially in turning corners.

If the stitching is added directly on the edge, turn the pocket wrong side out and trim away the material of the seam up close to the stitching, being careful, of course, to hold the seam away in trimming, so as not to clip the material.   When the pocket is stitched in position, remove the bastings and press it carefully.

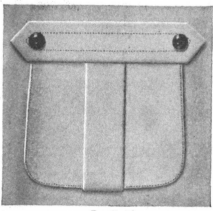

FIG. 41

53. Finishing the Pocket.—Lift up the strap and secure it underneath the flap, as shown in Fig. 39.   This may be done with slip-stitches, so that the thread will not show on either the right or the wrong side of the pocket. If a button is used, as in Fig. 39, rather than take stitches from the underneath side, slip the fingers underneath the strap and the flap and sew the button on, bringing the thread through the strap and the flap and thus holding these two parts together with the button.

In finishing off patch pockets, turn the garment so that it is wrong side up and take a few catch-stitches across the ends of the pocket. These stitches will keep it from pulling loose or tearing at the upper edge, as they serve to strengthen both the pocket edge and the garment.   If such a pocket is to be used a great deal, as, for instance, in children's school or play coats, it is advisable to put a stay strip at the back of the pocket, because such a strip prevents the pocket from tearing out.   This strip should be of the same material as that used for binding the seams of the garment.   It should be cut lengthwise and carefully slip-stitched to the material from the wrong side, so that the stitches will not be visible from the right side.

BOX-PLAITED PATCH POCKET

54. The box-plaited patch pocket, which is shown in Fig. 41, is similar to the patch pocket just described. The material for it is cut in much the same manner, except that 2½ inches is allowed in the center for the plait.

55. Making the Plait and Pocket.—The plait is brought together and basted, and then the edges are opened out smooth and basted carefully, as shown in Fig. 42. If the material is very firm, it is not necessary to stitch the plait before pressing it flat. It is

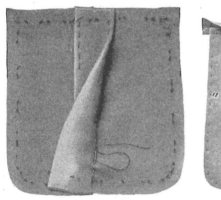

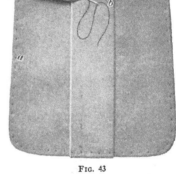

Fig. 42   Fig. 43

customary to leave the plait open, so as to give more freedom in the pocket. However, if the material is wiry or not firm in weave, the best plan is to stitch the plait and then press it so that it will be true and even and will hold its shape well.

Then turn the outer edge of the pocket and baste, as at *a*, Fig. 43, and bind the upper edge of the pocket with a bias strip of lining, as at *b*.

56. Making the Strap.—The strap, which finishes the top of the pocket, is cut crosswise of the material. It should be from 1¼ to 1¾ inches wide and extend just beyond the edges, as shown at *a*, Fig. 44. Line the strap with silk of a color to match the pocket, and stitch the strap in the manner shown in the illustration or in a way that harmonizes with the other stitchings.

57. Completing the Pocket.—With the strap made, fell the upper edge of the pocket to the strap, as at *b*. Next, pin the pocket in position on the garment. Lift the strap, as at *c*, and stitch the pocket all the way around on its outer edge, stitching to the box plait on each side, but as a rule not across it. In this case, the plait is left so that it may be securely slip-stitched from the wrong side.

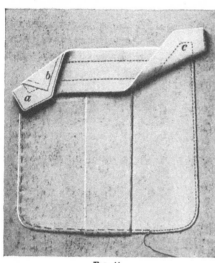

FIG. 44

Then stay the ends of the pocket from the wrong side, using either a stay strip or slip-stitches. Press the strap and the pocket so that they will lie flat on the garment.

If desired, a button may be added to each end of the strap so as to make the pocket more attractive; or if corded loops are used in trimming the garment, a little cord may be made to extend down from the button and be secured in place with a button.

PATCH-POCKET VARIATIONS

58. In Fig. 45 are illustrated several additional styles of patch pockets. Such pockets, as will be noticed, may be made in different shapes, as well as with different styles of straps, flaps, and other trimmings. However, as is true of the other pockets, patch pockets must always harmonize with the garment on which they are used, as a close study of the illustration will indicate.

BOUND POCKETS

59. In Fig. 46 is shown the type of pocket known as the **bound pocket.** This kind of tailored pocket, which is not unlike a regular slit, or welt, pocket, derives its name from the fact that the edges of the opening are bound, usually with braid. When garments trimmed with braid are in vogue, this style of tailored pocket is in

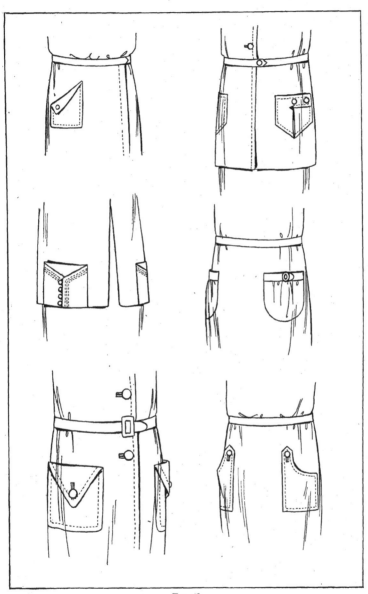

Fig. 45

great demand, but, of course, it would rarely, if ever, be used on garments that are not so trimmed.

For binding the pocket edges, braid that is ¾ inch wide is usually

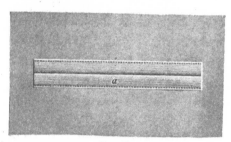

satisfactory, although for broadcloth suits or suits of fine, firm material, narrower braid of fine weave is sometimes employed. Military braid is possibly the most desirable of all braids for tailored work, because it is wieldy; that is, it may be stretched or shrunk to fit shaped

FIG. 46

edges and curves and yet is firm enough to give a satisfactory finish.

60. Making the Pocket Opening.—In making a bound pocket, it is necessary first, as in making other pockets, to determine its position and the width that the pocket opening is to be. With these points known, indicate the width of the pocket opening on the material, as shown by the chalk marks *a* and *b*, Fig. 47, and then at right angles to these lines draw lines *c* and *d*, placing them so that the distance between them is ⅛ inch less than the width of the braid, or equal to the width that the bound portions are to be, usually ½ to ¾ inch, as the braid on each bound edge shows from ¼ to

⅜ inch. With these points marked, stay the wrong side of the pocket with a stay strip, as for the welt pocket.

Next, cut two pieces of braid, each 2 inches longer than the pocket, and apply

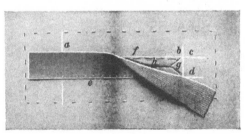

FIG. 47

them to the pocket with a small running-stitch, as shown at *e* and *f*, taking care to keep the outside edges of the braid exactly on the chalk line. When the braid is thus secured to the material, form the pocket opening by slashing the material exactly in the center of the space between the strips of braid and clipping to the corners in diagonal lines, as in the welt pocket, and as shown at *g*. In clipping these diagonal lines, be extremely careful not to clip the braid. With the opening cut, slip the braid of the upper edge through the opening to the wrong side and baste it, as at *h*.

61. Making and Applying the Pouch Pieces.—Cut two pieces of lining for the pouch portion of the pocket, making these pieces as wide as the braid is long and as deep as the pocket is to be and shaping them at the top to conform to the outline of the pocket opening. In this case, as the opening is straight, no difficulty will be encountered, but when it is crescent-shaped or shaped as in Fig. 25, as is sometimes the case, much care has to be taken in shaping the upper edge of the pouch portion to make it exact. With the

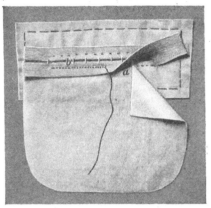

Fig. 48

upper edge and the sides of these pieces shaped, shape the lower edge as in Fig. 48.

Next, turn the garment wrong side up and place one of these pouch portions so that its upper edge is directly over the lining stitches, as at *a*, and baste it in position. Then bring the free edge of the braid of the lower portion over to the wrong side and secure it in position with basting. Next, turn the garment right side up and baste the two folded edges of the braid, or welts, together, as in making the welt pocket, exercising care to keep the fold even and in line with the weave of the braid.

Now turn under the triangular piece at each end of the opening and fasten it neatly and securely on the wrong side. Next, stitch along the lower edge of the braid, as at *a*, Fig. 46, so that the stitching on the wrong side will appear as at *b*, Fig. 48. This stitching serves to hold the pocket pouch in place. If the braid is very wide and extends far below the stitching line *b*, whip the edge down so as to hold it well in place.

Next, stitch a piece of the garment material to the upper edge of the remaining pouch portion, as in making the welt pocket. Then place the side that has the material attached directly over the opening, baste the upper edge to the braid, and then over the right side stitch the upper edge in the same way as the lower edge was stitched.

62.   Completing the Pocket.—Turn the wrong side up and stitch the sides and the lower end of the pocket portions together, and pull all threads through to the wrong side and fasten them in place. Finally, stay the ends of the pocket on the wrong side.   The ends on the right side may be left plain, as the illustration shows, or finished with arrowheads.

CHAPTER IV

TAILORED SEAMS AND PLACKETS

PRECAUTIONS IN MAKING TAILORED SEAMS

1. Tailored seams, many kinds of which are used in tailored costumes, require generous seam allowance and careful basting, stitching, and pressing. Their development is not difficult, however, and if you take the time to carry out each detail, you will undoubtedly obtain very gratifying results.

2. Seam Allowance.—In making allowance for tailored seams, be guided by the kind of material you are using. Fabrics that fray or ravel easily require a wider seam allowance than materials of firmer weave. Also, they require extreme accuracy, with regard to the marking of seam lines. Tracing, chalk marks, or basting-stitches, may be used, according to the kind of marking best suited to the texture of the material.

3. Mark-Stitching.—Too much emphasis cannot be laid on the value of mark-stitching along the seam lines that are indicated by the tracing, chalk marks, or basting applied with the pattern in position on the material, as this stitching will mark both sides of the garment exactly alike and show accurate positions for pockets or trimming features that are to be the same on both sides of the garment.

The method of making mark-stitches is shown in Fig. 1. After taking two short stitches with double thread, skip $\frac{1}{2}$ to $\frac{3}{4}$ inch and take two more short stitches, leaving a loop on the surface between each two groups of stitches, as shown at *a*. After basting the entire length of the seam in this way, draw the two thicknesses of material apart and cut the threads between them, as at *b* and *c*. Then short threads will be left in each piece to mark the pattern line accurately and the two pieces will be marked exactly alike.

It may seem to some persons that mark-stitching takes too much time; but it is the only way in which to make sure of a clean, exact line for basting or stitching in woolen materials, and the personal satisfaction derived in putting together a garment that has been carefully mark-stitched more than repays for the time consumed.

4. Basting.—Before basting the seams, to prevent stretching one edge and thus making it longer than the other, pin the edges together at frequent intervals, inserting the pins perpendicularly to the seam line so that they will not cause annoyance

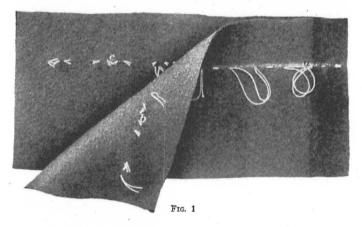

Fig. 1

while the basting is being done. Then baste with short stitches, being careful not to stretch the seam.

5. Stitching.—For stitching woolen materials, procure, if possible, silk thread that is just a tone darker than the fabric. Very dark and medium blues, as well as very dark reds and browns, come in so many different hues that it is frequently necessary to use black for stitching. In any event, in selecting thread, consider the fact that it will work up a little lighter than it appears on the spool. The proper way in which to secure a perfect match is to lay a single thread across the material in good daylight; artificial light can seldom be depended on in matching colors.

Another good point to remember in connection with thread used for tailored seams is that the manufacturer numbers the colors

on the spools; therefore, it is well at times to keep the spools as
they become empty, so that you may procure more thread of exactly
the same color if it is needed.

6. Before starting to stitch, test the machine-stitching on a
scrap of material like that used for the garment in order to make
sure that the tension, the length of the stitch, and the size of the
needle are correct. Very fine stitching is not suitable for tailored
garments, as it draws the material down and mars the smooth
surface. Very long stitches, too, should be avoided, but they are
permissible when the stitching is intended for decorative purposes,
this, as a rule, requiring heavier silk than would otherwise be used.

In stitching, strive always for extreme accuracy. The marked
seam line will serve as a guide when you are applying the first
stitching on the wrong side, this stitching being required for most
seams; but when stitching on the right side, use a sewing-machine
gauge or quilter or mark the line you wish to follow, unless your eye
is sufficiently well-trained to gauge spaces properly.

Attention must be given to the adjustment of the gauge or
quilter. Be guided by your sewing-machine instruction book when
placing either attachment in position, being careful to adjust the
quilter just high enough to permit the material to pass freely under
it. On some sewing machines, you will find it impossible to adjust
the gauge or the quilter on the left-hand side of the presser-foot,
and, in some cases, if you use the quilter as a gauge, you will
have to turn it backwards. In such instances, extreme care must
be taken to follow exactly along the edge that is to be stitched.

7. Pressing.—Pressing, too, is of decided importance. In
making tailored seams, press each stage of the work as you advance,
always pressing lengthwise of the seam and making it as flat as
possible. Also, press the finished seams. As a general rule, the
pressing may be done entirely on the wrong side of the material.

KINDS OF SEAMS

8. Plain Seam.—The plain seam is used even more extensively in woolen materials than it is in wash fabrics. Many distinctive dresses are assembled by means of plain seams, not a stitch
showing anywhere on the outside of the garment. When such is
the case, the responsibility of the seams is very great, for it is

through the perfection of their making and pressing that they take their place inconspicuously in a tailored garment.

Fig. 2

To make a plain seam, place the right sides of the material together so that one mark-stitched seam line is directly over the other; then baste along the mark-stitched line and, after the fitting of the garment, stitch on the basted line.

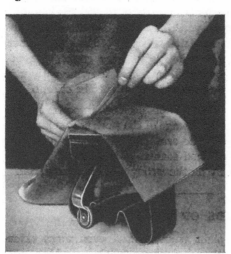

Fig. 3

In order to finish such a seam in woolen material, open it out, as shown in Fig. 2, and then press well on the wrong side with a moderately hot iron, or, if the material is not heavy, you may turn the seam edges together to one side if you wish. In some cases, it is not necessary to use any moisture in order to press the seam open satisfactorily, but if you find it difficult to make the seam edges lie flat without first dampening them, run a slightly moistened sponge or sponge cloth along the opened seam and then press it. The use of considerable moisture in the pressing of seams takes from the softness of finish that is generally desirable in women's garments.

9. Instead of pressing seams in velvet or in woolen fabrics having a nap that is not pressed flat, steam them open by running them over the edge of an inverted hot iron that has been covered with a damp cloth, as shown in Fig. 3. The velvet presser described in Art. **18,** Chapter I, is, of course, satisfactory, too.

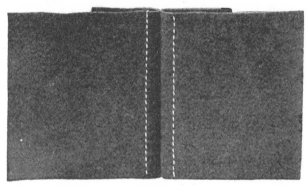

FIG. 4

10. Finish the edges of a plain seam by notching, pinking, overcasting, or binding them, according to the nature of the fabric, notching or pinking closely woven fabrics, such as flannel and broadcloth, binding those that fray readily, and overcasting those that do not require binding and yet need a more lasting finish than notching or pinking would provide.

11. Single-Stitch Seam.—The single-stitch seam, illustrated in Fig. 4, makes an attractive finish for a plain seam. To make this seam, first carefully press and baste both edges back from the stitched line of the plain seam; then stitch accurately on both sides the distance from the seam line you desire. The presser-foot of the sewing machine serves as a good guide in doing such work. It is well first to stitch along the right side of the seam, keeping the edge of the presser-foot in line with the plain seam, and then, when this side is stitched, to repeat the operation on the other side of the seam line.

4 W I—7

12. Double-Stitch Seam.—To make the double-stitch seam, which is illustrated in Fig. 5, baste as for a single-stitch seam; then baste back ⅜ inch or more on each side of the first basting. Add

FIG. 5

stitching on both sides of the plain seam, as just explained, making a single-stitch seam; and then stitch back ⅜ inch or more on each side of the first stitching, as is clearly shown in the illustration.

13. Cord Seam.—Make the cord seam, Fig. 6, as follows: Baste a plain seam, but do not stitch it, as the outside stitching is

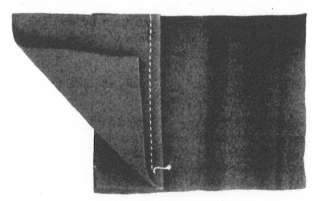

FIG. 6

all that is necessary; then, instead of pressing the seam open, turn both seam edges to one side and baste them. Next, with the presser-foot of the machine as a guide, stitch ⅛ to ¼ inch from the seam edge through the three thicknesses. When the basting is removed, the effect is similar to that of a corded seam.

FIG. 7

Instead of giving the cord seam a final pressing as suggested for tailored seams in general, press merely along the row of stitching, taking care not to let the iron extend over the outer edge, or corded effect, for a flat pressing would make the seam appear as a tuck rather than a cord.

14. Welt Seam.—The welt seam, which is shown in Fig. 7, should be made as follows: First, baste and stitch as in making a plain seam; then cut away one seam edge to within $\frac{1}{4}$ inch of the stitching, as shown at *a*, Fig. 8. Next, bind, notch, or overcast the wide seam allowance, and turn it back over the one that has

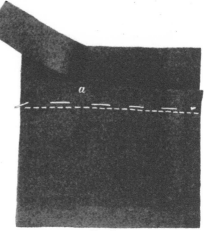

FIG. 8

been partly cut away. With the right side of the material up, as in Fig. 7, press the material away carefully from the seam with the fingers so that it will not overlap in any place. Next, baste along the seam edge and then back ½ inch, or almost the width of the stitching desired. Finally, stitch the desired width, usually ⅜ or ½ inch from the seam, using a sewing-machine gauge or quilter for this purpose, if you wish a guide to insure even spacing.

FIG. 9

15. Double-Stitched Welt.—To make the double-stitched welt, an example of which is shown in Fig. 9, follow all the instructions for making a welt seam, and in addition apply a second row of stitching on the seam turn, as is clearly shown at *a*.

FIG. 10

16. Tuck Seam.—The tuck seam, or *open welt*, as shown in Fig. 10, is made as follows: First baste as a plain seam, but do not stitch. Then turn both seam edges to one side and baste them as in making the cord seam. Then, from the right side, add another row of basting the desired tuck width from the seam edge, as shown in Fig. 11. Place a row of stitching the desired distance, usually $\frac{1}{4}$ to 1 inch from the seam edge; then remove the basting and mark-stitches, and the seam will appear as a tuck, as in Fig. 10.

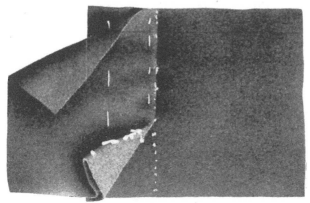

FIG. 11

17. Slot Seam.—The slot seam, which is illustrated in Fig. 12, requires an allowance of $\frac{3}{4}$ to 1 inch for each seam edge. Make the seam as follows: Baste as for a plain seam, with short, even bast-

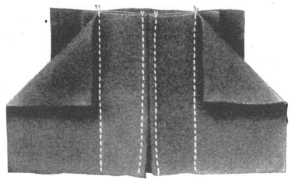

FIG. 12

ing-stitches, and press the seam open. Then cut a strip lengthwise of the material, making it a little longer than the seam and $\frac{1}{2}$ inch wider than the pressed-open seam measures from one edge to the other, as shown in Fig. 13. Place the right side of the strip to

the wrong side of the garment, pin the center of the strip **directly**
under the seam, as at *a*.   Take care that the strip is eased a trifle,
as it should not be stretched in the least.   Baste from the right

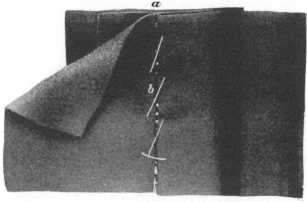

FIG. 13

side, with diagonal basting, as shown at *b*, holding the seam firmly
with the left hand and thus avoiding any possibility of stretching
the strip or the seam.   Next, baste and stitch $\frac{3}{8}$ to $\frac{3}{4}$ inch from the
seam on each side.   When the bastings are removed, the seam will
have the appearance of two tuck seams meeting.

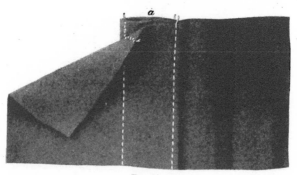

FIG. 14

If you wish to make the *slot seam with inside stitching*, as shown
in Fig. 12, lift the inside edges of the slot seam, or tucks, and
stitch directly on the edge of each, but do not stitch through the
underneath strip.

18. Tailored Fell.—The tailored fell, or *imitation strap*, as it is sometimes called, is shown in Fig. 14. To make the tailored fell, proceed as follows: Lap one piece over the other so that the

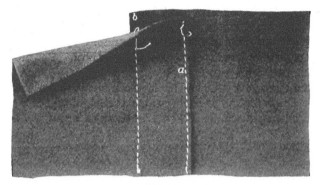

Fig. 15

mark-stitching lines meet exactly. Baste along the line of mark-stitching, or the seam line; turn under the edges so that they meet at the center, as at *a*, and baste the outer edges and stitch.

This seam, which is very similar to a machine fell, is extensively used in unlined coats and skirts, especially tailored wash skirts.

Fig. 16

19. Lap Seam.—The lap seam, illustrated in Fig. 15, is used only on heavy, firmly woven materials that do not fray. An allowance of $\frac{1}{4}$ to $\frac{5}{8}$ inch is necessary for this seam. To make the seam, lap the edges as in the tailored fell, but do not turn the outside edges under; baste and stitch the outside edges, making the rows of stitching absolutely parallel; then trim the material off close to the stitching, as shown at *a* and *b*. Do not use selvage edges.

20. Strap Seam.—The strap seam, an example of which is shown in Fig. 16, is simply a plain seam with a good seam allowance, over which, after the seam has been pressed open, is placed a bias strap of the same or some contrasting material. The procedure in making this seam is as follows:

For the strap, cut a bias piece of the material twice the width that the finished strap is to be; catch the edges together with a diagonal basting-stitch, as in Fig. 17, taking care that the basting

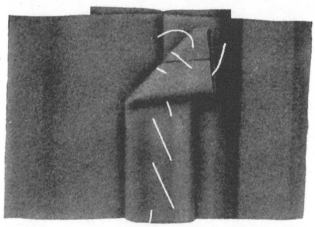

Fig. 17

does not show on the right side and that the edges do not overlap and cause a ridge after the seam is pressed; and then press the strap, being very careful not to twist it in the least. Next, place the strap directly over the seam on the right side, and baste it in position with diagonal basting, as shown. Finally, baste the outside edges down and stitch on each edge of the strap, so that it will appear, when finished, as in Fig. 16.

Sometimes, on garments where machine-stitching is not desirable, the edges of the strap are slip-stitched down or secured with a decorative stitch.

21. Variation of Stitching on Tailored Seams.—A seam may be made to take on an entirely different appearance by the way in which it is stitched.   Each season brings out a new mode of stitching that, when followed out in accurate detail, adds a great deal to the appearance of a garment and distinguishes it from models of a past season.

Very heavy materials require a seam broad and substantial in appearance, and the outside stitching is almost invariably applied in such a way that it will give this effect.   Light-weight materials do not require outside or decorative stitching, but if such stitching is used, it should not be placed too far from the seam itself, because the material does not have sufficient body to hold itself firmly between the original seam and the outside stitching.

Some plain seams in firm materials, such as broadcloth, have a wide seam allowance, the seam being pressed open and three or four rows of stitching added on each side of the seam from $\frac{1}{16}$ to $\frac{1}{8}$ inch apart.   Seams are also quilted with small circles, diamonds, and squares when Fashion favors this form of decoration.

REQUIREMENTS OF TAILORED PLACKETS

22.   Tailored plackets, or openings in skirts that permit them to be slipped over the head with ease, are not unlike wash plackets, yet because of the materials used in the construction of tailored skirts, the methods of making them differ and they demand greater care.   Tailored plackets require more basting and pressing than do wash plackets; in fact, extreme care must be taken with any tailored placket so as not to stretch either of its sides, for the woolen materials used in tailored skirts are almost ungovernable when they are once stretched.   Also, as the facing silk often used in the construction of tailored plackets differs in weight and texture from the skirt material, it, too, must be carefully handled, so that it will not appear drawn or too full in any place.   However, to make a placket that fastens up so perfectly that the skirt opening does not attract undue attention doubly repays any one for the time and effort that must be expended in its construction.

23.   Essentials of Placket Making.—To be able to make strictly tailored skirts successfully, it is imperative that these tailored plackets be thoroughly understood and mastered.   A good plan, therefore, is to procure pieces of woolen material of suitable size and to make the plackets in the order in which they are described; then, when it is desired to make a tailored skirt, the finishing of the placket will not seem difficult.

As in the making of tailored seams, the importance of accurately mark-stitched seam lines, careful basting, and frequent pressing in the development of tailored plackets cannot be overestimated.

Each seam and each edge of any tailored placket should be carefully basted and pressed before any stitching is done, because woolen materials will slip and stretch under the presser-foot of the sewing machine unless they are carefully held in place with basting. Especially is basting necessary in the application of the facing pieces.

24. Facing of Plackets.—To finish most tailored plackets properly, lengthwise facing strips of soft taffeta, satin, percaline, or sateen are needed, and, no matter which material is used, it is generally referred to as *facing silk*. If the skirt is to be a very fine one, a soft excellent quality of taffeta or a firmly woven satin may be used as a finish. For the majority of woolen skirts, percaline of the best quality is used, and for very heavy skirts sateen of close, fine, weave is desirable. In the selection of a facing, however, it is of the utmost importance to choose material that is in keeping with the material and the style of the skirt and that will wear equally as well as the skirt material. It is very unsatisfactory to use a facing material that does not correspond with the skirt material or that will wear out before the garment does. Also, as the facing of the placket must, in many instances, turn back over the rings of the hooks and come well up under the prongs, the facing material must of necessity be thin enough not to interfere in the hooking of the skirt.

KINDS OF PLACKETS

PLAIN-SEAM PLACKET

25. Nature of Placket.—A skirt having waist-line fulness does not require especial strength at the placket opening because there is very little strain on the opening. In such a skirt, the **plain-seam placket,** which is made very simple, as shown in Fig. 18, may be used. In a placket of this kind, there should be no suggestion of its finish on the right side. The usual position of such a placket is at the center side above a plain seam.

In a skirt having fulness at the waist line, the placket opening need not be so long as in a plain, fitted skirt and, for this reason, the plain-seam placket is generally made not more than 8 inches long, this length permitting the skirt to be slipped off easily.

26. Applying Placket Stay Tapes.—The seam lines that were mark-stitched in the cutting of the skirt are essential in the making

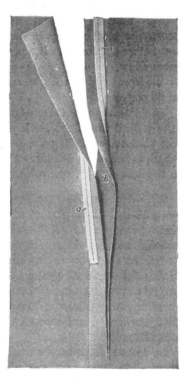

FIG. 18 FIG. 19

of the placket, for they serve as a guide for the placing of the tapes that are used as a stay for the placket edges and as a foundation for the fasteners. After stitching the side seam of the skirt, baste a piece of tape $\frac{1}{2}$ inch or so longer than the opening left for the placket, on the wrong side of the skirt, as at *a*, Fig. 19, so that one edge of the tape is in line with the mark-stitching that indicates the seam line on one side of the placket. Then stitch the tape through the center, thus making a row of stitching show on the opposite side of the seam allowance made in the material, as at *b*.

Baste and stitch a similar strip along the other side of the placket, also, as at *c*, making sure that the edge of the tape is exactly along the mark-stitched seam line. Then turn under the front, or upper, portion of the placket along the mark-stitched line and baste and press it flat.

27. Finishing the Seam Edges.—In most cases, the seam edges below the placket may be turned and pressed together over the front-skirt portion, but if a pressed-open seam is essential, clip the seam allowance on the back- or under-placket edge straight across at the lower end of the placket, in order to permit this seam edge to lie perfectly flat.

To finish the raw seam edges, overcast them or, if the material is of a kind that frays readily, bind the edges with a light-weight silk binding, extending the overcasting or binding along the full length of the seam, including the placket edges, and across the slash in the seam edge if one was made at the lower end of the placket.

28. Applying the Snap Fasteners.—Three or four snap fasteners are sufficient for a placket of this kind. In applying them, sew them directly over the lines of stitching that hold the tapes in position, as shown in Fig. 18, and take the stitches through the tape as well as the material, so as to make them very secure. When sewing the snaps along the upper-placket edge, however, be very careful not to catch the stitches through to the right side; take them through merely the turned-under placket edge and the tape, so that there may not be even a suggestion of the stitches on the outside of the skirt.

In sewing snap fasteners on a placket, always remember to begin at the bottom of the placket, for then if any slight fulness should, by any chance, work up on either side of the placket it can come out at the waist line rather than at the bottom of the placket.

29. Securing the Turned-Under Portion.—In order to hold the turned-under upper portion of the placket in position when the skirt is being worn, it should be secured with slip-stitching. In doing the slip-stitching, fold back about ¼ inch of the turned-under portion, as shown in Fig. 18, and take the stitches, as at *a*,

very close together, catching only a thread or two of the material
in the turned edge as well as in the material underneath so as to
avoid having these stitches show on the right side of the skirt.
Also, do not draw the stitches up tight; rather, permit sufficient
ease in them so that the edge that was folded back to facilitate the
slip-stitching will fall back over these stitches and lie perfectly flat.

WELT-SEAM PLACKET

30. The **welt-seam placket** is shown in Fig. 20. This style
of placket is used in fitted, gored skirts, usually at the left center-
side seam, or at the
left side of a front or
back panel. Also, it
may be employed on
a skirt finished with
plain pressed-open
seams as well as on
one having seam edges
turned to one side
and finished with out-
side stitching. The
placket here illus-
trated is at the left
side of a two-piece
skirt that has a raised
waist line supported
by an inside belt.

**31. Applying the
Facings.**—For the
welt-seam placket, cut

Fɪɢ. 20

two strips of facing silk, making each about 1¾ inches wide and
a trifle longer than the placket opening. After finishing the skirt
seam, clip across the underneath seam edge at the lower end of the
placket, as shown at *a*, Fig. 21. This clipping must be done on the
one seam edge to permit it to extend under the other and to make
the seam lie perfectly flat when the placket is lapped into position.
If a welt seam is used for the skirt, then it will not be necessary to
clip the seam at the bottom of the placket, because the edges of the

seam will then come over each other in the forming of the welt and
will not have to be pressed open.

Next, baste one of the strips of facing silk to the material,
placing its right side to the right side of the gore that is to form the
underneath part of the placket with the raw edges even.   Then
turn it to the wrong side, fold the raw edge of the strip over to meet
the raw seam edge of the placket, as shown, and crease and baste
the turned edge, as at b.   When this turned edge is folded back in

position, it will be close to
the mark-stitched line at c.

When this strip is basted
in position, proceed with the
other facing strip. Lay it
so that its right side is to
the wrong side of the skirt
portion, as at d, and the edge
of the facing is even with
the mark-stitched seam line.
Then baste this facing strip
in position, as at e, and baste
again, as at f, so as to hold
the facing silk well in position.

32. Stitching the Placket.
With the basting done, proceed with the stitching.
Stitch the underneath edge of
the placket portion where it
was turned over, as at a, Fig.
22, so that the edge will be
held securely in place. Then

Fig. 21

stitch the upper - placket
edge, stitching from the right side $\frac{1}{4}$ to $\frac{1}{2}$ inch from the edge, as at
a, Fig. 20, and continuing the line of stitching to the bottom of the
placket.   In stitching, hold the underneath portion of the placket
away so that it will not be caught in with the stitching; also, be
sure to use a gauge or to mark with basting threads the line on
which to stitch so that there will be no danger that the stitching
will appear crooked, for in a very plain placket of this kind the

workmanship must be as nearly perfect as possible, in order that the break between seam and placket may be imperceptible.

When you reach a point about $\frac{1}{4}$ inch from the bottom of the placket, lift the needle and the presser-foot and draw the material out just a trifle in order to leave a thread length of about $\frac{1}{2}$ inch between the end of the stitching and the needle.   Then, with the placket still under the presser-foot, turn the under-placket edge, or seam allowance, back underneath the upper portion and adjust

FIG. 22

the material under the presser-foot in order to continue stitching diagonally to the seam line, as shown in Fig. 20, without causing a break or unevenness in the line of stitching.   Before continuing the stitching, however, turn the spool of thread on the machine so as to wind up the extra thread length that was drawn out.   Then, when the stitching is continued, no loop of thread will show on the right side, but the extra bobbin-thread length will remain and loop over the under-seam edge without puckering it as would be the case if the extra thread length had not been provided.

After completing the stitching, pull the threads through and fasten them.   This diagonal row of stitching makes the bottom of the placket secure and holds the upper and underneath portions together.

If you prefer, you may omit the outside machine-stitching entirely and secure the turned edge by catch-stitching it through the facing silk to the right side of the skirt, making the stitches as tiny as possible so that they will be practically invisible on the right side.

33. Finishing the Placket.—Before putting on either hooks and eyes or snap fasteners, press the placket thoroughly so that it will lie perfectly smooth and not appear stretched or puckered in any place. If you use snap fasteners for fastening the placket, as in this case, fold the free edge of the facing silk on the upper edge of the placket back over the raw edge of the skirt seam, and whip it down directly over the stitching that is put in from the right side. If you use hooks and eyes, sew the hooks on first and then bring the strip over and hem it down underneath the prongs of the hooks themselves.

In a placket of this kind, always take care to overcast the lower edges so that the placket will appear neatly finished. When the placket is stitched and pressed, proceed to put on the fasteners, remembering always to begin at the bottom of the placket opening to mark their positions and to sew them on in the same order so as to have any fulness come out at the waist line.

34. Applying the Belting.—When the fasteners are in position, the inside belt should receive attention. As you will observe, on referring to Fig. 22, no stitching appears on the right side of the skirt at the waist line.

In order to make provision for this finish, the upper edge of the skirt should be turned over the belting when the skirt is being fitted. After the fitting is done, turn the belting back so that the upper portion of the skirt may be laid out flat, removing one pin at a time as you turn the belting back and reinserting it with care in order to maintain the correct line at the upper edge of the skirt. Then secure the skirt to the belting by taking small basting-stitches $\frac{3}{8}$ inch below the upper edge of the belting and through the edge of the skirt that extends over the belting.

After basting, trim the seam edge of the skirt quite close to the row of basting; then baste over the seam edge a narrow strip of bias silk that has its edges turned, and secure this on both sides with stitching, as is clearly illustrated in Fig. 22. The belting may then be turned back against the skirt and, as the illustration indicates, no stitching will show on the right side of the skirt.

Finish the ends of the belting with two or three hooks and eyes, according to its width, applying the hooks so that the ends of the prongs are just inside the end of the belting and the eyes so that the loops extend about ⅛ inch beyond the end of the belting, as shown.

35. Welt-Seam Placket in Tailored Wash Skirt.—The way in which to make a welt-seam placket for a tailored wash skirt is shown in Fig. 23. Apply the under facing for this placket in much

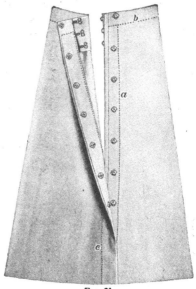

the same manner as for a similar placket in woolen material, but, instead of folding the facing under and leaving it loose, stitch it flat, as at *a*, ⅛ to ¼ inch in from the edge of the seam line of the skirt, so that it will not be seen when the placket is hooked up. Such stitching holds the facing more securely and prevents it from pulling out in the laundering. Apply the facing to the upper edge by first stitching it over the right side along the edge, then turning it to the wrong side and stitching it flat, as shown.

To secure the skirt to the belting, turn under the upper edge and whip this turned edge

FIG. 23

to the extreme upper edge of the belting, or stitch the turned-under edge to the belting, first turning the skirt portion back in order not to make the stitching evident on the right side.

If you wish outside stitching at the top of the skirt, as at *b*, you may apply this below the upper edge a distance that is the same as the width of the stitching on the welt seam, as at *c*, or somewhat narrower than this. You may take this stitching merely through the turned-back portion at the upper edge of the skirt, as shown, or through the belting, also, the stitching in this case serving to hold the skirt securely to the belting in the laundering.

4 W I—8

36. The **tuck-seam placket,** which is a form of opening much used in skirts that employ tuck seams, adapts itself very well to both wash and woolen materials. It is generally used on a straight seam down the center front or back of a skirt, but it may be employed on the edge of a panel having a tuck finish or when a tuck finish is used on a side gore. The method of making the tuck-seam placket differs somewhat in wash and wool materials, stay tapes being used in wash materials for the fasteners required on the opening and silk facing pieces being employed in woolen materials for this purpose. Both of the methods are given here so that you may be prepared to make the tuck-seam placket in any sort of material.

37. Tuck-Seam Placket in Wash Material.—In order to avoid a break in the stitching at the termination of the placket and still show only a single row of stitching on the right side, it is advisable to finish both sides of the placket before forming the tuck. For the stays that are required when the placket is used in wash material, use tape or narrow, bias, seam binding having its edges turned.

To apply the stays, stitch a piece of the tape that is a trifle longer than you desire the placket, over the left front of the skirt, as at a, Fig. 24, placing the tape about $\frac{1}{2}$ inch from the front edge preferably on the wrong side of the material and extending it from the waist line. Stitch a similar strip to the right front of the skirt, as at b,

FIG. 24

applying this in practically the same manner preferably over the wrong side of the material. The reason for applying the stays before forming the tuck seam is to prevent the stitching, as at c, from showing on the right side of the skirt when the tuck seam is completed.

38. Next, form the tuck for the center front by folding back the right front of the skirt the width of the tucks plus a generous seam allowance. Baste it the tuck width from the fold and stitch the tuck the full skirt length, also pressing it before joining it to the left front of the skirt.

In applying the stitching, be careful to stitch in a straight line and to make the stitching an even distance from the edge its entire length.

With the tuck stitched its full length, slip the front edge of the left front underneath the tuck, in order to bring the marked center-front line of the left front directly under the marked center-front line in the tuck, or right front. ·

With the center-front lines and the hip lines exactly matched, pin and baste the fronts together, taking the basting-stitches just a trifle to the right of the tuck stitching, beginning just above the lower end of the stay tapes and continuing to the lower edge of the skirt. This basting should hold the tuck to the left front, leaving the seam allowance of both fronts extending together underneath.

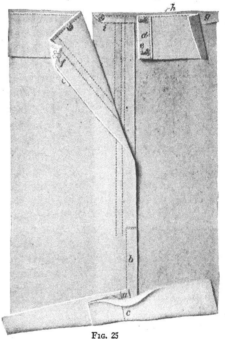

Fig. 25

39. In order to stitch the fronts together, first fold the right front back over the left front, as shown in Fig. 24; then, with your finger pressing the right front back over the stitching that secures the tuck, stitch the seam allowances together, as at *d*, as close to the fold as you can, but be very careful not to let this stitching catch the edge of the material that is folded back.

Start the stitching just above the lower edge of the stay tapes, and in order to make the finish secure and the tying of thread ends unnecessary, stitch from the inside of the seam allowance directly across to the outside edge, and then back over this stitching, as at *e.* Continue the stitching to the skirt edge.

40. In Fig. 25 is shown the wrong side of the completed placket. At *a*, a few of the stitches that secure the tuck are drawn out to illustrate the closeness of the two rows of stitching, one of which shows only on the wrong side, as at *b*, and the other on the right side, as at *c*. To make the inside belt, hems are stitched in the ends of the belting, as at *d*; then hooks are secured, as at *e*, and eyes, as at *f*. The upper part of the skirt is turned down as at *g*, and the belting applied, so that it comes slightly below the turned edge, as at *h*. The raw top edge in the lapping portion of the skirt may be covered with a narrow tape, as at *i*, secured with fine whipping-stitches.

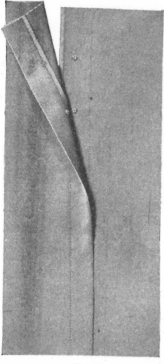

Fig. 26

41. Tuck-Seam Placket in Wool Material.—In making a tuck-seam placket in wool material, as shown in Fig. 26, plan to finish both edges of the placket separately, as in the case of wash materials, before stitching the seam. The first step in the making of this placket is to prepare and apply the stay pieces.

42. As a stay piece for the tuck, or upper, portion of the placket, cut a straight strip of facing silk about ½ inch longer than you wish the placket opening and ¾ inch wider than the distance from the raw edge to the basted or marked line indicating where the tuck should be turned. Then, as a guide for placing the stay piece for the tuck edge of the placket, turn back the tuck allowance on the skirt and press it in order to crease the edge. After creasing, open out the tuck, when the crease will appear on the wrong side, as at *a*, Fig. 27.

Apply the stay piece by first placing it over the wrong side of the skirt portion so that it extends about ⅜ inch beyond the creased line underneath, as shown, and then basting it to the skirt material through the allowance that will be turned back but as close to the creased line as possible in order to hold the stay strip close to the tuck edge when it is turned. Use silk thread that matches the color of the skirt material for this basting and take extremely fine stitches through to the right side and stitches about ½ inch long on the facing side, as at *b*.

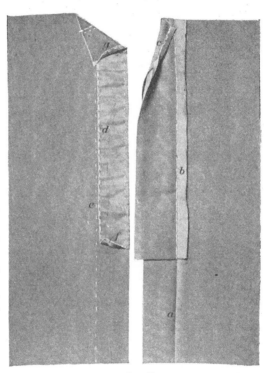

The stay strip is cut wide enough to form a binding for the raw edge of the tuck allowance, as at *c*, but before securing this in position, turn the tuck allowance

FIG. 27

back and press it again over the stay piece. Then, after turning the binding over the edge and whipping or stitching it in position, as at *a*, Fig. 28, stitch the tuck, as at *b*, its full length before applying it to the other front section of the skirt, as directed in making a tuck-seam placket in wash material.

43. For staying the under-placket edge, cut a straight strip of facing silk about ½ inch longer than you desire the opening and

½ inch wider than the distance from the raw edge to where the tuck, or upper-placket portion, will lap, as indicated in Fig. 27 by a line of

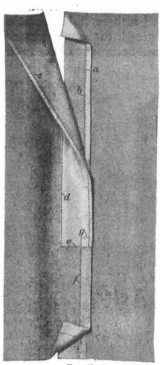

basting, which was applied directly after the cutting of the skirt.

Apply this by first turning under one lengthwise edge a scant ¼ inch and basting it, as at d, Fig. 27, to the wrong side of the skirt about ⅛ inch inside of the basted line on the skirt, as at e, which indicates the point to which the tuck edge is to overlap. When you reach the lower end of the strip, turn this under, as at f, to produce a neat finish; then turn the strip over to the right side of the material to provide a finish for the raw edge; turn and baste this in position, as at g, Fig 27, and stitch it, as at c, Fig. 28. Stitch the other edge of the strip, also, as at d, and whip or slip-stitch the turn at the lower end of the facing strip, as at e, before joining it to the tuck edge of the placket.

If the material has a smooth, fine finish that will be likely to show press marks, it is advisable not to turn the end of the facing strip, as at f, Fig. 27, but simply to overcast this raw edge.

FIG. 28

44. With both portions of the placket finished, place the tuck edge over the other edge of the skirt so that it is just even with the basted line made on the under portion, and baste these edges together. Then turn the right, or upper, front over on the other skirt portion and stitch the seam edges together, as at f, from the lower end of the placket opening to the lower edge of the skirt, stitching as close to the first row of stitching as possible in the same manner as previously directed for stitching the tuck seam in a wash skirt or, for a somewhat softer finish, join along the seam lines by hand, using running-stitches with an occasional back-stitch.

Joining the edges in woolen materials by hand is, in a way, some-what easier than stitching them together, for when the seam is being machine-stitched, extreme care is required to prevent the turned-back portion from slipping under the needle and being caught by the stitching.

In securing the two sections together, either by hand or by machine, take a double row of stitches across the seam allowance at the lower end of the placket, as at g, to serve as a stay and prevent the stitching from pulling out.

Apply the snap fasteners, as shown in Fig. 26, just over the stitching of the tuck, taking care to catch the stitches through the stay pieces underneath but not through to the right side.

HABIT-BACK PLACKET

45. The **habit-back placket,** shown in Fig. 29, derives its name from its orig-inal use as a finish for the opening in the plain back of a woman's riding skirt, or habit. Besides being used for riding habits in seasons when such a finish is favored, it may provide the center-back opening of a fitted separate or suit skirt.

As plackets made on skirts that fit snugly at the waist and hips require secure fast-ening, hooks and eyes are used instead of snap fasteners and are placed close together to hold the edges securely and neatly.

Fig. 29

46. For accurate development of the habit-back placket, a mark-stitched seam line, as at a, Fig. 30, is essential. After deter- · mining the placket length, as a rule, 8 to 11 inches measured from the waist line, stitch and finish the skirt seam from the lower end

of the placket to the bottom of the skirt.   Then, prepare to finish
the placket.

47.   Preparing the Fly and Applying the Facings.—A *fly*, or
extension, piece is required for the underneath portion of this placket.
For this, cut a lengthwise strip of the skirt fabric about $2\frac{1}{2}$ inches
wide and $1\frac{1}{2}$ inches longer than the placket opening, and mark the

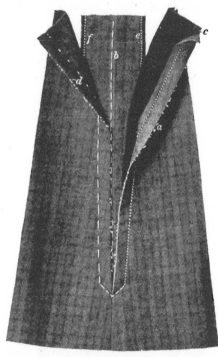

center of the piece with
basting thread, as shown
at *b*.   Also, cut a piece of
facing $\frac{3}{8}$ inch larger on all
sides than the strip of
material just prepared for
the fly and another piece
of facing the same length
as the first one and about
2 inches wide.

Slip this 2-inch strip
under the right-hand side
of the placket opening with
one end extending a trifle
above the material and one
edge well over the mark-
stitched line, as at *c*; baste
it in this position and then
turn the placket edge over
on the mark-stitched line
and baste, so as to avoid
stretching the placket edge
or facing in any place.
Next, turn the left-hand

Fig. 30

side of the placket on the
mark-stitched line, as at *d*, and baste it in position.

To make the fly, place the wrong sides of the strip of material and
the facing together; turn the facing over on each side of the strip
and baste it in position, turning under the edges for a neat finish.
With this done, turn the facing silk up over the lower end of the
strip the same as on the sides and baste it down, taking care to
finish the corners neatly and as flat as possible.   Then, as shown at
e and *f*, stitch around the strip so as to hold the facing in position.

48. Stitching the Placket.—Next, adjust the gauge on the sewing machine so that it will give a very accurate stitched line the same distance from the edge of the placket opening as the remaining seams of the skirt are stitched from the edge. If no ornamental stitching is to be added to the seams on the right side of the skirt, then the stitching should be a generous $\frac{1}{4}$ to $\frac{1}{2}$ inch from the edge. Light-weight materials require the narrow stitching, while

FIG. 31

heavy-weight materials appear to better advantage if the stitching is placed in $\frac{3}{8}$ to $\frac{1}{2}$ inch from the edge, the gauge being adjusted to give just the width that is desired.

Next, carefully press the placket edges, as well as the fly piece, so that they will be absolutely free from wrinkles. Stitch the right side of the placket first, stitching from the waist line down to within $\frac{3}{8}$ inch, or so, of the end of the opening, as shown in Fig. 30. At the end of the stitching, pull the thread through to the wrong side and fasten it. Also, turn the free edge of the facing back to within a scant $\frac{1}{4}$ inch of the edge of the placket, as at a, Fig. 31, and press it in position, but do not whip it down. Pressing is done at this time merely to insure a neat finish at the bottom of the placket; that is, so that the end of the facing will be held down between the skirt and the fly portion. Later on, when the hooks are in position, the free edge of this facing piece is whipped down under the prongs of the hooks, as at a, Fig. 29, thus covering the rings and stems of the hooks and giving a neat finish. This also prevents wear on the threads that hold the hooks.

49.   Applying the Fly.—Next, place the fly piece, which has been finished on two sides and one end, so that the cloth side is up and its center is exactly underneath the center of the placket opening, as shown in Fig. 30.   Bring the placket edges together directly over the basting that marks the center of the fly.   Then pin carefully from the bottom of the placket up to the waist line, and, after pinning, baste both edges to the fly portion.   It may not seem

FIG. 32

necessary to baste the right-hand side, since it is stitched, but it is well worth while.   If such basting is carefully done, it will insure a perfectly smooth placket, especially at the bottom, where, unless this precaution is taken, the material might appear drawn when the stitching is added to the left side of the placket.

When the fly is basted in position, mark diagonal lines that meet in an angle at the end of the placket to serve as a guide in the stitching, using tailor's chalk or basting thread for marking.

Stitch the left side of the placket next, beginning at the waist line and stitching down. For this work, adjust the sewing-machine gauge or quilter the same width as it was adjusted for the first stitching, so that the stitching will be the same on both sides of the placket opening.   When you reach the bottom of the placket, turn and stitch down on the chalk line to the center of the placket, as at *b*, Fig. 29; then turn the work and stitch up to the termination of the stitching that was put in on the right-hand side of the placket, as at *c*.   In this way, the stitching line will appear unbroken on the right side and, as shown in Fig. 32, on the wrong side.   As before, pull the machine threads through to the wrong side and fasten.

50. Next, remove the bastings and press the placket carefully. This is the most opportune time for pressing the placket, because it cannot be pressed well after the hooks and eyes are in position. With the exception of the band, the placket should now appear on the wrong side as in Fig. 32.

51. Hooks and Eyes.—Mark for the hooks and eyes next, taking care not to stretch the edge of the placket. Place the first hook and eye so that it will come about $\frac{3}{4}$ inch from the end. A hook and an eye are placed close to the lower end of the placket to prevent it from being torn out, the usual practice being to hook them and then press them very firmly, so that they will not come unhooked. The last hook and eye may come up rather close to the band, but this is a very good feature, for, if the skirt is inclined to be a little tight around the waist and the space between the hook and eye and the edge of the band is large, the placket might gape below the band.

As a rule, a No. 2 hump hook with a straight eye is satisfactory for a tailored placket of this kind. If the material is very light in weight, a No. 0 hook and eye may be used; but as this size is a little tedious to fasten, the No. 1 size is preferable.

52. Applying the Hooks and Eyes.—Apply the hooks to the right-hand side first, placing them so that the prong of each hook is $\frac{1}{8}$ inch from the edge of the placket and directly under the chalk mark and securing them with over-and-over stitches. It is not necessary to buttonhole them, as they will be covered with the facing; yet, the buttonhole-stitch gives strength, and if you can buttonhole rapidly it is well to use this stitch. In fastening the hooks in place, be sure to sew over the rings and underneath the prong of each hook, making them as secure as possible, so that none of them will pull out of position by the continuous fastening and unfastening to which they will be subjected in putting on and removing the skirt on which they are used. When all the hooks are in position, sew the edge of the facing underneath the prongs of the hooks and fell it down neatly, as previously mentioned.

Next, sew the eyes on with the buttonhole-stitch, placing the straight eyes directly opposite each mark on the right-hand side of the placket opening and straight with the edge of the placket, as shown at d, Fig. 29. For this work, use buttonhole twist that is as near the color of the material as possible. If the material is very dark, black buttonhole twist is usually satisfactory. In sewing the eyes on, you will find it well to hook up each hook and eye as the eyes are sewed in place, so that there will be no danger of their not hooking exactly right. The edges of the placket should come together in a perfectly straight line, as if they were a continuation of the seam; they must not appear drawn or too full at any place.

When the hooks and eyes are in position, trim the edges of the placket facing even with the edges of the skirt seam above the waist line, in preparation for applying the skirt to the band or belting.

53. Finishing the Waist Line.—The manner in which the waist line of a skirt may be finished with a narrow strip of light-weight silk or lining material so that another belt may be worn over it without causing undesirable bulk is shown in Fig. 31. Cut the strip for the belt of a length equal to the waist measurement plus the distance the placket edges overlap and an allowance for finishing each end.

To apply this strip, first baste it to the wrong side of the skirt, turn under the ends, as at *b*, and baste just below the edge of the tape that shows at *c*. This tape may be put on when the skirt is fitted and left in position so as to keep the band exactly the right size. When the size is correct, stitch the one edge of the band to the skirt, as at *d*, and then, after turning the band over to the right side, baste and stitch it all the way around and overhand the ends, as at *e*.

Complete the placket and the waistband finish by sewing hooks and eyes in place.

<hr/>

INVERTED-PLAIT PLACKET

54. The **inverted-plait placket** is shown in Fig. 33. Although it was one of the first tailored plackets in use, it is still very convenient and satisfactory. It is rarely used with narrow skirts, but is often brought into use with the advent of full skirts and is employed at the center back when skirts appear very plain around the waist and hips and full at the lower edge, for the plait itself can be stitched down to give an absolutely plain effect, and yet allow freedom for walking or fulness at the bottom of the skirt.

For figures that have large hip measures, a placket of this kind is more desirable than the habit-back placket, especially if the plait itself is stitched two-thirds of the placket length, as shown, because

it will permit the skirt to open out across the fullest part of the hips
and thus make the skirt appear to better advantage than it would if
the plait were omitted.

55. The allowance for the plait is usually made on the skirt
pattern itself. As a rule, it is extended 3 inches beyond the center-
back line at the waist line and twice this distance, or 6 inches, at the
bottom. This amount, of
course, is allowed on each of
the back gores, so that the
plaits will be uniform in size
on each side of the center-
back seam. In marking the
pattern lines of a skirt that
is to have an inverted plait,
mark-stitch both the center-
back line of the foundation
skirt and the pattern line of
the plait; then, when the skirt
is basted together, the pattern
lines of the plait become the
center back of the skirt and
the center-back line of the
skirt forms the placket edges,
which meet directly over the
center-back seam.

FIG. 33

**56. Preparing for Mak-
ing the Placket.**—To prepare
for the inverted-plait placket,
baste and stitch the center-
back seam of the skirt, which
is the plait extension, from
the waist line to the bottom of the skirt, and bind or overcast each
edge. Then press the seam open, and on the right side of the center-
back seam, exactly half way between the seam and the mark-stitched
line, cut the material down from the waist line at this half-way point,
making the slash as deep as the placket itself is to be, usually
11 inches for a skirt that is fitted closely. Fig. 34 shows where the
slash should be made, but as this illustrates the wrong side of the
skirt, the slash is naturally at the left of the wrong side of the seam.

57. Applying the Facing Strips.—To make the inverted-plait placket, first cut two lengthwise strips of facing silk, making one of them about 2½ inches wide and the other 2 inches wide, and each strip 1 inch longer than the placket opening.   Place the right side of the narrower, or 2-inch, strip to the right side of the cloth on the right-hand side of the placket with the raw edges even, and baste and stitch it to the edge, turning it up at the end before stitching.   Then turn the facing back to the wrong side of the placket and

Fig. 34

baste it down, as at *a*, Fig. 34, leaving a scant ¼ inch of the facing showing on the right side.   Then turn and baste the edge of the facing just over the line of the mark-stitches, as at *b*, in order to give a good, firm edge over which to turn the plait.

Next, join the 2½-inch piece to the opposite side of the placket in a similar manner.   Then turn the strip over to the wrong side so that it just meets the raw edge of the skirt, and baste it, as at *c*; crease it in the center and then turn it back on the skirt material and baste it again on the edge, as at *d*.   Turning the facing under in this way, thus making it double, produces a strong enough stay to hold the eyes in position at the lower end of the opening. Having turned back the lower end of the facing before stitching, secure these turned edges to the skirt with hemming-stitches. Then stitch the facing strips along the edges from the right side, as at a and b, Fig. 35, and afterwards take a few overhanding-stitches to hold the edges together at the end of the placket and prevent this from tearing down.

58. With these edges stitched, press the placket facings from the wrong side, so as to have them smooth and straight. Next, if

Fig. 35

the material is not very firm, baste a lengthwise strip of facing silk or seam binding a trifle longer than the depth you desire the outside stitching of the placket and $\frac{1}{2}$ or $\frac{3}{4}$ inch wide, to the wrong side of the skirt, along the mark-stitched line or plait edge to the left of the opening. This strip serves as a stay for one bias edge of the inverted plait and prevents it from stretching or sagging down. The facing strip for the opening serves this same purpose in the right-plait edge. Then turn the plait on the mark-stitched line back over the stay strip, turning from the right side, and baste it on this line all the way to the bottom of the skirt. The plait is basted the full length of the skirt to insure a true line.

When the edges of the plait are basted, bring them over and pin them in position, taking care to have their edges meet exactly over the seam and to baste very smoothly. In doing this basting, place the work on the sewing table, so that the weight of the skirt will not pull the plait out of position. First, determine the exact length that the placket is to be and mark it accordingly with tailor's chalk straight across from one edge to the other. Then baste from the termination of the placket to the bottom of the skirt on each edge, and on the left-hand side from the waist line down the entire length, basting through all thicknesses but taking care not to catch the stitches through to the front part of the skirt.

59. Stitching the Plaits.—Next, prepare to stitch the edges of the plaits. If the skirt is part of a suit, or if the other seams are stitched in welt or open-welt effect, the stitching on the edges of the inverted plait should correspond with the other plaits or seam stitching. After determining the distance that the stitching is to extend from the waist line, mark it as already explained for the placket length—in this case, about two-thirds the length of the placket—and stitch the right-hand side first, as shown at c, Fig. 35, stitching from the waist line down.

As has been mentioned, for very stout figures it is well not to extend this stitching the full length of the placket, so as to give more freedom over the largest part of the hips. For very slender figures, the stitching may extend farther down on the placket; but, in any case, it is best to make this stitching a little shorter than the placket, as such stitching gives a neater finish.

In terminating the stitching, as at d, you may run it diagonally upward or downward, as desired. Whichever plan you follow, mark the turn on both sides of the plait with tailor's chalk, so that the stitching on each side will correspond. Stitch through only the edge of the plait, as shown, pull the threads through on the inside of the plait, and fasten them securely. Next, stitch the left side of the placket, as at e. This side is stitched in the same manner as the right side, except that the plait is stitched to the skirt itself.

60. Applying the Hooks and Eyes.—With the stitching done, press the placket very carefully. Then place hooks on the right-hand side and eyes to correspond along the left-hand edge of the placket, as at *g*. In securing these fastenings in place, sew through the center-back seam of the skirt; this will give strength and prevent them from pulling away from the skirt material. As you will observe on referring to Fig. 35, the hooks and eyes at the lower end of the placket are placed midway of the portion used as the fly. This plan is an excellent one, as the fasteners keep the

placket in position and yet permit the plait to be open enough to allow for freedom at the bottom of the placket. Take the stitches to secure these lower hooks and eyes through the facing pieces as well as through the skirt material. Then, to prevent the bottom of the plait from tearing out at its lower edge and also to keep the placket in position, clasp the bottom hook and the eye, which are designated by *h*, and press them very firmly with an iron so that they cannot be unhooked.

FIG. 36

61. Finishing the Waist Line.—With the fastenings applied to the placket edge, finish the waist line in a manner suitable for the style of skirt you are making. The illustrations of the inverted-plait placket here discussed show a band of the skirt material with a lining of facing silk. The band is applied in the same manner as any other band, except that the two kinds of material are used and joined in a seam at the upper edge of the band, as shown in Fig. 35.

Sew the hooks and eyes on the band as in the habit-back placket. Then, when the placket is fastened up and in position, the wrong side will appear as shown in Fig. 33, and the right side as in Fig. 36.

4 W I—9

LOCATION OF PLACKET OPENINGS

62. Some designers say that when designing a garment they never consider the place where a dress or skirt will be opened. They get the desired style effect and then plan for an opening afterwards, placing it where it will in nowise affect line or trimming. This is a good point to remember in the placing of plackets. Also, unless an opening is to be made a trimming feature, it should be as inconspicuous as possible, and as few or as many fasteners used as the looseness or the tightness of the garment requires.

Sometimes, good workmen will use but one or two snap fasteners on a placket and perhaps put just a narrow strip of silk as a stay strip underneath, overcast the edges rather than bind them and make the entire opening in such a way that you would need to look carefully to find it.

And so there are two responsibilities in making openings in garments; first, to know how to make all kinds correctly; then, to know when to use them properly in accordance with Fashion's demands.

CHAPTER V

TAILORED SKIRTS

FASHION CHANGES

1. Wherever women are found, a keen and genuine interest in dress also is found. Weeks before the calendar announces a new season, groups of women the world over may be heard discussing the probable new features to be expected in dresses, suits, coats, and the like. Of the features discussed at such times, the length and fulness of skirts are in all probability the most popular topics. For it is such subtle changes as a few inches added to or removed from the width or the length of a skirt that herald the arrival of a new mode.

It is not the purpose of this chapter to present styles as they are found in any one season. A much broader and more useful task has been undertaken—that of familiarizing you with the various types of skirts that are worn at more or less regularly recurring intervals, the methods of constructing them, and the manner of finishing them in order to obtain effects characteristic of each. Further than that, this chapter shows how one style is developed from another, so that no matter what the fashion of the moment may be, the knowledge gained may be readily adapted and will be found adequate to the making of skirts in any style and of any desired material.

2. Achieving Smartness.—After one has learned the technique of sewing, to see a garment is all that is necessary in order to be able to copy it, and very often to improve upon it. And so if you are making skirts, you must see skirts. Watch the shops and magazines for new and desirable features. Then, you can make skirts that meet every need of service, attractive smartness, and

125

individual becomingness. Remember that a skirt designed for service alone is only half a skirt, that it can just as well be attractive and modish as otherwise. Perhaps one reason why "Ladies' Tailors" have become almost extinct is because so many of them have overlooked this, have refused to modernize their methods and to keep abreast of the times. Beware, then, of falling into the error of their ways, and when skirts are made of one width of fabric, slip over the head, and have imitation pockets, make yours likewise, though it may upset many of your tailoring principles. At times when skirts have nine gores and a tight waist line, transfer your loyalty to them. And all the while be content in the thought that a happy, intelligent interpretation of fashion will be yours if your interest in clothes is sufficient to keep you ever on the alert for correct methods of making them. Moreover, they will possess a smartness that will do you credit.

3.   Appropriateness of Tailored Skirts.—Just as the cut and the method of finishing skirts vary from season to season, so are there changes in the appropriateness of skirts to various occasions. The fickleness of fashion, which is responsible for these changes, has elevated them at times to a position of such prominence that a skirt with its accompanying blouse is considered proper for wear at even semiformal events. At other times, separate tailored skirts are considered appropriate only for outings, sports, and general business wear. However, whether it is a separate garment or part of a coat suit, a tailored skirt and a simple blouse or shirtwaist form a costume that is practically always acceptable, from a standpoint of good taste and service, for wear in offices, shops, stores, factories, and similar places.

MATERIALS FOR SEPARATE SKIRTS

4.   Skirts for different occasions are, of course, made from different types of materials; those for semiformal wear, for example, are made from soft, fine material, while those for sports and outings are made of coarser material that will withstand more severe strain. The seasons, also, must be considered as a factor in determining the suitability of materials to skirt making. Fashion again intervenes at times, demanding that materials be soft and dull in finish, or lustrous, or of some special weave. Having in mind all of these influences, one might make a very long list of fabrics that have, at some time or other, been popular for the making of tailored skirts, but of the helpfulness of such a list there is room for doubt. We may say in general, though, that materials for tailored skirts may be divided into two groups—woolen materials and washable materials. The washable materials include linen, cotton, and silk.

5. Woolen Materials.—The most successful woolen materials for separate skirts are fairly light in weight, even when the skirts are to be worn for the sake of warmth, and have a surface that is reasonably smooth in order to shed dust easily. Also as the skirt is subject to more or less cleaning, the material is of a color that does not fade and of a weave that holds its shape well. Firm, even-textured fabrics, such as flannel, homespun, and serge, fulfil these requirements best. Hair goods, such as wool alpaca, or mixed hair goods, such as brilliantine and heavy wool pongee, are very durable, though some object to them on the score that they are not so attractive as the softer weaves.

6. In choosing material for a woolen skirt, take into consideration the undergarment that will be worn with it. With a skirt of harsh materials, like camel's hair or cheviot, a petticoat must be worn, for bloomers do not offer enough protection for comfort. Another point worthy of consideration is whether the petticoat is soft and thin enough not to give undesirable bulk, yet of sufficient body not to cling unduly to the skirt and spoil the style effect. Sateen petticoats have a most disconcerting manner of gathering up in the front over the knees, and no skirt, however modish, can look its best under such circumstances. Silk jersey is probably the most satisfactory material to use for petticoats to be worn under woolen skirts.

7. The *colors* of wool skirts vary as much as the materials. Those for more or less formal wear are usually dark, conservative colors, such as navy blue, brown, black, or gray, while those for sports wear are often very brilliant. White or cream wool skirts, usually plaited, are favorites with many people for sports wear, but because they soil very readily they are impractical except for occasional use.

8. Linen, Cotton, and Silk Materials.—*Linen* skirts of white or delicate colors are cool, light, and easily laundered. The one objection to them is that they wrinkle very readily. The heavier dress linens, therefore, should be chosen for making skirts. Those called "non-crush" linens are more satisfactory than other kinds.

Cotton materials suitable for skirts include piqué, duck, galatea, cotton gabardine, such linen-finished materials as Everfast and Indian head, poplin, and basket-weave and novelty skirtings. Skirts of such materials are very satisfactory for summer wear because they are cool and may be laundered easily and successfully.

Although *silk* skirts are not generally considered tailored skirts, at times they follow tailored lines very decidedly. When this is the case, firm, heavy silks or the full ratiné weaves are employed, the same care being exercised in their construction as in the making of tailored skirts of woolen materials. Some of the silk materials that may be successfully used are pongee, Shantung, Canton crêpe, silk ratiné, heavy flat crêpe, corded silks, such as bengaline and faille, and, in some seasons, heavy satins.

WAIST-LINE FINISHES

9. For finishing the waist lines of skirts, there are four general methods, all of which are controlled entirely by fashion and which are as follows: (With an inside belting; with a waist lining or camisole top; with a casing for an elastic; and with a waistband that must be covered with a belt.)

FIG. 1

10. Finishing a Skirt With an Inside Stay Belt.—For a separate skirt that is not fitted extremely close at the waist line, and for one in which a slightly raised waist line is desirable, the inside stay belt is the correct finish to use. Such a skirt can be finished to wear either with or without a separate belt.

The inside stay belting may be had by the yard in several widths, varying from 1 to 6 inches, and made of either canvas or cambric. The cambric belting is boned for stiffness; the canvas, except the very light-weight grades, is heavy enough without boning. Both types may be had either straight or shaped. In case a shaped belting is needed and only a straight one can be obtained, it may be shaped by taking small darts from the top edge and tapering them out toward the bottom, as shown in Fig. 1. The position of the darts depends on the closing of the skirt. In placing them, determine the center front, take a dart there, and continue from that point. Fig. 1 shows a belt that is planned for a center-back closing.

11. Amount of Belting Needed.—In estimating the amount of belting needed, allow $1\frac{1}{4}$ inches for finishing the ends, and 3 inches as a safeguard in case the waist measure increases. Lay this 3-inch allowance in two plaits just deep enough to permit the belt to fit the waist line. If needed, this amount can be let out. .

A belt that has been cut too short may be lengthened by cutting it in half and inserting a piece of belting that is long enough to give the desired length.

There is also a patent belting that comes in adjustable lengths with the hooks and eyes attached. This saves considerable time and is a convenience in case the waist measurement changes. It costs a trifle more than belting that is purchased by the yard.

12. Sewing Hooks and Eyes On Belting.—When you are ready to sew the hooks and eyes to the belting that comes by the yard, turn hems in both ends, dividing the $1\frac{1}{4}$-inch allowance mentioned between the two ends, and stitch the hems securely. Then apply two or three hooks and eyes of medium size, regulating the number by the width of the belting. Place the hooks so that the prongs are back just a trifle from the ends of the belting, and sew securely. Place the eyes so that just enough of the curved portion extends beyond the end of the belt to permit the hooks to be slipped through them easily. This arrangement of the hooks and eyes will bring the ends of the belt exactly together, but not so that they overlap when hooked.

In addition to sewing through the rings of the eyes, take a few stitches over each side of the eye where it touches the end of the belting; and in addition to sewing through the rings of the hooks, take a few stitches under the prongs.

13. Applying Inside Stay Belt to Skirt.—*If the skirt material is light or medium in weight,* gather any fulness, using two rows of small running-stitches placed from $\frac{3}{8}$ to $\frac{1}{2}$ inch apart, the upper one $\frac{1}{4}$ inch from the upper edge of the skirt. Locate the center front

and back of the skirt and the prepared belt, and pin these together
so that the upper edge of the belting is half way between the two
rows of gatherings on the skirt.   Then turn the projecting edge
of the skirt over the top of the belting.   In this way, one row of
gathering will be on the right side of the skirt and one directly
under it on the wrong side.   Adjust the skirt fulness as desired,
pinning it in place, and try on the skirt to make sure that the
gathers are correctly adjusted.

On the wrong side of the belting, place seam-binding tape over
the raw edge of the skirt material so that the upper edge of the tape
just covers the line of the gathering threads.   Baste this tape in
place, being careful that you do not catch the threads through to
the right side of the skirt.   Now draw the belting away from the
skirt portion and stitch just inside the lower edge of the tape.   The
stitching, then, will be through only one thickness of the skirt
material, the belting, and the tape.   Finally, turn the belt
back to its original position and from the right side of the skirt
stitch along the line of gathering.   This stitching will be done
through two thicknesses of the skirt material, the belting, and the
upper edge of the tape.   Run the machine very slowly and use a
rather long stitch. · Some prefer to do this work by hand, using
back-stitches.

If the stitching on the right side is objectionable, stitch two
rows from the inside before the belting is turned back, keeping the
second line of stitching along the *top* edge of the tape.   Then
turn the belt down against the inside of the skirt and press the upper
edge carefully.   This method is especially successful for a plain-
fitting skirt having no gathers.

14.   *If the material is very heavy*, place two rows of gathering
threads around the top of the skirt, and draw the fulness in to fit the
top of the belting.   Before joining the belt and the skirt, lap a piece
of seam binding or light-weight material over the right side of the
upper edge of the skirt and stitch it in place.   Then turn the free
edge of this binding over the top of the belting with the edge of the
belting and the gathered edge of the skirt even.   This prevents a
bulky finish such as would result if the heavy material were turned
over the edge.   Pin and baste the binding to the belting.   Then
draw the belting away from the skirt portion and stitch along the
edge of the binding, through the belting and binding only.

15. *In applying an inside stay belt to a wash skirt,* first gather in any fulness with two rows of gatherings, as described in Art. **14.** With the right side of the material uppermost, lay the prepared belting over it so that the side showing the hems at the ends is up, and the lower edge of the belt just covers the upper row of gatherings. Baste and stitch very close to the edge of the belting. Then turn the skirt over to the wrong side and trim away any surplus material close to the top of the skirt underneath the belt, leaving only enough material to prevent the stitching from pulling out. This avoids bulk around the waist, which would be inconvenient in a wash skirt, as the skirt would not iron well nor have a trim, neat appearance at the top. As a final step, turn the belt down against the inside of the skirt and press.

FIG. 2

16. Finishing a Skirt With a Waist Lining or Camisole Top.—When low waist lines are in fashion, a simple, practical, and comfortable method of finishing the skirt waist line is with a waist lining or camisole top. This method is also commonly used for young girls' skirts. It gives a very good, straight hip line, and is more comfortable than a skirt band placed low on the hips. Fig. 2 shows the usual type of waist lining that is used for such purposes.

This lining has the neck and armholes finished with picoting, which is desirable in that it is dainty and provides a flat finish that will not mar the lines of the dress. It is not so desirable, however, from the standpoint of serviceability. A narrow hem, finished with a very narrow lace edge is quite as dainty and much more durable if the garment must stand hard wear. The closing in this case is at the center back, but it can be planned equally well to come at the center or side front. This will depend upon the location of the skirt opening.

The surplus fulness at the lower edge of the front is laid in a soft plait at each side. This method of removing the waist-line fulness is essential if the bust is at all prominent, or if a comparatively close-fitting effect at the waist line is desired.

The average figure requires 1⅛ yards of material for this type of lining. For the cutting, a plain-waist pattern having a shoulder dart may be used. If such a pattern is not available, use a pattern that does not have a dart and make provision for it by slashing the pattern from the center of the shoulder, on a line parallel with the front, to the lower edge of the pattern. Then, in placing the pattern on the material, separate the slashed edges at the shoulder and overlap them at the lower edge an amount sufficient to remove as much fulness at the waist line as desired.

Allow 1¾ inches for the 1-inch hems at the closing. Unless the lining material is rather heavy, it is not necessary to cut away the surplus material between the dart edges.

When the hems and darts are basted, slip the lining on the figure and fit it. At this time, pin the dart at each side front to remove the fulness at the lower edge. These darts are merely pressed in, no stitching being necessary. When the fitting is completed, make French seams on the shoulders and under the arms. Finish the neck and armhole edges as desired.

17. A camisole top is made from a straight piece of material. For a person of small measurements, one length of 40-inch material is sufficient. But if the material is narrower, or the figure larger, two lengths should be provided and a seam used under each arm. Still another method of cutting, one that is sometimes found to be economical, is to use the material lengthwise around the figure.

The camisole top is commonly made perfectly straight with no shaping whatever, and it is seldom necessary to provide an opening, as the garment slips on quite comfortably over the head. If a very close-fitting effect is desired, an opening can be arranged under the left arm. In this case, pin and stitch a dart at each side front to take in surplus fulness at the upper edge; or, if preferred, finish the top with a ½-inch hem, which may be used as a casing for a tape.

18. *To join the waist lining or camisole and skirt,* pin them together at the low waist line. Gather any fulness in the skirt, using two rows of gatherings ¼ inch apart, or lay it in small plaits or folds before joining it to the camisole. If it is necessary to lift the skirt in order to have it hang straight at the lower edge, trim away the required amount on the lining or camisole edge rather than the skirt edge.

When the lining or the camisole and skirt are pinned together satisfactorily, join them with a plain seam having its raw edges turned to the right side. Trim this seam close to the stitching, cover it with seam binding or a bias strip of light-weight material, and stitch along both edges of the tape or strip.

It is often more satisfactory, particularly in the case of separate skirts that are not washable, to finish the lower edge of the lining or the camisole and the top of the skirt separately and join them by means of snap fasteners. The camisole may be finished with a hem or straight facing, and the skirt with a band such as is described later in Arts. **20** to **22,** inclusive. No. 3 snaps, placed 3 inches apart, hold the camisole and skirt together very well and provide a simple means of detaching and joining them for convenience in cleaning.

19. Finishing a Skirt With a Casing for Elastic.—An elastic run through a casing is sometimes used on skirts made of light-weight material, or on those having considerable fulness. This is not generally considered, however, a very desirable type of finish for the skirts of children or of women who do not wear corsets as any tight band around the body tends to restrict the circulation somewhat.

If the skirt material is at all heavy, light-weight material of the same color should be used for the casing. Cut this twice the width of the elastic plus ½ inch for finishing, and as long as the skirt is wide at the top plus ½ inch for turning under at the ends. If there are plaits in the skirt, lay them flat before applying the casing.

Stitch the casing to the skirt in a ¼-inch seam, having the wrong side of the skirt and the right side of the casing together. Turn up the free edge of the casing ¼ inch and bring the turned edge over to the right side of the skirt, so that the edge of the crease just covers the first stitching. Baste it in place and stitch from the right side close to the edge.

Cut the elastic 3 inches shorter than the waist measure. Run it through the casing and fasten the ends of it securely by stitching them to the casing.

20. Finishing a Skirt With a Waistband.—The waistband that is covered by a separate belt is cut and applied in a manner quite similar to the casing for elastic just described. The greatest difference between the methods of applying lies in the fact that the casing is cut to correspond in length with the width of the skirt at the top before the fulness is drawn in, whereas the waistband is cut to correspond with the waist measure of the figure.

21. *If the skirt material is light in weight* and the waistband is to be made of it, cut a strip 2½ inches wide and as long as the waist measure plus ½ inch for finishing the ends and the width of the placket for lapping. Thus, if your waist measure is 27 inches and your placket is 1½ inches wide and you allow ½ inch for finishing the ends, the total length required for the waistband is 29 inches.

Measure in from one end of the band a distance equal to the width of the placket plus ¼ inch for finishing the end. Mark this point with a pin or a colored thread. Then mark ¼ inch from the other end of the band—the amount allowed for finishing each end. The distance between these two markings should exactly equal your waist measure.

Next, locate and mark the center front and the center back of the belt. Pin these to the corresponding points on the skirt, and proceed to apply the band according to the manner described for the casing for elastic. The waistband, however, receives one additional finishing touch. After stitching the lower edge of the band on the right side in the manner described, stitch also the top and ends, keeping very close to the edge and stitching on the right side.

22. *If the skirt material is heavy* and is likely to produce a bulky, undesirable finish, it is used for the outside only, and a thin lining material is used for the inside of the band. In applying a band of this sort, determine the length in the same manner, but cut it only 1½ inches wide. Then cut a piece of lining material of the same size to be used for the inside of the waistband, the skirt material being used for the outside. The upper edge of each is turned ¼ inch, and held in place by the stitching done on the right side around the edges.

HEM FINISHES FOR TAILORED SKIRTS

23. Influence of Style on the Finish of Hems.—Whether the hem or the facing of a skirt shall be stitched on the machine or put in by hand is a question controlled largely by fashion. There are seasons when garments are made to show as little stitching as possible; then hems are put in by hand. There are other seasons when machine stitching is made a feature of trimming; at such times hems are stitched, and very often with several rows of stitching.

The width of hems is likewise a variable feature. Some materials are attactive with wide hems, while others appear to advantage with hems of moderate width. There are times, too, when no hem is used, a binding or a band of contrasting color being used instead.

When skirts are circular or flaring, it is customary to finish them with fitted or bias facings rather than hems, in order to produce a surface on the right side that is smooth and entirely free from the creases that result from pressing over a fold or dart. When skirts are only very slightly flared, the fulness may be shrunk out and the hem finished as it would be in a perfectly straight skirt.

Besides always taking such points as these into consideration when planning a skirt, be on the alert for ideas as to how hems are being handled, as shown in the current fashion books and in the smartest models in the shops.

24. Plain Hem in Straight Skirt of Light-Weight Material. When the skirt is cut straight so that there is no fulness in the hem to be disposed of, and when the material is light in weight so that a $\frac{1}{4}$-inch turning at the top does not leave shiny creases on the right side after pressing, the method of hemming is similar to that used on cotton dresses and is as follows:

Mark the line of the bottom of the hem with a row of bastings. Turn the hem to the wrong side on that line, and run a row of bastings $\frac{1}{4}$ inch from the edge of the fold. With the Picken gauge, measure the width desired for the hem and trim it off to an even width at all points. Turn in $\frac{1}{4}$ inch at the top and baste in position. If it has been decided to secure the hem by hand, as is usually the case, hold the lower edge of the garment toward you and use either fine whipping-stitches or slip-stitches. Remove all bastings before pressing the hem, to prevent them from leaving imprints on the material.

To obtain an even flatter finish and render the slip-stitching of the hem easier, proceed as directed and, after turning in $\frac{1}{4}$ inch at the top, stitch it on the machine near the crease, as shown at *a*, in Fig. 3. This gives a firm edge and also protects the slip-stitches.

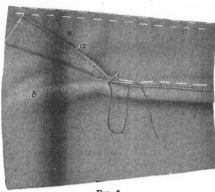

FIG. 3

To slip-stitch easily, hold the skirt side next to you, as at *b*, having the fingers of the left hand on the hem side and the thumb on the skirt side. Take up as little material as possible with each stitch. To avoid pulling or puckering the stitches, take a back-stitch every 6 or 7 stitches, as at *c*.

25. Plain Hem in Straight Skirt of Heavy Material.—Two methods are applicable to the finishing of hems in skirts of material that is so heavy that the turning in of the upper raw edge would cause an undesirable ridge. If the material does not fray nor ravel, the hem may be secured by catch-stitching the edge of it, as illustrated in Fig. 4. There is only one turn in a hem of this kind.

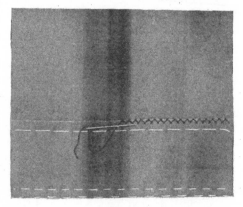

FIG. 4

This type of finish, of course, applies only to such skirts as are practically straight so that no fulness is present in the hem to be disposed of.

If the nature of the material is such that it frays readily, the most satisfactory finish is by means of a band of seam tape or ribbon. To make this finish, apply the tape to the right side of the material and stitch $\frac{1}{4}$ inch from the raw edge, as shown at *a*, Fig. 5. Baste the top of the hem in position. The stitching will then appear at the edge of the tape, as at *b*. Then join the free edge of the tape to the skirt with slip-stitching, as at *c*, also taking a back-stitch in the tape every 6 or 7 stitches.

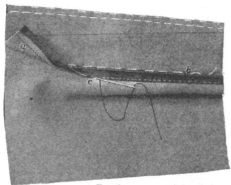

FIG. 5

26. Straight Facing on Straight Skirt.—In the hemming of a straight skirt, it sometimes happens that the skirt is not long enough to provide as wide a hem as desired. Or again, the material may be so heavy that the double thickness of it would make too heavy a lower-edge finish. In either case, a straight facing may be used and applied as follows:

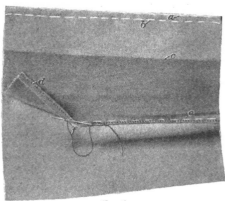

FIG. 6

Turn the skirt edge to the wrong side on the marking line of bastings, as at *a*, Fig. 6. Then baste it $\frac{1}{4}$ inch from the edge, as at *b*. Trim it off to an even width and with a plain seam join a straight piece of lightweight material to the top, as at *c*, having this strip wide enough to give the total hem width desired. Turn under the upper edge $\frac{1}{4}$ inch and stitch near the crease, as at *d*. Baste the facing in position, as at *e*, and slip-stitch, as at *f*.

27. Shrinking Fulness From the Hem of a Slightly Flared Skirt.
When a skirt is slightly flared, it is a little wider at the extreme lower
edge than where the lower edge of the hem will come.   Unless this
slight fulness is disposed of in some way, the hem will not fit
smoothly.   In cotton skirts, this fulness is frequently plaited or
gathered in, and in the case of such material there is no objection to
that method.   But if the same method were used in cloth skirts,
the resulting bumps and creases would produce a very unattractive effect.   There is, however, a means of removing fulness from
cloth without cutting and without leaving undesirable, shiny creases,
and that is by shrinking the surplus fulness out of the material.

28.   The first steps in the process of making such a hem are the
same as described for the plain hem in a straight skirt of light-

FIG. 7

weight material; that is, turn and
baste the lower edge of the hem, as
at *a*, Fig. 7, and measure and trim
the hem to an even width.   Then
run a gathering thread along the
top of the hem $\frac{1}{4}$ inch from the edge,
as at *b*.   Lay the skirt out on the
ironing board, dampen the hem,
and shrink out the fulness by bringing the iron up from the bottom
of the skirt and holding the fulness
in with the gathering thread until
the turned portion is the width of
the skirt where the top of the hem comes.   This work must be
done very carefully in order to take out all of the fulness, for, of
course, if fulness in any tailored skirt is plaited in, it will not look
well and will eventually show on account of the frequent pressings
that such a skirt receives.

Next, bind the upper edge of the hem with a bias band of silk,
sateen, or percaline.   Whatever is used in finishing the placket is
usually suitable for this binding.   Place the right side of the binding to the right side of the hem edge and baste them together with a
$\frac{1}{4}$-inch seam.   Then trim away the edge of the hem just below the
gathering thread, as shown.   Turn the binding over, taking great
care to turn it over the hem, rather than to turn the hem over, as
that would make an extra thickness at the top of the hem, and so

defeat the purpose of this particular finish. Stitch along the edge of this binding on the right side, as shown at *c*. Baste the upper edge of the hem to the skirt and finish it by hand or with machine stitching, according to the effect desired. Press the hem thoroughly.

29. Facings Used on Flaring Skirts.—Circular skirts and those having a decided flare cannot be hemmed successfully, even by shrinking out the fulness, for it is impossible to remove all of it in that way. The only satisfactory finish in such cases is a facing.

There are two kinds of facings, *fitted* and *bias*. Bias facings are successfully used when made of light-weight material and applied to a skirt that is not extremely circular or flared. The more flaring the skirt, the greater is the necessity for a fitted facing, which is usually made from material like that of the skirt.

30. Applying a Fitted Facing.—The term "fitted facing" implies that the threads of the facing material and of the skirt run in the same direction. To achieve this result, lay the skirt out smooth on the table and place the pieces of the material that were left from cutting out the skirt over the lower edge so that the lengthwise and crosswise threads of both match. As a rule, such a facing is from $2\frac{1}{4}$ to 4 inches wide.

In order to get the facing accurate as to shape and grain, lay the pieces over the edge of the skirt, rather than the skirt over the pieces. Arrange them to the best advantage; that is, so that the longest piece of the facing may be cut from each piece of material, thus obviating the necessity of a large number of piecing seams in the facing. Be sure to allow for any seams necessary for piecing the facing. These seams should follow either a lengthwise or a crosswise thread, as a bias seam is hard to match and likely to stretch. Join the facing pieces with plain seams and press them open.

When the facing is made ready, lay the skirt right side up on the table and put the right side of the facing down over it, matching the grain. Baste the lower edges in a $\frac{1}{4}$-inch seam, keeping the work flat on the table so that neither the edge of the skirt nor that of the facing will become stretched in any place. Stitch the seam and press it open, when it will appear as at *a*, in Fig. 8. Then turn the facing over to the wrong side of the skirt, bringing it up $\frac{1}{4}$ to $\frac{3}{8}$ inch from the bottom of the skirt to avoid any possibility of its showing on the right side.

31. If the skirt is made of broadcloth or any other firm material on which an imprint of this seam might show on the right side, additional precaution must be taken. Before pressing the facing in place, cut a bias piece of light-weight cambric a little wider than the seam and slip it in between the skirt and the facing so that it covers the seam and comes to the bottom of the skirt. Secure the cambric to the facing with long, uneven basting-stitches, using a harmonizing silk thread so that the stitches will not show prominently on the right side of the facing. This piece will receive the

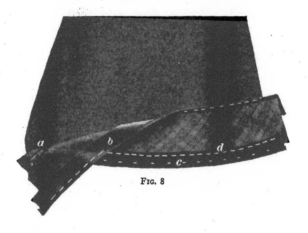

Fig. 8

imprint of the piecing seam and the edges, and thus keep the seam from showing through to the right side and prevent the ugly press marks from appearing when the hem is pressed.

When the facing has been turned up and the cambric section basted in place, press the facing and trim it off so that it is of an exactly even width at all points. Then bind the upper edge of the facing, as shown at *b*, and baste the top of the facing to the skirt. It is then ready to be stitched or hemmed by hand.

32. Applying a Bias Facing of Light-Weight Material.—In case the skirt to be faced is not extremely circular, or the skirt material used is too heavy to make a satisfactory facing, or there is not sufficient skirt material left for the facing, then it is well to apply a bias facing of silk, sateen, or percaline of good quality and of a color that harmonizes with that of the skirt.

In determining the width to cut the bias facing, bear in mind that the material of a woolen skirt should be allowed to extend $\frac{1}{2}$ to 1 inch above the bottom edge, as shown at *a*, Fig. 9. This plan prevents the facing from showing on the right side and it provides a more durable finish at the lower edge of the skirt, for the skirt material is usually of a stronger quality than the facing.

To allow for this turn-back on the skirt, run a row of bastings where the bottom of the skirt is to be, as shown at the lower edge of the skirt section illustrated in Fig. 9. Then trim off the lower edge of the skirt $\frac{3}{4}$ to $1\frac{1}{4}$ inches beyond the basting. This allows an extra $\frac{1}{4}$ inch for the seam that joins the facing

FIG. 9

to the skirt. In a wash skirt, it is satisfactory to have this seam $\frac{1}{4}$ inch from the lower edge.

33. When the finished width desired for the facing has been decided on and the amount that the skirt material is to be turned up has been deducted, add $\frac{1}{2}$ inch to provide for the seams at the top and the bottom of the facing. Cut and join enough bias pieces of this width to go around the bottom of the skirt.

Put the right sides of the bias facing and the skirt together with their edges even and join them in a $\frac{1}{4}$-inch seam. Bias facings of light-weight materials are very easily stretched when they are joined to heavier materials, so care must be exercised not to draw the facing tighter than the skirt material. It should be eased on very carefully, not loose enough to form a wrinkle but just slack enough to prevent it from pulling or drawing.

Turn the facing to the wrong side of the skirt, having the crease come along the line of basting that marks the lower edge of the skirt, and baste the skirt material $\frac{1}{4}$ inch from the edge as you would in putting in a hem, as shown by the middle row of bastings along the lower edge of the skirt section in Fig. 9.   Let both edges of the plain seam that joins the facing to the skirt turn upwards, and, smoothing the facing against the wrong side of the skirt, baste it to the skirt, taking the stitches through the seam, as shown by the upper row of bastings at the lower edge of the skirt.

Bias is very pliable and can be drawn quite readily into the position desired at the top so that the facing lies flat.   Turn in the upper edge, baste it in position, as shown, and finish with hand hemming or with machine stitching.

Fig. 10

34. Stitching as Trimming at the Bottom of a Skirt. As previously mentioned, there are times when stitching as a trimming is in vogue, and a number of rows may be placed around the bottom of a skirt to give a band effect.   Such trimming is very desirable, particularly on plain skirts.   The chief point to consider is the spacing, which should be worked out to give the most attractive result.   Often a number of rows are placed close together, then a space is left, and several more rows are added, as in Fig. 10.   This is usually decided in part by the proportions of the garment, or of the suit as a whole in case it is a part of a coat suit.

A skirt to be so trimmed should be faced with a light-weight bias facing in the manner described previously, basted, as shown, and thoroughly pressed.   Then turn back the facing and proceed with the stitching, which will go through the skirt material only.   The seam gauge must be used for this, because perfection of detail is an essential to a pleasing result.

35.   Stiffening the Lower Edge of a Skirt.—It is sometimes desirable to have the lower edge of a skirt stand out.   This is often the case when there are several rows of stitching on the lower edge of a skirt as just described. Crinoline cut on a true bias is used for the purpose of stiffening skirt edges.

Lay the bias crinoline on the bottom of the skirt, letting the lower edges of the crinoline extend from $\frac{1}{8}$ to $\frac{1}{4}$ inch below the row of bastings that mark where the lower edge of the skirt is to be turned. Dampen the crinoline and shape it a trifle by drawing in the upper edge a little so that it will fit the skirt exactly. It would be very detrimental to the appearance of the outside of the skirt to have any wrinkles form in the crinoline. To prevent this, run a warm iron carefully over the crinoline after it is dampened. This will shrink away any fulness and cause the crinoline to assume the shape of the lower edge of the skirt.

36. Baste the crinoline to the skirt with three rows of basting-stitches, as shown in Fig. 11. Then bring the lower edge of the skirt up and baste it from the right side, keeping the turn exactly on the line of the bastings that mark the lower edge of the skirt. This causes the crinoline to fold back, as illustrated, and is done to protect the skirt edge, for the cut edge of crinoline is composed of sharp, little, wire-like threads that would pierce through the material, if allowed to come in a crease, and would cause it to wear out quickly. A folded edge, however, is quite smooth and harmless. Catch-stitch the turned edge of the skirt to the crinoline, taking care that the stitches do not show on the

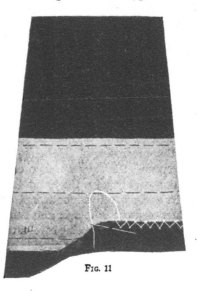

Fig. 11

right side of the skirt. Finally, cover the crinoline with a bias facing of silk or percaline, whipping it down neatly at the upper and lower edges.

37. Skirt Braid and Its Selection.—It is often necessary to protect the lower edge of a tailored skirt in some way. For this purpose, skirt braid, as shown in Fig. 12, is excellent. It is a woven, somewhat elastic braid that may be had in either wool or mercerized cotton, in widths varying from $\frac{5}{8}$ to $\frac{3}{4}$ inch.

In selecting the braid, be careful to have it harmonize closely with the color of the skirt. It can rarely be had to match exactly, as

black, white, light grays, and tans are practically the only colors in which it is made, but from one of these it is usually possible to select a color that harmonizes with the skirt material. For example, if the skirt is dark blue, a black braid would be chosen, while for a lighter blue skirt, gray would be a better selection. It is not essential for the braid to match exactly, as it is applied so that only $\frac{1}{8}$ inch shows at the lower edge of the skirt.

Fig. 12

For silk skirts or very light-weight woolen ones, a mercerized braid is more satisfactory than woolen braid, as it is not so thick and heavy. It also wears better.

38. Applying the Skirt Braid.—The skirt braid is most easily applied before the upper edge of the hem is stitched in. It is well, however, to have the hem basted temporarily.

Hold the right side of the skirt toward you and place the braid to the under side of the hem. Then, with uneven stitches, baste all around the extreme edge of the skirt, as shown at c, Fig. 8, taking care to keep the braid $\frac{1}{8}$ inch below the bottom edge of the skirt and perfectly smooth, not drawing or pulling it in any place. Then turn the skirt over and baste the braid again, this time at the top, as shown at d, being careful to take the stitches through the hem but not through to the outside of the skirt.

After this, open out the hem and, with the sewing machine, stitch along the top edge of the braid, through the braid and the hem or the facing. Join the ends of the braid in a flat fell, as shown at a, Fig. 12, so that the joining will be as flat and neat as possible, whipping the ends down on both sides of the braid with very close stitches so that they will not pull out. Then baste the hem again, finish the top edge as desired, remove the bastings, and press the lower edge of the skirt.

39. If you decide, after the hem of the skirt has been whipped or stitched in, that skirt braid is to be used, it is not necessary to rip open the hem. Merely sew the braid on by hand, being very careful not to have any stitches show on the right side of the hem.

MAKING TAILORED SKIRTS

PERFECTION OF DETAIL

40. Beauty of line, though primarily dependent on the design selected for the garment, must be supported by careful handling of the fabric. And careful handling of the fabric should begin with the sponging and shrinking of the material so as to keep it perfectly smooth and straight. Therefore, in constructing a tailored skirt, it is necessary not only to have it in harmony with Fashion's dictates, and to have the seam, placket, waist-line, and hem finishes suitable for the figure and the purpose for which the skirt is intended, but also to work for smooth, well-defined lines without permitting tight stitches, bulky seams, or press marks to show.

This perfection of finish necessitates the use of long, easy, blind-stitches in putting in hems or turned-back facings, in pressing open of all seams, and in pinking of all edges on which pinking can be done.

41. Pressing.—A knowledge of how materials should be pressed, particularly in the case of woolens, is very important in all tailoring, but it is in connection with skirts that the majority of women probably do the greater part of their pressing during both the making and the wearing. Consequently, the methods and cautions concerning pressing are given here in detail for your immediate use.

In pressing woolen materials, the first caution is to use an iron that is hot, but not sufficiently hot to scorch. Bear in mind, too, that wool scorches much more readily than cotton, and, although the press cloth comes between the material and the iron, use every precaution when hard pressing must be done, as in the making of tailored garments, for the heat from the iron soon penetrates the muslin press cloth and scorches the material.

42. To press a woolen skirt, first place it around the ironing board, generally with the right side uppermost except for the pressing of seams and other details in the process of construction, or for a material that takes on shine readily. If the material has a nap that is pressed flat, brush it straight with a whisk broom; then place the press cloth over the portion that is to be pressed and beat down any extra-heavy seam or thickness with the back of a long-handled tailor's brush or clothes brush. Next, dip the sponging brush in water, shake it to remove some of the water, and then pass it gently over the press cloth, taking care to distribute the moisture evenly.

With the press cloth thus dampened, proceed with the pressing, manipulating the iron with the right hand and smoothing the press cloth with the left. Keep the iron moving continually with a slightly rotary motion, and lift it, rather than push or drag it, from one part of the material to the next, so as to prevent an "ironed" appearance and to minimize the danger of wrinkles creeping in and of pulling the material or garment out of shape. Lift the press cloth with the left hand occasionally to make sure that the material is lying perfectly smooth and that no wrinkles have been formed anywhere, for, as is well known, wrinkles that are steamed and pressed can be removed only with great difficulty.

Another point worth remembering is always to place the iron on the stand, whenever a new place is to be sponged or pressed, so that both hands may be used to adjust the material and the press cloth properly.

If the material is of a kind that takes on shine readily, throw the press cloth back, brush the material quickly, and return the press cloth in position, continuing in this way as long as it steams freely and finishing the pressing as just described.

43. When the fabric is of a very soft nature, use only as much moisture as is absolutely necessary to give a flat, well-pressed appearance, and do not bear very much weight on the iron in pressing. If the material has a prominent nap, or pile surface, avoid pressing altogether, steaming open the seams in the manner explained in Chapter IV concerning the making of tailored seams and removing any wrinkles that may form in the material in practically this same manner.

44. Removing Shine.—Sometimes, in the construction of woolen garments, certain parts, especially seams and overlapping edges, become shiny, or glossy, if too much pressure is exerted on the iron or if the press cloth does not have sufficient moisture. To remove the shine, first place over it a press cloth that is slightly damper than one needed for ordinary pressing. Then hold a hot iron very close to the press cloth, but not on it, keeping the iron in one position for several seconds, or until the steam has had an opportunity to penetrate the fabric. Then lift the press cloth and brush the fabric so as to send the steam even deeper into it and to roughen its surface a trifle in order to make the shine appear less prominent.

Repeat this process until every trace of the shine is removed. Then, dry the steamed material thoroughly, holding the iron close enough to the press cloth so that the fabric will appear as though pressing had been carefully done, although the iron is not pressed to it for an instant.

45. Seam Allowances and Pattern Lines.—All of the illustrations in this chapter that show how to place a pattern on material, indicate an allowance for seams. Such an allowance is necessary, however, only with drafted patterns or tissue-paper patterns that make no provision for seam allowance.

Another point that should be taken into consideration in connection with tailored garments is the necessity for retaining accurate pattern lines in cutting. Because of this, it is often helpful to trim off the seam allowances when they are made, so that the pattern lines may be easily mark-stitched along the edges before removing the pattern from the material. In case this is done, seam allowance will be made on the material just as is done in the case of drafted patterns, or tissue-paper patterns that provide no seam allowance.

STRAIGHT ONE-PIECE SKIRT

46. Simplicity of Style.—To provide the beginner with those factors very necessary to good tailoring—experience in handling the heavier materials and in using painstaking tailoring methods—the straight one-piece skirt is well adapted. Its one seam and its waist-line and hem finishes provide this experience without wearying the worker and confusing her with a great amount of detail.

Some form of this type of skirt is in favor at all times. It is becoming to practically every figure, and may be varied to suit individual needs and desires by placing its seam in different places. Sometimes, the seam is found in the center back or the center front, or again over the left hip, or midway between the center front and the left hip, as illustrated in Fig. 13.

47. Material Required.—At times when Fashion permits of a skirt being as narrow as $1\frac{1}{2}$ yards at the lower edge, this skirt requires only one skirt length of 54-inch material, plus 2 or 3 inches for the separate belt.   If the material is narrower than 54 inches, or if wider skirts are favored, allow the lengthwise thread of the material to run across the figure.   In this case, the length purchased will equal the width desired for the skirt plus an allowance for the plait that covers the seam. Enough material for the belt can often be cut from one selvage, as the material is usually wider than is necessary for the length of the skirt.

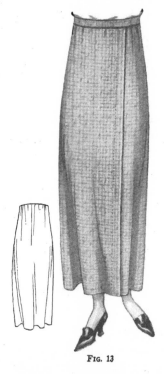

Any material that will hang gracefully and not be too bulky when gathered at the waist line, can be used for this type of skirt.   But when the skirt is to be made on a crosswise thread, the material should be plain; or, if figured, the design must be such as not to emphasize the crosswise cut.

48. Constructing a One-Piece Skirt.—The making of the skirt proceeds in exactly the same manner whether the material is placed lengthwise or crosswise around the figure. No pattern is necessary. Simply shape the front of the skirt slightly at the waist line.   To do this, measure down $\frac{1}{2}$ inch to 1 inch from the top on the center-front fold and cut from this point in a gradual curve toward the sides.   Before doing this, it is necessary, of course, to determine exactly where the plait is to be, so that the center front may be accurately located.

FIG. 13

After shaping the front, join the ends in a plain seam and form a plait over it.   Gather the skirt on the upper edge, and join it to an inside stay belt, arranging the fulness so as to have more at the sides and back than at the front. Make either a plain-seam or a tucked-seam placket under the plait at the left side.

When the top is finished, turn up the hem and choose the finish that is best suited to the material used, being guided by the suggestions given earlier in this chapter.

VARIATIONS OF THE ONE-PIECE SKIRT

49. Evenly Gathered Skirt.—Probably the simplest variation of the one-piece skirt is that which is gathered evenly at the front, back, and sides and has its opening under a plait at the center back. The material for such a skirt must be chosen with care, for, besides being of light or medium weight, it must be soft and wieldy enough to fall gracefully over the hips.

50. Wrap-Around Skirt.—A variation of the one-piece skirt that is well liked, particularly for sports wear, is the "wrap-around" model, so called because it is simply wrapped around the figure and lapped at the side front from 8 to 12 inches.   The rest of the fulness is gathered, and the skirt is attached to a belt or hung from a camisole.   The only fastening, as a rule, is at the waist line, below which the edges merely overlap.   If there is a tendency for the skirt to swing open, the edges can be tacked with *French tacks*, which consist of strands of thread reinforced by blanket-stitches.

51. *To make French tacks*, put the skirt on and pin the opening together in two places, one about 10 inches below the waist line and the other 8 or 10 inches below this one. Remove the skirt and mark the position of the pins with a tailor's tack on the upper- and underneath-skirt sections as a guide in placing the stitches.

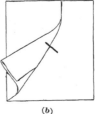

(*a*)   Fig. 14   (*b*)

Provide buttonhole twist for the work if your fabric is wool, or sewing silk or cotton if the skirt is made of lighter-weight material. Have ready a small piece of the dress material, about 1½ inches square, or a piece of tape for a stay piece for each French tack.

Take the first stitch in the upper skirt section through two thicknesses of material, if it is possible to do so without letting the stitch show on the right side, having the tack come quite close to the edge, or at least not beyond the depth of the facing or hem that finishes it. Take the second stitch in the underneath skirt section in a corresponding position through the material of the skirt and the stay piece, which should be held underneath. Do not draw the two parts close together, but leave a length of thread between, from $\frac{3}{4}$ inch up to 2 or 3 inches, as preferred. Take the third stitch in the upper section and the next in the lower, continuing in this manner until you have five or six strands, as shown in (a), Fig. 14.

As the next step, cover these strands with blanket-stitches, as shown in (a), making these close together and filling the entire length, as in (b). Fasten the thread securely in the dress material.

Proceed in the same manner in making the second tack, but make the lower tack a little longer than the upper one.

52. Draped Tailored Skirt.—A pleasing variation of the straight one-piece skirt may be had by draping it slightly at the left side as shown in Fig. 15. Extreme draping is seldom attempted in tailored skirts, for the material employed is usually too heavy and stiff to drape well. When draping is prevalent, however, or the lower edge of skirts is narrower than the upper part, a tailored skirt may be caught up on one side just enough to give a suggestion of the mode.

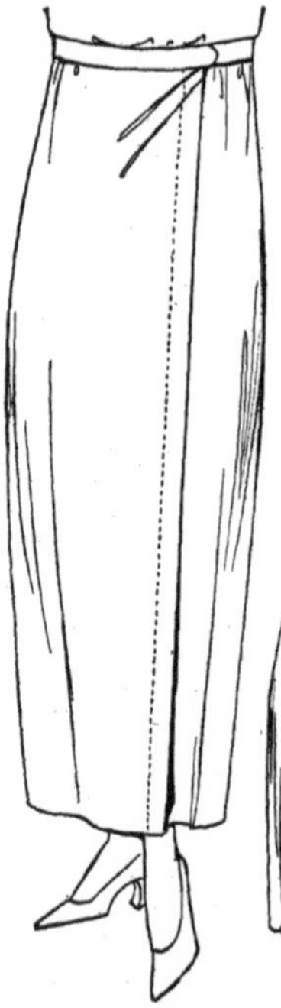

FIG. 15

53. The material provided for a draped skirt must be longer than would be necessary for a straight one, for the drape draws it up at the side front; and if an even hem line is desired, it must be cut off so that it is even with the shortest point all around.

In draping the skirt, draw the material around the form and pin it in the position desired at the waist line. Then put in the folds on the left-side front and pin them. This draws the edge of the material in a diagonal line from the top to the bottom of the skirt. When you are sure that the folds assume the desired appearance, turn the edge under so that a plait will be formed straight from top to bottom of the skirt. To secure this straight effect, it is necessary to turn under more at the lower edge than at the top. This may be trimmed off after the plait has been basted and stitched, as shown in the illustration. Since this brings the side-front plait on a slightly diagonal grain, the material used for this skirt must be such as will look well that way.

54. Make the skirt ready for the belt as directed for the plain one-piece skirt. After the belting is made ready and fastened around the figure or dress form, pin the material in place to assume the effect desired. Then tack the folds at the top and attach the skirt to the belt. If one is inexperienced in working freely with materials, it is best to make a muslin model first, which may then be taken apart and used as a pattern for cutting the skirt.

55. Varying Skirts With Trimming and Pockets.—Very often the most attractive skirts in the magazines or the shops, the skirts that look so "different" and so chic, are, when one comes to analyze them, merely straight one-piece skirts. Their smartness lies in the applying of an unusual braid, or buttons grouped in a different way, or a pocket placed to break the plainness. It is for such features that one must be ever on the alert, for they come to one only through observing not only the difference between two skirts, but their common similarity to a simple foundation. So, for such variations, which depend chiefly on style changes, no definite instruction can be given. The suggestions that have been given, however, will, if followed, prove to be of inestimable value.

STRAIGHT TWO-PIECE SKIRT

56. Only slightly more complicated than the one-piece skirt, and fully as becoming to all figures, is the two-piece skirt. A very simple form of this skirt is shown in Fig. 16. As will be noted, the front fits smoothly and the back is gathered in to fit the waist line. The closing comes under the left-side seam.

57. Material Required.—For the model as illustrated, provide two skirt lengths, allowing for the finish at the waist line and for a hem of the desired width. No extra allowance for the belt is necessary, as it can be cut from the pieces that are removed in shaping the skirt.

58. Cutting the Skirt.—It is not necessary to have a pattern for cutting a simple two-piece skirt of this type, since the back section is made of a straight piece of material and the front section is shaped only slightly.

The front and the back sections are usually the same width at the bottom, or very nearly so, and they are seldom as wide as the full width of the material. The first thing to do, then, after dividing the material in half, crosswise, is to determine the width desired at the lower edge of the skirt. Measure off half of this width on the back section, and half on the front. Cut a straight piece from one selvage in the back if the material is wider than half of the skirt width. No further shaping is necessary in the back.

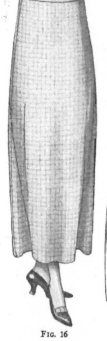

59. Fold the front section lengthwise so that the double part is equal to one-fourth of the finished skirt width. There will be an extension of a single thickness beyond one selvage equal to the width of the piece removed from the back section, if the material is wider than half the skirt width. It is not necessary to cut this off yet.

At the top of this section, measure from the fold one-fourth of the waist measure and place a pin. If slight fulness is desired in the front, 1 or 1½ inches may be added, and the pin moved to the new point. Next, lay a yardstick on the material, having one end touch the point just marked, and the other end touch the bottom of the double material at the selvage. Draw a diagonal line between these two points. Measure down 9 inches along this line from the top and mark a point, making sure that the distance from this point to the center-front fold is at least one-fourth of the hip measure. If it is not, draw a new

FIG. 16

line, keeping the lower end at the same point, but swinging the upper end out far enough to give the correct hip measure. Such a correction is seldom necessary, however.

Now cut through the two thicknesses of material on the diagonal line and shape the center front slightly at the top, as directed for the one-piece skirt.

60. Constructing the Skirt.—Join the side seams, leaving the left one open at the top for a placket, and finish this as either a plain-seam or a welt-seam placket, depending on the kind of seams used. Attach the skirt to an inside stay belt after gathering and adjusting the back fulness. Finish the hem as desired.

61. In order to keep the front section of such a skirt perfectly smooth and prevent the skirt from falling to the front, tapes may be applied to the side seams. These will hold the back fulness in place and keep this section from stretching out of place when worn. To do this, sew a piece of $\frac{3}{8}$-inch tape to one side seam about 7 inches from the waist line, draw it across the back so that it is firm but not in the least tight, and secure the other end to the opposite seam. Next, fasten one end of a piece of tape $7\frac{1}{2}$ inches long to the waist line at the center back and sew the other end to the center of the tape that extends across the back.

VARIATIONS OF THE TWO-PIECE SKIRT

62. Gathered or Plaited Skirt.—A very simple way to make a two-piece skirt of soft, light-weight material and one that is popular at times, is to cut the front section nearly as wide at the top as the back section, and gather it, drawing most of the front fulness away from the center front and distributing it over the hips. Part of the fulness is sometimes laid in plaits or tucks at each side, and these plaits or tucks are stitched from the waist to the hip line.

63. Skirt With Front and Back Plaits.—A two-piece model may be developed as shown in Fig. 17, by placing a seam at the center front and the center back, and covering each with a plait. When a skirt is cut in this way, there are no side seams and hence there is no side shaping. If there is too much fulness in the front part of the skirt, it may be taken out in darts over the hips. This makes the skirt fit more smoothly at the waist line. The shaping at the top in front is not done until the front plait has been made.   The opening is commonly arranged to come under the front plait.

64. Panel Skirt.—The two-piece skirt is sometimes varied by introducing panel lines in the front and the back.   These panels are usually composed of plaits, or of tucks that are stitched from the waist line to the bottom.   Fig. 18 shows a model having such a

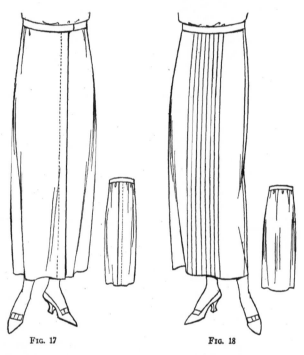

FIG. 17   FIG. 18

panel.   In this case, the panel decoration consists of pin tucks put in ¾ to 1 inch apart and pressed thoroughly.   Such a panel may vary in width, but ordinarily, to look well, it should be from 4 to 8 or 10 inches.

One method of making such a panel is to put the tucks in the center of the piece of material that is reserved for the front before this section is shaped.   Another method that may be followed, although not so good as the first one, is to allow ⅛ inch for each pin tuck desired and cut the front as usual, making the tucks after the cutting is done.

65. Plaited skirts in some form are in vogue at all times, especially for sports wear. Since they may be developed from any plain-skirt pattern or without a pattern, the chief requirement for making them is a knowledge of how to allow for the plaits in cutting, how to baste, stitch, and finish the skirt, and how to press the plaits. Once a woman is familiar with such details, she should encounter no difficulty in making any kind of plaited skirt, for the same principles apply to all.

66. Material Required.—The amount of material required for a straight side-plaited skirt, such as is illustrated in Fig. 19, must be based on the length desired for the skirt and the width it is to be at the lower edge when finished. Both are largely controlled by fashion, though the general rule for the width of a plaited skirt is that it be three times the hip measure. This allows for the plaits to meet throughout their length and overlap at the waist line. At times, however, narrow skirts and plaited skirts are in fashion at the same time. The usual procedure under such conditions is to make the plaits merely deep enough to hold their shape.

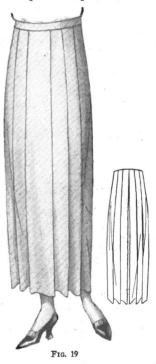

FIG. 19

To determine the width of the skirt, decide on the depth of each plait and multiply that by two, since each plait takes up two thicknesses of material. Multiply this amount by the number of plaits to be made, and add the amount thus obtained to the hip measure. The sum is the width to be provided for the skirt. Allow enough straight widths or fractions of widths of the material to provide this width, and add enough to take care of the seams that will be necessary to join them. Make these strips as long as you desire to have the skirt and add enough for the hem and the waist-line finish.

4 W I—11

67. Constructing the Skirt.—Join all of the edges of the material in plain seams. Mark the center front and the center back. Hem the skirt before arranging the plaits, for any changes to be made in the length while hanging it will be made at the top rather than at the bottom.

68. With this done, turn your attention to the plaits, bearing in mind the following suggestions, which will be helpful in arranging them:

1. Decide on the width of the plaits.
2. Plan the number of plaits. This equals the hip measure divided by the finished width of the plaits.
3. Plan the amount of material to be used in each plait. If the plaits are planned to meet throughout their length, the amount will equal three times the finished width of the plait. But if less is folded under, that is, if the plaits are shallow, the amount will be obtained by dividing the width of the skirt in inches by the number of plaits.
4. Plan the amount of material to be folded under each plait; that is, its depth. In case the plait edges meet, this will exactly equal the width of ·the plait. But if the plait is shallow, subtract the finished width of the plait from the total amount of material allowed for it, as determined in 3. The remainder is the depth, or the amount folded under.

Arrange the plaits at the hip line first, pinning them to make sure that they are correctly placed. This is most conveniently done by slipping the skirt over the ironing board. Baste the plaits lengthwise from the hip line to the hem. Then at the waist line overlap them as much as is necessary to conform with the waist measure, and baste them in position from the hip line to the waist line.

69. Before trying the skirt on, arrange for the placket. The most desirable arrangement is to have it come in a seam. In any event, it must come under a plait. If you cannot arrange the placket on a seam and there is a little uncertainty in your mind as to whether or not the plaits are correctly arranged and you are safe in slashing a placket opening in the material, open one of the seams for a few inches at the top as a temporary opening. This can be restitched when the permanent placket is located.

Try the skirt on and make any necessary changes in the plaits. At this time, pin the top of the skirt to an inside stay belt. Measure the distance from the floor, and make all adjustments in length by lifting or dropping it at the top. Then remove the skirt and complete it by finishing the placket and the waist line.

VARYING THE SIDE-PLAITED SKIRT

70. Skirt With Side-Plaited Panels.—A variation of the sideplaited skirt that is very often seen is shown in Fig. 20. The panel treatment, which it illustrates in one form, permits of infinite variety of arrangement. The panels may vary in width and in location, and the plaits of which they are composed may differ in depth or they may follow a symmetrical arrangement, as illustrated. Or, one panel only may be used and its location may be at the center front, side front, or over the left hip. Here, again, the habit of careful observation of models in the shops, on the streets, and in the fashion magazines, will serve you well in keeping your skirt modish.

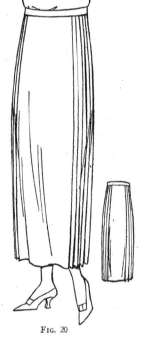

In planning for such a skirt, decide on the number of plaited panels and their width. Subtract the sum of the panel widths from the hip measure. The remainder will be the combined widths of the plain sections. To this, add three times the width of the combined plaited-panel widths and the sum will be the width needed for the skirt.

71. In making a skirt with plaited panels, sew up the seams and hem the lower edge as directed for the straight

Fig. 20

side-plaited skirt. Mark the center front and center back and the location and width of the plain sections. Plait the remaining material to conform to the width previously decided on for the plaited panels. Finish the skirt as directed for the plain side-plaited skirt.

STRAIGHT BOX-PLAITED SKIRT

72. The box-plaited skirt, as illustrated in Fig. 21, is more successful for young girls and for average than for stout figures, because the wide plaits tend to emphasize breadth of figure. Box-plaited skirts are very attractive and comfortable for sports wear.

73. Material Required.—A *true box plait* is one in which the plaits are so formed that the two edges come together on the wrong side at a point directly under the center of the outside of the plait, as shown at *a*, Fig. 22. The edges of true box plaits also touch on the outside. For a true box-plaited skirt, therefore, material equal in width to three times the hip measure is required, the same as for a side-plaited skirt. But if so wide a skirt is not desired, the plaits may be laid shallower; that is, the edges need not touch underneath.

Fig. 21

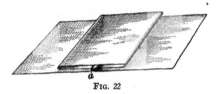

Fig. 22

These shallow plaits do away with considerable bulk over the hips and at the same time produce a very good effect.

74. Constructing the Skirt.—Beginning with the center-front plait, measure and pin the plaits in position. Take great care that each one follows a thread of the material. Then baste them and proceed with the finishing as for a side-plaited skirt.

MECHANICALLY PLAITED SKIRT

75. Varieties of Plaited Skirts.—In order to save time in the making of *side-* and *box-plaited skirts* and to have them mechanically accurate, many people have the plaiting done at a shop equipped with the necessary mechanical apparatus. The rest of the work involved in making the skirt can then be done at home. *Accordion-*

plaited skirts can be made only by this method, as it is impossible to do the plaiting by hand.

It is sometimes impossible to have work of this kind done in a small town, as there may not be such a shop. Where this is true, you may send the material to an establishment of this kind in a larger town, or your dry-goods merchant will be glad to send it away for you. In cities, some of the larger stores have a department where this work is done.

76. Preparing the Material for Plaiting.—For the *side-* and *box-plaited* skirts, proceed exactly as you would in preparing a skirt for plaiting by hand, but leave one seam open throughout its length. Hem the lower edge. If it is desired to have any particular point in the material for the center front, be sure to mark it clearly with thread, for otherwise the center of the material will be treated as the center front. This, of course, is important only in the case of a side-plaited skirt having a box plait in the center front with the opening at some point other than the center back.

Prepare the material for *accordion plaiting* just as described for the *side-* and *box-plaited* skirts. It is wise, however, in planning an accordion-plaited skirt, to add 1 inch to the length, as the plaiting takes up the material about that much in a skirt of average length.

77. Finishing the Skirt.—When the skirt is returned from the shop, join the last seam, and finish the side- or box-plaited skirt as you would a hand-plaited one.

Great care is necessary in joining the last seam of an accordion-plaited skirt, in order to have the plaits match perfectly. Leave an opening at the top of this seam for the placket. Since the plaiting is uniform, it makes no difference where the joining is located.

To simplify the joining of the accordion-plaited skirt to the inside stay belt, run a row of gathering-stitches $\frac{1}{4}$ inch from the top, using stitches about $\frac{3}{8}$ inch long. Draw these up to fit the size of the prepared belt, distribute the fulness evenly around the skirt, and join the skirt to the belt as you would in making a gathered skirt.

PLAIN-FITTED SKIRT

78. A fitted skirt may hang straight, it may decrease in width at the bottom, or it may flare as in a circular skirt. Such skirts require patterns and considerable fitting to make them assume, without gathers, the lines of the figure. Plain-fitted skirts may have from two to nine gores. In fact, Fashion has occasionally decreed the adoption of as many as fifteen gores.

79. Material Required.—It is quite difficult to estimate the amount of material required for a fitted skirt. The safest plan is to choose the pattern to be used and be guided by the instruction given on the envelope. The amount will be influenced, of course, by the length of the skirt and its width at the bottom. With a material having no decided "up and down," such as a nap or a figure, material may be saved in the cutting by placing the pattern pieces on the material so that the top of one is next to the bottom of another. Particular care is necessary in this case, however, to have each gore come on the correct thread of the material, for one or more gores cut incorrectly will interfere greatly with the proper hanging of the skirt.

80. Constructing the Skirt.—The making of fitted skirts gives more experience in the art of tailoring than the making of any other type of skirt. The large number of seams and the prominence given to them by the tight fitting make accurate stitching and pressing actual necessities. Also, the seam finishes that are in keeping with the material must be chosen with care. Welt seams are generally used, but corded seams and single- and double-stitched seams also are employed at times.

Choose the placket that corresponds best with the kind of seam used. The fitted-skirt placket demands special attention, particularly in the locating and sewing on of the fasteners, because there is considerable strain at the closing point.

In basting a fitted skirt, remember always to begin at the hip line and baste both upward and downward from there. Fit the skirt carefully before doing any stitching.

ONE-PIECE CIRCULAR SKIRT

81. When garments on gracefully curved and molded lines are in favor, the one-piece circular skirt illustrated in Fig. 23 is popular, not alone for its beauty of line, but also because of its simplicity, which enables one to make it with comparatively little effort. It does require careful handling, however, because of the bias seam at the center back.

82. Material Required.—It is very evident that the one-piece circular skirt must be made of material that is wide enough to form the entire skirt.   If the skirt is to be long, wide material, say from 52 to 56 inches wide, must be used; but if it is to be short, material from 36 to 44 inches wide will do.   A good plan is always to have the material at least 12 inches wider than the length of the skirt in front.   Such material will accommodate the skirt pattern, which is higher at the waist line in the center back than at the waist line in the center front, and will allow the requisite amount for the seam used in applying the facing at the lower edge.

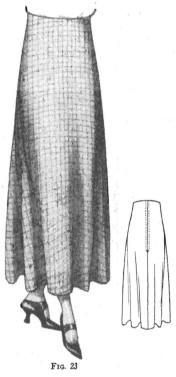

The exact amount of material to be supplied cannot be decided on accurately without the pattern, for circular skirt patterns differ in the width of their flares, and this, of course, influences the needed amount.   So here again, select your pattern, and then purchase the material.

As to the kind of material, a moderately plain weave is best. But if a plain color is not used, a conservative pattern should be

Fig. 23

chosen so as not to attract attention to the crosswise cut in the back.

83. Cutting Out the Skirt.—Fold the material crosswise through the center and pin the selvage edges together.   Pin the pattern on it so that the center-front line comes on the crosswise fold, as shown in Fig. 24.   In cutting out the skirt, allow ½ inch for a finish at the top and 1 inch at the center back, so that it may be finished in a slot seam if desired.   Since it is much easier to turn an even line at the lower edge of a skirt if more than a seam's width is allowed, particularly when it is on the bias, allow 1 inch for finishing the lower edge.

84.   Marking, Pinning, and Basting.—When the skirt is cut out, mark-stitch the waist line, hip line, and center-back seam.   To prevent the seam edges from stretching, lay the skirt out flat and double on the sewing table, with the two ends of the waist line and the two ends of the hip line coming together, and the edges of the back seam exactly meeting.   Measure down the placket length from the waist line and from that point baste to the bottom of the skirt, using $\frac{1}{4}$-inch stitches so that the edges of the seam will be kept smooth when it is pressed open to form a slot seam.

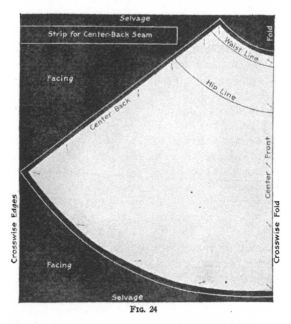

FIG. 24

85.   First Fitting.—When the skirt is basted as directed, slip it on merely to see if it is correct in size.   In doing this, be very careful to adjust the mark-stitching at the waist line so that it comes exactly over the waist line of the figure.   The ripple of a circular skirt begins well up on the hips, the skirt hanging quite free from the belt so as not to appear too tight and drawn around the hips.   For this reason, make no attempt to fit the skirt close to the figure.

86.   Making the Slot Seam and Placket.—Next, give attention to the slot seam.   If the material is wide and the skirt is not too long, the lengthwise strip needed may be cut without piecing. As indicated in Fig. 24, however, the top of the skirt reaches the selvage, making it impossible to cut this strip longer than shown. Where piecing is necessary in plaid or figured material, use great care in matching the design so that the piecing will not be noticeable.

After completing the habit-back placket, press both the seam and the placket very carefully under a damp cloth.

87. Overcoming Sagging.—At this stage of the work, it is advisable to hang the skirt up by pinning the waist line to a straight strip of muslin fastened to a coat hanger, or arranged in some other way that will permit the waist line to be pinned straight across and the bias back to have a chance to sag before the skirt length is measured.

While the skirt is shaping itself according to the weight of the material, the belt can be prepared.

88. Second Fitting.—Put the inside stay belt around the figure and hook it in the center back. Then, put the skirt on, adjust it correctly, and hook up the placket. Next, turn the top edge of the skirt over the stay belt and pin it securely all around, so that the top line is even and the skirt fits perfectly around the waist.

With the skirt pinned thus securely to the belt, measure the distance from the floor to the desired hem line, making the skirt $\frac{1}{4}$ to $\frac{1}{2}$ inch shorter in the back than in the front. This may be done while the skirt is on the figure by simply changing the skirt gauge properly, or the bottom may be turned an even length and the $\frac{1}{4}$- to $\frac{1}{2}$-inch difference taken care of when the basting line is put in. The reason for making the back shorter than the front is to allow for sagging. Since the front of this skirt is cut on a crosswise thread of the material, there will be no possibility of its dropping down; but no matter how carefully a skirt is made, any part that is cut on the bias will have a tendency to sag, especially at the back.

89. Completing the Skirt.—Remove the skirt, taking care to keep the upper edge pinned securely to the belt and not to lose any of the pins at the bottom. Baste the skirt to the stay belt and finish with a seam binding, as described in Art. **13**.

Since a circular skirt cannot be hemmed successfully even by shrinking out the fulness around the lower edge, the bottom of the skirt may be finished with a fitted facing or it may be bound.

90. Two-Piece Circular Skirt.—The circular skirt may be developed very satisfactorily by cutting the pattern in two sections so that a seam comes at each hip. Be very sure that the hip seams are located exactly as desired before cutting the material. A good plan is to cut the skirt from muslin in one piece and locate the seams as desired on it. Then use the muslin sections as a pattern.

The circular skirt cut in this way requires two lengths of material, each as wide as a single one of these sections is at the bottom. Fold

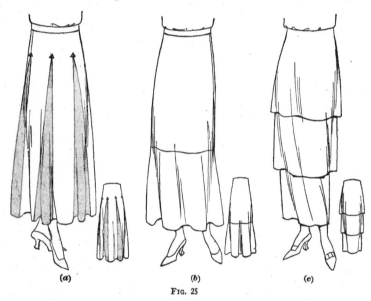

(a)   (b)   (c)

Fig. 25

the material lengthwise, and arrange both the center front and the center back of the pattern pieces on the lengthwise fold. By cutting the circular skirt in this way, the bias seam in the back is avoided and the possibility of the back sagging is overcome. The side seams are still bias, but the sagging at the sides can be overcome as described previously for the sagging at the back of the one-piece circular skirt.

Make the skirt as instructed for the one-piece skirt, except to use an appropriate placket and plain or cord seams. The opening is on the left hip.

91. The Godet Skirt.—An effective variation of the circular skirt is the *godet skirt*, so named because of the godets, or flaring sections, that are inserted in the lower portion of a plain skirt, as illustrated in (*a*), Fig. 25, so that a circular effect is produced. The godets vary in length and in width, depending on how much flare is to be added and how high the flare is desired to extend. Contrasting material is sometimes used for the godets to produce a particular effect.

92. The amount of material required for a godet skirt is the same as for a plain, two-piece skirt, plus a sufficient allowance for the godets. This additional allowance can be determined only when the length and width of the godets are known.

93. If it is not convenient to purchase a special pattern for a godet skirt, a plain, two-piece-skirt pattern may be used by slashing it at the points desired for the inserts to a depth corresponding with the depth of the godets to be used. To make a pattern for the godets, cut a circle having a radius equal to the depth of the godet. From this circle, cut a section as you would cut a piece of pie, making the section as wide at the outside as you want the bottom of the godet to be.

94. In a skirt of this kind, it is usually planned to have a godet come at each side seam, but before inserting the godets, the seams should be carefully basted with short stitches and the skirt evened off around the bottom. If this is not done, the godets are likely to be placed too low on the hips.

The skirt is not difficult to make, but the work must be done very accurately. Rip open the basted seams and set the godets in with great care, using plain seams for inserting them and clipping the skirt portion slightly at the point of each godet in order to have the seam lie perfectly flat. Work an arrow-head over each point to strengthen the material as well as to add decoration to the skirt. Finish the bottom of the skirt with a bias facing.

THE FLOUNCE SKIRT

95. A very good way to give a circular effect to a plain, two-piece, fitted skirt is to add a circular flounce, as in (*b*), Fig. 25. For best results with this skirt, a special pattern should be purchased.

Finish the side seams of the upper part, make a placket, and join the skirt to a belt. Then measure the distance from the lower edge of this part to the floor and trim it off to an even length all around before adding the circular flounce. Before finishing the seams of the flounce, make sure that the top edge of the flounce just fits the lower edge of the skirt section. When the flounce is made and attached satisfactorily, face the bottom with a bias or a fitted facing.

THE TIERED SKIRT

96. The tiered skirt shown in (c), Fig. 25, has a circular tendency. It may be varied by applying more or fewer tiers, each one flaring slightly over the one below, or by having the tiers very narrow and arranged in groups.

The pattern for this skirt has as its foundation a rather narrow, fitted skirt, which is made complete except for the belt, this, however, being basted on so that the foundation may be hung. Then the flounces are applied, beginning with the lower one. The top flounce and the foundation skirt are applied to the belt in one operation, following the general method given in Art. **13.**

The foundation skirt may be hemmed, but the circular flounces are finished with bias facings.

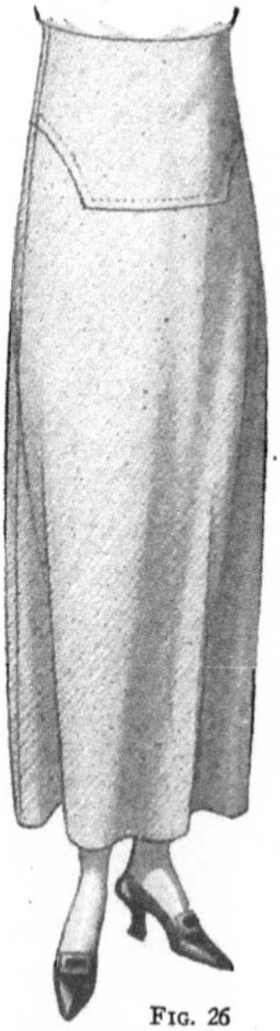

YOKE SKIRT

97. At times, simply by the use of fitted yokes at the top, skirts give the effect of being fitted without being either circular or composed of many gores. Yokes vary in outline, depth, and position, but their application is quite similar for all types.

Fig. 26

In Fig. 26 is shown a skirt that is fashioned with a yoke extending entirely around the skirt and cut deeper in the front than over the hip portions and at the back. A skirt with such a yoke is satisfactory only for the slender figure, as it would emphasize the hip breadth and decrease the apparent height of a large figure.

98. Material Required.—The amount of material required for this yoke skirt is the same as for a plain skirt, plus a sufficient allowance for the finish of the seam which joins the yoke and the skirt.

99. Constructing a Yoke Skirt.—Cut the yoke according to your pattern, sew up the side seams, and fit it to the figure. Then turn the lower edge ½ inch to the wrong side and press it flat.

Join the skirt seams as for a plain skirt. Then lay the skirt over a smooth surface, preferably over an ironing board, and place the pressed-under edge of the yoke over the top edge of the skirt. Pin and baste these together very carefully with short stitches, keeping a very even, straight line. Fit the skirt before stitching the yoke to the skirt portion. Make the placket finish as you would for any fitted skirt.

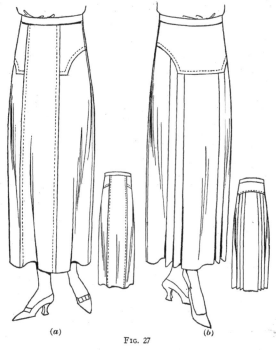

(a) Fig. 27 (b)

VARIATIONS OF YOKE SKIRT

100. Yoke Skirt With Panels. The yoke skirt may be adapted to the stout figure by breaking its horizontal line with front and back panels, as in Fig. 27 (a), which virtually makes of it a six-gored skirt. In making this skirt, first prepare the yoke sections. Then join the side-front and the side-back gores, and baste the yoke sections to these as directed for the yoke skirt. Next, baste the panels to the side sections in preparation for cord seams. Before stitching, fit the skirt thoroughly. Finish it as for any fitted skirt.

101.   Plaited Yoke Skirt.—A skirt that permits comfortable freedom by introducing plaits, yet retains its fitted effect over the hips, is shown in Fig. 27 (b).   It may be cut from the same pattern as the plain-yoke skirt shown in Fig. 26 by locating and basting the plaits in place before cutting, and then proceeding with the construction as for the plain-yoke skirt.

<hr>

CHARACTERISTICS OF GORED SKIRTS

102. (The term *gored skirt* is applied to any skirt made of gores, or shaped pieces, that are cut narrower at the top than at the bottom.) Such models are often popular, particularly when fitted skirts are in vogue, as the seams permit of a trim, well-fitting garment.

While practically all skirts are gored at least slightly, those of less than four pieces, or gores, are usually referred to as three-piece, two-piece, or straight skirts.

Skirts of four or more gores are a little more difficult to make than those with fewer pieces, because they usually require considerable fitting and sometimes much altering.   The method of construction, however, is practically the same for all gored skirts.

<hr>

SIX-GORED SKIRT

103.   The arrangement of gores in a six-gored skirt gives the effect of a front and a back panel and two gores over each hip. Fig. 28 shows such a skirt made from wash material.   A strictly tailored wash skirt, such as this, requires as much care in pinning, basting, fitting, and finishing as does a woolen skirt.

104.   Material Required.—Since the width of skirts at their lower edge varies so greatly from season to season, it is impossible to specify the amount of material that a skirt of any given number of gores will require, and have this amount hold with any degree of accuracy from one season to another.   The only safe way is to be guided by the material requirements given on the pattern envelope. For a six-gored skirt, this is likely to be from two to three skirt lengths, varying with the width of the material and the flare of the gores.

105.   Placing the Pattern and Cutting Out the Material.—Place the skirt material on the cutting table, folding it through the center lengthwise so that its right sides are together, and pinning the selvage edges together so that the fabric cannot slip when the pattern is pinned on.

When the pattern has been carefully tested as to its width at the lower edge and its length, so that it is as nearly correct as possible as far as style and becomingness are concerned, lay the pieces on the material, having the center-front and center-back panels, or gores, come on the lengthwise fold. In doing this, it is a good idea, provided the material has no up and down, to place the bottom edge of the center-front gore at one end and the bottom edge of the center-back gore at the other end. The material between may be used for the side gores, which require a little more material than the front and the back gores, for they must be arranged very carefully in order to have them come according to the thread of the material. By adjusting the pattern pieces and trying out different arrangements, it may be possible to save some material.

106. When all of the pattern pieces are placed, mark the pattern lines and either mark-stitch the hip line and waist line or mark them with basting threads. The use of a tracer for this purpose is not advisable in firmly woven materials, because it is likely to cut through and leave ugly marks in the finished skirt.

In cutting, allow on all seam edges $\frac{3}{4}$ to 1 inch if welt seams are to be used, or $\frac{3}{8}$ inch for plain seams. Save all pieces of material for the cutting of a fitted facing for the skirt.

FIG. 28

107. Marking, Pinning, and Basting.—When the skirt is cut out and the pattern removed, run a basting thread along the center of the front and the back panels. Then pin and baste the edges of the gores together from the hip line up and down, taking care to keep the pattern lines together. There is never a time when pattern lines may be overlooked, because on them are built the perfect lines of a garment.

The placket opening may be at the left side of either the front or the back gore, but it is usually preferred on the first gore because a placket placed in the back shows signs of wear more quickly. Measure down from the waist line on the seam where the placket is

to be located, to the depth desired for the opening.   Place a pin crosswise at that point and then run a basting thread along the pattern line on each side of the placket opening, so that there will be no danger of losing sight of the lines in fitting.

108.   First Fitting.—Put on the skirt and pin the placket opening as shown in Fig. 29, meanwhile adjusting the skirt smoothly around the hips.   If it is too tight, lift it a trifle at the waist line; or, if it is too loose, take off an equal amount on each side gore over the hips to make it fit correctly.   If there is too much fulness at the lower edge of the skirt, take in the seams so as to produce a narrower effect.   Practically the only point to consider in this first fitting is the fulness at the lower edge and the fit of the skirt through the hips.   The waist line and hem do not require attention until after the seams and placket are finished.

109.   Preparing for the Second Fitting. After removing the skirt carefully, stitch the seams, make the placket, and prepare the inside stay belt.   When welt seams are used,

Fig. 29

they serve as a trimming and should be as nearly perfect as possible.   Adjust the stitch to the correct length and tension and use the seam gauge so that the stitching is accurate.

110.   Second Fitting.—Place the stay belt around the waist line and hook the ends.   Put the skirt on, fasten the placket, pull the skirt up well on the belt, and turn the top edge of the skirt in between the belt and the skirt itself rather than over the belt.   Pin the skirt to the belt every few inches, so that it fits smoothly.   Measure the lower edge of the skirt an even distance from the floor at all points.

111. Finishing the Skirt.—Remove the skirt and run a row of basting-stitches along the top on the turn where the raw edges are turned under between the skirt and the belt. Unpin the skirt from the belt and join it in the manner previously described for the joining of an inside stay belt to a wash skirt, letting the edge of the belt come even with the row of basting.

Apply a bias facing to the bottom of the skirt. When the garment is complete, remove all bastings and press it.

SEVEN-GORED SKIRT

112. The seven-gored skirt differs from the six-gored one in that two gores are substituted for the center-back panel. Because of this, it opens in the center back. If desired, the opening may be finished with a habit-back placket such as was used for the one-piece circular skirt. Otherwise, use the welt-seam placket, finishing it without the outside stitching.

EIGHT- AND NINE-GORED SKIRT

113. The construction of eight- and nine-gored plain skirts differs so little from the construction of six- and seven-gored skirts, respectively, that a pattern with the correct number of gores is the only new consideration. The eight-gored skirt has three gores on each side, a panel in the front and another in the back. The nine-gored skirt provides for a front panel, which is cut on the fold of the material, three gores on each side and two in the back. Develop these two types of skirts exactly as 'you would the six- and seven-gored skirts previously considered.

SIX-GORED, INVERTED-PLAIT SKIRT

114. In Fig. 30, view (a), is shown the front and in view (b), the back of a six-gored, inverted-plait skirt. This style of skirt may be worn becomingly by the majority of women because it has straight lines. The inverted plaits provide a convenient and comfortable amount of fulness.

115. Material Required.—Since it is rather difficult to keep plaits in position if they are made of wiry or open-weave material,

4 W I—12

fairly firm material should be chosen for a plaited skirt. Two skirt lengths of material 54 inches wide will develop this skirt for an average figure.

116. Placing the Pattern and Cutting Out the Material.—A plain, six-gored-skirt pattern may be used for the inverted-plait skirt. In Fig. 31 is shown such a pattern, in average size, placed

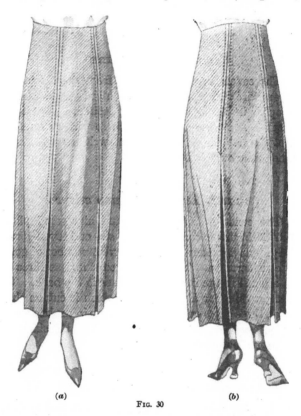

(a)   (b)

Fɪɢ. 30

on 54-inch material. In a smaller size, the gores may be slipped alongside of each other so that not quite so much material will be needed. On the other hand, for a large figure, three skirt lengths are necessary because the gores are wider.

One point that is well worth remembering and stressing in any case is that the pattern pieces must be laid on the correct thread of

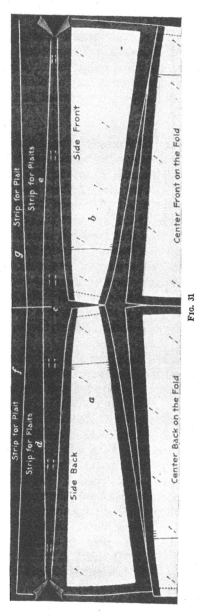

Fig. 31

the material, regardless of whether or not this arrangement requires more material than is deemed advisable, for a garment may be entirely spoiled if one piece is cut the wrong way of the material. Especially does this point demand attention in tailored garments because their extreme plainness makes every defect so clearly evident.

117. In laying out the material for this skirt, the usual custom is departed from in that two folds are made rather than one and the selvages are brought together, not on the edge, but about one-fourth of the width of the doubled material from the edge. The wider lap of the material thus laid is used for cutting the gores, and the narrower one for the strips that slip under the seams to form the plaits. Notice that, in the layout shown, the center-front and center-back pattern pieces are laid on the fold of the wider lap. Do not pin them until the side gores are correctly located as follows:

Pin the side gores indicated by *a* and *b* through only one thickness of material. Then if the material must be slipped over to provide the correct width for the front and the back gores, it will not be necessary to remove all of the pattern pieces.

Try out the location of the pattern pieces until you have them so placed that they require the least possible material.

To provide ample allowance for the plaits, locate a point $1\frac{1}{4}$ inches both to the right and to the left of the top of each gore and a point $2\frac{1}{2}$ inches both to the right and to the left of the bottom of each gore. Then connect these points with diagonal lines as shown, curving them enough to correspond with the original pattern lines, particularly at the top.

118. When the four pattern pieces that provide for the six gores of the skirt are placed and marked, bring the material over in the manner shown at c in preparation for the cutting of the strips that go underneath the seams to form the inverted plaits. These strips are very similar to the strips for the slot seams, but each strip must be twice as wide as the allowance for the plaits, at both the waist line and the bottom of the skirt, in order to have them fit exactly in position. If the pattern pieces of the skirt are very wide, provide an extra length of material for these strips. As the skirt has six gores, it is necessary to have six strips; therefore, cut two strips, as at d, two, as at e, and two more on the fold, as at f and g. That these strips may conform to the width of the plaits, take care in measuring for them to have each strip $2\frac{1}{2}$ inches wide at the top and 5 inches wide at the bottom.

Before cutting out the material, outline each edge of the pattern properly, allowing 1 inch at the bottom of each gore for finishing the lower edge. In cutting, be very careful to make true, even edges.

119. Marking, Pinning, and Basting.—When the skirt is cut out, lay each piece flat on the table and mark-stitch the hip line, the waist line, and all around the pattern edges. In removing the pattern pieces from the material, mark the gores at the hip line so that they may be put together in their correct order. Pin and then baste on the pattern lines, up and down from the hip line, using small stitches so that they will not pull out in the fitting and so that the edges of each seam may be held in correct line. This is very important because these seams are similar to slot seams and must have lines as nearly perfect as possible. For the placket, leave an opening on the left-hand side of the back panel, or on the left-hand side of the front panel. With the skirt thus basted, slip it on for the first fitting.

120. First Fitting.—In connection with the first fitting, it is well to remember that a plaited skirt should not fit too closely. It must fit smoothly, but a trifle loose, for when the strips that go underneath the plaits are put in place they will fill the skirt out a trifle. Of course, if the skirt appears to be really too large, it should be taken in enough to make it fit correctly.

121. Adding the Strips and Marking the Placket.—When the skirt is fitted, remove it and press the seams open, dampening them carefully and pressing them thoroughly, so that the edges will be as straight as possible. The attractive or unattractive appearance of the finished skirt depends considerably on this pressing.

Place one strip underneath each plait, pinning the center of the strip directly underneath the seam and easing the strip to the seam so that it does not appear drawn. Baste carefully in exactly the same manner as for a slot seam.

When all of the strips are in place, make the habit-back placket. With that completed, baste the strips from the right side of the garment so that they lie perfectly flat.

122. Second Fitting.—Slip the skirt on to make sure that the strips do not draw in any place and that the skirt fits smoothly. If any alterations are necessary, do the work very carefully so as not to interfere with the line of the plaits at each seam.

123. Stitching the Plaits and Strips.—Remove the skirt from the figure and sponge and press the strips from the wrong side in order to take up any fulness, and thus have them perfectly smooth. The skirt is then ready to stitch from the right side.

Determine the distance that the stitching is to extend downwards from the waist line, and the depth of the stitching from the seam edge, points that are controlled entirely by fashion. Lay the skirt out flat, measure from the waist line the depth decided on for each plait, and mark with a pin the point where the stitching is to end. Adjust the seam gauge on the sewing machine to the proper width; and in stitching, be careful to keep the material up well on the machine so that it will not pull or drag down, for it is impossible to stitch evenly or to keep the seam lines straight if the weight of the material pulls it away from the presser-foot. Stitch down on one side . of the plait until you reach the point marked for the end of the stitching. With the machine needle down through the material, use it for a pivot, turn the skirt to a forty-five degree angle, and stitch diagonally toward the point where the folded edges of the plait meet.

Stitch the other side of the plait from the waist line down in the same manner. The two rows of stitching will then appear as in Fig. 30. Bring the threads through to the wrong side and tie them securely. Never turn at the bottom of the first stitching and stitch back up to the waist line on the opposite side, for there is great danger of drawing and pulling the seam.

FIG. 32

124. When the plaits are all stitched, turn the skirt over and stitch the edges of the strips to the edges of the plait allowance on the wrong side. Have the stitching come from $\frac{3}{8}$ to $\frac{1}{2}$ inch from the edge, and begin it up on each seam about 3 inches beyond the termination of the stitching on the right side, as shown at a, Fig. 32, so that the seams will be in no danger of pulling out. When all the stitching is done, bind, overcast, or notch the seam edges from the waist line to the bottom of the skirt, as at b.

125. Third Fitting and Finishing.—Slip the skirt on, pinning it to a previously prepared stay belt, and mark the hem line. Remove the skirt, and finish the waist line as directed for the plain circular skirt. Bind the edge of the hem with a bias binding of light-weight taffeta or satin or fine percaline. Baste it carefully just above the turn and also at the top, and whip or slip-stitch it in place. Finally, lay in the plaits below the stitching as for a box-plaited skirt, and press the entire garment.

SIX-GORED, BOX-PLAITED SKIRT

126. Cutting the Skirt.—In Fig. 33, view *a*, is shown the front, and in view *b*, the back of a six-gored, box-plaited skirt. It is developed from the same pattern and in much the same manner as the six-gored, inverted-plait skirt just considered. The pattern pieces are placed on the material in practically the same positions, but they are kept closer together because the only seam allowances necessary are on the back edges of the side-front gores, on the front edges of the side-back gores, and at the top and bottom of the skirt. Seam allowances on the front and back panels, on the back edges of the side-back gores, and on the front edges of the side-front gores are unnecessary because these edges just meet underneath the plaits.

Instead of six strips for plaits, as in the inverted-plait skirt, only four strips are required for the box-plaited skirt, since they are used only along the panel edges of the front and the

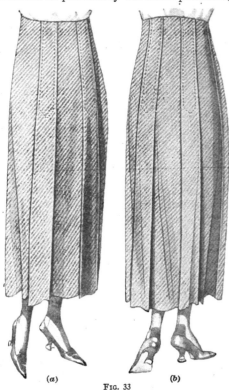

(a)   (b)

Fig. 33

back gores. The seams over the hips are uncovered. Each strip should be 5 inches wide at the top and 10 inches wide at the bottom, since no allowance is made on the gores for plaits. It is readily seen that this skirt requires about the same amount of material as the inverted-plait skirt.

127. Basting the Seams.—Mark with a basting thread the center of each strip that is to be used for a plait. Then fold under the raw edges until they meet exactly at the center of the strip. Baste the fold on each side of the plait thus formed, taking great care to have absolutely true edges.　Press the plaits carefully and they are ready to be applied to the skirt.

To make the skirt ready, bring together the pattern edges of the front and side-front gores, as well as those of the back and side-back gores.　Baste them with diagonal basting, as shown at *a*, Fig. 34, being very careful not to draw the seams in any place, nor to overlap them nor let them separate at any point, for, as no

Fig. 34

seam allowance is made on these edges, they must come together exactly.

When the gores are basted, pin the plaits over them.　In doing this, be extremely careful to keep the center of each plait exactly over the meeting edges of the gores, and hold each plait perfectly smooth so that it will be neither too full nor too tight in any place. When the plaits are pinned in place, baste them to the gores, having the line of basting come from $\frac{1}{2}$ to $\frac{3}{4}$ inch from each edge of the plaits and leaving an opening for the placket under the left side of the left-front plait.　Then pin and baste the side seams together.

128. First Fitting.—Slip the skirt on for the first fitting, and adjust it properly on the figure. If the skirt appears too tight, clip the basting that holds the gores together underneath the plaits at the seams where the extra fulness is needed. If the skirt is a little tight over the hips, let out the basting at the hip seams, thereby letting each gore out a trifle. If considerably more freedom is needed, rather than allow too much on the front edges and thus destroy the line of the gores, let out the edges of the back side gores and slip them out from under the plaits enough to allow for the necessary amount. If the skirt is too large, clip the bastings and slip the gores far enough underneath the plaits to take out the desired amount of fulness, or take up the hip seams a little. In any event, the amount let out or taken up should be at the seams where it is most needed.

129. Completing the Skirt.—After the skirt is removed, even up any seams that were opened in fitting and replace the necessary basting. Then press the skirt on the wrong side, after which apply the placket facing in the manner shown at *b*, Fig. 34. As will be observed, this placket is finished similarly to the plain-seam placket, in which straight facings are used and the edge is stitched down before the snap fasteners are sewed on.

Stitch the skirt, following the instruction given in connection with the inverted-plait skirt. Then slip the skirt on and secure it to a stay belt and turn the hem. Remove the skirt after the second fitting and finish the waist line and hem as described for the inverted-plait skirt. Press the whole skirt thoroughly.

NINE-GORED, SIDE-PLAITED SKIRTS

130. In Fig. 35, view (*a*) is shown the front, and in view (*b*), the back, of a nine-gored, side-plaited skirt. This skirt is somewhat similar in effect to the straight-plaited skirt previously described, except that the plaits are much farther apart and not so deep. Also, the stitching over the hips gives a more fitted effect than one is accustomed to seeing in the straight-plaited skirt.

131. Placing the Pattern and Cutting Out the Material.—If a special pattern for a nine-gored, side-plaited skirt is provided, it will not be necessary to make an additional allowance for plaits outside of the pattern edges. But if it is more convenient to use a plain nine-gored-skirt pattern that has no plait extensions, place the pattern pieces in position, as shown in Fig. 36. Put the center-front line of the front gore on the fold, and place the side and the back gores on the correct thread of the material. This arrangement can be followed only on a material having no nap and no decided up and down. If material with a nap is used, more must be provided.

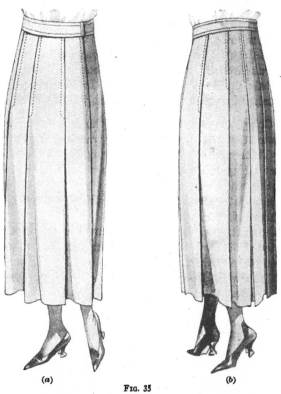

(a)　　　　　　(b)

Fɪɢ. 35

In placing the pattern pieces, remember that the plait allowance must be made on *both* sides of each gore. Before cutting, mark this allowance, adding $\frac{1}{2}$ inch for seams on each side. Since the plaits must be $1\frac{1}{2}$ inches wide at the top and $2\frac{1}{2}$ inches wide at the bottom, the total width of the allowance on each side of each gore will be 2 inches at the top and 3 inches at the bottom. The reason for narrowing the plaits at the top is to avoid a bulky finish at the waist line. Locate the points that correspond with these measure-

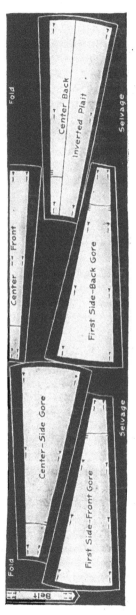

FIG. 36

ments, connect them, and cut the garment along the marked lines. A yardstick may be used in marking.

132. Mark-Stitching, Pinning, and Basting.—Mark-stitch on all pattern edges, the hip line, and the waist line. Turn the center-back pattern piece back on the inverted-plait line and mark-stitch it, so that this line may be folded in position when the skirt is put together. Then after removing the pattern pieces, turn the edges of the front gore over to the wrong side, and baste through the gore and its turned-under edge on the mark-stitched line. Place this gore over the edge of the first side gore, so that the mark-stitched line on the center-front gore just meets the mark-stitched line of the side gore, and the waist lines and hip lines of the two form two continuous lines. Pin the gores together in this position.

Next, turn under and baste the back edge of the first side gore; then lap it to meet the pattern line of the front edge of the center-side gore. Continue in this manner until all the gores are basted. Then turn the inverted plait back and baste on the original center-back line. Next, baste up the center-back seam for the first fitting.

133. First Fitting.—Slip the skirt on and adjust it well on the figure, taking care to see that each plait turns toward the back on the outside and toward the front on the inside, or wrong side, of the skirt. Do not fit the skirt too tightly at this time, for after it is stitched it will appear to fit closer than it does when the gores are just basted together, even though the basting-stitches are small.

If the skirt is too loose, move the front panel over an equal amount on each side of the first side gore and turn the inverted plait at the back in a trifle deeper. If this change is not sufficient, determine how much smaller the skirt should be and take an equal amount off each gore. This work may be accomplished without interfering with the turned edge of the plait by simply taking out the basting that holds the gores together and moving them over a little.

If the skirt is too small, let out the inverted plait a trifle, rip the basting on the front panel, or gore, and then make this gore a little wider on each side. If it is much too small, each gore must be let out enough to allow sufficient fulness.

134. Preparing the Skirt for Stitching.—When the fitting is done, remove the skirt and make any alterations that have been found necessary, taking care that the same amount is taken off, or added to, the corresponding gores on the right and the left sides of the skirt. If many alterations are made, it is wise to try on the skirt again to see whether or not they are made correctly. When the changes have been completed, press the skirt on the wrong side, so that the edge of each turned plait will be even and smooth before the stitching is added. Remove the bastings from the center-back seam so that the skirt may be placed in easy position for stitching, and stitch the plaits, taking the usual precautions as to marking for the termination of the stitching, adjusting the stitching gauge, and seeing that the thread matches correctly.

135. Stitching and Binding the Seams.—Before stitching the seams of this skirt on the wrong side, stitch all of the plaits except the inverted plait at the back. This is done in order to secure accurate results. Be sure to leave 4 or 5 inches of thread at the bottom of each plait so that each thread can be pulled through to the wrong side, threaded into a needle, and used to take several back-stitches for fastening. When the plaits have been stitched, turn the skirt wrong side out and stitch the gores together with $\frac{3}{8}$- to $\frac{1}{2}$-inch seams, as shown at *a*, Fig. 37. Trim them evenly and finish by pinking the edges, or by binding them as shown.

When all the rest of the seams have been finished, baste and stitch the center-back seam. Then make an inverted-plait placket, and extend the stitching down far enough to correspond with that of the side gores. Press·the center-back seam open and finish the edges.

136. Second Fitting.—Put on the skirt and adjust it at the waist line. If it seems a little tight through the hips, lift it a trifle at the waist line to allow the necessary fulness. Then pin a tape securely

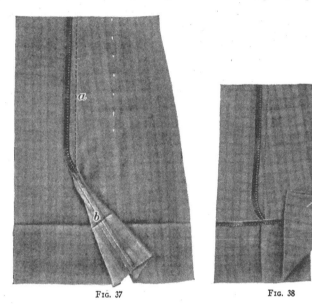

FIG. 37   FIG. 38

around the waist, so that the skirt may be trimmed off on an absolutely correct line. This skirt is finished with a waistband rather than an inside stay belt. Turn the hem and remove the skirt.

137. Finishing the Skirt.—Finish the waist line with a waistband, as explained in Arts. **20** to **22,** inclusive. Baste and press the lower edge of the hem and open it out, as shown in Fig. 37. Then, from the lower edge up to the seam binding, trim the seam edges to within $\frac{1}{4}$ inch of the stitching, as at *b*. Press open the seam to prevent it from forming a cord in the hem, turn the hem back in position, and finish it,using a method suitable to the material. Fig. 38 shows the finished hem where a seam meets it. Notice how the seam tapers to the point where seam and hem meet.

HANGERS FOR SKIRTS

138. Instructions relative to the making of tailored skirts would be incomplete if no information were given about skirt hangers, for to care properly for skirts when they are not in use, one must hang them up correctly. There are various kinds of skirt hangers, those most frequently used being tape hangers, frame hangers, clothes-pin hangers, and safety-pin hangers.

139. Tape Hangers.—The tape skirt hanger is made by sewing narrow strips of material, seam binding, or tape to the inside of the skirt band or belt, generally one strip on each side, so that the skirt may be suspended from two hooks spaced the correct distance apart to accommodate the hangers.

In making a hanger of this kind, turn the edges of a narrow strip of the facing material and stitch these edges together, or stitch together the edges of seam binding or tape. Then cut the material so that each strip for the hanger will be about $2\frac{1}{2}$ inches long, and secure them in position by overhanding the ends of each closely at the bottom of the band or the belt, placing them straight along the edge of the band or the belt. By securing the strips to the garment in this manner, there will be no possibility of the hanger material showing above the belt or the band when the skirt is worn.

140. Frame Hangers.—Another kind of skirt hanger that is used considerably is made of wood or wire. It is similar to the hanger used by men for hanging up their trousers, being arranged so that it may be slipped over the belt or the band of the skirt, clamped in position, and then hung over a hook or a nail. A hanger of this type supports the skirt so that there is no danger of its getting out of shape. It can be purchased in various stores.

141. Clothes-Pin Hangers.—A very popular kind of hanger consists of two clothes-pin clamps attached to a wire frame, which is supplied with a large hook or ring that can be slipped over a hook or nail.

142. Safety-Pin Hangers.—The fourth style of hanger is made by covering small metal rings with crocheting or twisted ribbon and then attaching a medium-sized safety pin to each one. To use such hangers, pin the safety pins in the belt of the skirt and slip the rings over properly-spaced hooks in the closet or wardrobe.

CHAPTER VI

TAILORED BLOUSES AND FROCKS

CHARACTERISTICS OF THE SEPARATE BLOUSE

1. Advantages.—In considering the advantages of the separate blouse, it is well to keep in mind its usefulness and practicability. It is conceded that a blouse worn with a separate skirt may not provide so artistic an effect as a one-piece garment, but at the same time its possibilities of daintiness and cleanliness cannot be overlooked. Then, too, much of the unpleasing appearance of such a costume can be avoided if particular attention is given to the belt and the height of the skirt finish, so that, in spite of all adverse criticism, the separate blouse has really become so much a part of a woman's wardrobe that it will undoubtedly continue to be regarded as one of the essential garments.

Nearly every woman is constantly aware of the economy and convenience of blouses and skirts, and, as they are inexpensive when made at home, it would seem that such blouses should be supplied in sufficient number to permit, at all times, an appearance of freshness, cleanliness, and smartness—points that are of importance to every woman who appreciates the necessity of always looking her best.

2. Significance in Wardrobe.—The tailored or semitailored blouse is of special significance in the wardrobe of the business woman for wear with tailored suits, and is also an essential part of certain types of sports outfits; in fact, such a suit or skirt cannot be correctly completed except by such a blouse. But the blouse must emphasize the same features as the garment with which it is worn, that is, the cut, fit, and finish must harmonize. That an appropriate blouse will improve considerably the appearance of a good-looking suit and the right kind of blouse worn with even a plain, inexpensive skirt will make it appear less ordinary are readily conceded facts, but on the other hand, it must be remembered that a cheap, machine-made blouse is entirely out of keeping with good-looking tailored clothes.

3.   Accessories.—Along with attention to the suitability of the blouse to the suit or skirt, special care should be given to the selection of neckties for wear with tailored blouses.   The tie should be very simple in line and design or definitely of the mode.   A bow or a narrow four-in-hand of a color that matches the color of the skirt that is worn with the blouse, or some light, striking color that is truly becoming is usually satisfactory.   To match the tie with the stripe or the figure of the blouse material gives an air of smartness that is very pleasing.   The woman who is short and inclined to be stout or the truly stout woman or girl will look better in the shirtwaist of this type if a long, narrow four-in-hand, rather than a short tie or a bow, is used, for such a long line of color will tend to add length to her figure.

The blouse is the first thing to greet the eye when the coat is removed; and, as the coat of a tailored suit is usually dispensed with while a woman is on a train, making informal calls, or while she is at work in an office or a shop, it is essential that the blouse and its accessories be smart and attractive.

4.   Style Changes.—Blouse styles change in much the same manner as the styles of other garments, but in their essentials they are very similar at all times.   The most pronounced changes called for by fashion are at the neck line, for it is usually in the shape and finish of the collar that this year's blouse may be distinguished from last year's.   The closing of the blouse is many times an indication of fashion changes, too, for there are periods when blouses with back closings or blouses that slip over the head are decidedly in vogue, particularly in semitailored types.   The changes in the sleeves, with the exception of their length, come so gradually that they are not very pronounced from one season to the other.

5.   Materials.—In planning blouses, just as there should be a reason for the choice of the particular collar, cuffs, front closing, and yoke, especially the shaping of the yoke, so should there also be a reason for the kind of material used, for it should harmonize absolutely with the design and its weight should be such as to emphasize the desired effect.

Because of the nature of the garment, the fabric selected for it should be washable; but even so, the range of materials appropriate for this use is wide. Choice may be made among silk or cotton broadcloth, dimity, madras, handkerchief linen, crêpe de Chine, pongee, or light-weight flannel, for any one of these may be cut and finished with that degree of perfection demanded in tailoring.

6. Types.—As an aid in the development of tailored blouses, it is well to know that there are only two distinct types; namely, the *mannish blouse*, and the *semitailored blouse.* Do not become confused by the names manufacturers use, because these are very often selected merely for advertising purposes, to give distinction to their line of blouses rather than to describe the essential style features of the blouse in question. Such names naturally lead to the belief that there are numberless types of blouses, but the fact remains that practically all tailored blouses are developed from the two standard styles.

Fig. 1

MANNISH TAILORED BLOUSES

MANNISH BLOUSE

7. The **mannish blouse,** an example of which is shown in Fig. 1, is almost the counterpart of a man's negligée shirt, a fact that accounts for its name.

The chief characteristics of the design of such a blouse are the back yoke extending over the front-shoulder line, the neck-line finish, which consists of a collar band and separate collar, and the cuffs. These are of the straight-band type and may be worn quite heavily starched, if desired. The mannish front plait and the seam finishes are other notable features of the mannish tailored blouse.

8. The blouse is necessarily severe, but it is this severity which makes it becoming to certain types and suitable for wear on certain

4 W I—13

occasions, for there are times when it is necessary to wear the mannish tailored blouse for correctness, such as when riding or hiking, since the costumes appropriate for these sports are necessarily untrimmed. The tailored suit is, of course, properly completed by such a blouse, but careful thought should be given before making the decision to wear it, for it will be found very trying to overplump or unusually thin persons. If there is a tendency toward excess flesh around the chin, or if there are hollows in the cheeks, it is better to wear one of the variations of this blouse, but for those who find the severely tailored finish becoming, there is nothing smarter or more trim.

9. Materials.—Suitable materials for mannish blouses are madras, linen, firmly woven wash silks, light-weight flannels, fine chambrays, and pongee. As a rule, 3 to $3\frac{1}{4}$ yards of material must be provided for such a waist, on account of the cuff, cuff finish, front plait, yoke, collar, and collar band. Although such pieces are very small, they really require considerable material, because each one must be cut on the correct grain of the cloth. If the person for whom a mannish blouse is to be made, knows exactly how much material she requires for a plain foundation waist, then this amount, plus 1 yard extra for the cuffs, yoke, collar band, etc., will generally be sufficient.

10. The thread to be used for the mannish blouse should be a trifle coarser than that which would be used in ordinary work; for example, if the madras to be used for such a blouse is of a weight that would seem to require No. 60 thread, then it would perhaps be better to use No. 50, so that the stitching, which must be accurate and straight, will show up to the best advantage.

In beginning to stitch such garments, where the stitching means so much to the finish of the article, it is well always to try the stitch on a scrap of the material to make sure that the machine is properly threaded and in good condition.

11. Pattern Requirements.—A mannish-blouse pattern of the right bust measurement and with satisfactorily shaped front plait, yoke, collar, cuffs, etc., should be provided, for these features have much to do with the style of the garment as well as the time required for making. If one cannot be found as illustrated, such details as cuffs can be changed as desired.

12. Cutting Out the Material.—Although a mannish shirtwaist is plain, it demands considerable care throughout its construction if satisfactory results are to be had. While it would seem that caution about cutting out so plain a garment would be unnecessary, yet as the back, front, and sleeve must be cut one way of the warp thread, the yoke, collar, and cuffs, another way; and as each pattern line must fit to the adjoining one perfectly, directions for placing the pattern pieces and cutting out the garment seem advisable. The most economical and convenient arrangement of the pattern pieces on the material is given with the pattern. This may be observed with good results, the following suggestions also proving helpful, particularly to one of limited experience.

13. Before placing the pattern pieces on the material preparatory to cutting out, baste the front plait in one side of one end of the piece of material that is to be used and the hem in the opposite side, making each of them a trifle longer than the front length of the pattern piece. The plait for the right-hand side of the blouse should be from $1\frac{3}{8}$ to $1\frac{3}{4}$ inches wide, a width of $1\frac{1}{2}$ inches, with stitching a generous $\frac{1}{4}$ inch from the edge, being usually satisfactory, and the hem for the left-hand side just one-half the width of the plait.

Press the plait and the hem carefully from the wrong side, and then lap them as they should be lapped, that is, with the center of the hem directly underneath the center of the plait. With this done, pin the pattern piece for the front part of the blouse on the material, placing it so that its center-front line is in line with and directly over the center of the hem; then cut the material directly across, allowing sufficient for shoulder seams and hems, if your pattern does not provide this allowance. Next smooth out the rest of the material carefully and proceed to pin it. If it is plain, pin the selvage edges together; if it is striped, pin the stripes together. This will permit each piece to be cut true and in line with the warp threads or the stripes of the material, as the case may be.

With the material thus made ready, place each of the remaining pattern pieces in position, using plenty of pins to secure them so that none will slip. Place the center back of the back part of the pattern along the fold. Place the sleeve pattern so that the lengthwise thread will run through the center from top to bottom, and the cuff, collar, collar-stand, neck-band, and cuff-opening pieces, so that the center of the long dimension of the pattern will come on a lengthwise thread of the material. In the case of striped material, this arrangement causes the stripes to run across these pieces.

A yoke crosswise with the back is also a desirable feature in such a garment; not only is it pleasing, but it sets much better, lasts longer, and may be ironed more easily than one cut the other way.

14. When all the pattern pieces are placed on the material as directed and securely pinned, trace all around the edges carefully so as to obtain accurate pattern lines. Then cut the garment out, allowing $\frac{1}{2}$ inch for seams on the front, back, sleeves, and yoke, and $\frac{1}{4}$ inch for seams on the cuffs, neck band, collar, collar stand, and cuff-opening strips, unless you are using a pattern on which seam allowance has been made. In this case, follow the outline of the pattern.

In cutting the slash for the cuff opening, do not try to cut through both thicknesses at one time; instead, cut one at a time, so as to be sure to cut along the warp threads and thus insure cuff openings that will appear neat when the cuffs are finished. At this time, also, cut a protection piece for the inside of the collar band, making it $3\frac{1}{2}$ inches long and of a depth equal to that of the collar band. The purpose of this piece is to provide an extra thickness in the back to protect the neck from the collar button that is used in holding the collar in position when the garment is worn.

15. Pinning, Basting, and Preliminary Fitting.—When each piece for the mannish blouse is traced and cut out, proceed to baste the shoulder seams together, seams to the right side, and to pin the under-arm seams in the traced lines, seams also to the right side. Then try the waist on to see whether or not it fits correctly at the shoulders, a procedure that is absolutely necessary before adding the yoke.

If the shoulder seams have to be taken up a trifle, do this work very carefully. If the neck fits up tight and close, let out the seam; and if the shoulders drag, make the seams deeper. Remember, however, that the neck must be kept absolutely correct, so that it will fit up close and smooth, and that any material difference made in fitting the shoulder will interfere with the fit of the collar band, which must correspond exactly to the neck size of the blouse; also, any perceptible change made in fitting the shoulder will make necessary the same change in the neck band to insure its fitting properly.

16.   Preparing the Cuffs.—The next step is to prepare the sleeve opening.   This is done exactly as in a man's shirt, detailed directions for which are given in Art. **23,** Chapter VIII.

When the cuff opening is completed, follow the instruction in Arts. **31** and **32,** Chapter VIII, for preparing the cuffs, for these also are made in exactly the same way as the cuffs of a man's shirt.

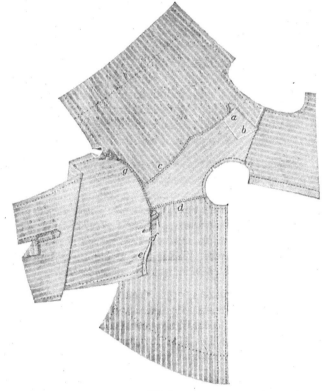

FIG. 2

17.   Applying the Yoke.—When the sleeve openings and the cuffs are neatly finished in the manner directed, arrange the yoke for the back of the waist, as shown in Fig. 2.   Pin the center back of the yoke to the center back of the blouse, having the notches at the neck exactly even.   Smooth the yoke out from the center back carefully, so as not to let a wrinkle creep in anywhere.   When it is smoothed in place well, turn the lower back edge under, as at *a*, and crease it carefully; then turn under the front-shoulder edges, as at b, and baste the entire yoke in position.

As will be observed, the grain of the yoke material runs in a direction exactly opposite from that of the material for the back of the shirtwaist, so pains must be taken to prevent it from wrinkling, as wrinkles in this part of the garment will cause great inconvenience in ironing or wearing.

In handling these sections, stretch the yoke a very little so that the under part will be a trifle fuller and prevent the yoke from appearing full or wrinkling near the armhole when ironed.   When the yoke is basted in position, stitch directly on the lower edge and on both of the front-shoulder edges, as at c and d.   If it is desired to make the joining of the seams show prominently, a second row of stitching may be added a generous $\frac{1}{4}$ to $\frac{3}{8}$ inch from the first stitching, as shown.   In doing this work, be sure to have your machine properly threaded and adjusted to produce a perfect stitch.

18.   Inserting the Sleeves.—The way in which the sleeves "set" in a tailored blouse or dress has much to do with the success of the finished garment.   They must present a smooth, well-fitting appearance without being too tight for comfort.   As a rule, it is not desirable that fulness show at the top of the sleeve, but every sleeve is cut a little larger than the armhole into which it fits in order to provide the requisite ease.   With careful handling, however, this fulness can be so disposed of as not to be noticeable.

19.   To insert the sleeves, begin about $4\frac{1}{2}$ inches from the under-arm seam line of the sleeve to run a row of tiny gathering-stitches $\frac{3}{8}$ inch from the edge and continue around to within $4\frac{1}{2}$ inches of the seam line on the other side.   Do not fasten the stitches nor unthread the needle, because the fulness must be adjusted in inserting the sleeve.

With the wrong sides of the blouse and sleeve together, match and pin the notches, the shallow part of the sleeve to the front of the waist, as at e, and the deeper part to the back, which is just the reverse procedure from that followed in inserting a dress sleeve. Adjust the gathering thread so that the sleeve is not full, but merely eased in over the top.   Use plenty of pins and put them in at right angles to the seam edges, being very careful to keep the lengthwise grain of the sleeve on the top in line with the shoulder seam.   Adjust the slight fulness until the sleeve hangs straight, looks well, and "sets" comfortably on the arm. Hold the sleeve in place with small basting-stitches.

20. Fitting the Blouse.—With the blouse at this stage, pin together the under-arm seams and also the sleeve seams, and then slip the blouse on to see whether or not the sleeves are placed exactly right. While the blouse is on, lay a cuff over the lower edge of each sleeve to determine just the proper length for the sleeve, remembering that a sleeve to which a stiff cuff is attached may be ⅜ to ½ inch longer than a close-fitting sleeve, as a stiff cuff looks well when it comes down over the hand a little farther than a plain sleeve. So that the cuffs may be placed correctly later, mark with pins just where the top edge of the cuff should come on each sleeve. At this time, also, trim the skirt portion, or lower edge, of the waist evenly, allowing from 3 to 4 inches below the waist line.

21. Stitching and Hemming the Waist.—Having observed all the points mentioned, remove the waist and, after opening up the under-arm seams, carefully trim the top of each sleeve to within ⅛ inch of the basting, as at *f*, Fig. 2; also, turn the armhole edge of the shirtwaist over on the sleeve, taking care to keep a true, even edge and to have the turned edge an equal distance throughout from the seam-line basting. When the armhole seam curves considerably, it is well to clip the seam edge of the shirtwaist every few inches, making the clips very shallow, but deep enough to permit the seam to lie perfectly flat and to give a smooth, even finish.

Next, stitch on the outer edge, as at *g*; then adjust the gauge or use the machine presser foot as a guide and stitch over the pattern-line basting the full length of the armhole. By doing both these stitchings from the right side the stitch will appear exactly the same, thus insuring stitching lines that are uniform.

With the armholes stitched, stitch up the under-arm and sleeve seams, using a flat-fell seam and lapping the back portion of both the waist and the sleeve over the front. Be extremely careful to have each armhole seam meet exactly at each under arm. Then, hem the skirt portion of the waist with a narrow hem and press the entire waist, so that the cuffs and the neck band may be neatly applied.

22. Applying the Cuffs and Neck Band.—Detailed instruction for applying the cuffs is found in Art. **33,** Chapter VIII. The instruction given there is for a man's shirt cuff, but is applicable in this case, since the mannish blouse cuffs are exactly like those of a man's shirt.

The directions for preparing and applying the neck band of a man's shirt, given in Arts. **29** and **30,** Chapter VIII, are equally applicable to the neck finish of the mannish blouse.

If a separate collar is to be worn with the mannish blouse, as is usually the case, an interlining should be placed in the neck band so that it will be sure to fit up close and not fall down, nor sag. Light-weight muslin, material of the same grade as is used for the cuff interlining, or material like that used for the garment itself, provided it is of smooth weave and is not too heavy, is satisfactory for interlining.

23.   Buttons and Buttonholes.—In a mannish tailored blouse the buttons and buttonholes are of great importance, for the reason that they must be extremely neat.   Three or four flat, neat pearl buttons about the size of a dime or smaller are usually satisfactory for the front.   Space them as in Fig. 1; that is, so that the distance between the neck band and the first button and that between the last button and the waist line will be the same as that between each pair of buttons.   Place the buttonholes exactly in the center of the plait, and cut them vertically and about $\frac{1}{4}$ inch longer than the diameter of the button.   As the plait of the blouse will in some cases be starched, buttonholes that are too small will be difficult to get over the buttons.   In making buttonholes for such garments, always take the precaution of barring the ends neatly to prevent them from tearing out easily.

Locate the buttonholes in the cuffs a little more than one-third the width of the cuff from the joining of the cuff and the sleeve, and parallel with the joining.

Place the buttonholes in the neck band horizontally and $\frac{1}{4}$ inch above the joining of the waist and the neck band.   Have the button-holes in the collar correspond with those in the neck band, except that they should be a scant $\frac{3}{8}$ inch above the lower edge of the collar stand, so that the collar will fit down well and cover the seam joining of the neck band when the waist is worn.

24.   Preparing the Waist for Wear.—It is sometimes advisable to launder a mannish blouse before wearing it; that is, if it is made of material that requires starch.   Such garments of silk material, however, require only a very careful pressing to complete them.

SEMITAILORED BLOUSES

ACHIEVING PLEASING EFFECTS

25. The semitailored blouse is frequently in vogue and invariably more popular than the strictly tailored, mannish blouse. It is less severe, and so is more generally becoming; also, it offers more opportunity for varying the style.

The styles of semitailored blouses here considered serve to bring out pleasing effects, but they need not be followed slavishly in the attempt to get suitable blouses for personal wear; rather, the details of construction and the many ways in which to render such garments attractive should be firmly fixed in the mind, so that it will be possible to evolve or create other garments equally pleasing and in harmony with the prevailing mode.

MANNISH OVERBLOUSE

26. In Fig. 3 is shown a style of semitailored blouse that may well be called a mannish overblouse. This garment is not far removed from the strictly mannish, tailored blouse already considered, as the tailored pockets and cuffs suggest the mannish type; yet, as the collar is different, the cuffs are double, and the material is soft, the blouse has a decidedly feminine touch and therefore may be placed in the semitailored class.

Fig. 3

27. Material and Pattern Requirements.—Any soft silk is suitable for a blouse of this kind. Especially desirable are the raw silks, such as habutaye, silk madras, shantung, pongee, or wash taffeta. If silk is not desired, cotton poplins, madras, flaxon, or dimity may be used satisfactorily.

A pattern similar to the style illustrated can usually be found in the fashion magazines. However, the blouse may be cut by a mannish shirtwaist pattern by making a few changes.

28.   Altering the Pattern for Fulness in Front and Additional Length.—It is desirable to allow fulness across the front of the waist pattern for the style of blouse here discussed.   In doing so, first determine how much is required; usually 1 to 2½ inches for each side is sufficient.   Locate a point midway of the shoulder seam, and then draw a line from this point exactly parallel with the center-front line to the bottom of the pattern.   Cut the pattern apart on this line, and place the two pieces of the pattern on another piece of paper or on the material.   Then separate the cut edges the desired amount at the shoulder, bringing them together at the lower edge; also, add sufficient length to both front and back to provide for the lowered waist line.

29.   Draping the Collar Pattern.—If you are using a foundation-waist pattern that does not have a suitable collar pattern, you may drape a collar such as you desire, after the blouse is partly completed, using muslin for modeling and draping.   The first essential for such a collar, which fits snug at the back of the neck, is to have the neck line of the blouse itself cut and fitted high enough to hold it well at the back.   Then when the collar is carefully fitted, a snug trimness is a certainty.

The collar may be planned directly on the person for whom it is made or on the dress form.   If you intend to drape it on the form, first try the blouse on the person who is to wear it and decide on a becoming line and depth for the neck line.   Then place the blouse on the form and outline the neck line with tailor's chalk or pins, inside of the neck edge, directly on the form, making sure that the line is even and true.   You are now ready to begin the draping.

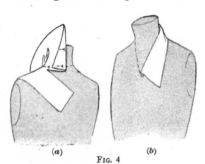

(a)   Fɪɢ. 4   (b)

30.   For this type of collar, use a piece of muslin from 4 to 6 inches longer than the depth of the collar, and torn off the full width of the material.   At one selvage, turn back about 2 inches on a diagonal line, tapering the turn to nothing at the other edge.

Pin the muslin at the fold to the center-back neck line of the form.

Place the narrowest part of the fold so that it will extend above the neck line, as illustrated in Fig. 4 (a), allowing about 2 inches to extend below at the back.   Place at least two pins, one at the neck line and one about 2 or 3 inches above, as illustrated.   The placing of the upper pin should be governed by the height of the roll you wish the collar to assume in the back.

31.   Begin to cut on a curve, cutting not more than $1\frac{1}{2}$ to 2 inches at a time, and then smoothing the material.   Continue in this way, following the marked neck line.

After the inner edge of the collar has been cut, turn down that part of the muslin which extends above the neck line and smooth it into the proper effect.   Keep it quite high at the center back and have the roll become gradually less until it lies flat at the front. Now mark and cut the outer edge, shaping it to obtain the outline in Fig. 4 (b).

32.   Cutting Out the Collar.—In cutting the collar, lay the muslin model on the material so that the center back will come on a lengthwise fold of the fabric.   If the outside edge of the collar is to be bound, allow in cutting from the muslin pattern just $\frac{1}{4}$ inch on all edges for seams.   If the collar is to be of two thicknesses of the material with the seam concealed inside, allow $\frac{3}{8}$ inch on the outer edges.

33.   Constructing the Garment.—The method of cutting out, fitting, and finishing for this type of blouse is practically the same as that for the mannish blouse.   In fact, the only difference lies in the shoulders, which in this garment are gathered, the cuffs and collar, and in the application of the pockets.

Full instructions for making the bound pockets, which form a very distinctive feature of the blouse, are given in Arts. **59** to **62**, inclusive, Chapter III.   Follow these instructions in detail, making allowance, of course, for the difference in size.

34.   As will be observed, the hip fulness is confined by small loops and buttons.   In making these loops, use thread of a color that matches the blouse.   Knot the end of it and bring the needle up through the material at a point where it is desired to have one end of the loop.   Then take three or four stitches through the material, one over the other, leaving loops on the right side, slightly loose and long enough to allow the button to slip under them easily.

Cover these loops with over-and-over stitches or with single-purl buttonhole-stitches.

In taking stitches over the foundation threads, you will find that by inserting the blunt, or eye, end of the needle first you will be able to work more rapidly and avoid catching any of the stitches through the material underneath, thus making sure that the loop is open its entire length. When you reach the end of the loop, insert the needle through the material and fasten the thread with several tiny stitches on the wrong side. The loops are placed $\frac{1}{2}$ inch in front of the under-arm seam and the buttons are placed just back of the seam.

35. Prepare the cuff opening on the sleeve by finishing it as a simple, continuous placket. For the placket facing, cut a lengthwise piece of material $1\frac{1}{4}$ inches wide, and twice the length of the opening, plus 1 inch. Turn both sides of the finished placket back flat against the wrong side of the sleeve, as this form of finish does not provide for lapping the opening. Then gather the lower edge of the sleeves as directed for the mannish blouse.

36. If crêpe de Chine or other sheer material is used for the blouse, it is well to interline the cuffs with a single thickness of some thin cotton fabric, such as lawn or India linon. Cut the interlining the same size as the cuff sections. Lay the two silk pieces together with their right sides in, and over them place the interlining. Using a $\frac{1}{4}$-inch seam, stitch around three sides, leaving free the edge that is joined to the sleeve. Trim the edges of the interlining close to the seam, turn the cuff right side out, work out the corners well, and press carefully. Then join the cuff to the sleeve.

37. To join the cuff to the sleeve, first adjust the fulness at the lower edge of the sleeve carefully, and baste the under thickness of the cuff to the gathered portion so that the seam will come to the right side. Stitch carefully. Now turn in the raw edge of the upper section a seam's width, bring it up over the seam and baste. Replace the basting with stitching. Stitch again around the entire cuff $\frac{1}{4}$ inch to $\frac{3}{8}$ inch from the edge to correspond with the stitching of the seams. After this, turn back the cuff so that the edge covers the stitching that joins it to the sleeve. Four buttonholes will be necessary in each cuff.

Follow the same general directions in making, finishing, and applying the collar as were given for the mannish blouse.

OVERBLOUSE WITH HIP BAND

38. In Fig. 5 is shown a semitailored blouse that is gathered into a hip band.   This style of blouse, though plain and practical, is always attractive when neatly made.   The Buster Brown type of collar makes it particularly youthful and becoming, softening the effect of an otherwise strictly tailored blouse.

39. Material and Pattern Requirements.—Crêpe de Chine, dimity, batiste, or handkerchief linen are suitable for a blouse as simple in design as this.   The usual requirements are $1\frac{7}{8}$ yards of 40-inch material, or $2\frac{1}{4}$ yards of 36-inch material, and about one dozen buttons.

The mannish blouse pattern is employed in the development of this blouse, as the lines of these two patterns are practically the same.   Before cutting out the garment, lay the front plait in the material, as described for the mannish blouse.

Fig. 5

40. Draping the Collar Pattern.—For draping the Buster Brown collar pattern, provided it is necessary to do this, practically the same amount of muslin is needed as for the roll collar discussed under the mannish overblouse.   Also, the same general directions hold true, although the specific method differs slightly.

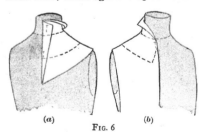

(a)   (b)

Fig. 6

At one selvage, turn back about 2 inches on a diagonal line, tapering the turn to nothing at the other edge, and pin carefully.   About 2 inches below the cut edge at which the turn is widest, pin the fold of the muslin to the center-back neck line of the form, as shown in Fig. 6 (a).   Pin again at least once more below the neck line directly at the center back, as illustrated, so as to have the folded edge held firmly in its proper place.   Smooth the material down over the shoulder toward the front and pin, as in (b).

With your shears, clip the muslin on a slightly curved line that will follow the neck line marked on the form. Clip downwards in two or three places toward the front, if necessary, so that the collar will not have a drawn appearance at the neck line. Continue cutting and smoothing the muslin, as already suggested, until you reach the center front.

In cutting the outer edge, use a row of pins as a guide in outlining the finished shape of the collar. Place the pins as indicated by the dotted line, Fig. 6 (a) and (b). Then trim off the excess muslin, following the line of pins, and you will have one-half of a Buster Brown collar exactly the size and shape you wish, and one that will lie flat and smooth and fit accurately at the inner edge.

41. Another easy and satisfactory method of forming a flat-collar pattern, such as the Buster Brown, is to outline it directly on the waist pattern. In order to insure accurate results, use the neck line of the waist pattern as the neck line of the collar pattern.

To outline the collar in one piece, lay the back portion of the pattern so that its shoulder line meets that of the front, and the neck ends are exactly even. Then outline the collar, making it of the depth you desire at the center front, shoulder, and center back and shaping it according to the design you are copying.

42. With the designing finished, prepare to form a complete collar pattern by folding lengthwise through the center a piece of paper large enough to accommodate the collar size and slipping this under the outlined collar pattern without changing the position of the front and the back waist-pattern sections. Pin this piece of paper in position so that its folded edge is exactly under the center-back line of the collar pattern and the remainder of the paper extends under the marked collar outline. Then trace the neck line and outer edge of the collar, and after removing the pins that hold the paper in place, cut on the traced lines in order to form the complete collar pattern.

43. Constructing the Overblouse.—The construction of the overblouse with the hip band differs but little from that of the mannish blouse.

Prepare the cuffs by putting the wrong sides of the two pieces together, unless an interlining is used, when it is placed between them. Baste the edges together carefully, and bind the two ends and one edge exactly as you would bind a single thickness of material. To apply the binding, put the right sides of the cuff and the bias binding together and stitch $\frac{1}{4}$ inch from the edge. Turn the free edge of the binding to the wrong side, and in turning under the raw edge for the second stitching, baste it in such a position that the crease extends slightly beyond the first stitching. Stitch the second time on the right side, letting the row of stitching come on the cuff proper, in the crease formed where the bias was turned over, and not on the bias itself.

After the collar has been bound with bias self-material, in the manner described for the cuffs, apply it and the cuffs to the blouse with a bias facing.

The making of the stand pockets is described in detail in Chapter III, Arts. **4** to **20,** inclusive. Place the pockets in the waist front and in the hip band before the latter is applied, having their sizes consistent with their use. The material for interlining and for the pouch should be of a weight suited for use with the quality of fabric used for the blouse.

44. In applying the hip band, gather the fulness at the lower edge of the blouse. In gathering the front, overlap the front opening, and run the gathers across the overlapped hem and plait. Gather the front and the back separately, and adjust the fulness so that very little comes directly in the center front, but more toward the sides. The back fulness is quite evenly distributed.

If the hip band is too tight to slip on comfortably over the head, leave each under-arm seam open 2 inches at the lower end and use the seam allowance in making a tiny hem on each side. In this case it is well to allow $\frac{1}{2}$ inch additional on the length of both the front and the back band, to take care of the lap. Then apply the front and the back bands separately, finishing the ends of each even with the short opening and sewing snaps on for fastening. Usually, however, it will be found that, with the full-length front opening, no side openings are necessary. In that case, join the front and the back bands with plain seams before applying them.

Attach one edge of the band to the lower edge of the blouse first, with the seam to the right side. Turn in the free edge a seam's width, bring it up over the first seam and baste. Stitch accurately and evenly just on the turn.

PERFECTION IN TAILORING FROCKS

45. Many of the principles involved in the making of the tailored and semitailored blouses can be carried over into the construction of dresses, for the very same perfection of detail that gives the tailored blouse its charm is the most notable feature of the tailored frock. And the skill gained in making these blouses will be invaluable when applied to the making of the complete tailored garment.

46. Tailored dresses are so generally becoming and lend themselves to development in so large a range of materials that they can be made to fill numerous needs. For the summer season, when wash dresses are in order, linen, linen-finished cottons, ginghams, cotton crêpes, crêpe de Chine, flat crêpe, and even voile, may be chosen. For cotton and silk, more particular work is required than for wools, because every stitch shows in its entirety and one cannot sponge and shrink or press away imperfections. So on such materials the work must, from the beginning, be as nearly perfect as possible.

When tailoring wash fabrics, such as cotton, linen, and silk, be sure that your machine is in excellent condition and will make a small, perfect stitch, for your stitching should be as dainty as your fabric. Do not use a needle or thread that is too coarse. Press all seam edges with as much care as for woolens, dampening, however, rarely proving necessary.

47. For winter, the choice of materials for tailored frocks goes to charmeen, serge, twills, wool crêpe, wool Jersey, soft flannel, broadcloth, and similar fabrics.

Spring and autumn usually find flannel, reps, basket weaves, tweeds, and kasha on the list of the most desirable fabrics for this type of dress.

48. Tailored garments need not fit snugly but they should fit perfectly; therefore, if a pattern is used, it must be accurate. When buying one, study the catalog carefully to make sure that the lines are placed where they will be becoming, for in tailoring the location of each seam is important. In fact, it is in just this careful attention to detail that the success or failure of the finished garment lies.

Remember always that, because of its simpler style and more durable construction, a tailored frock lasts longer than any other kind, so any extra time given to perfect accomplishment is justified.

TAILORED FROCKS CUT WITHOUT PATTERNS

ECONOMY OF TIME AND MATERIAL

49. One of the oldest notions in regard to tailoring is that one must have perfect patterns in order to obtain perfect results. That is all very true in regard to a certain severely tailored type of garment that fits the figure closely and has numerous seam lines, darts, and trimming features that make patterns necessary. There is, however, a more popular form of dress that is truly tailored but with a softer effect and that is cut entirely without a pattern. Made of various materials, it is seen in straight-line, one-piece effects and in models that are cut across at the waist line. The method of cutting is economical of both time and material, and is so flexible that it changes as fashion changes, allowing one to follow closely the vagaries of the mode.

Before cutting a dress by either of the following plans, read the instruction carefully at least twice, observing the illustrations carefully. Be *very* sure that you know what you are going to do before you cut the material.

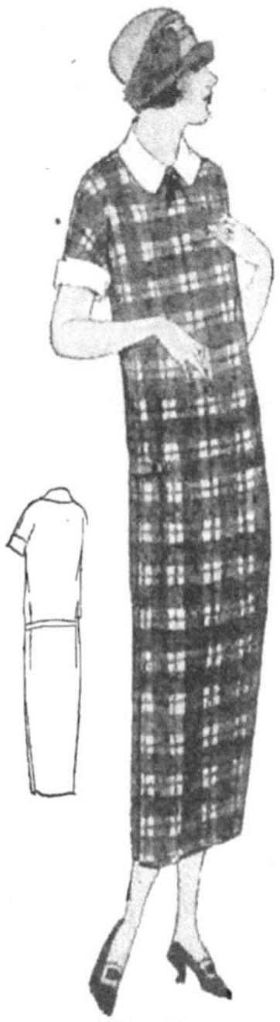

STRAIGHT-LINE, ONE-PIECE DRESS

50. A typical dress of the straight-line, one-piece type is shown in Fig. 7. Many variations of it are possible, but this serves to illustrate the simplicity of the method of cutting.

51. Materials Required.—The 54-inch wool fabrics, such as flannel, wool crêpe, fine Poiret, or

FIG. 7

charmeen, cut to best advantage in this dress, though the 32-, 36-, or 40-inch material is satisfactory also. One length plus $\frac{1}{4}$ yard of the 54-inch material is sufficient; two lengths of the narrower widths are necessary, unless one chooses to use a tunic band at the bottom; then, one and three-fourth lengths are sufficient.

If 40-inch silk is used, a luxuriously long scarf may be made of the strip that is cut from the side.

52. Taking Your Measurements.—Four measurements are required, and these are taken as shown in Fig. 8.

For your *blouse length*, put a pin in the dress you have on a little below your normal waist line or in line with the hip bones, to mark the waist line for the dress you are to make. If you are rather short, this is usually 2 inches below your normal waist line; if medium height, 3 inches; if tall, 4 inches. Measure from the

Fig. 8

pin in front, over the shoulder, and down the back to a point opposite the pin.

To obtain your *skirt length*, drop the end of the tape measure about 1 inch below the skirt length you want and measure from there to the pin. The extra inch will be taken up in the dart and the fitting at the waist line.

For your *hip measure*, measure around the hips at the fullest part.

For your *armhole measure*, measure around your arm at the shoulder, holding the tape moderately tight.

53. Preparing the Material.—After taking the measurements and before cutting the material, straighten the edges by cutting or tearing. If wool is used, tear or cut the material straight at both ends before shrinking it, and, if necessary to make it perfectly straight, pull it from the corners on the bias. All fabrics are woven straight, but in the folding they sometimes become crooked. Printed fabrics with large designs are the only kind that cannot be made satisfactory for cutting by tearing or cutting on a crosswise thread. These should be cut with regard to the design.

54. Folding the Material.—First, lay out the material folded wrong side out through the center lengthwise, selvage edges toward

Lengthwise fold

With the material wrong side out, selvage edges toward you, fold lengthwise through the center and place pins along the fold.

Selvage

Fig. 9

you, as in Fig. 9, and pin along the fold. Measure half the distance from the lengthwise fold minus the selvage width, as at a, and put a pin through both thicknesses. Then turn the top selvage up over the fold b, with the selvage itself extending beyond this fold. Turn over the entire piece of folded material so that the other half is on top and bring the selvage edge down to meet the other selvage. Smooth the material out carefully and pin through both folds the full length of the piece, when the folded material will appear

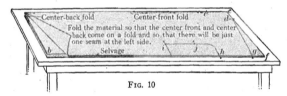

Center-back fold   Center-front fold

Fold the material so that the center front and center back come on a fold and so that there will be just one seam at the left side.

Selvage

Fig. 10

as in Fig. 10. This places the material so that the upper part, or fold, makes the front of the dress and the under part, or fold, the back, and brings the one seam on the left side.

55. Cutting the Neck Opening.—Next, locate the shoulder point at the neck by measuring down, or toward you, 2 inches from c at one end of the upper fold and marking d. Measure to the left on the upper fold 5 inches from c and locate e. Then cut on a straight thread from c to e to obtain the front-neck opening.

56. Shaping the Shoulders.—Now, to shape the shoulders, measure, for most figures, on the selvage to the left of the corner, or *f*, 4½ inches, and locate *g*. Very square shoulders require 2½ to 3 inches. Sloping shoulders require 4½ to 5½ inches. Then cut through the four thicknesses from *g* to *d* to make the shoulder line. A good plan is first to draw a chalk line along a ruler from *g* to *d* and then cut on this line to insure accuracy. Next, mark the width of the sleeves by measuring to the left from *g* one-half the arm-hole measure and placing a pin, as at *h*.

57. Cutting the Waist-Line Dart and Under Arm.—Now measure down from the shoulder line one-half the blouse length, and over from the fold one-fourth the hip measure, plus 1½ inches, and locate *i*. Cut on a straight grain from the selvage edge in to *i* through all thicknesses. This gives the waist-line dart and provides for the plait.

Prepare the under arm by measuring straight to the right of *i* 8 or 10 inches, depending on the depth of the armhole desired, and locating *j*. Then cut in a curved line from *h* to *j*, and straight down from *j* to *i*.

58. Completing the Sleeve Cutting.—Complete the cutting of the dress by removing the selvage from line *g h* and by slashing the fold on the under sleeve, doing this so that both sleeves are of the same length.

The neck is not shaped at this time, as it is advisable first to fit the collar at the neck and then to cut the surplus material away.

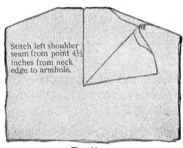

Stitch left shoulder seam from point 4½ inches from neck edge to armhole.

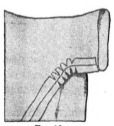

Fig. 11   Fig. 12

59. Sewing Up the Seams.—Prepare to sew up the dress, which has five seams. Begin the right-shoulder seam at the neck edge and stitch out to the armhole, using a ⅜-inch seam. Begin the left-shoulder seam, as shown at *a*, Fig. 11, 4 inches down from the neck edge to allow for the opening. Stitch the curved under-arm seams, beginning at the edge of the sleeve and stitching around the curve and down to the waist-line dart. In doing this, keep the edges together accurately by means of pins or baste carefully so that the material will not slip.

Next, stitch the side seam of the skirt part, beginning at the waist-line dart and stitching down. When the seams are all stitched,

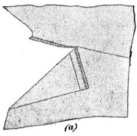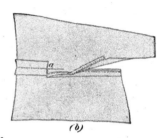

(a)   (b)

FIG. 13

clip the selvage edges every 6 to 12 inches to prevent their drawing; then clip the under-arm seams at the curve, as in Fig. 12, making about five clips in the turn, about 1 inch apart.

Pin the skirt plaits in place, allowing each to come toward the front or back, as you prefer, but with the outside edge of each in direct line with the under-arm seam.

60. Finishing the Neck Opening.—Finish the neck opening with stay tape or ribbon, as shown in Fig. 13, view (a) showing the right side and view (b), the wrong side. First clip the shoulder seam, as at a, view (b), so that the seam will lie flat, and then face the front edge with the tape or ribbon and bind the back edge. Make sure that the back-shoulder binding is as long as the front facing and take narrow seams so that the shoulder seam will not pull up.

61. Putting in the Hip Dart and Side Plaits.—Pin in the dart, taking up $\frac{3}{4}$ inch of the material at the seam for the average figure and tapering it to nothing about 2 to $2\frac{1}{2}$ inches on each side. On the wrong side, the dart will appear as in Fig. 14. Pin the hem up the amount allowed, turning an even line all the way around. The evenness of the lower edge of the skirt for this type of dress is determined by the hip dart, all fitting being done there. So turn the hem the amount allowed, evenly all the way, usually 3 to 4 inches.

At this time, it is advisable to slip the dress on to make sure that the darts are pinned to give an even line at the bottom, also that the hem is turned so as to make the skirt the correct length.

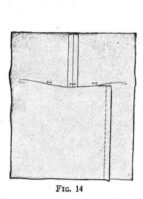

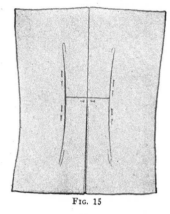

Fig. 14   Fig. 15

Pinch the side plaits in, as in Fig. 15 along both sides of the dart to get the effect desired. These plaits really fit the dress to the figure, controlling the fulness enough to make a belt unnecessary. However, one may be used across the back or front or all the way around, if desired.

Remove the dress, stitch the dart carefully, taking up just what was pinned in; then press the dart down, when from the wrong side

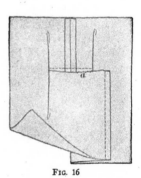

Fig. 16

it will appear as in Fig. 16. Turn the dress right side out, stitch the pinched plaits down, stitching ¼ inch from the edge and about 2 inches above the dart and 1 inch below.

Turn the dress wrong side out and prepare to stay the edge of the plait to the dart. First smooth the dress so that the plait will lie flat and on the straight of the material. Then take a few secure stitches, as at *a*, Fig. 16, to hold it firmly in position.

62.   Finishing the Sleeves, Hem, and Neck.—Finish the lower part of the sleeves by using seam tape or ribbon. To do this, apply the tape to the right side and stitch ¼ inch from the sleeve edge.

Turn to the wrong side, when the stitching line will appear as *a*, Fig. 17; then press down and slip-stitch or stitch in place, as at *b*.

To make a good hem finish, follow the directions in Art. **24 or 25,** Chapter V.

When fitting the dress, try on the collar that you choose to wear with it. Mark and cut the neck line that it requires, allowing for seams. Make sure that both sides of the neck are trimmed the same. Face the neck with a bias strip of silk or other suitable material. Sew two snap fasteners on the shoulder closing.

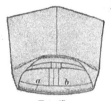

Fig. 17

63. Completing the Dress.—If a belt of the material is desired across the back, seam a 2-inch lengthwise strip together, using the pieces cut from the under arm for this. Stitch the folded material the full length,

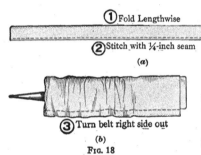

about ¼ inch from the torn edge and across one end, as in Fig. 18 (*a*). Turn the belt right side out. An easy way to do this is to place the blunt end of a pencil against the end seam and pull the belt down over the pencil, as in (*b*), until it is turned right side out. Then slip out the pencil. Press the belt and stitch across the open end.

If buckles are used, finish as shown in Fig. 7; otherwise, slip the ends of the belt strip underneath the front pinched-in plaits and secure them in place by means of ornamental buttons, tacking-stitches, or machine stitching.

Complete the dress by pressing it and adding the collar and cuffs.

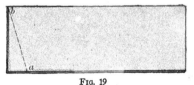

Fig. 19

64. Cutting and Applying Long Sleeves.—If long sleeves are desired, fold in the center, lengthwise, a piece of material as long as you want the sleeve and as wide as the armhole measure, as in Fig. 19. Measure down on the lengthwise edges 1½ inches, locating point *a*, and then draw a diagonal line from *a* to the end of the fold *b*. This gives a pointed sleeve that will fit perfectly into the straight ·armhole, as shown in Fig. 20.

Baste the sleeve in the armhole and stitch in before the under-arm seams are stitched, as shown. Start at the shoulder seam, as at *a*, to baste and stitch so as to bring the point in exact position and avoid stretching either the sleeve or the dress.

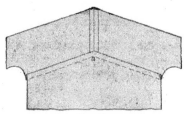

Fɪɢ. 20   Fɪɢ. 21

For long sleeves of this type, an effective wrist finish is shown in Fig. 21. Fit the sleeve at the wrist with pinched-in plaits and make a turn-over, center-stitched binding at the lower edge, as shown in Figs. 34 and 35, Art. **77**.

SLENDERIZING ONE-PIECE DRESS

65. If the figure is larger than 40-inch bust and it is desired to use 54-inch material, buy one length plus ½ yard, and use ¼ yard to put a crosswise panel in the center front of the dress, as shown in Fig. 22. This panel may be stitched in crosswise-tuck effect and used as a feature for a slenderizing dress. Or, if the hips are small in proportion to the bust, do not purchase any extra fabric, but plan for a plain seam covered with braid, as in Fig. 23. The seam may come at the center front or left-side front or right-side back. In any event, the panel or plain seam should

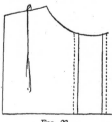

Fɪɢ. 22

Fɪɢ. 23

be made complete before the dress is cut out, as it is difficult to fold the material to make accurate allowance for either of them.

66. Cutting Out the Dress.—Place the material, which is now in the form of a tube, lengthwise, so that the center of the panel makes one fold and this fold is toward you. Then fold the material in half lengthwise, turning the panel fold up, or away from you, when it will be in the position shown in Fig. 10 with the exception that there will be a fold where the selvages are shown, as this dress has no side seam. Then cut the dress out as explained and shown in

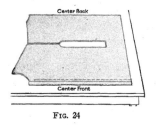

FIG. 24

Fig. 10. When the dress is cut and opened out, the upper part will appear as in Fig. 24.

67. Shoulder-Seam Dart.—If the bust is slightly full, and ease across the front is desired, or if plaids or checks are to be matched at the shoulder seam, a dart may be placed 1½ inches from the neck curve on each shoulder, as shown in Fig. 22. This may be pressed in ¾ inch deep (1½ inches altogether), and caught just at the shoulder seam, or it may be stitched down, dart fashion, for 2 or 3 inches. When this is done, the front-shoulder line will be made shorter than the back, which will have to be trimmed off. Stitch in the usual way, but trim off the lower sleeve edges to make an even line. Use the front as a guide in cutting the back-sleeve line.

68. Applying the Hip Plait and Belt Straps.—The plait at the side over the hips should be pressed back to form an inverted plait, thus making a box plait on the wrong side, as shown in Fig. 25, and

FIG. 25

an inverted plait on the right. Catch the box plait securely to the under-arm seam with the overcasting-stitches, as shown.

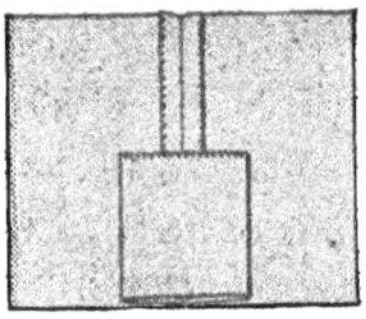

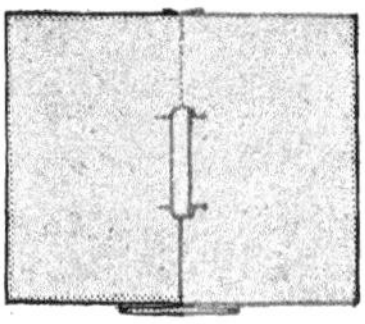

To hold the belt in position, wee belt straps are secured

FIG. 26

in place from the right side just above the inverted box plait, as shown in Fig. 26. Cut these 1⅜ inches wide and 2 inches long, overcast the raw edges together, and press the strap carefully. Then tuck the ends under, pin the straps in place, as shown, and apply them to the dress by means of invisible stitches. Be careful to have the two straps exactly opposite each other on the two seams.

SIMPLICITY TWO-PIECE DRESS

69. For materials of 36- or 40-inch width, the plan of cutting used for the simplicity two-piece dress, shown in Fig. 27, is ideal.

The fact that it is a little less tailored than the straight-line, one-piece dress makes it more adaptable to a variety of fabrics from cottons to wools; in fact, any fabric that does not have a definite nap can be used. Stripes are very smart used lengthwise in the blouse and crosswise in the skirt. Heavy silk crêpes and wash fabrics are also suitable.

The design of this dress makes it most becoming to the slight figure, so that when the bust measurement is large, the straight-line, one-piece dress will be more satisfactory.

70. Measurements and Width of Materials. Take the measurements exactly the same as for the straight-line, one-piece dress, Art. **52.**

If your bust measures more than 38 inches use 40-inch material. If it measures less than 38, 36-inch material is satisfactory. And if you are less than 34, 32-inch material may be used. From 3 to 3½ yards of 36- or 40-inch material is required.

Fig. 27

If you are tall and slender, the only waste in cutting the dress will be that cut out in shaping the neck. This type of dress is desirable for children, too. The measurements are taken in the same way as for an adult and the dress is cut the same except that the neck is made smaller and a 4-inch opening is made at the center back to allow the dress to slip over the head.

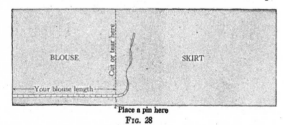

Fig. 28

71. Dividing the Material.—You now divide your material into two parts, one for the blouse and one for the skirt, as in Fig. 28.

Measure off from one end the *blouse length,* and place a pin in the edge of the material to mark the point. Clip through the selvage and cut or tear across, following the suggestions given in Art. **53.** The shorter part is for the blouse; the longer part, for the skirt.

72. Cutting the Armhole and Under Arm.—Fold the shorter piece of material, or the blouse length, first lengthwise, selvage edges together, and then crosswise, as in Fig. 29. (Bring one cross-wise end up 1 inch to make the front longer than the back and allow for fulness over the bust.) Measure to the left from the cross-wise fold *a* along the selvage one-half the armhole measure and place a pin, as at *b*. Measure from the fold *c* one-fourth the hip measure plus 1½ inches and place a pin, as at *d*.

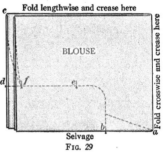

Fig. 29

To obtain the armhole curve, measure straight to the right of *d* 8 or 10 inches and place a pin, as at *e*.

Next, cut straight in from *b*, turning as the pin at *e* is approached and making a smooth, even, under-arm curve. Then continue to cut straight down from *e* to *d*, as shown by the dotted line.

73. Shaping the Waist Line and Sleeves.—To shape the waist line of the blouse, measure up from the bottom ½ to ⅝ inch and place a pin, as at *f*. On the upper piece, which is for the back, taper a curved line from *f* to a point half way between the under arm and the lengthwise fold. For the front, cut in a curved line on the lower piece from *f* toward *c* to a point slightly more than half way, as shown.

If a pointed sleeve is desired, measure up 1½ inches from *b* on the sleeve line and then cut in a diagonal line from *a* to the 1½-inch point.

74. Cutting Out the Neck.—Now, to cut the neck, as in Fig. 30, open out the blouse on the crosswise fold and turn it so that the folded edge is toward you and the back, or short part of the blouse, comes to your left. Measure up on the crosswise crease 4½ inches and mark with a pin, as at *a*. Measure 1 inch on the back fold from the crosswise crease and mark with a pin, as at *b*. Measure to the right from the crosswise crease 4½ inches and mark with a pin, as at *c*.

Cut the front-neck curve by cutting from *c* to *a* and the back curve by cutting from *b* to *a*.

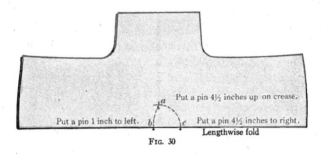

Put a pin 4½ inches up on crease.
Put a pin 1 inch to left.   Put a pin 4½ inches to right.
Lengthwise fold

FIG. 30

75. Utilizing the Under-Arm Sections.—When the blouse is cut, it should appear as in Fig. 31, which shows also the sections cut out at the under arms. Use one of these sections for cutting 1½-inch bias binding for finishing the neck, the bottom of the sleeves, and the pockets, and the other for 6- by 9-inch pockets, as shown. Shape the flaps of the pockets if the sleeves have been shaped, but if they are straight, cut the pockets the same size but with a straight turn-over at the top.

If pockets are not desired and the sleeve is cut straight, the under-arm pieces may be used as straight cuffs to extend the length of the sleeve.

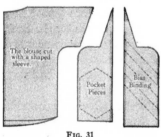

The blouse cut with a shaped sleeve.

Pocket Pieces

Bias Binding

FIG. 31

76. Proportioning the Skirt. Now cut the belt and skirt from the larger piece of material, as in Fig. 32. For the belt, measure 2½ inches from one selvage edge and cut a strip the full length of the material, cutting on a lengthwise thread. Measure the skirt length from the cut edge down toward the selvage. The material that remains may be used for a hem.

The skirt material should be wide enough to provide for the hip measure plus 6 inches for ease and 20 inches for plaits, each of the two large plaits taking up 8 inches, or 16 inches for both, and

each of the four small plaits 1 inch, or 4 inches in all. Thus, if your
hip measure is 40 inches, you will need 40+26, or 66 inches.

The dress is now cut and ready for stitching.

Selvage

Measure off 2½ inches and cut on a lengthwise thread.

The material left is the skirt length
The material left is the hem.

Selvage

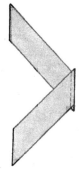

FIG. 32   FIG. 33

77. Binding the Neck.—The first step is to seam the binding
strips to make a center-stitched binding for the neck.   To do this,
join two or three bias pieces, as in Fig. 33, by placing the lengthwise edges together, stitching in a ¼-inch seam, and pressing open
with the fingers.   Sometimes two and sometimes three pieces are
required for the neck, as the length of the pieces depends on the
width of the material and the size of the hip measure.   Piecings are
not objectionable in the bindings, provided the seams are carefully
stitched, surplus edges trimmed away, and the seams then pressed
open.

Bias bindings may be bought prepared ready for use.   Some of
these are lovely, and many are made in organdie, lawn, and silk,
so they are suitable for all fabrics.
Hercules braid, also, is desirable as a
finish for silk or wool tailored dresses.
In using Hercules braid, fold it lengthwise and press it carefully before starting to apply it as binding.   The crosswise ends will join more neatly if a row
of machine stitching is placed across
each one to avoid stretching.

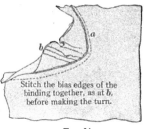

Stitch the bias edges of the
binding together, as at *b*,
before making the turn.

FIG. 34

Place the right side of the binding to
the wrong side of the neck and stitch in a ¼-inch seam, as shown
at *a*, Fig. 34.   Begin stitching at one shoulder and stitch across

the back of the neck and around toward the front. Do this easily and without stretching either the neck or the binding. Stitch all

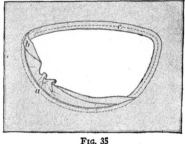

FIG. 35

the way around and join the binding in a bias seam where it meets, as at *b*, that is, on a lengthwise thread, just as the other joinings were made.

Crease the binding on the under side up from the stitching line *a*, Fig. 35. Then turn the free edge of the binding over ⅜ inch, as at *b*, drawing the edge up smooth and even and creasing as straight as possible. Turn the creased edge *b* down well over the stitching line *a*, and stitch through the center, as at *c*. Begin the stitching at the shoulder and proceed around the back as before.

78. Finishing the Sleeves.—To bind the two sleeves, join three strips of the binding, press open the seams, place the right side

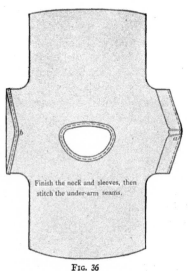

Finish the neck and sleeves, then stitch the under-arm seams.

FIG. 36

of the binding to the right side of the sleeve, as at *a*, Fig. 36, and stitch in a ¼-inch seam. Turn the binding to the wrong side and make a center-stitched binding. Turn back in cuff effect, as shown at *b*.

When the material is attractive on the wrong side, a turnover center-stitched binding, as in Fig. 37, may be made from

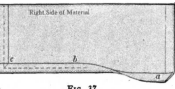

FIG. 37

the sleeve itself or as a cuff finish without using a binding piece. To make this, turn ⅜ inch to ½ inch, as at *a*; then make another ½-inch turn, as at *b*.   Stitch directly in the center.   This will give the same effect as the center-stitched bias binding that is used at the neck.

When this finish is applied, as in a cuff or a cascade, turn the edges in at the corner in square effect and stitch, as at *c*.

79. Completing the Blouse. With the sleeve finish completed, sew the under-arm seams, wrong sides together, for a French seam. Turn and complete the seams. When you reach the bottom of the sleeves, turn and stitch back in the stitching line just made about 1 inch to secure the cuff edge and to stay the thread ends.

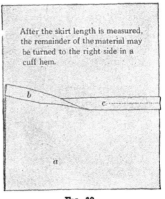

After the skirt length is measured, the remainder of the material may be turned to the right side in a cuff hem.

Fɪɢ. 38

80. Putting in the Skirt Hem. Now, with the blouse stitched, proceed to make the skirt, which has just one seam.   Before seaming it, decide on the hem finish.   A plain hem may be turned and machine-stitched in or it may be slip-stitched, directions for both being given in Arts. **24** and **25,** Chapter V.

A simple yet smart and attractive finish and an excellent substitute for a hand hem is the cuff hem shown in Fig. 38.   This should be put in before the skirt seam is stitched.

To make a cuff hem, turn the hem portion to the right side, as at *a*, creasing on a lengthwise thread.   Turn the edge over ⅜ inch, as at *b*, and turn the fold ½ inch, as at *c*. Press down and stitch directly in the center.

If the material frays, trim the seam neatly before French seaming

Fɪɢ. 39

81. Seaming the Skirt.—If a cuff hem is used, prepare to French seam the skirt, as in Fig. 39.   Pin the bottom *a* and top *b* of the hem ends together so that they will be perfectly even and cannot slip during stitching. These ends must not vary even slightly in width.

Contrary to the regular rule, begin the stitching of the skirt at the bottom.   Stay the end of the seam by beginning 1 inch from the bottom, as at *c*, stitching to the bottom, and then turning and stitch-

ing the full length of the seam.   Turn wrong side out and complete
the French seam, remembering to stay each end.

If you desire, the hem may be omitted and binding or braid used
to finish the bottom of the skirt.

82.   Putting in the Skirt Plaits.—Lay a 4-inch plait on one side
of the skirt, having the seam come at the inside of the plait, as shown
in Fig. 40.   This plait may be laid toward the back or the front, as
desired, and should be pressed in straight from top to bottom of the
skirt.

About 1½ inches each side of this plait, lay a small plait, about
½ inch deep, as shown, to take up all extra fulness.   As both sides are
alike, measure half way around the skirt and pin three similar
plaits in the opposite side.   The edge of each deep plait should come
in line with the under-arm
seam of the waist

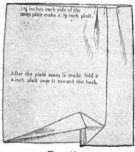

Fig. 40

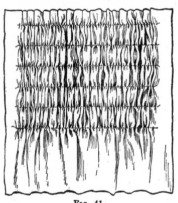

Fig. 41

If the figure is full across the back in the hips, an inverted plait,
with each plait made 2 inches deep and edges turned to meet, is
more satisfactory than the deep 4-inch plait.

·If soft material, such as crêpe, is used, the sides may be shirred in
instead of plaited, as shown in Fig. 41, five or six rows of shirring
placed 1 inch apart being desirable.   When gathered up, the shirring
should take in the allowance of the plaits on each side.   A loose,
long machine-stitch permits a quick, satisfactory shirring.   The
thread ends of the shirring should be secured with a needle.

83.   Making the Waist-Line Joining.—Next, proceed to pin the
skirt to the waist, as shown in Fig. 42, having the edges of the deep

plaits, if they are used, meet the under-arm seams.   Slip the skirt over the waist with the waist-line edges together, and hold the dress carefully while you pin the blouse and the skirt, together, thus preventing its being drawn too tight.

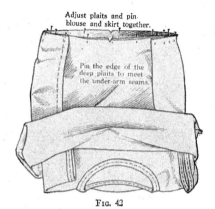

Adjust plaits and pin blouse and skirt together.

Pin the edge of the deep plaits to meet the under-arm seams.

FIG. 42

FIG. 43

To the notched center front and center back of the waist, pin the centers of the front and the back of the skirt, and place several pins in between these points.   By easing in the waist material, the skirt should fit on very well, but if necessary the plaits may be adjusted slightly.

When the waist and skirt are pinned together, stitch all the way around by machine, using a $\frac{3}{8}$-inch seam and overlapping the stitching for a couple of inches.   Then overcast the raw edges, as in Fig. 43, taking up a number of stitches at one time in order to do the work quickly.

For materials that are too heavy to French seam, overcast the other seams by means of this group overcasting, as shown.

84.   Making the Pocket and Belt. If pockets are used, finish the upper edge with a center-stitched binding, as in Fig. 44.   Turn the lap over to the right side and pin the pockets accurately in position, turning in the edges $\frac{3}{8}$ inch.   Begin

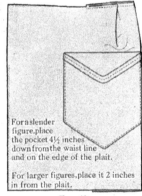

For a slender figure, place the pocket 4½ inches down from the waist line and on the edge of the plait.

For larger figures, place it 2 inches in from the plait.

FIG. 44

$\frac{1}{2}$ inch from the top, stitch to the top, and then back to stay the top edge securely.

4 W I—15

Make the belt as explained in Art. **63** of this chapter for the one-piece dress. Then, to make a tailored bow for the belt, cut off a piece of the belt material 5 inches long. Fold the ends to meet in the center, as shown in Fig. 45, and tack down. Cut off

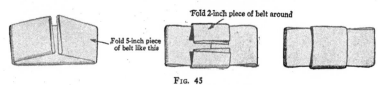

FIG. 45

another piece **2** inches long, fold this around the first piece at the center, as shown, and tack down.

Sew the tailored bow to one end of the finished belt. If the belt will slip over your shoulders, sew both ends of the belt to the bow. If not, put snap fasteners on the belt. Secure the bow just in front of the left-side seam.

TAILORED FROCKS CUT WITH PATTERNS

TAILORED FROCK OF CONTRASTING MATERIALS

85. The type of dress shown in Fig. 46 is equally attractive for indoor or street wear. It is the sort of dress that readily forms a part of a three-piece suit merely by the addition of a coat of material like the skirt.

The method of cutting provides one vertical dart from the shoulder, running down gradually to 7 or 8 inches below. Also, the dress has two horizontal darts on each under-arm seam at the bust line which serve to lift the grain of the material up parallel with the waist line, and give ease over the bust. Such darts are therefore especially desirable for a well-rounded figure.

86. Materials.—For the skirt and trimmings, flannel of a plain color, or one cross-barred in a contrasting color, is used; or, if preferred, any cloth of suit weight may be selected. The material for the blouse section should be of lighter weight than that used for the skirt. Wool crêpe is an excellent choice, but if a coat is to be added, crêpe de Chine or flat crêpe of a color that matches the skirt or harmonizes with it will be a better selection.

87. Pattern Alterations.—If an exact pattern cannot be obtained, one may be developed readily from any well-fitting, plain foundation-waist pattern. To change such a pattern to allow for the darts this dress contains, to remove width, and to keep the straight-line effect, apply the following suggestions:

Lay the front section of the foundation pattern on a piece of paper and trace around the edges of the pattern. Remove and cut on the traced lines, making all changes on this duplicate pattern. In this way, the original pattern is not damaged.

Locate a point on the shoulder seam half way between the neck line and the shoulder tip. From this point, draw a line to the lower edge of the pattern parallel with the center-front line and cut along this line. Then, as in Fig. 47, lay the two pieces thus obtained on another piece of paper, 8 or 10 inches longer than the pattern, separating the pieces at the shoulder from $1\frac{1}{2}$ to 3 inches, depending on the size of the bust, and overlapping them at the lower edge, as shown.

88. Determine the length of the blouse by pinning a tape around the hips at the point where it is desired to have the skirt and the blouse join, and measuring on the center front of the figure from a point close up at the base of the neck down to the tape. Ex-

Fig. 46

tend the center-front line of the pattern until it equals in length the measurement just taken. Extend the under-arm line as shown, in practically the same direction that it follows in the foundation pattern. To form the lower edge of the blouse, draw a straight line at right angles to the termination of the center-front line. Measure this and if it does not equal at least one-fourth the hip measure at the point where the tape was tied around the figure, plus 1 inch, change the slant of the under-arm line so that it will.

The width added to the shoulder line will allow for the vertical dart, while the extra length on the under-arm seam, made by cutting the bottom straight instead of curved, will take care of the two small horizontal darts under the arm.

As a rule, the only change necessary in the back pattern is to lengthen it to correspond with the front length. Make sure that the width across its lower edge is correct, usually one-fourth of the hip measure plus $\frac{1}{2}$ inch. The back of the dress will thus be 1 inch narrower than the front.

89. Such a foundation pattern usually has a plain-sleeve pattern which can be used with little or no alteration. The sleeve, as shown in Fig. 46, has a dart from the lower edge nearly to the elbow. The position and depth of this dart are determined during the fitting of the dress.

Fig. 47

To make a pattern for the convertible collar, cut a straight strip of paper 4 inches wide and twice as long as the pattern measures at the neck line from center front to center back.

For the skirt, no pattern is necessary, as it is perfectly straight with an inverted plait at each hip.

90. Cutting Out the Dress.—Lay the center-front edge of the blouse pattern along a lengthwise fold of the material. Cut along all other edges. Lay the center-back line of the lengthened back pattern on a lengthwise fold, and cut around all other edges.

For the skirt, the lengthwise grain may be used around the body, a length of material equal to the hip measure plus 20 inches usually being the amount needed. When the material is used in this way, there will be a rather wide piece cut off from one selvage because the width of the material exceeds the length of the skirt. From this piece may be cut the belt, the sleeve and pocket trimming, and the neck and collar binding.

If the weave, or pattern, of the material makes it desirable to have the lengthwise grain run up and down, use two lengths with seams at the sides. In this case also, the width of the skirt should be 20 inches greater than the hip measure, unless, of course, fashion demands a straighter silhouette; then 10 or even 6 inches extra will be sufficient. As two full widths will be much too wide, unless the material is comparatively narrow and the figure rather large, the material for the bias trimmings will be supplied by the extra width.

Cut the collar lengthwise of the material. If the fabric is light in weight it may be used for the lining; otherwise, use an appropriate silk.

91. Fitting the Blouse of Dress.—After the waist and the sleeve sections have been basted together, cut on the center-front fold from the neck down to give space enough for the head to slip through, then try the blouse on. Arrange the darts so that it fits correctly. Then cut the neck opening to the point where it is desired to have the opening end, making this a becoming depth. Pin in a dart at the lower edge of the sleeve, having it toward the back of the arm and about in line with the little finger. Have this dart deep enough at the wrist to make the sleeve ᾿close - fitting, tapering the dart to nothing as it approaches the elbow.

92. The Collar and Neck Finish. Finish the shoulder seams in order that the convertible collar may be applied. Very often in a garment of this type, there is an underfac-

FIG. 48

ing that extends from the shoulder seams to a point an inch or two below the front opening. But in this case, if the material is alike on both sides, it is unnecessary to use a facing because of the wide bindings that finish the edges of the front slash and collar. How-

ever, it is advisable to have the collar lined in order that the seam
may be finished properly.

93. Baste the two collar pieces to the neck line so that the blouse
comes between them, as at *a*, Fig. 48, keeping the right sides of the
collar pieces turned toward the blouse in
both cases. Keep all edges even while
basting in position. Then replace bastings with stitching. Press the collar, so
that the corresponding edges of the two
pieces, as *b* and *c*, come together in the
position shown at *d*. Then baste the
edges to keep them from slipping while
applying the binding. Do not turn the
raw edges in before basting, as this would
make the finished edge too bulky.

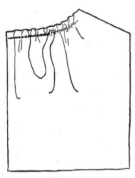

FIG. 49

In putting on a collar of this kind, it is
advisable, especially if the back neck is
full, to run a gathering thread along the neck line in the back,
as in Fig. 49, in order to prevent stretching the seam edge of
the collar where it joins the back and bring the collar close to the
back of the neck.

94. Before applying the bias binding to the collar and neck
opening, reinforce the lower end of the opening by cutting a small
triangle of material and apply-
ing it at the end of the opening
on the right side of the material,
as shown in Fig. 50. Tack it
carefully with back-stitches very
close to the end of the slit, as
at *a*, leaving it loose except at
this point. This completed, turn
the triangle to the wrong side,
and clip just a thread or two of
the material diagonally away
from each side of the tacking-
stitches that hold the reinforcement in place, so that it lies flat.

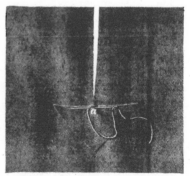

FIG. 50

Prepare bias binding of the skirt material, $1\frac{7}{8}$ inches wide. Fold
this lengthwise through the center and press a crease in it so that the

right side is out. Then turn the two edges in toward each other, making each turn ¼ inch wide. Bring the turned edges together so that they meet exactly, and press them.

95. In applying the band, begin at the reinforced end of the opening, placing the prepared bias on the wrong side of the dress, so that the center fold is over the tacking-stitches, as at *a*, Fig. 51,

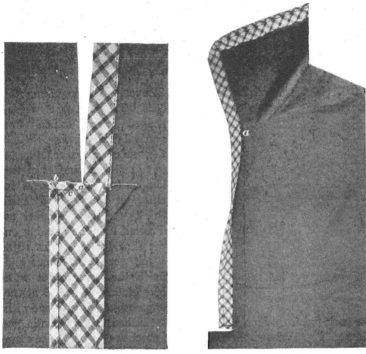

Fig. 51   Fig. 52

and the end of the bias band and the upper edge of the triangle are even, as at *b*. Secure the bias band to the triangle with back-stitches, as at *c*, but not to the dress proper. Then turn it up so that the back-stitches just made are inside and the center crease of the bias band lies directly over the edge of the front-opening slit. Baste the band on the wrong side of the dress, continuing around the collar and the other side of the opening. Then baste it on the right side, as in Fig. 52, keeping the turned edge of the band on the right side directly over that underneath, as at *a*.

When the basting is completed, stitch, beginning at the lower end of the opening and stitching on the right side until the point is reached where the collar folds over and exposes the opposite side. Cut the thread at this point and fasten the ends securely. Then turn the material and stitch around the collar on the side that will be exposed until the corresponding point on the opposite side is reached. Cut and fasten the thread as before, turn the material, and continue until the stitching is completed. In all of this stitching, take every precaution to keep it close to the edge in an even, straight line, and to catch both turned edges. Fig. 51 illustrates the wrong side of a finished band.

96. Making and Inserting the Sleeves.—Before joining the sleeve seams, prepare to finish the dart. Trim out the wedge-shaped piece which was marked during fitting. Stitch the two cut edges together to within about 2 inches of the lower edge of the sleeve to allow an opening and finish this in the same manner as directed for the opening on the shoulder seam, Art. **60.**

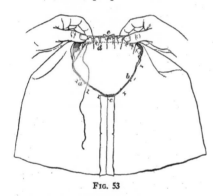

FIG. 53

Join the sleeve seams and finish the lower edges with bias bindings stitched at the upper edge to correspond with the neck finish. When the sleeves are finished, insert them in the blouse. Fig. 53 shows the matching of notches at a and b, the seam lines at c and e, and the adjustment of fulness at d.

97. Making the Skirt.—In case the lengthwise grain of the material is used around the body, there will be only one up-and-down seam, and this can be arranged to come in one of the left-side plaits, as directed in Art. **82.**

If the other method is used, and the lengthwise grain runs up and down, there will be two seams. In order to have each of these come in a plait, let the one on the left side come in the front plait, and the one on the right side in the back plait. The center front and center back of the skirt will in this way fall to one side of the exact center of the width of the material, but this will not affect the appearance of the skirt in any way.

98. Joining the Blouse and Skirt.—Turn the right sides of the skirt and blouse together and follow the suggestions given in Art. **83,** trying the dress on before stitching. At this time, make sure that the line of the joining of the blouse and skirt does not sag at the sides, the front, nor the back. To remedy a defect of this sort, should one occur, change the depth of the joining seam on the blouse section only. Make no change in this seam on the skirt section, as the line of the seam must follow the straight grain of the material. Decide on the position of the pockets at this time.

When the joining seam has been adjusted, replace the basting with stitching, leaving a 3-inch opening on each side in the front for a little stand pocket. Detailed instruction for making these is given in Arts. **4** to **20,** inclusive, Chapter III.

99. Hemming the Skirt.—A smart effect is the end in view in making any tailored frock, and one of the most important means to this end is care in turning and securing the hem, which should be as nearly as possible on a straight grain of the material. In a frock such as this, it can be exactly on the grain because of the hip-line seam and the horizontal darts at the bust line. Secure the hem by hand, following the method given in Art. **25,** Chapter V.

100. Applying the Belt.—Because of the severity of tailored garments, such a small thing as a belt assumes great importance in its effect on the finished whole. It must be neither too wide nor too narrow; if bias, as in this case, it must be on an *exact* bias. It must be stitched and pressed with great care. And the placing of it must give evidence of a fine feeling for balance and the relation of the lines of the gown to those of the figure. It is only when each detail of the whole garment is carried out with such a sympathetic appreciation of its importance that the finished garment becomes a truly tailored frock.

TAILORED FROCK WITH ARMHOLE DART

101. To supply necessary fulness over the bust and at the same time retain a becoming line in a dress is often a problem. One of the most satisfactory methods of accomplishing this is by the use of the armhole dart. This is a feature that is advantageous to the small, extremely thin figure, for it does much toward concealing thinness, and also to the figure having a large bust and a rather flat chest, for the ease given by the dart will help to maintain an appearance of proper proportion.

Fig. 54 illustrates a tailored frock that embraces this commendable feature in a becoming one-piece model. The simple lines of the design make it adaptable to both the very young girl and the woman of middle age.

The severity of the neck-line finish emphasizes the tailored idea, while the fact that the collar is easily removed for laundering is a point in its favor. A bit of brightness may be introduced in the narrow ribbon tie, which may be cut long enough to reach well down on the skirt of the dress, provided the lengthening line is desirable.

For a less tailored effect, the pockets may be omitted, and a more elaborate neck-line finish provided, but just as it is, the dress will prove suitable for home, street, and office wear.

102. Materials.—Silk crêpe is perhaps the best material for this design because it is soft and wieldy; but such materials as linen and linen-finished cottons are not inappropriate, and of the soft wools, wool crêpe and Jersey cloth are good. For the collar, use linen on a wool dress, or on silk or wash materials, a collar of the same material as the dress. White or cream color is preferred in most cases.

FIG. 54

103. Pattern Requirements.—To make this model, it is necessary to have only a plain foundation-waist pattern with a one-piece sleeve that fits well, unless a pattern that is a duplicate of this style is available.

If the plain foundation-waist pattern is used, it is a good plan to cut a duplicate of the original pattern, making all changes on it.

104. Forming the Armhole Dart.—The method of forming an armhole dart in a plain-waist pattern and then extending the lines of the waist pattern to form a skirt portion is shown in Figs. 55 and 56. Mark the armhole dart at the point you desire it, as in Fig. 55; for the average figure, a dart placed about 4 inches

FIG. 55

below the shoulder line and made about 2½ inches long is usually satisfactory.

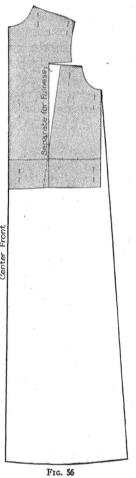

FIG. 56

In order to straighten the lower edge of the pattern and provide fulness in the lower edge of the dart, slash on the line marked for the dart and also from the inside end of the dart on a line parallel with the center front to the lower edge, as shown in Fig. 56. Then, in pinning the pattern to the large piece of paper in preparation for forming the dress pattern, separate the lengthwise slashed edges at the top ¾ to 1¼ inches, as shown, and overlap them at the bottom to take out as much width as you desire. See that the lower edge of the side section does not extend below the other pattern piece, for this would give an undesirable slant to the dart line.

105. Completing the Pattern.—With the pattern pieces securely pinned in position, draw the lower dart edge, extending it on a straight line from the inside end of the dart to the armhole end of the lower dart edge of the waist pattern. Then draw the under-arm line, making sure that the pattern measures, at the point where the hip line will come, at least 2 to 2½ inches more than one-fourth the hip measure, and that it gives as much width as you desire at the lower edge of the skirt. Then draw the line for the lower edge.

Make the back portion of the pattern without an armhole dart, as this is not needed and, besides, might prove undesirable.

In drawing the back under-arm line, be sure that the hip line of the back-pattern piece measures at least 1 inch more than one-fourth the hip measure.

Drape a muslin model for the collar pattern, following the instruction given for draping the collar of the mannish overblouse in Arts. **29 to 32,** inclusive.

106. Cutting the Garment.—Lay the front- and back-pattern sections on the material with the center front and the center back along the lengthwise fold of the material, and cut along all edges except the fold.

Cut the sleeves according to the foundation pattern, allowing for the slight flare at the lower edge if necessary and providing sufficient length for the tuck and the hem finish.

Shape the pockets as shown in the illustration, allowing for a hem at the top deep enough to come down below the bound buttonholes.

For the belt, cut a lengthwise strip of material 2½ inches wide and long enough to make the loops and long tie-ends as illustrated.

107. Putting the Dress Together.—Gather the lower and longer edge of the shoulder dart ¼ inch from the cut edge, using very small stitches, and draw it in until it fits the upper, short edge. Adjust the fulness evenly and baste to the short straight edge. Do not stitch the darts until the shoulder and under-arm seams have been basted and the dress has been fitted. When any necessary changes have been made, stitch the darts and the shoulder and under-arm seams.

108. Making the Sleeves.—Before sewing the sleeve seams, finish the lower edges of the sleeves by turning 2½ inches to the right side, as at *a*, Fig. 57. Above this, make a 1¼-inch tuck and turn it down over the portion that you have just turned up, so that the raw edge of the 2½-inch turn lies exactly in the fold of the tuck,

as at *b*. With this carefully pressed and basted in position, stitch
the tuck from the right side, 1 inch from its lower edge, as at *c*.
In this way, the stitching is through four thicknesses of material,
catching and confining the raw edge of the 2½-inch fold as well as
the tuck. Pin and baste the seams so that the tucks and hems
come together accurately. Stitch and press. When this is done,
insert the sleeves in the dress, following the method described in
Art. **96.**

Bind the center-front opening with a bias piece of the material,
and finish the neck edge in the same way if the material is not too
heavy. (The neck is
finished separately, as
the collar is removable.)

**109. Cutting and
Finishing the Collar.**
Place the collar pattern
on the material so that
its center back is on a
lengthwise fold, and
cut, allowing a ⅜-inch
seam. Finish the outer
edge of the collar with
a bias facing with the
corners mitered, or use
a fitted facing, which
is a more satisfactory

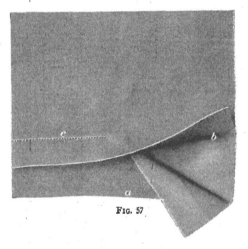

FIG. 57

method, particularly with heavy material, such as linen. To cut
this, follow the outline of the outer edge exactly, having the grain
of the facing material the same as that of the collar. Then
measure in from the edge as far as is necessary to provide the
width desired for the facing, and add a ½-inch allowance for
seams.

In applying the facing, put the right sides of the collar and facing
together, and baste and stitch ¼ inch from the outer edge. Then
turn the facing to the wrong side and turn the edge under ¼ inch,
clipping the corners diagonally ¼ inch to facilitate the turning.
If the facing is to be finished with machine hemstitching, merely
baste in place. If not, hem it down by hand or machine. Bind the
neck edge with bias binding.

The collar may be basted to the dress or applied with snap fasteners, the latter method being preferable as it allows of a quick transfer when necessary.

110. As an *economic method of sewing on snaps*, you will welcome the following: On one half of the collar, use the part with the projection; and on the other half, the flat part. Use them in reverse order on the neck of the dress. Then, when you sew snaps on a second collar, you do not have to throw away six or eight good halves because they have no mates. The same trick may be used on cuffs by sewing the flat part to one cuff and the part with the projection to the other.

If time for the trimming of dresses is very much limited, the above means of adding distinction by a variety of collar-and-cuff sets, either ready-made or of the kind quickly made at home, will be appreciated. Each dress may have two or three sets, all different, and if these are attached by means of snap fasteners, it is the work of only a minute to change them, and the dress takes on new freshness.

111. Making the Pockets.—Make the bound buttonholes, following the intructions given in Arts. **36** and **37**, Chapter II. In this case, the pocket hems, which are blind-hemmed by hand after the buttonholes have been completed, take the place of the facing or under thickness of material.

After turning under the pocket edges, place each pocket in the desired position on the garment, taking care to have the front edges of the small pocket on the blouse portion and of the larger one on the left side of the skirt come exactly in line. When the pockets are satisfactorily located, stitch them in position and add a button to the dress at the point where the upper edge of each buttonhole comes.

112. Completing the Dress.—Sew the edges of the belt together and turn it right side out, tacking it to the dress in two or three places to make sure that it will always be in the desired position. Exercise great care in locating it in order that it may come at the most becoming point. The suggestions in Art. **100,** regarding the belt of the tailored frock of contrasting material apply equally well to this dress, and in fact, to all tailored dresses.

Make the hem as directed in Art. **25,** Chapter V.

TAILORED FROCK WITH VEST EFFECT

113.   One of the most typical of tailored frocks is that which has
a vest effect and a convertible collar.   These details are very smart
and mark a frock as truly tailored, but do not add enough masculinity
to deprive it of its feminine charm.
In the model shown in Fig. 58, the
two rows of machine couching simulate a vest or waistcoat front by their
outline.

Comfortable looseness is given to
the blouse by three shoulder tucks,
and to the skirt by a plait at each
hip.

**114.   Material and Pattern Re-
quirements.**—Because of the general
characteristics of the design, including such details as the shoulder tucks
and the rather full sleeves, this model
is most happily developed in a soft
material, such as crêpe de Chine, flat
crêpe, wash silk, pongee, or voile.
Light-weight wool, such as wool crêpe
or challis may be used, too.

If you have a pattern similar to
this style, use it; if not, your plain
foundation-waist pattern with plain
sleeves will prove a satisfactory guide
for cutting the frock.   By making a
few changes, the other features are
easily added.

**115.   Changing the Pattern for
Shoulder Fulness.**—Cut a duplicate of
the foundation pattern, and on it locate
a point on the shoulder line half way
between the armhole and the neck line.

Fig. 58

Draw a line from this point to the bottom of the pattern parallel
with the center front, and cut the pattern in two on this line.   Lay
the two sections on a piece of paper that is long enough to accommo-

date the length required for the whole dress pattern, as shown in Fig. 59. Separate the two pieces from 1 to 1½ inches at the shoulder and very slightly at the lower edge. In separating

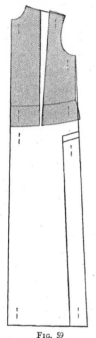

them, keep the corresponding lines, such as the two sections of the waist line and the bust line of the pattern, on the same level. To prevent an angle on the shoulder seam, connect the neck line and the shoulder tip with a straight line, as shown.

116. Extending the Pattern for Length. Measure the figure from a point well up at the base of the neck down to the bottom of the skirt and add to this a hem allowance. Extend the center-front line of the pattern, as shown, to correspond with this measurement.

Extend the under-arm line on a slight slant, making sure that the pattern measures at the hip line, one-fourth of the hip measure plus at least 2 inches. Connect the lower ends of the center-front and under-arm lines with a straight line.

FIG. 59

117. Altering the Pattern for the Hip Plait.—Measure the figure from a point well up under the arm down to the point where it is desired to locate the low waist line. On the pattern, locate a point on the under-arm line so that the distance from the armhole to this point corresponds to the measurement taken plus a ⅜-inch allowance for the dart. Then, from this point, draw the dart line 3 inches long, slanting it so that the inner point is 1 inch lower than the outer. Next, draw a line from the inner point to the bottom of the skirt, having it parallel with the extended under-arm line. Draw a second line parallel to the dart line ¼ inch below it.

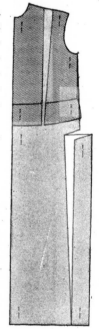

FIG. 60

118. Now cut out the new pattern, following all outside edges and cutting on the dart line and lengthwise to the bottom of the skirt. Trim off the small section which is above the second line, and lay the pattern on another piece of paper, as in Fig. 60. Arrange the long, narrow piece so that it touches the pattern proper at the lower edge, as shown, spreading the two pieces apart at the top so that the new under-arm skirt line is parallel with the center-front line. Then, draw a line connecting the two sections, as illustrated. This provides a hip dart that will lift the grain of the material at the side where it would otherwise drop and an allowance that gives the straight line at the side of the skirt and enables the plait to fall straight and hang correctly.

119. Changing the Back Pattern.—Pin the back pattern to a piece of paper long enough to accommodate the full length of the garment. On the figure, measure the center-back length from a point well up at the base of the neck, making the same allowance for the hem that was made on the front pattern. Extend the center-back line, as in Fig. 61, to correspond with the measurement just taken. Then draw the under-arm line parallel with the center back and equal in length to the under-arm line of the waist section in Fig. 59, minus ⅜ inch, which is taken out of the front in the dart seam. The distance from the point where the plait extension begins to the center-back line must be one-fourth of the hip measure. Draw the line for the plait allowance at right angles to the under-arm line and equal in length to the plait allowance on the front section. Draw the lower under-arm line equal to the corresponding line of the front-pattern piece in Fig. 60. Then draw a straight line for the bottom of the skirt. In

Fig. 61

cutting out the back pattern, cut along all of the outside edges.

120. Making the Underfacing Pattern.—Cut a duplicate of the front-waist pattern, and on this outline the underfacing, as in Fig. 62, keeping it the width that is most becoming to the individual figure, usually 7 or 8 inches across, and of a depth that is in good proportion to the front-waist length. To make the pattern, draw the lower line equal to one-half of the finished width plus ¼ inch for seam allowance. Place the point where the underfacing joins the shoulder line about 1 or 2 inches from the neck line (for the vest must be attached to the shoulder seam). The lengthwise line of the underfacing should be parallel to the center front, or it may be slanted very slightly toward the center front at the lower end if

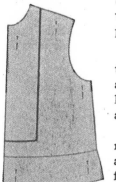

this gives a more pleasing effect. When the vest is satisfactorily outlined, cut out the pattern.

121. Cutting Out the Dress.—Lay the center front and center back of the dress pattern and the center front of the underfacing on a lengthwise fold of the material, cutting along all edges that are not on the fold.

Lay the sleeve pattern on the doubled material with the lengthwise grain running up and down, following the markings of the foundation pattern.

Fɪɢ. 62

The collar and collar facing are cut together in one piece, so that the outer edge of the collar is a fold. Use a straight, lengthwise piece of material, 8 inches wide and twice as long as the pattern measures at the neck line from center front to center back, adding 1 inch to the length to insure sufficient ease. If this is not needed, it can easily be trimmed off.

Cut the belt along the lengthwise thread, $2\frac{1}{2}$ inches wide, and long enough to encircle the low waist line and provide tie-ends and loops.

Cut the tie-cuffs on a lengthwise thread, but only 2 inches wide, making them long enough to tie around the wrist and leave loops and ends, or simply ends, as desired. For loops and ends, about 30 inches is sufficient. For ends only, 15 inches will suffice.

122. Machine Couching.—On the wrong side of the front section of the dress, make chalk lines where it is desired to locate the two rows of machine couching that simulate the waistcoat front effect. In doing this, measure accurately and use every precaution to keep the lines on the right and left sides at equal distances from the center-front opening.

To do machine couching, wind the bobbin with embroidery silk, but do not thread the bobbin case except for a long bobbin. With the bobbin in its proper position, loosen the upper tension slightly, lengthen the stitch, and use common sewing silk for the upper thread. Try out the stitching on scraps of the material to make sure that it is as it should be. Then stitch as usual, following the chalked lines on the wrong side of the material. This brings the heavy embroidery thread to the right side, and makes an attractive and very easily applied trimming.

123. Seaming the Shoulders and Applying the Underfacing. After fitting, stitch the shoulder tucks, locating them between the lines of couching-stitches and the armhole lines.

Turn back the straight edges of the underfacing once and stitch as at *a*, Fig. 63. Avoid using two turns, as for a hem, as the result would be a bulky ridge that would leave a mark on the right side of the dress when pressed over. Put the underfacing on the front of the dress with the right sides of the underfacing and waist together and the edges of the neck line and center-front opening, the depth of which has been determined during fitting, exactly matching.

Baste and stitch the front opening edges together, keeping the seam ¼ inch deep from the top to within 3 inches of the lower end of the opening. Then gradually taper it off, as at *b*,
running it out to almost
nothing at the point, as
at *c*. On the opposite
side, begin with almost
nothing at the point and
gradually slant the seam
so that it is ¼ inch wide
3 inches above the point,
and then keep it an even
depth to the end of the
seam.

Stitch the shoulder
seams of the dress, but
draw the shoulder line
of the underfacing, as
at *d*, Fig. 63, away from

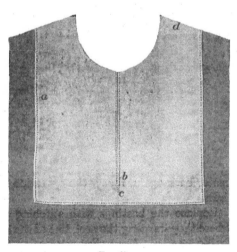

FIG. 63

the garment so that it will not be secured in the seam at this time.

124. Applying the Collar.—Crease the collar lengthwise through the center, as at *a*, Fig. 64. Then mark the center back of

the collar and the center back of the dress at the neck line and
bring the dress and one edge of the collar together at that point, as
at b, basting the edges together in a $\frac{1}{4}$-inch seam.   When the
joining of the dress and the underfacing at the front opening is
reached, as at c, bring the ends of the collar together, and stitch,
as at d, slanting the joining slightly to form a pleasing line in continuation of the front-opening line e.   Then continue the basting from c
along the neck edge of the underfacing to f.   Beginning at the

Fig. 64

center back again, repeat the operation on the opposite side of the
dress.

Replace the bastings with stitching and press the seams open
where they lie along the neck line of the blouse front and the underfacing, as at g.   Along the back section, press the seam so that both
sides of it will extend up over the collar, as at h.

With this completed, turn the collar right side out, and bring the
underfacing to the wrong side of the dress, so that the point f lies
over point i.   Tack these together securely, turn under the collar
edge j $\frac{1}{4}$ inch and slip-stitch it to the neck edge h of the dress.   Tack

the hemmed edge of the underfacing to the dress in a few places, taking the tacking-stitches through the machine couching-stitches, not through the dress.

125. Finishing the Under-Arm Line and Dart Seam.—Stitch the hip dart, joining the edges in a plain seam without fulness in the lower part, allowing the excess material to extend beyond the under-arm line of the waist.   Then join the under-arm seams, beginning at the jutting section at the hip and sewing upwards to the arm-hole.   Then return to the hip line and sew across the jutting line and on down to the bottom of the skirt.   Form a plait at each hip by turning the jutting edge back so that it lies over the dart seam. Baste and press the plait carefully throughout its length.

FIG. 65

126. Making and Applying the Sleeves.—To finish a sleeve of the type shown in this model, cut a 3-inch opening at the lower edge, locating it along the back of the arm in line with the little finger.   Bind this opening with a very narrow bias binding of self-material, as at *a*, Fig. 65.

127. To apply the tie-cuff, first gather the lower edge of the sleeve, using small running-stitches, and drawing them in as tightly as it is desired to have the sleeve fit at the wrist.   Then pin the tie-cuff to the gathered sleeve so that the right sides are together and the centers of each meet with their edges even, as at *b*.   Beginning at one end of the opening, baste the tie-cuff to the gathered edge and stitch it.   Folding the cuff lengthwise through the center with the right sides in, baste a ¼-inch seam from the end of the stitching down to the end of the tie, slanting off the corner. Repeat this at the other end of the tie and stitch along the line of the bastings. Then turn the tie-ends right side out, when the sleeve will appear as in Fig. 65. Turn in the raw edge of the cuff, opposite the gathers, $\frac{1}{4}$ inch, as at c,

bring the turned edge over the line of the first stitching, and hem it down by hand, as at d.

128. Insert the sleeves in the arm-holes, following the instruction given in Art. **96.** Make and apply the narrow belt according to the directions in Arts. **63** and **100.** Hem the skirt as described in Art. **24,** Chapter V.

TAILORED FROCK WITH MANNISH YOKE

129. While the frock illustrated in Fig. 66 is, strictly speaking, a tailored frock, it is slightly less formal than many because of its short sleeves. These, together with the rather low neck line and the trim loose-ness provided by the tucks at the shoulder, make it a particularly comfortable type for summer wear. Moreover, these same features combine to make it especially appropriate for development in the cool, wash materials, such as silk crêpe, wash silk, linen, and linen-finished cottons.

130. Pattern Requirements.—A plain foundation-waist pattern, with a few changes, will prove sufficient guidance in cutting this dress. Choose one that has a plain, smooth-fitting sleeve, and cut all seam allowances from your duplicate pat-

Fig. 66

tern before making any changes. Then allow for the seams when cutting out the pattern after all changes have been made.

131. Changing the Pattern for Yoke and Front Fulness.—Determine the depth desired for the mannish-yoke effect, measure down this distance from the shoulder line along the neck and armhole edges, and connect these two points with a straight line, as shown in Fig. 67, 1½ or 2 inches being the usual depth of such a yoke. Cut along this line and save the piece of the pattern that you cut off, for this is to be added to the back pattern later.

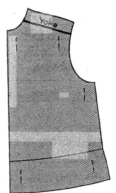

To make allowance for the tucks, slash and spread the remainder of the front-waist section as directed in Art. **115.** Have the space between the cut edges on the shoulder line equal to the amount desired for the tucks, but allow the lower edges of the slashed pattern nearly to meet, as in Fig. 59. They must, however, be spread far enough apart to provide sufficient width through the hips.

Fig. 67

(A dress of this type should measure at the hip line, when finished, at least 7 inches more than the hip measure of the figure.) This width is best distributed by having each half of the front measure 2½ inches more than one-fourth of the hip measure, and each half of the back, 1 inch more than one-fourth of the whole hip measure. If the figure is larger than average, add a little more width to insure comfort and to prevent strain on the dress in sitting.

Fig. 68

132. Adding Length to the Front Pattern. Measure on the center front of the figure from a point well up to the base of the neck down to the point where it is desired to have the bottom of the dress located. Add to this the width of the hem. On the paper to which the pattern was pinned, draw an extension of the center-front line, so that it is equal to the measurement just taken. Extend the under-arm line, and connect the lower edge of the front with the side, with a line that curves upward very slightly toward the under-arm line.

133. Changing the Back Pattern.—Place the pattern on a piece of paper a little longer than the finished pattern is to be at the shoulder line, and pin to the paper the piece that was cut from the shoulder of the front pattern when making the new yoke line, placing this edge to edge with the back-shoulder seam, as in Fig. 68. This will supply the proper extension and the correct neck and armhole lines to give the desired yoke effect. Extend the under-arm and center-back lines, observing the precautions in regard to the hip measurement just given. Then connect the center back with the side line to form the bottom of the skirt, having the line curve upward slightly as it approaches the under arm.

134. Cutting Out the Dress.—Before doing any cutting, lay all of the pattern pieces on the material and make sure that you have the best and most economical arrangement possible, laying both the center front and the center back of the pattern along a lengthwise fold of the material. Cut along all outside edges, allowing a $\frac{3}{8}$-inch seam except at the bottom where the depth of the hem must be considered, but do not cut the fold, not even for the front opening, for it is safer to decide on the size and depth of the neck opening during the fitting.

Measure from the shoulder tip down to the point on the arm where the sleeve is to end, folding back the lower end of the pattern to correspond with this measurement and cutting the sleeve.

Cut the belt lengthwise, $2\frac{1}{2}$ inches wide and long enough to tie a bow with loops and tie-ends.

For the collar, cut a lengthwise piece of material, 8 inches wide and twice as long as the neck line of the pattern from center front to center back. To this add 1 inch to insure sufficient ease in attaching the collar.

The cuffs are merely straight pieces equal in length to the measurement of the lower end of the sleeves. If a heavy material such as linen or flannel is used for the collar and cuffs, provide a thin lining for them, lawn for the former, and crêpe de Chine or China silk for the latter. If they are made of sheer material, cut them double. When cutting double cuffs, cut them on a doubled-over piece of goods so as to have a fold at the top edge and add $\frac{1}{2}$ inch for seams on the other three edges.

The vest is cut straight, as wide as the neck opening at the point where the top of the vest comes, plus $2\frac{1}{2}$ inches, and at least 2 inches longer than the measurement from the top of the vest to the V point of the collar. Plan the revers facing as directed for the underfacing in Art. **123,** having it long enough to accommodate the depth of the neck-line opening.

135. Baste the shoulder tucks in position, taking in just enough material to have the front- and the back-shoulder seams of equal length, and locating the tucks where they will be most becoming to the wearer.   They look best if not too wide, $\frac{1}{4}$ inch to $\frac{3}{8}$ inch being a pleasing width.

Baste the shoulder and the under-arm seams, and fit the dress. While the dress is on the figure, mark the depth of the neck opening and cut directly down the center front from the neck line to this point.   After making any necessary alterations in fitting, replace the bastings with stitching, securing the tucks first.   In order to do this, rip the basted shoulder seams after carefully marking their exact location.

136. Making Sleeves, Cuffs, Collar, and Vest.—In making the double cuffs, sew the ends together in a plain seam.   Then turn each cuff, bringing the seam inside and the two raw edges together.   If the cuffs are lined, join the lining to the cuff on the length first, then sew the ends together and proceed as for double cuffs.   After finishing the under-arm seam in the sleeve, join the cuffs to the sleeves by means of bias facings.   In joining them, have the under-arm seam and the seam in the cuffs come exactly together, so that one appears to be a continuation of the other.   Insert the sleeves in the dress as described in Art. **96.**

Follow the instruction given in Art. **124,** for applying the collar and underfacing, having point *a* a seam rather than a fold, if the collar is lined rather than cut double.

Make the vest double unless heavy material is used, when it is well to hem or face all edges or use a lining.   If it is to be double or lined, place the two wrong sides of the material together and join the top and the two sides with a narrow seam.   Then turn right side out, pressing it and slip-stitching the lower edges together.   Fasten one side of the vest by slip-stitching it securely to the dress with small stitches underneath the revers.   Use snaps on the other side.

137. Finishing the Dress.—Make the belt as directed in Art. **63,** and tie it at the point where it is most becoming, adjusting it very carefully.   Then, using pins for marking, decide on the location of the pockets.   They must not be too close together, nor yet too near the side seam.   The proper distance from the belt is best ascertained by trying out different locations for their effects.   As a general rule, a more pleasing proportion is maintained by having the distance between the pockets and the belt slightly less than that between the belt and the end of the collar.

Make the pockets according to the instruction given in Arts. **4** to **20**, Chapter III, using the variation at the upper left of Fig. 15.

Measure the dress length very carefully, and make the hem according to the directions given in Art. **25**, Chapter V.

TAILORED SATIN DRESS WITH TUNIC BLOUSE

138. One of the smartest of tailored frocks is the trim, neat, slenderizing model in Fig. 69. (It can be the most useful dress in one's wardrobe because it is appropriate for street wear as well as for informal occasions.)

The tunic effect adds interest and makes the outfit practical, too, for several overblouses can be worn with one skirt, provided, of course, the color and material form a pleasing combination. The decided break in the length of line makes the dress more becoming to taller figures, but when the material of the blouse and underskirt are the same, a style of this type may be worn by shorter women also, provided, of course, the bust and hip measurements are not too large.

139. Material Required.—For the best effect, use black satin for the dress and white satin for the trimmings. Other colors and materials can be employed, of course, but they do not give quite the chic appearance that results from the black and white combination.

If satin is used for the entire underskirt, which is attached to a camisole, the requirement for the average figure will be about $4\frac{1}{2}$ yards. By shamming the upper part of the skirt with the material of the camisole, it is possible to reduce this amount from $\frac{1}{2}$ to $\frac{2}{3}$ yard.

FIG. 69

The camisole will require one or two lengths, depending on the width of the material. For it, a light-weight black silk, such as radium, China silk, or light-weight crêpe de Chine is advisable.

By following the diagram in Fig. 70, it is possible, if a seam in the back of the collar is used, to cut the double collar, vest, and double bias cuffs from $\frac{3}{4}$ yard of white satin, 40 inches wide.   If it is desired to cut the collar without a seam in the back, provide $1\frac{1}{4}$ yards of satin.

140. Pattern Requirements and Changes.—A plain foundation-waist pattern may be used for cutting the tunic blouse.   Merely lengthen the under-arm, the center-front, and the center-back lines the desired amount, having a slight outward slant on the under-arm seams.   Outline the V-neck line during fitting, keeping comparatively straight lines from the shoulders to the end of the point.

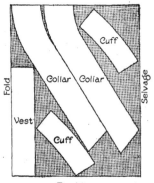

Fig. 70

For the skirt, no pattern is required, as it is straight with slight fulness over the hips and requires only the removal of about 11 inches from each of the two widths of material required for its making.

To drape the collar pattern, follow the instruction given in Arts. **29** to **32**, inclusive, for the collar of the mannish overblouse, illustrated by Fig. 4.   In order to increase the length, merely add a longer wedge-shaped piece of muslin when pinning it on the form.

Make the cuff pattern, shown in Fig. 70, by following the outline of the lower end of the sleeve pattern and allowing for the seams.

141. Constructing the Dress Foundation.—Make the camisole as described in Art. **17,** Chapter V.   Then join the side seams of the skirt, gather the fulness at the top or arrange it in plaits at the sides, and join it to the camisole as explained in Art. **18,** Chapter V.

Measure the skirt length and trim the hem to an even width.   Do not turn under the edge of the hem, as that makes a bulky finish.   Instead, follow the directions in Art. **25,** Chapter V.

142. Making the Tunic Blouse.—Before basting the front and back sections of the blouse together, make the welt pockets, following instruction given in Arts. **31** to **43,** inclusive, Chapter III.

Prepare the narrow belt sections, and baste the unfinished end of each to the under-arm line of the blouse front at the point where it is desired to have the belt located. The ends will then be joined in the under-arm seams.

Join the under-arm and shoulder seams of the blouse, basting them and fitting the blouse before stitching the seams.

Make and insert the sleeves as directed in Art. **96.**

Hem the bottom of the blouse as described for the foundation skirt.

Overcast all seams and press them open.

Sew up the back seams of the collar pieces. Then put the right sides of the two collar sections together, baste and stitch $\frac{1}{4}$ inch from the edge along the ends and outer edge. Turn right side out, pressing the collar and finishing the neck edge with a bias binding.

Finish the cuffs in the same manner as the collar, and attach both collar and cuffs either by basting or with snaps.

Tack the necktie of satin or ribbon under the collar as indicated in the illustration.

CHAPTER VII

TAILORED SUITS, COATS, AND CAPES

ORIGIN AND PURPOSE OF THE TAILORED SUIT

1. All dress, whether of the simplest or the most elaborate kind, is governed almost entirely by the use to which it is to be put. In former years, before women became athletic in their ideas and tastes and before they entered business pursuits, there was little call for the varieties in dress demanded by the women of today. Our sisters of half a century ago were not interested in the sports that give so much pleasure to women nowadays, nor did they choose to leave their homes daily to go to business. Their time was occupied with the affairs of the household and with amusements of a less vigorous kind. They knew little of such recreations as tennis and golf, and the automobile was not known. However, as women gradually accepted the more strenuous diversions and took up with men the affairs of the business world, they found need for clothes that would be appropriate for such wear and still be attractive and becoming.

It was probably the adoption of the bicycle by women and their acceptance of golf as a recreation that influenced them to favor the man-tailored suit, which made its appearance in England even before 1888. In that year, tailored suits for women began to take on an elegance of line and finish that was unexpected and even somewhat surprising; but, from then on, this type of garment has been improved and developed until it would now seem as if there were no more variations possible.

2. The tailored coat and skirt correspond to the regulation man's suit, and the woman who understands the real purpose of such a suit will readily admit that it is the backbone of her wardrobe. Of course, to some, the initial cost of a tailored suit in time, energy, and money may seem high, but when its advantages are realized it will be seen to be a better investment than can be made for any other part of a woman's outfit.

3. ⟮ The chief recommendation of the tailored suit lies in its practicability, for it is economical, convenient, and perfectly dependable for numerous occasions; in fact, the service that such a suit renders undoubtedly accounts for the great favor in which it is held and its widespread adoption by women in all walks of life. ⟯

In its principal use, it is a general-utility garment whose place cannot be filled by any other garment in a woman's wardrobe, no matter how simple and conservative in design, fabric, and finish the other garment may be. Thus, the business girl or woman who possesses a well-tailored suit and a good supply of neat, attractive blouses will have little difficulty in appearing just as she should. On the other hand, a tailored suit of good material, together with several plain blouses and at least one dressy one and a smart hat, may constitute a woman's entire street or afternoon dress without danger of embarrassment or the need of other costumes for wear outside of the home.

It will be well to remember, also, that the tailored suit that is in accord with fashion may be worn at all times, except at formal and semiformal evening affairs. Indeed, when worn with a dressy blouse and an appropriate hat, it is in just as good taste for informal evening wear and for afternoon social affairs, as it is for shopping, business, or travel when worn with a plain blouse and a tailored or a simply draped or trimmed hat.

Thus, as is evident, besides being a utility garment, the tailored suit is an emergency garment, a "standby" that can always be pressed into service and worn with confidence, comfort, and pleasure, provided the right accessories for different occasions are chosen and worn with it.

_____

ESSENTIAL FEATURES OF THE TAILORED SUIT

_____

STYLE AND INDIVIDUALITY

4. Pattern lines and proportions are possibly the first of the essential features of the tailored suit to consider, and these, of course, are controlled by the style that is to be adopted. Dress in its common-sense form, and the tailored suit in particular, is based on practical requirements, but to serve its full purpose, it must also be artistically worked out. On this principle alone may clothes be made that will give outward expression to the best conception of clothes knowledge. In the tailored suit, probably more than in any other garment, there is opportunity for simplicity, which is the keynote of culture and a most important element in all matters of dress.

It will be well to bear in mind that the strictly tailored suit is always of conservative style, whether skirts are long and narrow or short and full, whether coats are fitted, semifitted, or loose, and whether they are elaborately trimmed or devoid of fancy or extreme details of design. Of course, to have a stylish suit, its general lines should follow the prevailing lines of the modes that are in vogue at the time the garment is made; yet they should be modified to such an extent that the suit will remain in fashion long after any extreme garments of the period have been discarded.

5. A knowledge of past and present fashions, as well as an intelligent anticipation of fashions to come, is imperative if a garment that will long withstand the whims of fashion is desired. If at the time of planning a tailored suit, extremely full skirts and fitted coats are the vogue, the suit should be designed and cut with less fulness in the skirt and more fulness or looseness of fit in the jacket. In spite of the apparent sudden changes of fashion, there is really nothing abrupt nor radical in them; in fact, such changes are slow and consistent. Therefore, by a slight variance, or drifting, as it were, from the current mode toward that which is known to be coming, the suit may be so planned and constructed that it will never be radically out of fashion.

SUITABLE MATERIALS

6. In planning a tailored garment, there should be considerable thought given to the choice of material, for the fabric selected will have a decided bearing on the finished appearance of the outfit. Then, too, the necessity for thorough pressing limits one's choice because certain materials are better adapted than others to the frequent dampening and smoothing with the iron which go into the making of a tailored suit. Serge is a serviceable fabric and answers practically all of the necessary requirements, while various other twilled weaves, such as tricotine, Poiret twill, charmeen, and kasha are appropriate too. An all-wool tweed or a firm flannel will tailor well, and for certain occasions will be more appropriate than the other fabrics suggested.

<hr/>

LININGS, FINDINGS, AND TRIMMINGS

7. Linings.—Fashion usually influences the color and design, or lack of design, of the lining for a suit coat. It may be figured, striped, checked, or plain, and it may either match the suit material in color or be in direct contrast or pleasing harmony. If it is selected with the idea of harmonizing, it should usually be a tone or two lighter rather than darker. Frequently, it is of the same color and material as the blouse to be worn with the suit. However, good taste and the desire for practical service should govern one's attitude toward the fashion elements that enter into the selection of the lining of the coat. A neutral gray or tan or a cream white is often chosen; still, as will be admitted, lining of a color that is too light will not give the same service as a reasonably dark lining.

8. While the color and the design of the coat lining should receive proper consideration, its wearing qualities also are of extreme importance. It should be selected with the idea of giving service not only in actual wear, but also in durability of color and endurance of form and shape. It is a well-known fact that a flimsy, stretchy lining is not a serviceable one, no matter how attractive its color and design may be. Neither is the weight of the lining material an assurance of its durability, for often one that is light in weight possesses better wearing qualities than a heavy one. Then, too, a heavy material gives a bulkiness that may prove detrimental to the fit of the garment and also cause an uncomfortable feeling in the wearing. Therefore, instead of purchasing a lining of heavy weight, such as a cotton-back satin or a silk substitute, as, for example, heavy sateen, it is better to select a closely woven silk, such as crêpe de Chine or satin of good quality; or, if the expenditure must be kept within a certain limit, a percaline or a similar highly mercerized cotton will answer very well. Cotton linings and some silks stick to the blouse, making one's coat difficult to remove. So beware of this and choose that which allows the coat to be removed gracefully.

9. For firmness or for warmth, according to the character of the material, the style of the garment, and the season when it is to be worn, a foundation, or interlining, is sometimes introduced in tailored coats. For firmness alone, light-weight muslin or soft tailors' canvas is generally used, while for warmth, light-weight flannel or lamb's wool interlining is employed. When a foundation for firmness is used, it should be of reasonably good quality and should be properly shrunk.

10. Findings.—In the matter of findings, the thread used for stitching the seams and for all other stitching is the most important detail. To insure the best results, silk thread should always be used. Some persons may think that cotton thread is more economical, but there is really no economy, nor value either, in using any thread except silk for a tailored suit; besides, the difference in cost between the two kinds is too trifling to be considered in figuring the cost of the findings.

As will be remembered, the value of silk thread lies in its elasticity, its toughness, its durability, its fastness of color, and the smoothness and evenness of the stitching that it produces in both hand and machine work. Stitches made with silk thread do not flatten nor pucker the edges and seams of garments, and for this reason they conform very well to the woolen material that is usually employed for a tailored suit. Cotton thread, on the other hand, produces flat stitching, which impairs the appearance of the garment.

Another point in favor of silk thread is that it retains its color and will not collect dust, whereas cotton thread grows rusty and fades more quickly. A matter not to be overlooked, however, is that silk thread grows lighter in tone when it is worked up in both the lining and the suit material. This fact makes it necessary to purchase a thread that is slightly darker than the material with which it is to be used. As a general rule, sewing silk is employed for tailored-suit sewing, a light-weight, fine silk for whipping in the lining, and a somewhat heavier silk for felling in the lining.

11. Trimmings.—While the effect of the tailored suit depends considerably on the trimmings that are used, the range of the available trimmings is somewhat limited. In fact, buttons, braid, and a contrasting material for the collar and cuffs comprise the list from which trimmings that have to be purchased are chosen. Most of the other trimmings are made out of the material itself, and while the making requires time, such trimmings do not enter very largely into the expense.

In order that the buttons used on a tailored suit may be in keeping with the style of the garment, bone or composition buttons or self-covered ones are the best kinds to use. Of course, it is permissible to use novelty buttons when such are in vogue, but good taste demands that, in general, the choice of buttons be conservative rather than extreme, irrespective of the material of which they are made.

12. Braid is frequently used as binding for tailored garments and is usually applied flat. It may be put on in straight lines or in fancy designs of more or less elaborateness, although, on the strictly tailored suit, designs and figures that are extremely ornate should be avoided. This does not mean, however, that it is not permissible to work braid or other trimming into artistic forms on a semitailored suit, provided, of course, the braid and the design used are in harmony with the color, texture, and design of the suit. When bindings are to be used as trimming on a tailored suit, braid will prove a very satisfactory material. In such case, it may be applied not only to the edges of the coat, the skirt, the pockets, the collar, and the cuffs, but in some seasons to the seams of both the skirt and the coat.

13. In addition to braid and buttons, other trimmings, such as plaits, stitched bands, and pockets, are frequently applied to the tailored suit. When plaits are so employed, they may be stitched to the pieces of the garment or they may be applied. Pockets may serve for utility or ornamentation, or both, but they are always considered as trimming, regardless of the purpose for which they are used. Stitched bands may be plain or shaped.

Machine-stitching, whether put on bands or on the suit itself, gives a pleasing effect and is always in good taste. It should be remembered, however, that such stitching should always be of silk and, except in rare instances where fashion permits of a contrasting color or of a lighter or darker tone, it should be of a color that exactly matches the suit.

Hand-made crowfeet and arrowheads done with sewing silk or buttonhole twist add a desirable finish to a tailored suit and at the same time serve as a form of trimming. It is often advisable to improve the appearance of a suit by just such little embellishments as these.

ADDITIONS TO THE TAILORED SUIT

14. Since the tailored suit is so often used for other occasions than those for which it was originally intended, it sometimes becomes necessary to relieve the severity of the lines and to strive for a dressy appearance. This result may be accomplished very satisfactorily if a woman will study her suit until she finds just the right touch to add. She may use a fur piece, a fabric scarf, a frilly jabot, or a pretty collar; or, if it is in fashion, she may insert a frill in the inside of the collar or place an attractive bow at her neck. There are not many women who can stand the dark, hard lines of the tailored collar as the only outline for the face and bare neck, so it is well to know just how to soften these lines.

A bright little nosegay, consisting of a single flower, or a bouquet of artificial flowers made of ribbon or silk, a crocheted ornament, or a combination of several of these provides a bright bit of color for the tailored suit and helps to give that "dressed-up" appearance so desirable not only for personal gratification and assurance but also for smartness.

The hat to be worn with the tailored suit also provides, by its color and design, a means by which the severity of the lines of the suit may be relieved. Even an exceedingly pretty woman cannot afford, by the style of her tailored suit and accessories to rob herself of that dainty, feminine appearance which expresses the best of womanly traits and characteristics, and if she is careful to select a hat that is becoming and in accord with the suit, the costume in its entirety will be far more pleasing.

MAKING THE TAILORED SUIT

DESCRIPTION OF SUIT

15. A garment that embodies the constructive details usually met in the work of tailoring suits is illustrated in Fig. 1. It is severely cut and tailored, and because of its tailored simplicity, occupies an important place in the wardrobe.

It must not be inferred that all tailored suits are developed in the same way, for as with every other type of garment, there are variations from the standard which are often more desirable, more becoming, and more appropriate. At the same time, it is true that a

FIG. 1

thorough knowledge of the ways and means of fashioning a strictly tailored suit is all that is necessary in order that its variations may be properly developed. So the information that is given here is for you to study, master, and adapt to your own needs and taste.

The coat is cut with a panel effect front and back and with the seam-line joining accentuated by stitching. Such a plan makes the coat particularly becoming to the full figure; but by the use of a flared effect below the waist line, when such is in vogue, it may be made suitable for the slender type also. The mannish notched collar and the close-fitting sleeves are appropriate details.

The skirt is slender in effect, but really quite roomy as there are plaits allowed at the side-front and side-back. The center front is finished with a tuck. The instruction given in Chapter V on the making of tailored skirts will help you in the construction of this model. If you wish to follow another style, do so, making sure that its lines are in keeping with those of the coat.

16. Material and Pattern Requirements.—In tailoring, as in any other form of garment construction, it is essential that the quality, weave, and weight of the fabric harmonize with the design chosen. For such a suit as that illustrated in Fig. 1, serge, tricotine, Poiret twill, or kasha is a wise choice, an all-wool tweed or a firm flannel being more appropriate, however, provided a suit of the sports type is desired.

For this model, $3\frac{1}{2}$ yards of 54-inch material without an up and down is required for the average figure. If the material has an up and down, as broadcloth, 4 yards is needed. Of single-width material, that is, material not more than 36 or 40 inches wide, 6 yards is required. In addition, $2\frac{1}{2}$ yards of 40-inch lining should be supplied.

17. As a guide in cutting the suit, supply what is commonly known as a box-coat pattern of the proper size and a foundation skirt pattern that may be cut in five sections. Test both carefully and make all changes that seem necessary in order to suit the pattern to the measurements of the individual.

PREPARING THE MUSLIN MODEL

18. One of the chief requisites in a tailored coat is perfection in fitting, so extra precautions must be taken in order to have the finished garment satisfactory in this respect. It is not enough that the usual rules of fitting be put to use, but you must also take care to stress those details peculiarly related to the fitting of a tailored coat. The muslin model is the safest means of insuring a smooth-fitting garment, for if the pattern is first cut from trial material, it is a simple matter to make any changes necessary to provide an appearance of smoothness and grace of line.)

Cut the muslin with the aid of your coat pattern, taking every precaution to have each piece on the proper grain of the material, exactly as the cloth would be.   Mark the bust line and the waist line with pencil directly on the muslin.   Baste up the various pieces, using rather small stitches, and insert the sleeves; in fact, prepare the muslin coat for a first fitting.

19.   Shoulder Alterations for Rounded Figure.—In Fig. 2 are illustrated examples of alterations that may be required as well as

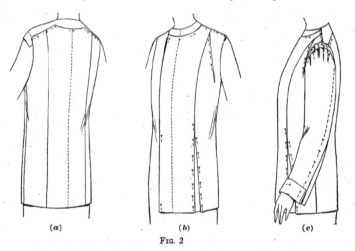

(a)   (b)   (c)

Fig. 2

the means of accomplishing them.   In fitting the more rounding figure, one or all of the changes shown at (a), (b), and (c) may be necessary.   When the shoulders and the figure just below the back-neck line are rather full, you will find that the coat draws up, appearing short-waisted and uneven at the bottom and very often projecting out in a point at the back.   To remedy these defects, rip the shoulder seams and insert a piece of muslin across the back-neck line, extending it out to the end of the shoulder and to the center-front line and making it 3 to 4 inches deep.   Shape this to follow the curve at the base of the neck, being sure to cut it rather high, as the feeling of comfort in a coat, as well as its smartness, is lost if it does not fit up closely at the back of the neck.

20. Now place the upper part of the back-coat section against the figure just where it seems to look best. Do not make the mistake of dropping it too low, as this will cause the armhole at the under arm to be too deep; usually a distance of from 1 to 2 inches below the center-back neck line is sufficient. Place a pin at the center back, and then smooth the muslin out toward the armholes and pin across the back-neck line and out to the armhole, as in view (a). Follow the same plan with the front, taking every precaution so that the upper part of the muslin model may appear just as you would wish the coat to look when finished.

At this time, it is well to decide on the position of the shoulder line on the new section of muslin. Mark this accurately with pins, placing them in a straight line just at the top of the shoulder. It may happen that the front section does not require any change in its position, and when this is the case, its shoulder line may be used as a guide in determining the position of the new one. When this alteration has been successfully completed, the coat should appear smooth for its entire length. If it does not, make any further changes that seem necessary.

If there is an appearance of fulness in the front between the side-front seam and the armhole, pin this out in the form of a dart, as in view (b). If necessary, rip the seam down a little from the shoulder, provided the dart deepens as it approaches this seam; however, if the alteration is slight, the seam need not be disturbed.

21. Hip Alterations for Rounded Figure.—View (b) shows also a change to add width to the lower portion of the coat. Rip the side-front seam from the bottom up to the waist line and add a wedge-shaped section of the muslin, pinning it in position on both sides. Have plenty of length in the inserted section so that the change will be gradual and not abrupt. Such an alteration may be made at the side-back seam, too, or at the under-arm seam, provided the coat requires more width at these points. In fact, add to or take away from any seam to bring about perfection in fit. Locate the new seam line at the center of the added section.

22. Deciding Upon the Length of the Coat.—With the necessary fitting in the coat portion accomplished, turn your attention to the adjustment of its length. It is sometimes difficult to decide what the length of a coat shall be, merely because there is uncertainty as to the proper relation between becomingness and style.

It is a mistake to assume that when fashion decrees that suit coats be long, the length of all such coats must be uniform as to inches. A little serious thought will readily show that a 30- or 40-inch coat will appear different on a tall woman from what it does on a short woman. A good point to remember is that the coat of any tailored suit should not be of such length as to give its wearer the appearance of being cut in two, or of being too long or too short in either legs or body. This test should always be the determining factor in deciding on the length of the suit coat, for if the length looks wrong, it is wrong, despite any decree of fashion. However, as will be readily seen, this *right look* cannot be determined unless the length and the width of the skirt and the proportions and needs of the figure, as to size and height, length of arms, and width of shoulders, are taken into consideration.. Also, if a belt is used, its width and position should be determined before the coat length is decided on, for, as a rule, the coat must be longer when a belt divides the length.

A wise plan is that of turning the lower edge of the muslin model up at various lengths to determine just which one seems best. Mark the correct length with pins, having the coat straight around, if desired, or sloping definitely longer in the front.

23. Sleeve Alterations for Rounded Figure.—After the body portion of the suit is fitted, notice the appearance of the sleeves. If the extra width produced by the change, which was made at the shoulder and which will naturally affect the size of the armhole, is not needed, it may be taken out at the under-arm seam. If the extra width is required, the sleeve must be altered to accommodate it. The well-rounded figure finds a short shoulder line most becoming, so a small section should be added to the top curve of the sleeve to provide length, which at the same time will cause the sleeve to fit better into the enlarged armhole, as in view (c). If the top curve of the sleeve seems to be pronounced enough, let out the front and back seams of the sleeve so that its size will correspond with that of the armhole of the coat.

Notice the sleeve below the elbow. Usually a slight change will be required to make it appear trim and straight. Make the alterations the same depth on the front and back seams of the sleeve, or rip the back seam and make such a change as is shown at (c), changing, if necessary, the location of the fulness so that the ease comes just at the bend of the elbow where it is needed. Turn up the sleeve to the proper length, which should be well below the wrist, as a short sleeve in a coat, unless it is intended to be short, is always awkward.

24.   Fitting Model on Slender Figure.—In Fig. 3 are shown types of alterations frequently necessary when fitting a coat on a more slender figure.   Notice in view (a) how a tuck has been pinned in

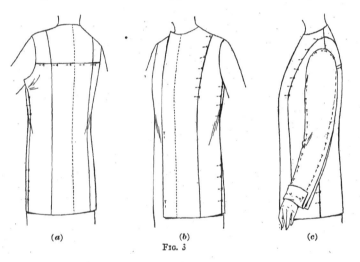

(a)   (b)   (c)
Fig. 3

across the back to raise it.   This change should be made when the back appears long and the back armhole seems to stand away from the figure.   Make this tuck as deep as is desirable, even though it may seem to bring the armhole too high up under the arm, as indicated, as the armhole can readily be trimmed out to the proper size after you first dispose of any excess fulness at the under arm. Pin this in at the seam, as illustrated, graduating the alteration to nothing as it approaches the waist line, which is not usually changed unless fashion favors the "pinched-in" effect.   Pin the seam in slightly at the hip, if required.

When these changes have been accomplished, notice the front of the coat.   It may be that there will be a slight bulge just above the bust line approaching the shoulder line, but the alteration shown in view (*b*) will take care of this. Graduate the depth of the fold to nothing toward the bust line and toward the top, provided the shoulder line is of the correct length. If it is too long, rip it and make a change at the side-front seam, duplicating this change in the length of the shoulder line on the side-back seam.

In considering the sleeve for such a type, make alterations as shown in view (*c*); that is, on both the front and back seams. Change the length of the sleeve and the position of the elbow fulness, too, if necessary.

25. Uses of a Muslin Model.—A fitted model for a coat is used as any other muslin model would be; that is, as a guide in the actual cutting of the garment. After ripping the fitted model apart and marking the changes made in fitting, press it carefully. You now have a pattern that fits you, so if the cloth for your suit is cut over exactly the same lines and is accurately basted and stitched together, it should fit you perfectly. The improvement in the appearance of a coat made with a muslin model over one made without this aid is easily seen; in fact, it is often impossible to obtain a satisfactory effect without the use of a fitted muslin guide pattern.

However, even with this extra precaution, there are certain subtle changes that may be required in fitting the actual coat, so each seam and edge must be carefully noted, and, if necessary, altered and evened to produce perfection.

CUTTING THE GARMENT

26. Sponging or Shrinking the Suit Fabric.—With a properly fitted pattern on hand, turn your attention to the cutting of the fabric with the aid of this pattern. Before cutting, however, make sure that the material has been properly sponged or shrunk, complete directions for such work being given in Chapter I, Arts. **27** to **31** inclusive.

27. Placing the Pattern.—If you are using a commercial pattern, the diagram accompanying it will help you, but the layout shown in Fig. 4 will be of additional aid.

Place the muslin sections in position for the coat, making sure that each is correct in relation to the grain of the material. It is a little more difficult to place a muslin pattern than a paper one, which is usually perforated to indicate its position on the fabric.   However, if you see that the straight, lengthwise threads of the muslin lie along the straight, lengthwise threads of the cloth under it, the coat will be correctly cut.

Arrange all the pattern pieces on the material before cutting in order to make sure that the nap of the material runs the same way in all of them; also, as shown, put the pattern pieces fairly close together but take every precaution to allow enough material so that the seams will be the proper width throughout.   Provide for an allowance of $\frac{3}{8}$ to $\frac{1}{2}$ inch for seams around the armhole, down the front closing of the coat, on the front facing, and entirely around the collar sections.   On all other cut edges, an allowance of at least 1 inch is required.

28. Marking the Pattern Lines.—With the pattern pieces in position, mark along the pattern lines first with tailors' chalk and then, when the garments are cut out and the pattern removed, with tailors' tacking.

29. Cutting the Coat Lining. The pattern used for cutting out the coat material is also used for cutting out the lining, but the lining material is cut a little larger on all seam edges, so that when in

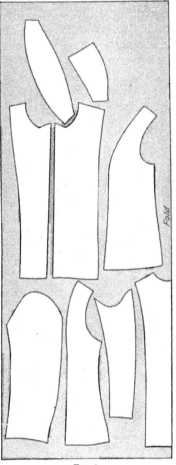

Fig. 4

place, it will be full enough not to tear apart nor to draw the coat when worn.) Before cutting out the lining, pin the two back sections of the coat pattern together, seam lines meeting, so that the back lining may be cut all in one piece.   Place the pattern pieces so that the waist or bust lines, as well as the elbow line of the sleeve pattern, are on the same grain of the material, as directed for cutting out the coat. The front section of the lining may be omitted, because the facing comes so far over that if the side section of the front is cut 1½ to 2 inches wider on the front edge, it will be wide enough to reach to the facing. To allow for a tuck in the center back of the lining, place the center-back line of the back-pattern piece ¾ to 1 inch from the fold of the material. This tuck will provide freedom through the shoulder and thus prevent the lining from tearing out.

Cut the sleeve with the elbow line on a crosswise thread of the material and with a 1½-inch seam allowance at the top, so that the lining will not draw when it is in place.

THE FOUNDATION OF THE COAT

30. After the coat material and the lining are cut out, give attention to the foundation of the coat. By those engaged in the tailors' trade, this is referred to as the "coat makings," and includes the muslin or canvas interfacing used on the inside of the coat to assist in making the garment take on a "tailored look." Every part of this foundation must be carefully made and correctly shaped if the finished coat is to have desirable tailored lines.

The usual tailored coat, developed at the present time, is made with a foundation of muslin only, although some tailors prefer an interfacing of linen canvas of the softest quality. You may follow the plan that seems best suited to the demands of Fashion, to your needs and your ability, as well as to the time that you can give to the making. Both methods are given here.

31. **Interfacings.**—To fulfil its mission, a coat foundation must be pliable and must "set" well on the figure after it is worn. This means, then, that it should be so constructed as to mold itself into the outer coat and not be apparent from the outside. For the main part of such a foundation, very soft, thoroughly shrunken unbleached muslin or the softest quality of all-linen canvas should be employed. The most desirable kind for this purpose is generally 36 inches wide. For a coat of the length shown in Fig. 1, 1 yard of canvas or muslin will be sufficient for a foundation, a three-quarter or a full-length coat requiring a piece as long as the coat is to be.

Fig. 5 (a) indicates the shape of the various pieces used for interfacing. The section *a* will provide a foundation for the fronts, *b* for the back armhole, *c* for the back-neck line, while *d* is cut with the aid of the collar pattern.

32. Preparing the Interfacing Pattern.—To prepare the front portion *a*, make use of the two front-pattern sections by pinning them together for the length of the seam, with shoulder lines even, and drawing on them a line that will indicate the size and shape desired for the interfacing. Start this line at the under-arm seam about 3 or 4 inches below the armhole. Continue it over toward the lengthwise seam, curving it downward for a space of 2 or 3 inches; then, using the seam line as a guide, continue the line to the bottom of the pattern so that the width from the center front to the edge of the interfacing is a seam's width wider than the front-pattern piece.

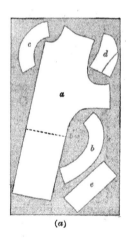

(a)   (b)   (c)

Fig. 5

To give body to the back armhole, mark on the back-pattern piece a section about 3 to 4 inches wide, having it follow the curve of the armhole. Prepare a facing for the back-neck line in the same manner, tracing this, the front you have just marked, and the armhole facing through to a piece of paper placed underneath the pattern. Trace in the bust line, the waist line, and the front seam of the front-pattern section, as well as the outline of each of the interfacing pieces.

33.   Cutting the Interfacing.—As in Fig. 5 (*a*), place the patterns on a half-bias grain of the muslin, which has first been thoroughly shrunk. Also, cut a foundation for the bottom of the sleeves, indicated at *e*, if you care to use one, making this the width of the sleeve and from 3 to 4 inches deep. Mark around each of the pattern pieces and mark also the bust line, the waist line, and the position of the front-seam line.

34. Follow the same plan if you wish to use linen canvas instead of muslin, but cut the two front sections of the coat separately and sew them together. If a still further tailored appearance is desirable, use muslin to reinforce the canvas. In such case, the canvas is treated separately, a coat of this kind naturally requiring much more time for its completion. To cut these muslin sections, follow Fig. 5 (*b*), which shows how the side and front pieces of the coat pattern are laid together in order to cut the extra muslin section for reinforcing the fronts. The dotted lines at *a* and *b* indicate the outline of the muslin.

To prepare these fronts, fold a piece of muslin 18 inches square diagonally across from a point 3 inches below one corner to a point 3 inches above the opposite corner; then cut along the diagonal line to produce pieces exactly the same in size, and arrange the pieces thus formed so that the straight edges are together, as at *c*. On these lay the front-pattern pieces, placing them so that their side-seam edges meet from the shoulder to the bust line. With the pattern pieces in this position, cut the muslin along the under-arm line from the bottom to the armhole, around the armhole to the shoulder line, and along the shoulder line to within $\frac{3}{4}$ inch of the neck line. Then, as shown by the dotted line, cut on a downward slant, as at *a*, rounding off the bottom of the muslin, as shown. Finally, slash the muslin, as from *d* to *e*, so that it can be lapped over to fit the canvas when the canvas is sewed together.

In addition to these muslin fronts, cut two circular pieces of muslin from $3\frac{1}{2}$ to $4\frac{1}{2}$ inches in diameter, as shown at *f*. Apply these pieces at point *e* of the bust line to hold the center of the foundation of the coat together, to prevent it from stretching and pulling out of shape, and to give strength to that portion of the garment.

35.   Armhole and Sleeve Pads.—This type of coat makes it necessary to supply small pads for the armhole and sleeve tops, so cut and finished that they will fill in the hollow at the front of the armhole and prevent the coat from falling in or sagging at that point.

Fig. 5 (c) shows the pads in detail and also indicates how the underarm sections of the pattern are laid together on a piece of cambric, from which foundation pieces for the pads are cut.   The width of these pads varies with the size of the figure, but the relative proportion of the pad to the pattern itself is shown when the pattern pieces are laid together.   At their greatest width, which is from a to b, these pads are wider than the pattern at any place.   The back part of each pad, as at c, is cut so that it will extend a trifle beyond the side seam of the back, as at d, and thus prevent any break at the seam.   The pad in front is cut off from 3 to 4 inches below the shoulder line, so as to avoid bulk at the top of the shoulder.

36.   Preparing the Armhole Pads.—Cut two pieces of cambric for the pads, making one from $\frac{1}{4}$ to $\frac{3}{8}$ inch narrower than the other.

Then place the smaller one on top of the larger.   Thus, the outer edge of the padding will decrease in thickness and there will be no ugly lines where it meets the coat.   Pin the two sections of the cambric together, as shown at e, and then quilt them with the padding-stitch, as shown at f.   In quilting these pieces, work from the upper side, taking the stitches back and forth, so that they will hold firmly, and running them through into the cambric at the under side.

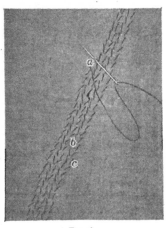

Fig. 6

37.   The Padding-Stitch Used for Quilting.—The stitch used for quilting is similar in effect to diagonal basting except that the stitches are much smaller than basting-stitches would be, that is, about $\frac{3}{8}$ inch long.   The method is illustrated in Fig. 6.

In taking each stitch, place the needle, as at a, so that the stitch underneath will be at direct right angles to the stitch on top.   When you have reached the edge of the section being quilted, do not turn your work, but take the next row of stitches toward you. The second row of stitches, as at *b*, will then slant in the opposite direction to the first, as at *c*, while the third row will duplicate the first, the fourth, the second, and so on.

38.   Preparing the Sleeve Pads.—With this quilting done, prepare the pads for the top of the sleeve. For each one, cut two thicknesses of cambric, as shown at *g* and *h*, Fig. 5 (*c*), making each of them one-half as long as the armhole measurement and about 4 inches wide, but cut the inside piece a trifle smaller than the outside one. Place the smaller one on top and then fold them together so that, when folded, they will be 2 inches wide.

CONSTRUCTING THE COAT

39.   Marking the Coat Pieces.—With all the materials cut out and the foundation ready, take up the actual construction of the coat. The first steps consist in mark-stitching all the pattern edges with reference to the notches on the pattern that you used for cutting your muslin guide as well as the changes in fitting made in the guide pattern. Mark the waist line, the bust line, the line indicating the turn-over portion of the collar, and the position of the fulness at the elbow of the lower- and upper-sleeve sections.

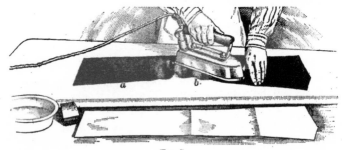

Fig. 7

40.   Shaping the Back of the Coat.—The tailored-suit coat, following as it does the dictates of Fashion, naturally changes in silhouette, sometimes being fitted and at other times straight in effect. The outline of a pattern for a straight coat will naturally omit the curves, which are a part of a more fitted style. For a semi-fitted coat, the center-back line may be curved slightly, but to accommodate this it is not necessary to cut the cloth to provide a seam; instead, you may place the center-back pattern piece on a fold as usual and then shape it by shrinking to make it conform to the lines of the pattern, taking out about ¾ inch of the center back at the waist line. To do this, mark the fold of the center back with a basting thread, as shown at *a*, Fig. 7. Then, with a brush, dampen

FIG. 8

the wrong side of the material from a point within 6 to 8 inches of the neck line to 6 inches below the waist line.

After the material has been dampened, especially at the center, proceed to shrink it with an iron that is not too hot, working across from the outer edge toward the fold and down to the waist line. Draw the material toward the center, so that it will shape in, as at *b*, and continue to run the iron gently over the material; but do not press too hard, or the imprint of the iron will show on the material. After working in this way until the fulness is taken out above the waist, proceed to remove the fulness below the waist. To do this, begin at the lower edge of the piece and work up toward the waist line, as shown in Fig. 8, working in the same way as above the waist line and dampening as frequently as is necessary.

41. When the back has been carefully shaped, lay the center-back pattern piece *a*, Fig. 8, on the back portion *b*, in order to see whether it is shaped enough to conform to the center-back line. In this connection, a little stretching on the cut edge will help a great deal. If the pattern shows that not enough of the fulness has been taken out, dampen the material again and repeat the pressing until it does assume the shape of the pattern piece at the center-back line. Do not be discouraged if the desired result is not obtained in the first or second attempt. Sometimes the material will have

4 W I—18

to be dampened and pressed as many as three times before it will assume the correct shape.

As soon as the correct shape is secured, pin the pattern piece in place and mark-stitch the material all the way around the outer edge. Then trim the seam edges even.   Finally, clip the seam at the waist line as well as above and below it, as shown at *a*, Fig. 9, so that the seam will shape in satisfactorily when it is basted to the side-back portions.

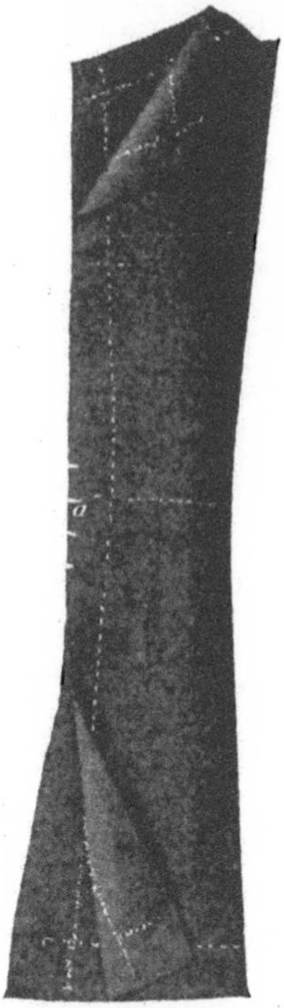

42. Basting the Sleeve. The next step in the construction of the coat consists in basting the sleeve. As shown in Fig. 10, place the two pieces of sleeve material so that the marks *a* and *b*, which indicate the points above and below the elbow where the fulness is to be held in, will meet the corresponding points on the underneath part.

With these marks pinned together, gather the fulness with small stitches. Pin the sleeve sections together so that the mark-stitched lines of the armhole, as well as those of the wrist, meet, and then

FIG. 9

FIG. 10

pin the seam from the armhole to the elbow and the wrist to the elbow, taking care that the sleeve seams are not stretched in any place.

With the pattern lines of the sleeves securely pinned, baste them carefully with moderately small stitches, keeping the basting directly in the mark-stitched lines, so that the correct seam line will be retained. This basting is only temporary, being used merely to determine whether the sleeve is of the proper length and width.

43. Putting Coat Together for First Fitting.—The coat is now ready to be put together for the first fitting. Therefore, baste together the side-front section and the center-front section of each front, being careful that the waist line, the bust line, and the shoulder lines meet exactly.   After attending to the front sections, baste the side-back sections to the center-back panel, using similar precautions regarding the various lines.

(a)   (b)

FIG. 11

Each of the four seams thus formed is to be finished with an open-welt seam.   Therefore, turn each seam allowance and baste it back, preparatory to making the open-welt seam, as at a, Fig. 11 (a), so that the seam will lie flat during the fitting.

44.   With the coat advanced to this stage, it is ready for the muslin or canvas sections of the coat foundation.   In putting these in the coat, place the marked seam line of the front interfacing directly underneath the seam line of the coat, the waist and bust lines matching.   Baste the armhole and neck-line facings across the back also with seam lines matching.   If canvas is used and there is a seam corresponding to the seam in the coat, arrange it in a similar manner, having the raw edges of the canvas seam on the side that will come next to the lining rather than next to the coat.   This is done to provide the smoothest possible effect on the right side.

Baste the canvas or muslin to the front sections of the coat with several rows of diagonal basting-stitches, as shown in Fig. 11 (a), starting the stitches at the waist line and running them up and down from this line so that the material will lie smooth on the interfacing. Turn the front-seam edges back over the foundation and baste them, as at b, in order that the width of the lap may be determined in the fitting.

45.   After all interfacing pieces have been attached to the coat material, baste together the shoulder seams, as at c, and also the under-arm seams, placing the seams on the right side, so that any necessary alterations can easily be made in the fitting.   Do not feel disappointed because the coat at this point seems to be a webwork of bastings; rather, be encouraged by the fact previously suggested that in careful basting and in the use of the flat-iron lies much of the success of tailored garments.

46.   First Fitting.—With the coat basted in the manner directed, you are ready for the first fitting.   To facilitate this work, it is well to have on hand a piece of tailors' chalk with which to mark any alterations that are necessary, for if these are accurately marked they can be made very readily after the garment is removed.

Slip the coat on carefully and adjust it to the figure, as in Fig. 11 (a), lapping the center-front lines and pinning them, as at d.   In adjusting the coat to the figure, take care to put it on so that it assumes the correct position across the back, across the front, at the neck, and at the waist line.   The reason for this precaution will be understood if it is remembered that the pattern is constructed from the bust line up and down.   In reality, the chief point to bear in mind in fitting the front of the coat is that it should "set" straight and easy around the bust.   It very often happens that a coat will appear slightly long just at the front edges.   Do not make any change in the garment because of this, as the tape that is applied later will draw up this edge a trifle.

47. Next, give attention to the shoulders. The coat may appear too full from the bust line to the shoulder. If this is the case, take it in slightly at the shoulder seam, fitting it rather close and shaping it so that it will appear snug and tight at this point. It is always well to remember that a graceful shoulder line is absolutely essential in a tailored garment. On the other hand, a shoulder that is straight stands out prominently from the figure and prevents the collar from fitting the neck as well as it should.

Notice the manner in which the coat laps at the bottom. If the amount of the lap increases as it approaches the bottom, take up a slight amount at the front shoulder near the armhole. On the other hand, if the coat separates at the bottom, let out the under-arm seam.

The first time the coat is fitted, it will doubtless appear a trifle loose around the armholes and at the under-arm seams, but this need not cause any alarm because there must be a certain amount of ease for the lining. The under-arm seam should appear on the figure as in Fig. 11 (a), but if it should drag or pull down, take it in a trifle at this time. In case the coat appears to be too snug under the arm, let the seam out enough to allow sufficient room for the lining and the foundation. Remember that the under-arm seam should be entirely free from the body, especially at the waist line, unless the waist line is definitely defined, and that an easy, graceful under-arm seam is a very important detail of a tailored suit. Mark the under-arm seam at this time with chalk in order to insure a true line for finishing.

48. In fitting the sleeve, which is the next detail to consider, take care to have it fit on the arm just as it will appear when it is sewed in place. To accomplish this, pin the sleeve in place at the top, as shown at e, Fig. 11 (a).

With the sleeve thus pinned, verify its length, taking care to have this accurate. It should not be so long as to have a clumsy appearance, but it should be long enough in the beginning to allow for the shortening up that will come through wearing. If the sleeve is too long at the armhole, turn in the surplus material, but be careful not to shorten it so much that the sleeve will draw and be uncomfortable when the elbow is bent and the hand brought up close to the face.

After the length of the sleeve has been definitely decided, mark with tailors' chalk where the sleeve is to be turned and also where it is to join the coat. If this is done in the first fitting, the basting lines may be put in and the sleeve basted in place before the second fitting.

49. A point that sometimes causes unnecessary alarm during the first fitting is the slight fulness that often occurs at the upper part of the sleeve, especially in the back. Much of this is required when the arm is brought forward, but if there appears to be too much fulness, it should be sponged and shaped out during the process of pressing rather than removed by cutting off the material from the back of the sleeve. In fact, no attempt should be made to trim off the back of the sleeve until it is definitely known just how much length will be required there.

If the sleeve is found to be too short from the shoulder to the elbow, it is best to lower the fulness at the elbow a trifle and then to fit the sleeve in below the elbow, so as to allow the turn in the arm to come where it should.

50. The back of the coat should appear in the first fitting as shown in Fig. 11 (*b*). It will be observed from this illustration that the coat should "set" correctly on the figure, that the shoulder line should shape into the shoulder, and that the sleeves should hang straight when they are properly fitted in place and the length at the top and the bottom has been determined.

Other points to be noted are the position of the crease that represents the fold at the center back, the markings that indicate the bust line of the pattern, the waist line, the width of the panel, the fit of the under-arm line, and lines *a* and *b*, which show where the fulness is held in at the elbow of the sleeve. At this time, too, verify the coat length previously decided on, making sure that it is becoming and in harmony with the length and fulness of the skirt with which it is to be worn.

51. Dissembling the Coat.—When every point in the first fitting has received attention, carefully remove the coat from the figure and strengthen all the chalk lines that indicate where alterations are to be made. Then proceed to *dissemble* the coat, as the operation of taking it apart is called by tailors. Remove the sleeve from the armhole and gently rip out the shoulder and under-arm bastings; then take out the basting-stitches that hold the underfacing and the coat pieces together and separate these pieces, provided the interfacing is of both canvas and muslin. If either has been used alone, merely loosen the bastings near the seam lines before proceeding with the stitching of the seams.

52. Stitching.—After the coat is dissembled, make the necessary alterations; and, after these are made and the coat is rebasted, proceed with the stitching. From the right side, stitch the side-front seams and the side-back seams to form open-welt seams, as previously mentioned. If a welt seam is preferred, remove the basting from the right side of the coat, and then stitch the seams on the pattern lines and turn and baste on the right side. Of course, other types of seams may be used in stitching a tailored coat, depending on your own preference. However, all stitching on a tailored garment must harmonize. After these seams have been stitched, remove the bastings and press each seam very carefully so as not to stretch it, especially from the waist line to the shoulder, for as will be observed from Fig. 11 (a), the seam edge of the side-front section comes considerably on the bias and it is therefore likely to stretch unless it is handled carefully.

53. If the coat is to have a breast or side pocket, proceed at this time to make it. It may be a stand, a welt, or a flap pocket, directions for making all of these being given in Chapter III. Carefully mark its position on the left-side front or lower right side, and after completely finishing it press it thoroughly.

Then join the shoulder and under-arm seams on the wrong side and stitch them. Finally, clip the edges of each of these seams so that they will lie perfectly flat, and dampen and press them well.

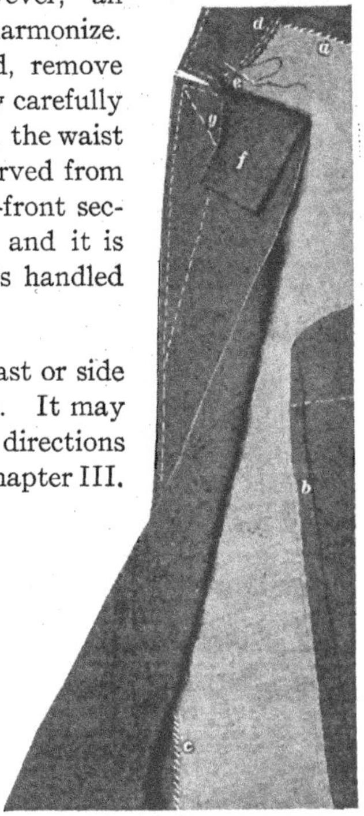

FIG. 12

54. Preparing the Foundation.—If muslin has been used alone for the interfacing, trim off the edges so that each comes to the seam line and not beyond it. If you used canvas also, stitch up the seams, press them open, and trim them, as well as the seam allowances for the armhole, under-arm, and shoulder line. Slip these trimmed edges under the pressed-open seams, and catch the raw edges of the seams to the muslin or canvas with loose whipping-stitches, as at *a*, Fig. 12. The interfacing will then be held in place without a drawn appearance. For further security, place a row of basting-stitches, strengthened by an occasional back-stitch, through the interfacing and a single thickness of the side-front seam allowance after the seam has been pressed open, as at *b*, fastening it to the seam edge that is turned toward the front. Replace the bastings around the neck edge and the armhole line, keeping the interfacing smooth and straight.

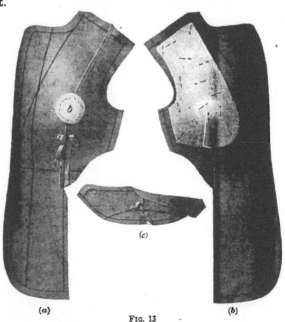

(c)

(a)   Fig. 13   (b)

55. If the plan you are following requires the use of a reinforcement for the canvas, place the coat on a hanger to keep it from becoming wrinkled and then proceed to prepare the canvas and muslin foundation. Sew up the side-front seams, press them open, and then trim the edges to within $\frac{1}{4}$ inch of the stitching, as shown at *a*, Fig. 13 (*a*). Over the bust point of each of these seams, lay a small circle of muslin, as at *b*, and baste it in position. With this done, place a second section of muslin over the front of the foundation, making it of the shape and size indicated in view (*b*) and having it come just inside the armhole line of the canvas and not quite to the seam line on the shoulder. Stitch these extra pieces in place, but first mark with a piece of tailors' chalk lines corresponding to *a*, *b*, and *c*, Fig. 14 (*a*), making these lines $\frac{1}{2}$ to $\frac{3}{4}$ inch apart.

After these lines are marked, turn the canvas over so that the inside will be uppermost, as in view (*b*), and then, as shown at *a* and *b*, chalk this side with lines about 1 inch apart, being careful to place the lines on the canvas in the same position as illustrated here.

As a careful study of Fig. 14 will reveal, the chalk lines on the wrong side of the foundation do not correspond in position with those on the right side. Those on the canvas are on just the opposite part of the front to those on the muslin, so that together they cover the entire piece of muslin. This arrangement permits of doing a part of the quilting, which is the next step in the making of the foundation, on one side, and the remainder on the other, and thus prevents the foundation from losing its shape or from being stitched irregularly.

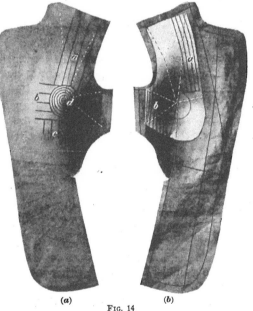

(*a*)   (*b*)
Fig. 14

56. The first step in the quilting consists in padding the small round pieces that were placed between the canvas and the muslin. Begin on the right side at point *d*, Fig. 14 (*a*), and then, with padding-stitches, work from this point around and around until the entire piece is covered. These padding-stitches should be about $\frac{3}{8}$ inch long and in rows about $\frac{1}{4}$ inch apart. Next, with the right side still uppermost, quilt with the padding-stitch on all the chalk lines and half way between them. When all the chalk lines on the right side and the spaces between them are covered, turn the foundation over and quilt on the opposite side in the same manner. After one front has been thus quilted, prepare the other one in exactly the same way.

57. Pressing the Foundations.—When the foundations, which in this stage of the development are called *bust forms*, have been quilted, they are ready to be pressed. Use considerable care in pressing them, for the shaping of the foundation has much to do with the "set" of the coat. In fact, some tailors regard the pressing of the bust forms as one of the very important points in the making of a tailored suit, since, during this process, the line from the shoulder to the waist, which must be absolutely smooth and graceful, is shaped.

To get the best results in pressing bust forms, a tailors' cushion should be used. Pressing them carefully over such a cushion will not pull out the point that is sometimes prominent at the bust line, but, rather, will have a tendency to remove this point and produce a line that runs down gracefully from the shoulder to the waist and "sets" straight and easy all the way. In pressing such a form, or foundation, lay it right side up over the tailors' cushion and press it all very carefully, rounding it slightly over the circle of muslin that is used

Fig. 15

to form the center of the foundation, and being extremely careful not to misplace the bust line by making the line from the shoulder to the bust either too long or too short. When the bust forms have been properly shaped by pressing, pin them up by the upper edge or the shoulder seam and allow them to dry thoroughly, so that their shape will be permanently retained.

58. Preparing the Collar.—You are now ready to begin the preparation of the collar. Stitch the bias seam at the center back in the material, and then press this seam open and lay the seam edge of the interfacing directly over the pressed-open seam. Pin the interfacing to the material, as shown in Fig. 15, and then baste

around the lower edge and through the line indicating the stand
portion, as at *a*.   Next, with the sewing machine, quilt the lower
section from *b* to *c*, using the same kind of silk thread as is used for
stitching the garment and making the rows ⅛ inch apart and as even
and neat as possible.

With this done, quilt the interfacing to the material by means
of padding-stitches, working from the center-back seam and the break
line toward the edges.   Make one row of the stitches, taking care
to have each stitch catch the cloth of the collar but not come entirely
through it; then turn the work and make the second row about
¼ inch from the first.   Continue in this way until the required surface
is covered, having the direction of the stitches alternate in each row.

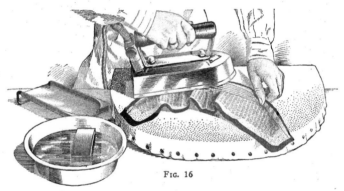

Fig. 16

59.   Shaping the Collar.—With the interfacing quilted in place,
the collar is ready to be shaped.   It should be remembered that the
collar of a coat is one of its important features and that the proper
fit of this part has much to do with the appearance of the entire coat.
This is emphasized by the fact that many custom tailors, in advertising their work, use such slogans as, "The coat that fits snug around
the neck," "The collar that fits the neck," etc.   They do not mean
by this that only the collar fits properly, but that every part of the
garments they make fits correctly.   Then, too, just as well-groomed
men are particular about the fit of the collar and shoulders of their
coats, so should women be careful about these points in their tailored
suits.

60.   The pressing and the shaping of the collar demand extreme
care.   To get correct results, lay the collar out carefully on the press
block and dampen the machine-stitched portion with a wet brush.

Then, as in Fig. 16, hold the collar with a moderately hot iron and stretch the neck edge around while the iron is in place.   This part of the collar must be stretched to assume almost a half circle, but care should be taken not to run the iron beyond the machine-stitched

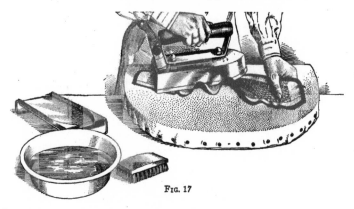

FIG. 17

lines, as only the stand portion of the collar is to be shaped at this time.   Run the iron over the stitching several times in order to dry the material and to make certain that the stand is shaped well.

61.   After the stand portion is shaped, turn the collar around as in Fig. 17 and shape the quilted, or collar, portion.   To do this, hold the collar at one end with the left hand, thumb on top, and with the other hand run the iron gently over the collar, stretching the outside

FIG. 18

carefully.   The next step in shaping the collar consists in pressing the stand portion in position.   This is done as shown in Fig. 18; that is, by turning it back over the quilted part of the collar and pressing on the break line.   When the pressing has been completed, the collar should be similar in shape to the one shown in Fig. 19. After it has been pressed and fitted, place a chalk mark outside the padding-stitches, as shown, to mark the outer edge of the canvas, which must be trimmed away when the exact line has been determined.

FIG. 19

62. Preparing the Sleeves.—In making a sleeve, first stitch up the inside seam and press it open. Then, in order to prevent the seam from drawing and to permit it to shape to the arm, clip its edges as at *a*, *b*, and *c*, Fig. 20. Next, place the bias interfacing over the sleeve as shown, taking care to have it extend beyond the

FIG. 20

seam line of the under-arm section, as at *d*. When the interfacing is properly placed, baste it diagonally through the center and then all around the edge so as to hold it securely in place. Next, as shown in Fig. 21 (*a*), turn the lower edge of the sleeve up over the interfacing on the line that was marked for the lower edge of the sleeve in the first fitting, pin this turned edge in place, and then baste it. Then, as shown in view (*b*), turn the material of the under-arm portion of the sleeve over the interfacing edge that extends beyond the seam line, as at *d*, Fig. 20. The interfacing is extended in this way so that the upper portion of the sleeve may lap over the under portion. After this is done, overcast the raw edge of the material to the interfacing, as in Fig. 22 (*a*), taking care that the stitches do not draw and that they do not extend through to the right side. Then miter the corners, and, as at *a* and *b*, overhand them with a silk thread

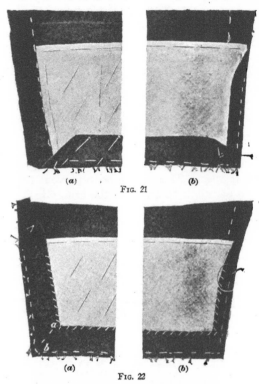

(*a*)   (*b*)

FIG. 21

of a color to match the suit. Also, overhand the raw edge around the sleeve on the under‑arm sleeve section, as shown in view (*b*).

63. After the interfacing is thus secured in place and the lower edge is in position, proceed to stitch the outside of the sleeve, provided stitching is desired. Sometimes stitching is placed on the sleeve in cuff effect; sometimes, it is placed merely at the bottom of the sleeve; and sometimes, if Fashion decrees, it may be cuff deep and in lines $\frac{1}{4}$ to $\frac{1}{2}$

(*a*)   (*b*)

FIG. 22

inch apart. However, the two kinds of stitching most frequently employed for a woman's tailored coat are those shown in Fig. 23 (*a*) and (*b*).

64. After the sleeve has been stitched, it is next in order to baste the outside seam and the joining of the

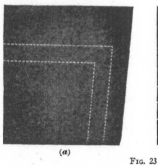

(*a*)

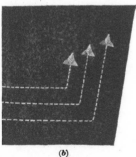

(*b*)

FIG. 23

lower, or cuff, portion. First, pin the mark-stitching together at a point that indicates where the elbow fulness is to be adjusted, as at *a*, Fig. 24; then pin up and down on the seam from this point. Proceed to baste the seam, basting downwards, as at *b*, from the armhole to the top of the cuff. Clip the top of the cuff, as at *c*, so that the seam will lie flat. Then remove the pins that were placed to hold the lower edge of the sleeve or cuff portion, and bring the edge *d* over and fell it down to the material, as at *e*, so that the cuff joining will show an overlap on the right side. Use silk thread to join these edges and make the stitches by hand, having them small and close together. Next, stitch the seam, beginning at the top of the cuff portion and stitching to the top of the sleeve or armhole

FIG. 24

line. Then, press the seam open over the sleeve board so that the rest of the sleeve will not become wrinkled

65. The sleeve is now ready to be prepared for the armhole.

FIG. 25

Therefore, gather the upper edge, using two rows of gathering-stitches, and draw the material and the thread until this edge is the same in size as the armhole of the coat. Then, from the wrong side, directly over the gathering threads, dampen the material and shrink out the fulness in the manner shown in Fig. 25. In doing this, hold the fulness gently with the fingers and lift the iron lightly over the material so as to shrink the fulness more by steaming than by actual pressing.

66.   Basting the Lining in the Sleeve.—After shrinking the fulness out of the upper part of the sleeve, prepare the lining by basting both seams and then stitching and pressing them.

To put the lining in the sleeve, turn both sleeve and lining wrong side out, and place the two side by side with the inside seam edges of each coming together, as in Fig. 26.' Baste them together, beginning

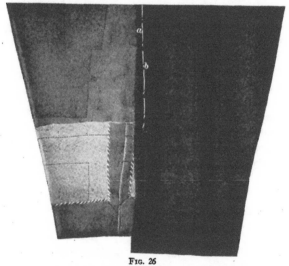

FIG. 26

at the top of the sleeve and basting through the seam allowance of the sleeve and the lining, as at a, down to the sleeve opening, which has been previously finished.   Use rather long basting-stitches and an occasional back-stitch, as at b.

A sleeve lining fastened in this way has an advantage over one that is secured only at the top and the bottom in that it is not likely to be pulled out of place in putting on and taking off the coat.

When this seam is basted, turn the sleeve right side out so that the lining is inside, and, to hold the lining securely, baste across the sleeve three times—at the elbow line, midway between the elbow and the lower edge of the sleeve, and about 3 inches from the top of the sleeve, having the stitches catch both lining and sleeve. Finally, turn the lining along the lower edge at least $\frac{1}{4}$ to $\frac{3}{4}$ inch from the lower edge of the sleeve, and fell it down carefully with medium-close, neat stitches, using silk thread of a color that matches the lining.

67. Placing Foundation Inside of Coat.—Provided you have used the canvas foundation reinforced with muslin, it should be secured permanently in the coat at this time. First, baste the canvas fronts, or bust forms, in position. To do this, pin the waist line of the foundation to the waist line of the coat and pin the center-front lines of each together, pinning up and down from the waist line; then gently smooth the material over the foundation, pinning it in place and taking every precaution to prevent wrinkles from forming in either the foundation or the material. When these fronts are pinned securely, baste every part of them very carefully, as shown in Fig. 27, so that the coat will not slip out of position in any place. Before securing the foundation in position, trim away the seam allowance so that the edges of the foundation just meet at the seam line. Slip these under the seam allowances and whip them in position as in the case of the canvas or muslin foundation used alone, shown at a, Fig. 12.

Fig. 27

68. Provided you are using an interlining for warmth, whether of Canton flannel or lamb's wool, insert it in the same manner, cutting it so that its edges come to the seam lines of the coat proper and whipping or catch-stitching it in place with the same stitches that hold the foundation.

In order to have the turn of the lapel smooth and trim, it is necessary to join the foundation to the cloth of the coat from the turn of the lapel out to its edges. Make this joining by means of the padding-stitch, working from the canvas side, but being sure to catch each stitch through to the coat fabric. Start the stitches just on the turn and continue the lines until the triangular section, which forms the lapel, is completely covered.

69. Taping the Fronts and the Collar.—When the foundation, whether of muslin, canvas, or a combination of the two, is secured in the coat, the fronts of the coat are ready to be taped. Taping is done to produce firm, true edges and to prevent them from stretching.

As a rule, a shrunken linen tape ⅜ inch wide is used for this purpose.

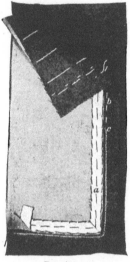

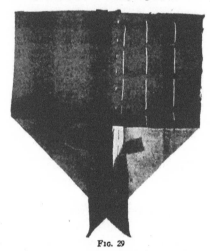

FIG. 28   FIG. 29

To tape the fronts, first baste the tape around the pattern line on the interfacing, as at *a*, Fig. 28. Hold the tape easy in all places with the exception of a 3-inch space just below the waist line; here, hold it firm to prevent the coat from having a stretched appearance at this point. To tape the collar, proceed in the same way, holding the tape easy, but not loose, all around the collar and keeping the tape just inside the line marked for the outside edge of the collar.

Be careful to miter the tape neatly at each corner. Then, with silk thread, whip both edges of the tape, keeping the stitches in the interfacing moderately loose, so that they will not appear drawn nor show on the outside of the front or collar. These stitches are permanent and always hold the tape in position, thus insuring a true, firm edge that will not stretch out of shape.

70. Applying the Front Facings.—With the taping done, place the front facings over the right side of the fronts of the coat and baste along the outside of the tape with ⅛-inch stitches, as at *b*, Fig. 28, leaving free the neck edges where they are to join the collar. Then stitch just outside the basting-stitches, as at *c*. Next, trim the seam thus formed in the manner shown in Fig. 29; that is, trim one seam edge to within a scant ¼ inch of the stitching and the other edge a generous ¼ inch, so that the thickness of the seam edge will be evenly distributed. Now, turn the seam allowance so that all thicknesses lie flat against the tape and whip the cloth to the tape with small stitches, as shown at *c*, Fig. 12, thus insuring a flat, sharp edge.

Next, turn the facing to the right side, smooth out the corners carefully, and place a row of small basting-stitches from the waist line up to the end of the lapel and then from the waist line down to the bottom of the coat and around to the end of the facing section.

Fig. 30

71. Second Fitting.—The second fitting is more exacting than the first and should therefore receive greater care. First, put the coat on the figure properly, being careful to have it come well up in the back and to "set" square on the shoulders. Then, at the center front, lap it as much as it will be lapped when it is worn, and pin it securely. Pin the center back of the collar to the center-back line of the coat, as in Fig. 30, and continue to pin around each side from the center back to the center front, taking care to keep the break line of the collar up close to the neck.

When the collar has been securely pinned to the coat, turn it down, as in Fig. 31, so that it will lie flat and smooth. If the chest of the person for whom the coat is intended is flat, bring the collar pieces down in front a little below the mark-stitched collar line in order that the lapels may lie flat where they join the collar; and, even if the figure is not flat-chested, extend the edge of the collar beyond the pattern line, as a general rule, because each side of the collar usually stretches from $\frac{1}{4}$ to $\frac{3}{8}$ inch.

FIG. 31

When the collar is in place, put the sleeves in, turning in the upper edge of each and pinning it in place, as shown in Fig. 30. Mark with chalk the point of the sleeve that comes opposite the shoulder seam of the coat, so that when the coat is removed and the sleeve is to be basted in, there will be no difficulty in determining accurately the position that it should have. Also, as shown in Fig. 31, put a chalk mark around the armhole of the coat to indicate just where the line of the sleeve should come in order to give a good line around the arm.

Another factor that demands attention in the second fitting is the length of the coat. Therefore, before removing the coat from the figure, turn the lower edge at the proper place and pin it securely, remembering the caution given as to the correct length and taking care that the garment is not even the least bit longer in the back than in the front, unless, of course, a definite difference is desired.

Mark with chalk the position of the buttons, also the depth of the opening of the under-arm seam, provided it is desired to have this seam open for part of its length.

72. Covering the Collar Foundation.—After all points that require attention in the second fitting have been completed, remove the coat, take out the sleeves, and mark the turn at the bottom of

the coat with basting-stitches.   Then proceed to attach the collar.
First, trim off the excess interfacing on the marked line; then
overhand the stand part to the coat with silk thread, using very close
overhanding-stitches.   Next, carefully mark the center back of the
upper collar piece, or collar facing, and pin its right side to the material side of the collar proper.   Begin to pin directly over the seam of
the collar, pinning carefully with several pins and stretching the
upper collar portion, or facing, slightly but evenly so that it will be
tight, but not so tight as to draw in
any place.

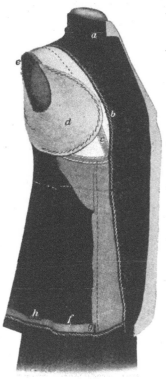

When the collar material is pinned,
baste the outer edge, and then stitch
just outside the interfacing edges.
Finally, trim the seam edges and turn
the collar over to the right side.

73. Turning and Felling the Fac-
ings.—Having turned the front facings
right side out carefully and evenly,
and having brought the edge of the
collar and that of the facing together,
as at *a*, Fig. 32, turn the raw edges
of the collar in carefully from the
shoulder line to the front and baste
in position as at *d*, Fig. 12.   Now
whip the free edge of the neck-line
seam flat to the interfacing, as at *e*,
Fig. 12.

When this is done, bring the front
facing section *f* up so that it lies flat
against the coat and turn in its edge *g*
to meet the turned edge of the collar.
Then proceed to join these turned
edges with very fine slip-stitches.
This slip-stitching process, known as

FIG. 32

stowing in the tailoring trade, packs the edges together closely so
that the joining is firm and scarcely visible.

After these edges are stowed together, whip the free, or neck, edge
of the collar and the inside edge of the facing to the foundation with
diagonal basting-stitches, as at *b*, Fig. 32.

74. Padding the Coat.—The seam edge of the dart in the canvas, provided you used canvas, should now be covered in the manner shown at *c*, Fig. 32. For this purpose, use a bias strip of cambric ¾ inch wide and whip its edge to the canvas directly over the seam. Next, place the padding pieces prepared according to the directions in Art. **36,** under the arm, as shown at *d*, and secure them to the canvas and muslin with diagonal basting-stitches, placing these all around the edge and making them loose enough not to draw in any place. As has been stated previously, these padding pieces are not to be employed unless a foundation of canvas and muslin is being used. After the padding pieces have been secured in place, trim them around the armhole so that the line of the padding comes exactly even with that of the armhole, and overcast the entire armhole, as at *e*.

75. Inserting Strip at Coat Bottom.—The next step in the making of the tailored coat consists in putting a strip of light-weight muslin or cambric around the inside of the bottom of the coat, as at *f*, Fig. 32. For this, cut a bias strip 2 inches wide and long enough to go around the entire lower edge of the coat so that its lower edge rests on the marked line that indicates the bottom of the coat.

Attach this strip to the interfacing, as at *g*, and then to the seam of the coat with cross-stitches, as at *h*, running it around the lower edge of the coat and fastening it at similar places on the other front. With this strip in place, turn the lower edge of the coat up over it, turning on the mark-stitched line, and then catch the edge of the hem to the muslin with diagonal basting-stitches, as shown. The purpose of this strip is to hold the lower edge of the coat firm and to give it a little extra weight.

76. Outside Stitching and Pressing.—Fig. 33 shows the way in which the inside of the back of the coat should appear before the lining is put in; that is, with the padding in place at the back of the arm, the bias piece of the interfacing material at the back of the neck, and the facing of the front section extending for a little distance over the back. You understand, of course, that this coat is built upon a canvas and muslin foundation. If muslin or soft canvas alone had been used, the padding pieces at the armholes would not have been necessary.

As will be observed, the mark-stitching at the waist line remains although all the other bastings are removed. These mark-stitches are retained so that the lining may be correctly placed, for the waist line of the lining must correspond with that of the coat.

If stitching is to be added to the outside edge of the coat, it should be done while the coat is in this condition.   Beginning at the break line of the lapel, stitch around the collar to the same point on the opposite side, and then from this break line down to the bottom of the coat on each side.   Where the stitching breaks at the bottom of the lapel, take care to have the new stitching come up well under the lapel and to put one row directly over the other, so that the joining will not be visible.

If each side of the coat is stitched down in this way, there will be no possibility of its drawing, as would be the case if one side were stitched up from the bottom and the other side down from the lapel. This plan makes it possible, also, to do all the stitching from the right side and thus to produce more attractive work, especially since the stitching must be done through several thicknesses of material.

When the stitching has been completed, press the coat carefully, particularly the lower edge, the body seams, and the collar, dampening the material with a wet cloth

Fig. 33

and pressing gently with the iron, so as to leave no impression.

77. Inserting the Sleeves.—In putting the sleeves in the coat, first baste them in, following the marks that were made in the second fitting, so that they will be in the correct position.   In doing this, use short basting-stitches in order to indicate whether or not each sleeve is in the correct position; loose sititches will not show the little defects or wrinkles that might appear at the armhole.

When both sleeves are basted in place, try the coat on to make certain that they are exactly right. If they are in the proper place and fit correctly, stitch them in, stitching outside the basting lines all the way around. Of course, if the sleeves are not put in correctly, they must be made right before they are stitched in place.

When the sleeves are stitched in, steam and press the armhole seams very carefully, so that a true line may be obtained and each sleeve may look as if it were set into the armhole, rather than over it. To do this pressing, place the coat over the pressboard so that the sleeve seam edge at the armhole is up and push the sleeve out of the way so that it will not interfere. Now turn the armhole seam into the sleeve portion and press again.

After this seam is pressed, turn the coat right side out, pull each sleeve, in turn, over the point of the board, place a damp cloth over it, and steam and press the entire sleeve.

78. Padding the Top of Sleeves.—In a tailored suit in which a canvas-and-muslin foundation is used, the shoulder and armhole seams are heavy because of the extra material. On account of this weight, the coat material, which is of only one thickness, will fall limp from the armhole seam, especially across the top of the sleeve, back of the shoulder seam, and will thus produce wrinkles in the sleeve. These wrinkles will make the sleeve appear too full, even though the armhole seam is absolutely free from wrinkles or excessive fulness. To overcome such a defect in a coat, prepare for each sleeve two oblong pieces of cambric, sewing these together with the padding-stitch after folding as described in Art. **38.** Then, with the armhole seam turned out, place the cambric pad directly over the seam, as in Fig. 34, and with long, medium-loose stitches catch the edge of the cambric flat to the armhole seam. When the sleeve is turned right side out, the padding should roll up easily but close to the seam, and should hold the shoulder out in a round, graceful line.

Fig. 34

The rounding shoulder of a man's coat shows the roll that a tailored coat should have, this pleasing effect being produced by padding the armhole properly. Padding such as this is invariably omitted, however, when the narrow, short-shouldered effect is in vogue.

79. Pressing and Making Buttonholes.—At this stage of the work, press the coat thoroughly, using a medium-damp cloth and a press block or cushion, and taking care to prevent any shine from appearing and to avoid the formation of wrinkles. Next, mark for the buttonholes and put them in, following the directions given in Arts. 16 to 31 inclusive, Chapter II.

80. **Placing the Lining in the Coat.**—Baste the tuck in place at the center back of the lining and stitch it on the wrong side from the waist line to the bottom only; or, if preferred, omit the stitching altogether. With the tuck pressed, place the back section of the lining so that its waist line comes on the back waist line of the coat, and pin it in position. Then, with long diagonal stitches, baste along the waist line and up and down from this point for about 2 inches on each side of the center-back line. Next, run a line of basting-stitches along the shoulder seams, around the armhole, and down the side seams, in each case about 2 inches from the seam line.

With the back portion of the lining basted in position, pin the waist line of the front pieces to the waist line of the coat, lap the under-arm seams of the front over the under-arm seams of the back, and turn under the allowance made for the front under-arm seams. Pin these securely and then baste the waist line and these seams with long diagonal stitches. Next, turn under the front edges and baste them. Bring the upper part of the front lining up around the arm-hole and shoulder line, and baste it in place in the same manner as the under-arm seam. Then, turn under the armhole seam allowance made on the sleeve lining and pin and baste this over the coat lining.

81. Some tailors prefer to stitch the under-arm and shoulder seams of the lining before placing the lining in the coat. If you follow this plan, press the seams after stitching and then put the lin-ing in place, pinning it carefully. After this, with a medium-length basting-stitch and an occasional back-stitch and with silk thread to match the coat, sew the under-arm and shoulder seam allowances of the lining to the corresponding seam edges of the coat in order to hold the lining in place. To do this, reach up between the lining and the coat. At this point in either process, you are ready to finish off the lower edge of the lining. Turn the edge so that it will come about $\frac{3}{4}$ to $1\frac{1}{4}$ inches above the lower edge of the coat, the distance usually depending on the width of the turn of the coat material, and baste the lining along this edge, not directly on the turn, but at a slight distance from it.

When the lining has been basted so that it is in its proper position, secure it in place.   In securing it along the bottom of the coat, as well as along the lower part of the sleeves, take the stitches from $\frac{3}{8}$ to $\frac{1}{2}$ inch above the turned edge on the inside in order to give additional length to the lining and thus prevent it from appearing drawn or too short.   For this work, use a stitch that has the strength of a whipping-stitch, but that slips under the turned edge of the lining, as a slip-stitch, and is concealed.   For the armhole, use a close, even overhanding-stitch.

In securing the lining, use silk thread that matches the color of the lining; and, to insure neat stitches, use a medium-fine needle.

82.   As in dressmaking, the use of weights in tailoring helps to give an appearance of trimness not to be overlooked.   Use the flat weights in preference to the weighted tape, and cover each one carefully with the same material as is used for lining the coat.   Secure the weights in position, one at each side of the center front, just inside the front facing and two more at the back in line with the side seams.   Take as many stitches as seem necessary to hold the weights in proper position.

83.   Final Pressing and Finishing.—After the lining is secured in place, press the entire coat lightly from the right side, so as to press the lining in position.   Then press the lower part of the lining and the under-arm seams from the wrong side, using a dry press cloth over the lining and pressing carefully, at the same time adjusting the material every little while so that no wrinkles will appear on the right side.

After the pressing is done, put the coat on to verify the position of the buttons; then, sew the buttons on.

VARIATIONS OF THE TAILORED SUIT

THE BOYISH TAILLEUR

84.   From season to season, there is a variation not only in the silhouette of the tailored suit, but also in the method of making it. When fitted coats, severe in outline, are in vogue, the interfacings used must be such that they will help to keep the shape of the garment and do their part in the effect being stressed.   When Fashion decrees a less tailored outline, there is a corresponding change in the type of interfacing used; in fact, in some cases interfacing is entirely omitted or cut from a soft sheer muslin only.   At the same time, a knowledge of the making of a strictly tailored suit acquired through study of the preceding pages of this Chapter and the application of the principles described, will make it a simple matter for you to develop the less tailored forms of suits, for these do not approach the strictly tailored suit either in severity of effect or difficulty of making.

85. Description of Suit.—A youthful style, varying little in outward appearance from its severely tailored sister, is the boyish tailleur, or tailored suit, shown in Fig. 35.   The coat does not lap but is held together by link buttons.   The mannish notched collar has a certain appeal, while bound pockets add a trimming note quite in keeping with the general effect.   The outfit is completed by a two-piece skirt of a becoming length and width. This suit depends for its foundation on a single thickness of a very thin muslin, not much heavier than a firm cheesecloth.

86. Material and Pattern Requirements.—The pin-striped serges are particularly good for a suit of this type, although a plain twill material, tweed, or flannel is also suitable. Crêpe de Chine is an excellent choice for the lining.   You will need 3 yards of 54-inch material for the suit and 2 yards of silk for the lining.

FIG. 35

87. A plain box-coat pattern of the correct size and a two-piece skirt pattern are the only guides necessary for the cutting of the

suit; or, if you wish, you may develop the skirt without a pattern.
If your coat pattern laps, plan to turn back the extra width on the
center-front line before cutting your material.   For a large bust
measurement, purchase or prepare a pattern showing a dart at the
shoulder.

88.   Construction of Coat.—Cut the coat from firm muslin, fit
the muslin carefully, and use it as a pattern for cutting the cloth for
the coat.   Cut, baste, and fit the coat accurately and carefully.
If you wish, you may allow, in cutting the front sections, enough to
turn back for facings instead of applying the facings as separate
pieces.

Follow the suggestions already given for making, omitting all
interfacings with the exception of the front sections, which should
be cut from muslin over the lines of *a*, Fig. 5, view (*a*).   No taping
is necessary.

The steps in fitting are the same as for the strictly tailored suit,
as are also the placing of the lining and the finishing of the coat with
the exceptions of the seams, which, in this case, are stitched plain.
Make sure that your machine is in good condition for stitching, for
the seams must be straight and even if the effect is to be all that is
desired.

Directions for the making of the pockets are given in Chapter III,
and for the buttonholes in Chapter II.

89.   To finish the bottom of the coat, turn and baste the hem in
the usual way.   Then, without turning in the upper raw edge, hem
it down to the coat, following the directions given in Art. **24,**
Chapter V, making the long stitch in this case much longer than
if you were hemming a skirt, in fact, at least 1½ inches.   The small
stitch, of course, should be very small so as to be invisible from the
right side.

Another method of finishing the bottom of the coat is to stitch
the lining by machine to the hem.   To do this, stitch the lining
pieces together, press carefully, and baste the lower edge to the
hem allowance of the coat, having the lining so placed that the row
of stitching will come at least 1½ inches above the turn of the coat and
the raw edges inside.   Replace the basting with stitching, turn the
lining up, and smooth it in place.   Now, baste the under-arm seam
allowances of the lining to the under-arm seam of the coat, and
finish the application of the lining by hemming it down to the front

facing and the neck edge. Bring the sleeve lining out over the body lining and sew it in place.

Careful and thorough pressing means quite as much in a coat of this kind as it does in the mannish tailored model, so be especially careful with each seam as well as with the finished coat.

THREE-PIECE SUIT

90. Description of Suit.—In Fig. 36 is shown a suit consisting of a dress having the blouse portion of silk and the skirt of cloth, and a coat of the same fabric as the skirt. The coat is unusual in cut, and so constructed that the seam lines are made a decoration further emphasized by the unusual pockets and trimmings. The wide sleeves and slightly surplice lines of the coat are other interesting details.

FIG. 36

The dress portion consists of a simple straight blouse with set-in sleeves and a two-piece skirt attached to the waist at a low waist line. Both are decorated by the same trimming arrangement as that used on the coat. In such a model, no interfacings are used nor is tape employed along the front edges.

91. Material and Pattern Requirements. — Charmeen is an ideal material for such a suit, while fine Poiret twill would make up attractively over these lines also. If a silk suit is wanted, bengaline or any firm-ribbed silk would be appropriate. The material of the blouse should be matched for the lining, while trimming of flat silk braid and embroidered banding add interest to the collar, pocket, and sleeves.

If the lining and blouse are made of the same fabric, 4 yards will be needed, while for the coat and skirt, 3 yards of 54-inch material should be provided. These amounts, of course, are for the average figure.

92. If you are unable to procure a similar pattern, a box-coat pattern will be a satisfactory guide. Pin or baste the under-arm seam, lay the pattern out flat and mark the panel lines in front and back, also the line at the top of the pocket, letting this terminate the panel lines. Trace entirely around the outside of the pattern onto a new section of paper, allowing for a generous lap in front, and trace also the new lines that you have just placed. Then cut the new pattern apart on these lines, having the coat proper in one piece and the under-arm section in another. This will mean that, when you cut the coat, there will be no seams except the shoulder seams and those by which the under-arm sections are joined to the coat. The sleeves, too, will be cut wider; in fact, the sleeve may be cut in one piece rather than two, with the inside seam line quite straight.

Straight lengths of material form the skirt, which is attached at a low waist line to a simple round-necked blouse with elbow-length, set-in sleeves.

93. Construction Details.—A coat of this kind requires the use of a muslin model, as the method of cutting, which the design of the coat makes necessary, provides very little opportunity for fitting. The model, however, may be accurately fitted by taking in folds or inserting sections as large as may be necessary to insure a smooth appearance.

Cut the coat as previously suggested, that is, without a seam below the top of the pockets. This means that 54-inch material is required; otherwise, an under-arm seam may be introduced. The collar is double and an extra section is provided to form the front facings.

After the first fitting, apply the trimming to the pockets and face the upper edge. Stitch the seams in cord effect as described in Art. **13,** Chapter IV, except the shoulder seams, which are, of course, stitched plain.

Make the small tie, which fastens the coat, of self-material, cutting a strip about 3 inches wide and 36 to 40 inches long. Stitch

the raw edges together the full length, turn the strip, press carefully and then cut the strip into two equal parts.   When stitching
the right facing, insert one of these pieces at the most becoming
position for the closing, and attach the other just in front of the left
side-front seam, having both equally distant from the bottom of the
coat.

Apply the trimming to the collar and sleeves; then finish the
fronts of the coat by attaching the facings.   Stitch the two sections
of the collar together, leaving the neck edges free.   Turn in the raw
edges separately, baste carefully, and slip the neck edge of the coat
between them.   Stitch in position, having the
stitching correspond with that for the cord
seams.   Insert the lining, following the usual
method, and press again.

94.   Lining   Cut   Without
Pattern.—Fig. 37 illustrates a
lining method that is simple
and   permits a saving of material.   The   fabric   used   is
crêpe de Chine, which, because
it has no definite difference
between   its   crosswise   and
lengthwise   weave,   is   used
crosswise   of   the   material.
Allow a plait at the center
back and plan for a dart at the
front shoulder to provide ease over the bust.   A lining of this sort

(a)   (b)

FIG. 37

may be planned with the aid of a dress form by putting the coat on
the form wrong side out.

After cutting off the selvage, pin the silk around the bottom of
the coat, placing the pins no farther than 1 inch apart.   Now
smooth the lining up to the neck line in the back, keeping a straight
thread on the center-back line of the coat.   Take a small plait in the
lining, as shown in view (a), pin carefully, and cut on a curve toward
the shoulder, being careful to follow the neck line of the coat and to
allow a proper amount for turning in and finishing.   Then pin it up
smoothly at the under arm and around the back armhole.   Now
follow the line of the shoulder while trimming off the back to form
the back-shoulder line, and allow for a generous seam here, too.

Cut the lining at the back armhole, cutting from the shoulder down to a point that would be at the position of the under-arm seam if there were one.

Next, prepare to cut the front. In order to make the cutting of the front-armhole line accurate, pin the material here and cut, following the armhole line of the coat and allowing for finishing. When planning the front shoulder, lay in the small plait as in view (*b*); then cut the material up to the front facing, adding a generous seam allowance.

Trim off any excess material in front, having the front line of the lining extend a seam's width beyond the edge of the front facing. Secure the lining in place at the lower edge and the front with slip-stitches, and at the shoulder with whipping-stitches. Cover small dress shields with the lining material and tack them in the armhole before bringing the sleeve lining up over the raw edge of the body portion at the armhole. Turn in a proper seam and whip the sleeve lining in place with close, even stitches.

The loop at the side in view (*b*) is a straight strip of the lining material cut double and carefully sewed in place with small back-stitches. It is matched by a small button on the inside of the left front so that the underlap of the coat may be secured.

SUIT DRESS

95. In these days of one-piece dresses and a desire for unbroken length of line, many business women prefer to wear the coat of a suit throughout the entire day, feeling that their appearance in a separate skirt and blouse is not so attractive as they would wish. Such a plan is thoroughly satisfactory, because there is a certain trimness about a tailored suit that cannot be expressed by any other garment. Then, too, the use of two materials, one for the skirt and the other for the coat, provides an appealing change from the usual model developed entirely of one fabric. However, if it seems more desirable to have the entire outfit of one color and material, by all means have it so.

96. Description of Suit.—With the desire for the appearance of a suit without the bulkiness of a blouse under the coat, the model illustrated in Fig. 38 was planned. The coat is cut on raglan lines, which make it particularly becoming to the broad-shouldered figure.

A dart is used in the front for ease over the bust, and another is used on the top of the shoulder in order to allow for fitting, thus providing the means of securing a smooth appearance at this place.

The straight skirt is built upon a camisole foundation with a side-front closing, as shown in Fig. 39. Notice how the fitting is accomplished by means of the small stitched-in plaits at each side of the front and at one side of the back. Three plaits, each 2 inches deep, finish the closing at the other side of the back and provide a desirable amount of width without taking away from the narrow appearance of the skirt.

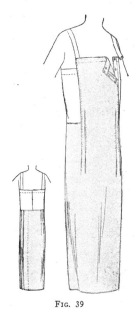

FIG. 38   FIG. 39

97. Material and Pattern Requirements.—A combination of flannel of a small plaid for the skirt with Poiret twill of a harmonizing color for the coat would be ideal for this outfit, although it

4 W I—20

could be made of any medium-weight wool or of a heavy silk if desired for wear in warm weather. For the camisole foundation, crêpe de Chine or a similar, supple silk is preferred. If the coat and skirt are to be made of contrasting materials, provide 1½ yards of 54-inch material for the coat and 1½ yards for the skirt, which is cut on the cross of the material and thus requires but one seam, it being joined under the tuck at the side back. If 40-inch material is to be used, 1½ yards will still be sufficient for the skirt, but you will need to provide 2¼ yards for the coat.

98. Any simple, raglan-sleeve coat pattern will be satisfactory for a guide in cutting this coat, or it may be developed from a box coat with kimono sleeves. In the latter case, mark the raglan lines first; then cut the pattern apart on these lines. Slash the front-pattern section from the raglan line to the bottom of the coat and place the resulting sections on a new piece of paper, having the slashed sections meet at the bottom but separated the desired amount, from 3 to 5 inches, for the dart at the top.

99. Cutting and Making.—Because of its simplicity of construction, such a garment may be satisfactorily made without the use of a muslin model, although, of course, the model will be found helpful both in cutting and fitting. After cutting the coat, baste in the front dart; then baste up the seams. Try the coat on and, if necessary, let out or take up the seams and dart. It may be that the coat will fit smoothly at the shoulder without a second dart, but if it does not, do not hesitate to fit the coat closer at the neck line, tapering the dart out to nothing as it approaches the tip of the shoulder.

FIG. 40

Finish the collar with a trimming band of the skirt fabric and attach the collar to the neck edge, following Fig. 64 and the directions in Art. 124 of Chapter VI, but having the facing extend the full length of the coat instead of part way down, as described in the making of the dress. Directions for making the pockets are given in Arts. 41 to 43 inclusive, Chapter III.

Notice in Fig. 40 how the seams are finished by pressing and overcasting. Bind the edge of the front facing and the hem with a ½-inch bias of a firm silk and slip-stitch to the coat, being very careful not to have the stitches show through to the right side.

100. The skirt portion requires careful fitting. Provide a smooth-fitting camisole foundation, with or without a seam at the center back, and pin the skirt to it, pinning in the darts at the side front and back and arranging the depth of the plaits and tuck at the back. Replace the pins with basting and stitching, and finish the opening at the side front by the use of a placket facing unless the garment is for a slender figure, when no opening is necessary. Try the garment on again to mark the proper skirt length and to ·make sure that there is no bulkiness at the waist line or just below it. Finish the raw edges underneath by overcasting and the hem by following either of the methods described in Art. **2 5,** Chapter V.

TAILORED COATS

SEPARATE TAILORED COAT

101. In considering tailored outer garments, the top-coat is next in importance to the tailored suit. Such a coat is both service-able and attractive, and may be developed out of light or heavy fabric, so that it is suitable for wear in any season. In silk or linen, such a coat is a protection from the dust of traveling, while in the heavier fabrics, it can be worn for shopping or on errands of business; in fact, when simplicity of cut and finish dominate the mode, the tailored coat is suitable for wear on any day-time occasion. The fact that it is usually made of a firmly woven fabric helps to keep it looking well so that the length of time given to repairs and pressing is reduced to a minimum, which is, of course, a point in its favor. Indeed, the tailored coat is practically indispensable to the girl or woman who spends even a small amount of time out-of-doors.

102. Description of Coat.—Fig. 41 shows a practical model of the top-coat, which follows the lines of the regulation box-coat. The double-breasted effect makes for protection and warmth, while the plait at the back gives ease through the lower part. The stitching, placed about $\frac{1}{2}$ inch from the edges of the fronts, collar, and cuffs, provides a neat finish and adds to the tailored effect. Bone buttons are the means of fastening.

103. Material and Pattern Requirements.—Camel's hair, tweed, cheviot, or wool velour may be the choice of material for this coat, or for summer wear, pongee in a heavy quality might be used.

Supply 3 yards of 54-inch material and 6 bone buttons. A spool of heavy silk for the stitching may be included in the list of requirements, or you may use sewing silk. Because the lining of the coat extends only part way, you will need but $1\frac{3}{4}$ yards of the lining silk. Crêpe de Chine or a medium-weight satin or sateen are appropriate for this purpose.

104. Patterns of this type are usually available, but if you should wish to use a foundation box-coat with a one-piece sleeve, the alterations necessary may readily be made. Extend the center-front, center-back, and side lines the desired amount and plan for the plait at the back. Provide also a generous allowance at the fronts for lapping and add from $\frac{1}{2}$ to 1 inch to the lapel and collar, since the design of the coat requires an appearance of greater width through the collar and lapel portions.

Locate the position of the top seam in the sleeve by pinning the sleeve pattern into the arm-hole; then mark a point just at the shoulder line on the sleeve. Unpin the pattern and draw a straight line from the armhole to the wrist of the sleeve pat-tern, using this point as a guide. Mark the depth of the cuff on the bottom of the sleeve and trace this line and the bottom of the sleeve through to a separate piece of paper to provide a pattern;

FIG. 41

then cut the sleeve pattern into two sections, following the guide line drawn previously. The belt may be cut from muslin and the pockets, too, are best cut in the same manner. Cut the coat from muslin and fit the model carefully, making any necessary changes in fitting.

105. Cutting Out the Material and Lining.—After preparing the muslin pattern for the coat in the manner directed, place it on the material, being careful to have the center front and the center back of the pattern pieces come on a lengthwise thread, and the elbow lines of the sleeve on a crosswise thread of the material. Arrange the back-pattern piece so that it is from 8 to 12 inches from the fold to allow for the plait at the center back, provided you did not make this allowance on the muslin.

When the muslin guide pattern has been properly placed and securely pinned, cut out the coat material, allowing for seams and marking the pattern lines in the usual manner. Next, give attention to the lining. Cut the material for this the same as for the outside, but let it extend only to a point about 3 inches above the normal waist line.

106. First Fitting.—With the material for the box-coat cut out, baste the garment together for the first fitting. The purpose of this fitting is to see whether the position of the shoulder and under-arm seams, as well as the length and width of the sleeve, is correct, and also to determine whether the plait in the back is just as it should be. If these points need any altering, give attention to them at this time, keeping in mind the instructions for the fitting of the tailored suit.

Cut a straight length of muslin of a becoming width for the belt, usually about 2 inches, and cut one pocket from muslin. Arrange the belt around the coat and pin it in place. Pin the pocket on, too, making it smaller or larger than your pattern if a change seems advisable. Mark the position of the buttonholes on the belt so that the marks may be transferred to the cloth when it is cut.

Do not lose sight of the fact that the coat in this fitting should fit a trifle loose, especially at the under arms, in order to leave room for the lining and possible interlining which, when inserted, will cause the coat to fit a little more snug.

107. Developing the Coat for the Second Fitting.—When all points that should be noticed in the first fitting have received attention, take off the coat and dissemble it by removing the sleeve and the basting in the shoulder and the under-arm seams Then, on the wrong side, baste and stitch these seams and press them open so that they will lie smooth and flat. Also, baste, stitch, and press the sleeve seams, and then baste the sleeves into the coat. Make the collar and apply it as for the tailored-suit coat.

To prepare the cuffs and pockets, interline them with well-shrunken muslin cut on the bias and then line them with silk. Baste the cuffs to the sleeves and prepare to face the lower edge of each cuff and sleeve, joining with a bias piece of lining or covering with the sleeve lining, provided such a lining is used. When these are ready, place the facing on the front.

108. Second Fitting.—The coat is now ready for the second fitting, which is similar in every way to the second fitting of a tailored-suit coat. During this fitting, do not fail to mark with a row of bastings the line near the lower edge of the coat where the hem is to be turned later; also, be careful to observe every detail, for any alterations that have to be made later will cause much trouble and will detract from the appearance of the coat.

As a finish for the seams that are not concealed by the lining, as well as the inside edges of the facing, use a binding of a firm silk, such as taffeta or satin, cut bias, or a light-weight sateen or cambric.

Fig. 42

109. Finishing the Coat.—Before the finish at the bottom of the coat can be completed, the hem allowance must be made even by measuring from the line of bastings to the raw edge and trimming off any necessary material. To give weight and body to the hem, a finish is used that requires a strip of bias silk 1½ inches wider than the hem. Baste this bias facing over the right side of the coat material, keeping the edges even. Stitch ¼ to ⅜ inch from the edge, and turn the bias strip over the raw edge of the coat material to the wrong side, being very careful not to make a turn in the coat material itself as that would produce a bulky edge. Press the crease in the silk facing. The free edge of the facing now extends on the wrong side to ¾ or 1 inch above the line of basting-stitches that mark the position for the bottom of the hem.

When the hem is turned, which is the next step, this bias facing is turned along with the coat material, thus producing a firm edge for the bottom of the coat.   Baste the hem in position and slip-stitch the binding to the coat by hand or stitch on the machine, as preferred.

Make and apply the patch pockets and make the buttonholes, using either the worked or the bound buttonhole; the latter is usually most appropriate for this type of coat.   Directions for both are given in Chapter II; for the worked buttonhole, in Arts. 16 to 30 inclusive; and for the bound buttonhole, in Arts. 35 to 39 inclusive.   At this time, put in the lining in a manner similar to that of the tailored-suit coat and hem the edge with a ½-inch hem. Fig. 42 shows how the inside of the coat should look after the lining is in place.   When every point in the making has been at-tended to, press the coat thoroughly and then sew on the buttons.

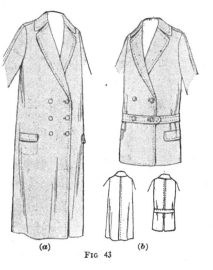

(a)   (b)

FIG 43

VARIATIONS OF THE SEPARATE TAILORED COAT

UTILITY COATS

110.   In Fig. 43, views (a) and (b), are shown two types of coats cut over exactly the same lines as the model in Fig. 41, but being very differ-ent in effect.   View (a) is slightly more fitted, omits the back plaits, and consequently eliminates the belt.   View (b) is of the mackinaw type, and for the girl actively engaged in sports, would be very attractive made up in a heavy plaid wool.   Such a coat is serviceable and practical for the school girl, too.

The materials appropriate are those mentioned for the coat shown in Fig. 41, and the method of making is exactly the same.   In any of these coats, a full-length lining may be employed if it seems desirable.

CHILD'S SERVICE COAT

111. No form of tailoring is easier of accomplishment or more pleasurable than the making of coats for the smaller members of the family. The designs to be followed are, or should be, simple; and the simplicity of the fitting lessens considerably the work of making such a coat.

112. Description of Coat.—The coat shown in Fig. 44 is suitable for school wear for girls of from 6 to 16 years. The lines are

much like those of a coat appropriate for a grown-up, but they have also a certain youthful air that should characterize a coat for a child or a young girl.

The raglan line of the sleeves simplifies fitting and finishing, so a coat of this type is a wise choice for one's first attempt at coat construction. The notched collar and the tailored belt and pockets are appealing features, while the fulness allowed in the plait at the center back gives the young wearer ease and freedom for play and sport.

113. Material and Pattern Requirements.—For service, tweed is an excellent choice for a coat of this kind, while camel's hair, polo cloth, and similar coatings will look well and wear well too. There is also a novelty coating that makes up to advantage, the right side having a woolly surface and the wrong side being plaided and smooth

FIG. 44

and therefore eliminating the need for a lining.

For an 8-year-old girl, supply 1½ yards of any 54-inch material and 2½ yards of lining, provided the lining is to be used in the entire coat. From 1¼ to 1½ yards will be plenty for a partial lining. Supply also 3 bone buttons and a buckle for the belt.

114. Supply a raglan-coat pattern of the proper size, which should be readily procured. If there is difficulty in finding such a pattern, a kimono-sleeve coat may be used by marking in the raglan lines and providing for the plait at the center back.

115.   Directions for Making.—A muslin model is helpful but not really necessary, although such a trial garment is to be recommended for the inexperienced sewer.   Whether it is used or not, cut the cloth for the coat in the usual way and cut also an interfacing of light-weight muslin for the front of the coat and the collar.   Insert this carefully after fitting as previously described, and proceed with

the making of the coat.   Finish the seams with binding, provided no lining or a partial lining is used.   As a finish, place rows of stitching at the joining of the raglan seams, on the pockets, on the cuffs, and also down the center back of the coat to hold the plait in place.   In this case, the stitching for the plaits extends to the belt line, but very often it is extended only to a point about half way from the neck line to the waist line. The necessity for careful pressing is to be emphasized in this coat, as well as in any other type of tailored garment.

——————

DRESSY COAT FOR SMALL GIRL

116.   Description of Coat.—A coat cut over the same lines as those of the coat in Fig. 44 is shown in Fig. 45. This model, however, is distinguished by a certain softness of finish and the addition of a fur collar, so that it is appro-

FIG. 45

priate for special occasions.   The plait at the back is omitted, its place being taken by a simulated slot seam made decorative by heavy stitching.

117.   Material and Pattern Requirements.—Such materials as wool velour, bolivia, or any of the dressier pile fabrics are appropriate for this coat, while it may also be developed of bengaline or velvet, the former for spring and summer and the latter for fall and winter wear.   In 54-inch fabric, $1\frac{1}{2}$ yards of cloth will be needed; in

40-inch widths, 2½ yards is required for a coat for an eight-year-old child. For this type of coat, 2½ yards of lining is the usual requirement, together with a strip of fur 6 inches wide and long enough to extend around the neck line of the coat, usually about 14 inches. A cloth-covered button provides the means of fastening.

118. Making the Coat.—The cutting, fitting, and finishing of this coat are quite the same as for the coat illustrated in Fig. 44 except that the finish of the collar and the center back requires different treatment. To hold the sides of the simulated slot seam, place two rows of stitching; but if you wish, both stitching and seam may be omitted and the back made plain.

119. Cutting the Fur.—Considerable care and experience are essential to obtain satisfactory results in the cutting and finishing of fur pieces; for this reason, fur of good quality justifies the expense of being handled by an expert. If you purchase new fur or have on hand fur pieces that you would like to use, a furrier will prepare these for you, shaping the collar according to the pattern you submit.

In case you prefer to do this work yourself, proceed with the greatest of care so as to bring out the full beauty of the fur and prevent any suggestion of amateur workmanship.

In cutting the fur, first mark with tailors' chalk the cutting line on the pelt, or skin, of the fur; then cut on this marked line, using a very sharp knife or razor blade for this purpose.

120. If piecing of the fur is essential, apply the pieces before cutting the collar, planning the piecing so that the hairs, or nap, will run in the same direction in all sections, thus making the piecing entirely inconspicuous. To join the piecing, lay the upper, or nap, sides of the fur so that they face each other and overhand the edges of the pelt, or skin, together with fine, close stitches. Use waxed cotton or linen thread and a rather coarse needle for the sewing, unless the pelt is very soft and thin, when a fine needle should be employed.

121. Making the Fur Ready for Application.—Unless you purchase the fur pieces already prepared, it will be necessary to tape the edges, and, in some cases, such as when you use mole or soft squirrel, to provide an interlining.

To tape the edges, first place the tape along the edge of the fur so that it faces the hairy side rather than the pelt; then overhand the edge of the tape to the extreme edge of the pelt with short, firm stitches. If an interlining is required, use one layer of sheet wadding cut the exact size and shape of the pelt, or skin part, of the fur, and baste this around the edge, taking very short stitches through the pelt; then turn the tape back over the edge of the pelt and interlining and baste its free edge flat through the pelt and the interlining.

122. To finish the coat collar, cut a single thickness of interlining a seam's width smaller on all edges than the collar itself. Place the interlining on the wrong side of the collar and, bringing the edges of the collar up over it, catch-stitch them in place and attach the collar to the coat. Then slip-stitch the fur collar to the collar of the coat.

123. Finishing.—Provide a loop of the cloth of the coat and a button of the proper size for fastening.

Baste and sew the lining in as usual, allowing the plait for width at the center back.

WRAPS

ESSENTIAL FEATURES

124. A *wrap* is distinguished from a coat by its very deep armholes and loose, baggy lines, few of which follow the lines of the figure, and is often characterized by the appearance of being drawn loosely around under the arms and held together at the front, thus giving the wrappy effect from which its name is derived. Practically every season, wraps of a more or less elaborate nature, intended for evening wear, are in vogue; and other times the use of wraps is popularized to the extent of being adapted for almost every purpose but general utility wear. In this case, they are made of more practical materials and on more conservative lines than the typical evening wrap, but invariably the fabric is of a soft quality that drapes well and the general effect is more elegant than that of a coat.

125. Wraps are suitable for either winter or summer wear, velvet, fur, and soft, luxurious woolens being chosen for cold weather and soft, light-weight woolens and silks of prevalent fashion finding favor for warm weather. With the heavier materials, a lining is almost invariably used, and sometimes an interlining is provided for additional warmth, but when the wrap is intended merely for slight protection, the lining may be omitted altogether or used only in the waist portion of the coat.

In selecting the design and materials for a wrap, take into consideration not only the styles and the texture and color of the fabrics sanctioned by Fashion, but also the places where the wrap will be worn. If the wrap must serve for afternoon and evening wear, it should be of fairly conservative design and of unobtrusive color. This same suggestion applies if the wrap is for evening wear alone, but must be worn on a public conveyance such as a street car. If a private conveyance is available, the wrap may be as luxurious in effect and as brilliant in color as fashion, good taste, and the individual type permit.

126. In making wraps, keep in mind the fact that precise tailoring is undesirable. Work for softly finished rather than hard-pressed edges and for style rather than a carefully fitted effect. If you find it necessary to use interlining as a stay for any of the edges or portions of the wrap, choose a very soft quality and try to avoid any suggestion of this interlining in the outside appearance.

RAGLAN-SLEEVE WRAP

127. A conservative type of wrap, having raglan seam lines and comparatively straight front and back sections with slight draping at the under arm is shown in Fig. 46. It has a convertible collar and cuffs of fur, which make a warm and attractive trimming for cold-weather wear. If preferred, however, the collar and cuffs might be made of self-material and trimmed with stitching or in some other manner that accords with prevalent styles. For a wrap made of silk, a softer type of collar having shirrings, cordings, or fabric trimming would be pleasing.

128. Material and Pattern Requirements.—To develop the raglan-sleeve wrap as illustrated, 4 yards of 54-inch fabric, 4 yards of 40-inch lining material, and fur collar and cuffs already cut or 1 yard of fur banding 6 or 7 inches wide for the cuffs and a piece of fur for the collar about $\frac{3}{4}$ yard long and 7 inches wide are needed. For staying the front edges, the bottom of the sleeves, and the collar, provide about 2 yards of soft muslin.

129. Developing a muslin model is the safest method of obtaining a pattern for a wrap or any unusual coat design. As a guide in shaping the model for this wrap, you may use a commercial pattern having deep raglan lines, or a kimono-coat pattern on which you may indicate the raglan lines.

In cutting out the muslin for the modeling, merely mark the raglan seam lines through the lower portion, leaving an abundance of material to work with so that the lines may be changed as much as desired.

130. Pin the sections of the muslin model together on the form and then work for the draped effect at the under arm, shifting the seam lines as much as you wish and adding piecings of the muslin, if necessary. When you have produced the effect you desire, baste the muslin model, "smoothing" the curves in the seam lines. Then try on the model again to make sure that it is correct and to make any adjustments that seem essential. If care is given to the making and fitting of the model and it is made correct as to length

Fig. 46

and the amount of fulness, little or no fitting will be required in the development of the wrap.

Model the collar in muslin, also, making it roll as much as desired and cutting it to make it of becoming shape and width.

131. Cutting Out the Wrap.—After carefully marking the seam lines of the muslin model, remove the bastings and use the model as a pattern for cutting out the wrap. Arrange the coat-pattern sections on the material as previously suggested, placing the raglan sleeve so that its lengthwise center is over a lengthwise thread of the fabric. For a very soft finish along the front edges, you may plan to omit the seam that joins the facings and cut the facings in one with the wrap fronts; this, of course, will make a practically straight front line essential. For the collar, provide merely a facing of the fabric.

Cut out the muslin sections and the lining, also the fur, as previously suggested.

132. Making the Wrap.—Proceed with the construction of the wrap in the usual manner, basting, fitting, and then finishing the seams. However, if you are working on velvet, duvetyn, or a velvety woolen, steam the seam edges open instead of pressing them,

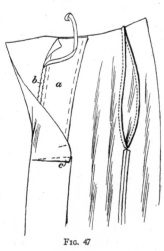

FIG. 47

running the inside of the seam over the edge of an inverted hot iron that is covered with a damp cloth. There are boards specially constructed for the pressing of velvet that prevent the nap from being flattened. If you have such a board, you may press the seams over this. However, ordinary pressing should be avoided for fabrics of velvety texture, for it has a tendency to flatten the nap and leave undesirable marks.

If allowance for a facing has been made on the wrap fronts, baste the interlining, as at a, Fig. 47, in position along the marked front edges, tape this in the usual manner, as at b, and through the revers, or turn-over, portion supply padding stitches to hold the muslin to the wrap fabric.

Then fold the facing allowance back and, if it appears to have any surplus length, smooth this from the top and the bottom toward the point where you desire the fastenings and pin a dart in the facing, as at c. Finish this dart with pressed-open edges.

Make the collar ready for the application of the fur by applying the interlining, and then turning the raw edge of the fabric over the muslin, catch-stitching it in position.   In this condition, join the collar to the coat.

133.   Interlining for Warmth.—If you wish to provide an interlining for warmth, you may use Canton flannel or lamb's wool. Such an interlining need extend only through the body portion of the wrap, terminating above the waist line but running the full length of the sleeves.   Cut this with the aid of the wrap pattern, making no allowance for seams.   Then, in applying it, first pin it carefully in position so that the edges just meet over the center of the pressed-open seams and then catch-stitch the edges of the interlining together, taking the stitches through the seam edges underneath but exercising extreme care not to take them through to the outside of the wrap.

134.   Finishing the Wrap.—Finish the cuffs by facing them with the wrap-lining material; then slip them over the finished lower edge of the sleeve and slip-stitch them in position.

Secure the fur collar in position by slip-stitching its taped edges to the interlined collar facing.

Tape and turn under the lower edge of the wrap; then make and apply the lining, as previously directed, and supply an ornamental buckle or a button and loop for the fastening.

CAPES

STYLES AND REQUIREMENTS

135.   A *cape* is a loose, sleeveless garment that hangs from the neck and shoulders and may be cut in decidedly circular fashion and fitted snugly over the shoulders or made of slightly shaped or straight pieces of material and gathered at the neck line.   Like wraps, capes are almost always suitable for evening wear and every now and then become popular for day-time wear, also.   As a day-time garment, capes, unlike wraps, are sometimes used for general utility or service wear, often being developed for this purpose on tailored or military lines and from fabrics of a sturdy nature.

136.   Material and Pattern Requirements.—In regard to the selection of designs and fabrics as well as their construction, practically the same suggestions that apply to wraps should be followed for capes, with the exception of capes of the tailored or military variety, which require just as careful tailoring as do coats.

As to the cutting of capes, many styles do not require a pattern, being made merely of straight pieces of material. If a cape is to be fitted over the shoulders, however, a regulation cape pattern should be used as a foundation for the cutting. A pattern having side-seam lines may be used to cut a seamless cape if the pattern is laid on the material so that the seam lines just meet from the shoulder tip to the lower edge. This will leave an open space between the upper edges of the side seam, which must be taken in as a shoulder dart.

In the cutting of an extreme circular cape, the shoulder dart may be omitted, for, in this case, the upper, or shoulder, edges of the side seam may be placed together and the lower edges separated to provide flare.

EVENING CAPE

137. A youthful and pleasing style of evening cape that is very easily made is shown in Fig. 48. This consists simply of straight pieces, a straight

FIG. 48

gathered section for the main portion of the cape, a wide band for the lower portion, and a straight standing piece for the collar foundation. The trimming consists of large flowers of self-fabric, which almost completely cover the collar foundation and the band at the lower edge.   This style is particularly lovely in velvet, duvetyn, heavy silk crêpe, or taffeta.   When intended for winter wear, the cape should be lined and interlined throughout, but for summer wear, both lining and interlining may be omitted.

138.   Material and Pattern Requirements.—For the average figure, about $4\frac{1}{2}$ yards of 40-inch fabric that may be used crosswise, or $3\frac{3}{4}$ yards of the same width that must be used lengthwise, and 3 yards of lining are required for this style.   In addition, if velvet or duvetyn is the fabric selected for the cape, $\frac{3}{4}$ yard of matching silk in a crêpe or plain weave is needed for facing the flower petals.

Although no pattern is required for this style, it is advisable to try out the design in muslin in order to determine a becoming length and the fulness that is needed, as well as the correct size for the collar and the band at the lower edge.

139.   If the cape is being made of a material having an up and down, such as velvet, a seam will be necessary at the center back. In this case, cut two straight lengths for the main portion of the cape, making these as long as you desire the finished cape minus the width of the band, which is usually about 9 inches.

If material without an up and down has been provided, cut about a $2\frac{1}{2}$-yard length of this to be used crosswise.   If the cape is to be held close to the neck line, a little extra length will be required at the sides in order to insure an even line at the bottom, but for the effect that is illustrated, no shaping at the upper edge is required.

As illustrated, the band at the lower edge is about $1\frac{1}{2}$ yards around and 9 inches wide, and the collar is the same width and about 25 inches long, the collar strip being doubled.   In cutting these from the cape fabric, provide two strips the full width of the material, planning to have the extra length that is not needed for the collar serve as a piecing for the band at the lower edge.

A cape without lining should have the band at the lower edge made double.   In this case, more material will be required and the band and collar may be cut lengthwise of the fabric.

140.   Making the Cape.—Line the main portion of the cape before applying the collar and the band to it, first facing the edges of the slashes for the arms and then slip-stitching the slashed edges of the lining to these facings.   Turn back at least 1 inch of the cape fabric along the front edges so that the lining may terminate inside of the turned edge.

4 W I—21

Gather the lining and outer portion of the cape together and join them to the band.   Then make the collar ready, interlining this with crinoline or with several thicknesses of muslin padded with close

rows of stitching in order to make the collar stand upright.   Seam or slip-stitch the ends of the collar; then join it to the gathered upper edge of the cape.   Complete the cape by making and applying the flower trimming, then lining the band at the lower edge, and supplying hooks and blind loops for fastening at the neck line.

REVERSIBLE CAPE

141. (The cape illustrated in Fig. 49 has many interesting features.   First of all, it is reversible, a wool material being used for one side and a silk for the other.   Thus, it becomes two wraps instead of one, the wool side being worn out when a service cape is desired and the silk side, when a dress-up wrap is needed. The simplicity of the style of this wrap makes possible the cutting of it without a pattern, as the directions that follow indicate.   The fact that the fulness of the cape is placed in plaits rather than gathers makes it better suited to the well-developed figure than most other forms of capes.)

142.   Material Requirements. For the wool side of this cape, fine Poiret twill, kasha, or tricotine are suitable materials, and for

Fig. 49

the silk side, satin in a comparatively heavy but supple quality.   If the wool is a 54-inch width, supply one length plus 4 inches; of the satin, two lengths are needed. It is not advisable to use 40-inch material for both sides of the

cape because of the waste.   Supply also a strip of fur 6 inches wide
and from 25 to 27 inches long for the collar.

143.   Making the Cape.—Turn a 2½-inch hem on one edge of
one length of the satin, place this over one edge of the other length,
and baste and stitch the full length, forming a tuck by stitching
through the three thicknesses.

In order to provide enough width in the silk for the bands that
finish the center front of the wool side, measure from the center of
the tuck out toward the selvage a distance equal to one half of 54
inches, or 27 inches, plus 6 inches for the band and ½ inch for seam
allowance, that is, 33½ inches.   Trim the satin off beyond this on
each side.   The strips remaining, one of which will be wider than the
other because of the tuck, are to be used for lining the collar and
also for the strings of the cape.

Now place the wool section over the satin, front-seam lines meeting, baste the two together on these lines, and stitch.   Press the
seams carefully.   Smooth out both sections so that the satin at
the front will be a double thick-
ness, 3 inches deep, and the
remainder of the cape be entirely
without wrinkles.   Stitch the
two together across the bottom.
Then turn the cape right side
out, baste entirely across the
bottom and down the fronts,
and press carefully.

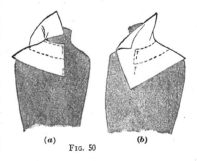

(a)   Fig. 50   (b)

To provide a trimming band of
the satin on the wool side and also
to add a little extra weight to the bottom of the cape, turn the lower
edge up 3 inches on the right side, and slip-stitch it in place.

144.   So that the cape will not be bulky at the neck edge, a small
yoke to which the cape may be attached is provided.   Model this in
muslin first, as shown in Fig. 50, view (a) showing the front and view
(b), the back.   The inner edge should follow the neck curve and the
outer edge should duplicate the larger curve, as shown.   Using this
muslin as a pattern, cut a yoke from muslin also, and build up the
cape on this.   Start with the center back, wool side out, pinning
the center back of the cape to the center back of the yoke; then
match the center fronts of the cape and yoke and pin these care-

fully, too. Now prepare to pin the plaits in the cape portion so that
around the upper edge its size will match the size of the lower edge
of the yoke.   Place an inverted box plait about 2 to 3 inches deep
at the direct center back; then on each side of this place a single
plait of the same depth or slightly smaller.   Just at the curve of the
shoulder, you will need another plait, with perhaps a small dart on
top of the shoulder, too.   A single deep plait on each side of the
center front is usually all that is necessary, but if the figure should
seem to require more, do not hesitate to add two smaller ones.

With the yoke attached, the front of the cape should appear as in
view (a) and the back as at view (b), Fig. 51, which show clearly the
position of the plaits. You will do well to follow these guides
exactly in your work, varying the depth of the plaits slightly, if necessary, so as to have the cape and the yoke match exactly in size.

145.   Now remove the cape and baste in the plaits carefully
below the yoke without catching the yoke portion with your stitches.
Mark the position of the yoke on the cape portion also; then remove

the yoke and use it as a pattern
for cutting the permanent yokes,
one of satin and one of the cloth.
Mark the shoulder darts, if you
used them, and repin and baste
them, turning them so that the
excess material in both the satin
and the wool is between the two
thicknesses of the cape.   Stitch the
darts, tapering the stitching carefully so that the end of the dart
will lie flat.   If the effect is bulky,
trim off the darts to within a
seam's width of the stitching.   Press
the seams open carefully.   Trim
off the top of the cape, if necessary,
to within a seam's width of the
yoke line.   Turn in the lower edge

(a)   (b)

Fig. 51

of the wool yoke and baste it down over the cape.   Replace
the basting with stitching.   Now turn in the raw edge of the satin
yoke, baste it so that it conceals the raw edge of the cape and the
wool yoke and slip-stitch its lower edge in position.   Turn

the neck edge of the two yokes in a seam's width and slip-stitch these together.

146. Prepare the fur of the collar as described in Arts. **119** to **124** inclusive, and line it with a strip of satin. At this time, also prepare the strings of the satin. Cut strips 3 inches wide and 27 inches long, seam them on the length, and turn to the right side. Press carefully, keeping the seam in the center of the strip rather than at the edge. Slip-stitch the ends together and sew them in place at the ends of the collar, as shown in Fig. 52.

FIG. 52

The collar is fastened to the cape by means of snap fasteners so as to be interchangeable and consequently adaptable to both sides of the cape. Provide two sets of medium-size snaps and sew one every $2\frac{1}{4}$ inches. Attach the hole or socket parts of the the snaps both to the satin and to the cloth sides of the cape. Then sew the knob or projection parts of one set of the snaps to the collar. This plan, as illustrated, enables you to fasten the collar to either side of the cape with no loss of time.

CHAPTER VIII

GARMENTS FOR MEN AND BOYS

ADVANTAGES OF HOME-MADE APPAREL

1. Although such garments as shirts, blouses, night shirts, pajamas, undergarments, smoking jackets, house coats, lounging robes, or bath-robes, and similar garments for men and simple coats and suits for boys are not generally included in dressmaking, they offer an excellent opportunity for the woman in the home to do a service that will mean a step toward economy and much satisfaction to the male members of the family. Men are more interested in such wearing apparel than the average woman thinks, and there is real economy in making these garments at home. As a rule, material better than that used in ready-made garments can be purchased for much less money than the made-up garments themselves, and it is always possible to keep enough of the material on hand for patching and making new collars and cuffs, so that the life of such garments can be lengthened.

The making of garments for men and boys also offers excellent possibilities to the woman who wishes to specialize. For example, a good business may be built up by making well-fitting shirts of unusual materials, or coats for barbers, surgeons, etc., or suits for small boys.

2. Many women hesitate when it comes to making garments for men and boys because they imagine that the work is difficult. In this, however, they are in error, for when such garments are understood they are simple to construct and the work is easily accomplished. Just as in making garments for women, the chief essentials are suitable materials, exactness of measurements, accuracy in

320

planning and cutting, care in basting, neatness and skill in sewing, correctness in the joining of all the parts, and care in pressing and finishing.

MEN'S SHIRTS

TYPES OF SHIRTS

3. Shirts for men are really of four types—the *dress shirt*, the *negligée shirt*, the *outing shirt*, and the *work shirt*. The distinguishing feature of the dress shirt is its bosom, which may be plain, plaited, or tucked and which must always be starched in laundering to have it give the proper appearance when worn with a dress suit. The other three shirts—the negligée, the outing, and the work shirt—are made without bosoms, although, for semidress occasions, negligée shirts are sometimes made with plaited fronts. These three types differ from one another chiefly in material, because the purpose for which the shirt is intended determines the material of which it is constructed.

4. Front Closings.—Any of the types of shirts mentioned may be made with a front-plait closing when the shirt must be slipped over the head in putting it on. Shirts may be made in the more general style of what is called a *coat shirt;* that is, a shirt that opens all the way down the front and may be slipped on in the same way as a coat.

5. Yokes.—Shirts are made with a shallow yoke in the back and some fulness below it, so as to allow for perfect freedom and thus overcome any danger of splitting because of the expanding of the shoulder muscles. Flannel shirts are sometimes made without gathers in the back, however, such shirts being often worn without a coat as part of a uniform.

6. Neck Finishes.—The neck of a *dress shirt* and a *negligée shirt* is usually finished off with a neck band, to which separate stiff or soft collars may be attached, although in some cases, a permanent collar of the same material as the shirt is put on.

The neck of an *outing shirt* may be finished with a band to which stiff or soft collars may be attached, but generally a permanent turn-over collar is attached.

A *work shirt* is always made with an attached, soft, turn-down collar of the same material as the shirt.

7. Sleeve Finishes.—The sleeves of *dress shirts* are finished with bands that are 1 inch wide when finished. Straight, stiff cuffs are attached to the bands when the dress shirts are worn.

There are three distinct ways of finishing the sleeves of *negligée* and *outing shirts;* namely, with regular cuffs, with French, or double, cuffs, or with wristbands to which separate cuffs may be attached. Separate cuffs are not so much in evidence as attached cuffs, but, as is the case with other articles of wear, styles control the width and particular cut of the cuffs and collars of these two types of shirts.

The sleeves of an *outing shirt* are usually made full length; however, they may be made short or the lower part of the sleeve may be made detachable, generally at a point above the elbow, thus making the shirt an ideal garment for outdoor sports.

The sleeves of a *work shirt* are always made full length and are practically always finished with wristbands.

SHIRT MATERIALS

8. Varieties of Materials.—The materials suitable for shirt making are numerous. Chief among the plain materials are radium silk, crêpe de Chine, tub silk, silk broadcloth, silk lajerz, pongee, habutaye, soisette, linen, oxford cloth, poplin, percale, chambray, sateen, galatea, duck, denim, khaki, and flannel.

Equally as popular as the plain materials are some of the novelty cotton shirtings, which come in great variety, with striped, figured, and basket-weave effects. Of these materials, madras is probably the most popular because of its attractive designs and excellent wearing qualities. There are also numerous striped flannels, silks, and linens, which make attractive shirts. Hickory shirting, a coarse, cotton, striped material, is extensively used for work shirts.

9. Suitability of Materials.—Although the use to which a shirt is to be put governs the material of which it is to be made, taste and judgment must be exercised in selecting materials.

For *negligée*, any of the light-weight fabrics mentioned may be chosen, depending on the use that is to be made of the shirts, the season of the year in which they are to be worn, and the outlay that it is desired to make.

For *outing*, or *sports*, *shirts* that are to be used for hunting, camping, and similar outdoor sports in which they will be subject to hard wear, materials possessing good-wearing qualities, such as chambray, flannel, sateen, galatea, denim, khaki, and the like, are the ones from which to choose. The weight of the fabric for such shirts will depend on the taste of the person who is to wear them, as well as on the season of the year and the climate in which they are to be worn, and the coloring and the texture will depend on personal taste. As a rule, if such shirts are built on good lines and of shrunken material, they are sure to give satisfaction.

If sports shirts are to be used for town wear, as in playing golf, tennis, and similar outdoor games, such fabrics as fine linen and silk should be considered. Such shirts offer excellent opportunity for the expression of good taste so far as color schemes and textures are concerned.

For *work shirts*, materials that will give service should always be selected, such materials as those mentioned for outing shirts intended for hunting and camping being particularly good, as is also hickory shirting.

10.   Findings for Shirts.—Attention should be given also to the thread and buttons to be used in shirt making. The thread to be used for stitching will be governed by the material that is employed. Cotton and linen fabrics are generally stitched with cotton thread, and silk and woolen fabrics, with silk thread. The size of cotton thread to use will depend on the texture of the material, although, as a rule, the thread should be reasonably coarse so that the stitching line will be clearly defined. Of course, good thread is absolutely necessary for men's shirts, because the stitching should be even and smooth and should hold fast until the garment is worn out.

Small, flat, untrimmed buttons should be employed for men's shirts, the better grade of pearl buttons for shirts made of the finer fabrics and the cheaper grade for heavy outing and work shirts. Three, five, or seven buttons are required for each shirt, depending on the front closing.

11.   For the bosoms of dress shirts and for the front plait, collar band, and wristbands or cuffs of negligée shirts, it is necessary to provide material to be used as interlining. Generally, such material

as butchers' linen or medium-weight muslin is suitable for this
purpose, the linen being used for expensive materials and the muslin
for the cheaper grades.

Instead of making collar bands for shirts, it is advisable to purchase them ready made, especially if time is an item in shirt construction. Collar bands complete even to the buttonholes and
ready to attach can be bought for a small sum in nearly all dry-
goods stores. If such a band is to be used, purchase it according to
the neck measure. These bands have an allowance for shrinkage, so
it is not necessary to shrink them before attaching them to shirts,
as both will shrink together.

12. Quantity of Material Required for Shirts.—The quantity
of material required for a man's shirt depends on the width of
the fabric of which the shirt is to be made, the size of the person for
whom it is to be made, and, to some extent, the type of the shirt.

As a rule, a person with a 14½-inch neck and a 34-inch chest will
require about 3¼ yards of 32- to 40-inch material; a person with a
15- or 15½-inch neck and a 36-inch chest, about 3½ yards; a person
with a 16-inch neck and a 40-inch chest, about 3¾ yards; and so on.
Generally, the 36-inch material cuts to better advantage than the
narrower widths. For interlining, more than ½ yard of 36-inch
material is seldom required.

13. In order to determine the exact quantity of material required
for a shirt, a good plan is to arrange the complete shirt pattern on
paper that is as wide as the material that is to be used and then
measure the length of the paper covered by the pattern. For a
work shirt, it is always advisable to procure enough material for
replacing the collar and wristbands as they wear out, as well as for
an extra thickness that will be needed in making the collar. It is
well to bear in mind, also, that if two shirts are cut out at one time,
the cutting can be done to better advantage and time will be saved
in both cutting and making. Of course, for negligée and sports
shirts, some men may object to having two garments of the same
pattern or design, but for work shirts such a plan is entirely practical.

After the amount of material required for a shirt has been
accurately determined, it is an excellent plan, whether a woman
makes shirts for members of her own family or is engaged in the busi-

ness of shirt making for regular customers, to keep a memorandum of it for future use.

14. Shrinking Material and Setting the Color.—If colored material is to be used for making shirts, it is often considered advisable to set the color and to shrink the material before making it up. As shirts are very easy-fitting, however, it is not necessary to do this work if the material is not likely to shrink very much. Of course, not all colors will fade, but when there is any likelihood of such an occurrence, it is always advisable to set the colors.

NEGLIGÉE SHIRT

15. The making of a negligée shirt is considered first, as this is the style of shirt used most. Two styles of negligée shirts are shown in Figs. 1 and 2. The shirt shown in Fig. 1 has a 1½-inch plait and French, or soft, cuffs, and the one shown in Fig. 2 has simply a hem at the front closing and cuffs or wide wristbands that are to be s t a r c h e d. Otherwise, these shirts are identical, each having a yoke across the back and an opening that extends the full length of the front, thus m a k i n g t h e m coat shirts.

Fig. 1

16. (**Shirt Pattern.** In purchasing a pattern for a shirt, three measurements must be considered; the neck, the chest, and the length-of-sleeve. The neck measurement, however, is the one that governs the size of pattern to be purchased. If this is correct, the other measurements may be altered satisfactorily.

In making a shirt, it is a good plan to use as a guide a shirt that has proved satisfactory. From this garment, the pattern pieces may be altered.

For example, the length of the sleeve may be measured from the tip of the shoulder to a point where the cuff joins. Then this measurement may be used to adjust the tissue-paper sleeve pattern. If it is too short, slash the pattern through the center at the elbow point and separate the pieces. If it is too long, fold the pattern in the form of a tuck to shorten it. In either case, before cutting out the material, make the outer lines of the pattern even where it was altered.

Fig. 2

17. Placing Pattern Pieces on the Material. After the pattern pieces have been measured and altered, if necessary, place them on the material in such a way as to permit the material to be cut to the best advantage. As shown in Fig. 3, lay the material out on a flat surface and place on it first the front-pattern piece, keeping it 1½ inches from the edge of the material. Take care, if striped material is used, to have the center front of the pattern come exactly on a stripe or in the stripe, so that when the plait is turned in position it will lap evenly with the stripe of the material.

In this case, the front plait is cut separately and applied. This is a decided advantage in striped material in order to have the stripes appear well in the plait. However, in most cases, the hem or plait may be cut in one with the center front and then turned and basted before cutting out the fronts so that the stripes will come in the desired location.

Next, place the center back on a fold and place the yoke and the

cuff-pattern pieces so that the lengthwise threads run crosswise when
the garment is worn. Place
the plait section on a single
thickness of material.

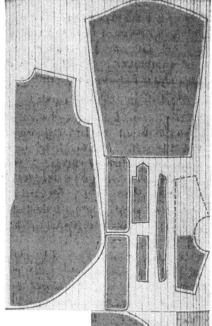

The collar band is shown
in Fig. 3, but this may be
made of a lighter-weight
fabric than the shirt, or,
as previously explained,
may be purchased ready-
made.

The remaining pattern
pieces are shown in posi-
tion in Fig. 3.

**18. Allowances for
Seam and Edge Finishing.**
In cutting out the shirt, if
no seam allowance is pro-
vided in the pattern, make
an allowance of $\frac{1}{4}$ inch for
the seams or finish on the
neck edge of the fronts, the
neck and the lower edges
of the yoke, the upper edge of the back,
the lower edge of the sleeves, all edges of
the sleeve facings, cuffs, or wristbands, the
collar or neck band, and the plait. For
the other edges of the front section of the
shirt, the yoke, the back of the shirt, and
the sleeve, make a $\frac{3}{8}$-inch allowance.
Whether a plait is used, as in Fig. 1, or
simply a hem, as in Fig. 2, there should be
an allowance on the upper center front of
the shirt for over-lapping. It is always
advisable to place a mark on the neck
curve exactly at the front line of the
pattern to represent the center of the

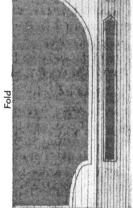

Fig. 3

shirt front, so that this point will not be overlooked in making
the garment.

In cutting shirts for men that are very large, it is sometimes necessary to provide four shirt lengths of material instead of three, and to piece the sleeve in the back with a lengthwise piece of material about one-third of its width. If this piecing is done neatly with a flat-fell seam, the joining will not be noticeable. By observing custom-made shirts, it will be seen that the sleeves are pieced in many instances, the piecing being done to save material in cutting a number of shirts at a time.

19. Making the Front Plait.—After cutting all the parts required for the shirt, the first step in its construction is to finish the front closing. For a coat closing, that is, an opening that extends the entire length of the shirt, the plait is finished in a manner similar to that shown in Fig. 1. The length of this plait is a little less than the length of the opening, extending from the neck to the skirt section of the shirt.

Cut an interlining of lawn or cambric to be used under the plait and baste this interlining to the wrong side of the plait section to hold it in place.

In applying the plait, place the right side of the plait to the wrong side of the shirt on the left-hand side, and then baste and stitch. Press the seam open and turn the plait over on the right side, creasing it so that the seam is back from the edge about ¼ inch on the inside of the shirt. Next, turn in the seam allowance on the other edge of the plait and baste and stitch the plait flat to the shirt, placing the stitching about ⅛ inch from the edge. Then add stitching to the outside edge of the plait to correspond with the stitching on the inside edge. The lower edge may be finished straight across or pointed as in Fig. 1.

20. Making the Front Facing.—The next step is to cut a strip of plain white, light-weight material for facing the right front of the shirt. Cut it 2 inches wide and as long as the strip cut for the plait. Fold this facing lengthwise through the center and place it to the right side of the material on the right-hand side of the shirt, having the raw edges of the facing to the outer edge of the shirt. Baste and stitch. Next turn the facing to the wrong side and crease the seam edges back away from the facing, having the joining back about ¼ inch from the edge. Baste to the shirt. Then apply a row of stitching from the outside about ¼ inch from the edge of the shirt. The folded edge of the facing is left free.

On some patterns, an allowance is made for the finish at the front. In this case, the usual method is to turn both sides in a hem.

If a hem is to be turned for the front closing, as in Fig. 2, it is necessary simply to insert a strip of interlining in the hem and to stitch it in place.

21. Making the Yoke.—The yoke in a shirt is made double and extends above the back portion.   Therefore, gather the back section on each side and place it so that the top will come between the two thicknesses of the yoke. Arrange the gathers so that they will come over the shoulder blades when the shirt is worn, or 3 or 4 inches each side of the center back.   Place the inside-yoke section with its right side to the wrong side of the back. Pin the yoke and back portions together and baste.   Then pin and baste the other yoke portion in position, having the right sides of the back and yoke together. Next, bring the right side of each yoke portion up so that the armhole and neck edges come together and baste about 1 inch from the outer edge, taking care to have the yoke portion very smooth.   S t i t c h across the yoke directly

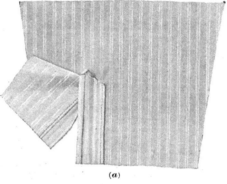

(a)

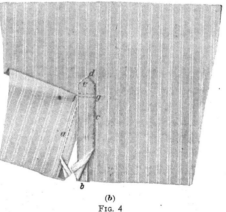

(b)

Fig. 4

on the lower edge where the yoke and back portions join, and then stitch ¼ inch above so that the stitching will harmonize with the flat-fell seams that are to be used in the side and sleeve seams.

22.   Making the Shoulder Seams.—After the yoke is applied, join the front portions to it, concealing the shoulder seam between the two thicknesses of the yoke.

23.   Finishing the Sleeve Openings.—Prepare the sleeves next by finishing the cuff openings.   To do this, lay the sleeve right side down and place the two strips that are cut for the openings so that their wrong sides are up, the larger strip on the front of the sleeve, its shorter side toward the opening, and the smaller one toward the back of the sleeve; baste the strips in position, and then stitch with a ⅛-inch seam, as shown in Fig. 4 (*a*).

With this done, turn the free edge of the smaller piece over ⅛ inch on the side and the upper end and crease the edge.   Bring it over to the right side and stitch it down, as at *a*, Fig. 4 (*b*).   Then pull

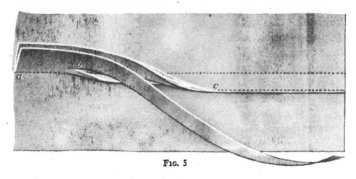

Fig. 5

the longer strip to the right side of the opening and turn the sleeve right side up, creasing the free edges, as shown in Fig. 4 (*a*).

Next, press open the seam that joins the larger piece to the sleeve and crease it down smoothly, as at *b*, Fig. 4 (*b*).   Bring the edge over to the right side and baste it down, as at *c*, taking care that it overlaps the seam edge of the under piece so that this piece will not show when the cuff is fastened.   Also, if striped material is used, be careful that the stripes match, as at *d*.   When the pointed end *e* is turned under, clip away any surplus material and baste this part down very carefully.

When this is done, proceed to stitch, beginning at *f*, which is close to the end of the shorter strip, stitching across to *g*, and then back again ⅛ to ¼ inch above the first cross-row, being careful to stitch through the shorter strip underneath with both rows of stitching. Stitch around the point and down on the inside edge, and then from *f* on the outer edge to the bottom of the opening.

24. Inserting the Sleeves.—The next step is to join the sleeves to the armholes. To do this, baste them in position and finish with a flat fell, as shown in Fig. 5, first stitching in a plain seam, as at *a*, trimming away one edge, as at *b*, and then turning the other edge under and stitching, as at *c*. Remember that it is best to have the two stitchings visible on the right side in making this seam.

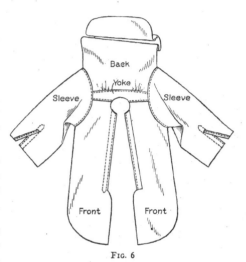

FIG. 6

25. Making the Under-Arm and Lower Finish.—The shirt is now ready to have the under-arm seams stitched. Finish these, also, with a flat fell and stitch them from the ends of the sleeves to a point about 8 inches from the bottom of the shirt, or to the point indicated on the pattern. Fig. 6 shows how the inside of the shirt appears before these seams are stitched.

After stitching the under-arm seams, finish the front, bottom, and side edges of the shirt with narrow hems.

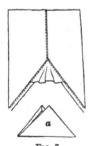

FIG. 7

26. Making the Gussets.—Gussets are placed at the bottom of the side seams to reinforce them. For each seam, cut a square of material that measures 1¾ inches on all sides, fold each square diagonally through the center, as at *a*, Fig. 7, turn the raw edges to the inside, making a very narrow turn, and then baste the turned edges together.

After the under-arm seams are stitched and the hems at the bottom of the shirt are in place, place the gusset with the folded, or diagonal, edge down, the point joining the under-arm seam of the shirt, at its termination, and the straight edges lying along the hems of the lower portion. Stitch the gusset securely in place, as shown in Fig. 7. This prevents the shirt from tearing or ripping at the under-arm seams, thus affording considerable protection.

27. Neck Bands.—As stated, neck bands may generally be purchased ready-made. This is a decided advantage, as they are accurate and inexpensive, too. Furthermore, it requires considerable work to make a neck band. If, however, it is not possible to purchase a neck band, one may be made in the following manner.

28. Material for Neck Bands.—It is not always desirable to make the neck band of the same material as the shirt, as this is often heavy or has cords running through it that will not permit of a smooth finish. Firm, even-weave cambric or long-cloth is especially suitable for neck bands of cotton shirts. Also, an interlining is required so that the band will fit up close and not sag. This may be of lawn or the same material as the band.

Fig. 8

29. Making a Neck Band.—Put the right sides of the two pieces of the neck-band material together and over them place the interlining, which has been cut the same size as the neck-band pieces. Then stitch around the band, beginning at the lower edge of the center-front at one end, continuing around the curved end, across the top, and around to the lower edge on the opposite end, leaving the bottom free. After stitching, trim the edge close to the stitching, say to within about ⅛ inch, then turn the band right side out, and smooth the curved edge carefully, pressing the rounding corners back with a hot iron, if necessary, so that they will lie perfectly flat.

With the band thus prepared, draw the two thicknesses apart, leaving the interlining with the under piece of the band, as at *a*, Fig. 8. Then cut a piece of material about 3 inches long and as wide as the collar band, as at *b*, and place it on the outside against the upper part, or single thickness of the band, directly over the center back, with the right sides of the two together. This piece serves as a protection across the back of the collar.

Next, stitch it ⅛ inch from the edge, turn it over on the inside of the neck band, and stitch across the piece, as at *c*. Turn the band right side out and stitch across the upper edge, as at *d*. This stitching will catch the raw edge of the protection piece and hold it in place across the upper edge of the band.

Remember that when the band is lapped for the front closing, it should measure exactly ½ inch larger than the neck measurement to allow for shrinkage. If it should happen that the band is too large or too small, the alteration should be made equal on both ends

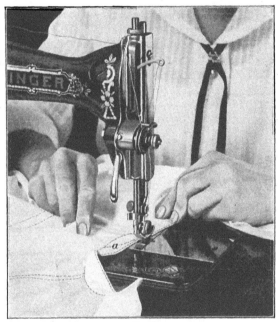

Fig. 9

of the band, so that the shape of the band and the position of its center-front and its center back will not be changed.

30. Applying the Neck Band.—The neck band is now ready to be applied to the shirt. To do this, draw the lower part of the band and the interlining apart and crease the free edge of each of these toward the other. Then place the neck of the shirt between the lower part of the band and the interlining, having the interlining over the right side of the shirt. Baste this in place and then machine stitch, beginning at a point 2 inches from the center back and continuing across the center back to a point 2 inches beyond it on the opposite side.   Then bring the upper layer of the band down and baste it in place across the bottom, leaving the center back free for a space of 3 inches.   Next, stitch across the bottom of the band and up around the center-back opening, as shown at a, Fig. 9, thus leaving a section at the center free, so that the buttonhole may be made through two thicknesses of material only.

If the band, while being stitched on, should appear a trifle large, after it has been tested and found to measure exactly correct, stretch the neck of the shirt enough to permit the outside edge of the front plait and the hem to come exactly even with the ends of the neck band.   Or, if it should seem to be a little small for the neck of the shirt after its correct size has been determined, hold the· neck of the shirt a little full, but without a wrinkle, so as to adjust it in the band.   The safest way to do this is to run a fine gathering thread around the neck edge so that the fulness will be evenly adjusted.

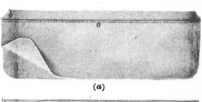

(a)

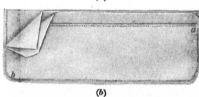

(b)

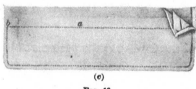

(c)

FIG. 10

31.   Preparing Cuff Interlinings.—Cuffs for a shirt, whether they are to be soft or stiff, require an interlining to give body and enable them to shape well.

For interlining *soft cuffs*, if the material is fairly heavy, one thickness of the material of which the garment is being made will answer; but if the garment material is light in weight, an interlining consisting of two thicknesses of firmly woven material, such as lawn or cambric, should be used.

To prepare an interlining for soft cuffs, if one thickness is to be used, cut the interlining the same size as the cuff, but when two thicknesses are used, make one the same in size as the outside-cuff portion and the other $\frac{1}{2}$ inch narrower, as shown at a, Fig. 10 (a).

For *stiff cuffs*, use butcher's linen or heavy muslin, using two thicknesses, and cut as directed for soft cuffs.

32. Making Stiff Cuffs.—As shown in Fig. 10 (*a*), put the lower edges of two thicknesses of interlining together, baste and stitch along the upper edge of the narrow one, as at *a*, and then clip off the

FIG. 11

corners of the other thickness, as at *b*. With the interlining thus prepared, lay the two pieces for each cuff so that their right sides are together, and on them place the prepared interlining, as shown in (*b*). Next, baste and stitch along the sides and the lower edge in the pattern lines, beginning the stitching at a point about $\frac{3}{8}$ to $\frac{1}{2}$ inch below the top of the cuff, as at *a*, and extending it around to the same distance from the top on the other side. Stitching in this manner will permit the cuff to be sewed to the sleeve with ease.

Next, trim the interlining up to within $\frac{1}{8}$ inch of the stitching, as at *b*, and clip the ends, as at *a*, Fig. 11; then, with a small hammer, proceed to hammer the rounding corners, as shown at *b* and *c*. Hammering the edges down in this way insures a good, flat finish, doing away with all bulky edges, which not only are troublesome to iron over, but give the finished cuff a poor appearance. A hot iron may be used to press down the edges.

When the cuffs are stitched and trimmed and have their edges pressed down, turn each right side out and crease it very carefully all around the outer edges. If this work is well done, so that the edges are perfectly even, and each is then carefully pressed, it will not be necessary to baste them before another stitching, because the interlining will aid in keeping the outer portion of the cuff smooth. To insure a true, even edge, it is sometimes well to work the edge out with the point of a pair of scissors or a stiletto.

Before laying the cuffs aside, stitch them at the ends and the lower side and also $\frac{5}{8}$ inch from the upper edge, as shown at *a*, Fig. 10 (*c*),

so as to make them ready to join to the sleeve.   Stitching their outer
edges before joining them insures against the twisting of either the
upper or the lower section or the interlining.   Such stitching serves
to hold the cuff sections together, so that, in laundering, the iron will
not push them unevenly.

33.   Joining the Cuffs to the Sleeves.—With the sleeve wrong
side out, as in Fig. 12, gather the lower edge of the sleeve by hand,
beginning just beyond the finished edge of the cuff opening on the
upper side and gathering to a point about 4 inches from the seam of

the sleeve, as shown at *a*;
also, from the opening
on the under side, gather
about $2\frac{1}{2}$ inches toward
the seam, as at *b*.   Turn
the underneath edge of
the opening back to the
wrong side and pin it in
place, or turn its edges
in and finish off neatly
and let it protrude as
at *c*.   Then pin and
baste the cuff to the
sleeve, as shown, joining
the interlining and one
thickness of the cuff to
the wrong side of the
sleeve, so that the cuff
may be turned in and
stitched from the right

Fig. 12

side, and also so that there will be only one thickness of material to
turn, thus insuring a neat finish.   The seam of the sleeve should
come at a point about one-third the length of the cuff from one end
of the cuff, as shown between *a* and *b*.

When the cuff is basted on, stitch in the pattern lines.   Then
trim the seam edge close and turn the upper edge of the cuff over
neatly, after which proceed to turn the seam ends in and to stitch
them in position.   In this way, a neat finish will result and a bulky
seam will be avoided.   Begin to stitch at the termination of the
first stitching, as at *b*, Fig. 10 (*c*); then turn and stitch across the

upper edge. As in every case of stitching in the shirt, remember to keep a good stitch, to stitch straight, and to secure all machine threads.

If the ends of the cuffs are not so neat as they should be, overhand the edges together so that a perfectly smooth line will be obtained.

34. Making Separate Shirt Collar.—If a turnover collar is to be worn with the shirt, one made in the following manner will be satisfactory.

Place the two right sides of the collar material together as in making the cuffs, and over this place an interlining of smooth, lightweight material. If the material of which the collar is to be made is very heavy, an interlining will not be required in the turn-over por-

tion; in such a case, just a firm, very lightweight interlining of one thickness in the standing part of the collar will be sufficient. When the collar is made ready, stitch around the edges as for the cuffs, leaving free the edge that is to be joined to the stand. Trim the seam edge close,

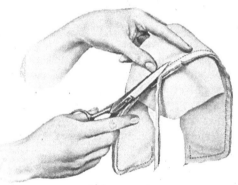

Fig. 13

as shown in Fig. 13, press the rounding corners, turn the collar right side out, and crease and stitch around its outer edge.

Next, prepare the stand section in the same way. To allow for lapping, this section is longer than the upper piece; therefore, in stitching this section, be sure to stitch around the points. Then trim the edges, as described for the collar edges. Turn the stand right side out, press the seams carefully, and turn in the free edges at the upper edge. Insert the edges of the collar between the turned edges of the stand, and baste carefully. Then stitch close to the edge all around the stand.

35. Attaching Separate Collar to Shirt.—Sometimes the stand section of a collar is omitted and the collar is attached directly to the shirt. The method of construction is the same as for a soft stand collar that is to be applied to a shirt, except that the lower part of the collar is left free and the neck of the shirt is inserted between the edges of the collar and stitched flat as in stitching the cuff.

36. Buttons and Buttonholes.—The buttons and buttonholes of a shirt are of great importance because of their prominent position down the front.   Small, flat, pearl buttons are satisfactory and they should be spaced as in Fig. 1; that is, so that the distance between the neck band and the first button and that between each two buttons will be the same.

The buttonholes should be placed exactly in the center of the plait, and they should be cut vertically and about $\frac{1}{4}$ inch longer than the diameter of the button.   As the plait of the shirt will in nearly every case be starched, buttonholes that are too small will be difficult to get over the buttons.

The buttonholes in the cuffs should be located a little more than one-third the width of the cuff from the bottom if single cuffs are used.   In double cuffs, a second buttonhole should be placed the same distance from the top, or the joining of the cuff and sleeve, as shown in Fig. 1.   Also, a buttonhole is worked in the lap finish just above the cuff, as this illustration shows.

The buttonholes in the neck band should be horizontal and placed $\frac{1}{4}$ inch above the joining of the shirt and the neck band. The buttonholes in the collar should correspond with those in the neck band, except that they should be a scant $\frac{3}{8}$ inch above the lower edge of the collar stand, so that the collar will fit down well and cover the seam joining of the neck band when the shirt is worn.

37. Preparing the Shirt for Wear.—It is always advisable to launder a shirt before wearing it; that is, if it is made of material that requires starch.   Such garments of silk material, however, require only a very careful pressing to complete them.

38.   The work shirt differs from a negligée shirt chiefly in that it is made of different material and has an attached collar and wristbands instead of cuffs.   After the material is selected, the shirt may be cut out with the aid of the same pattern as is used for a negligée shirt, or a special work-shirt pattern may be used.   As a rule, a work shirt requires a yoke that is 2 inches deeper than the yoke used for a negligée shirt, so as to give the wearer protection over the shoulders. Therefore, if a negligée-shirt pattern is used in cutting out a work shirt, it is well to remember that the yoke should be made deeper and the back portion shorter to accommodate the increase in size of the yoke. A work shirt should also have a little more allowance for fulness across the back. This allowance—usually 4 inches is enough—may be provided by placing the pattern piece for the back so that its center-back line is 2 inches from the fold of the material.

The collar and wristbands of the work shirt require an interlining, which may be of any of the materials previously mentioned. It is advisable, however, to use an extra thickness of the material for the interlining, because, when these parts become worn, there will then be this extra thickness underneath to which the worn part may be darned. It may be well to note, also, that the collar of a work shirt may be reversed when it becomes worn. This may be done by simply ripping the stitching that serves to hold it to the collar band and then turning it and stitching it back in place.

Fig. 14

MEN'S HOUSE COATS AND ROBES

HOUSE COATS

39. For comfort in the home, perhaps no garment is more enjoyed by men than the house coat, or smoking jacket, one style of which is shown in front and back view in Fig. 14. For such a garment, the proper selection of material is the chief essential. Double-faced, wool-knit fabrics, closely woven Jersey, soft home spun, corduroy, velvet, and quilted satin are materials from which a selection may be made. Generally, a house coat requires the same amount of material for its construction as does a man's negligée shirt. The coat is, of course, shorter than a shirt, but the material is needed for the seams, which are

wider than those of a shirt; also for the shawl collar and the two
patch pockets at the lower side fronts.

40. Cutting out the House Coat.—Before cutting such a garment, to have it a satisfactory length and to have the sleeve correct,
test the pattern as directed for testing the shirt pattern. Then
place the pattern as for a shirt. Provide a lining if the outer
material is such as to require one.

41. Constructing the Coat.—In seaming such material as is
used for house coats, extra precaution must be taken to baste each
seam with small stitches. If this is not done, the thickness of the
material will cause the edge nearest the presser-foot of the sewing
machine to slip forward and thus produce an uneven seam. If no
lining is used, the seams should be so made that the garment will

appear as neat on the
under side as on the
right side. For the closing of a house coat,
simple, durable frogs,
like those shown in the
illustration, are gener-
ally satisfactory.

**LOUNGING ROBE OR
BATH-ROBE**

42. Another com-
fortable and convenient
man's garment for home
use is the lounging robe,
or bath-robe, two styles
of which are shown in
Fig. 15.

Fig. 15

As bath-robes are used
as house coats and also as beach coats, the material varies and
may include brocaded velvet or silk corduroy, silk poplin, faille,
Jersey, soft homespun, eiderdown, light-weight flannel, mohair,
ratiné, terry cloth, and blanket cloth. Those used only for lounging robes are, as a rule, quite conservative in color and conventional
in material. One would not use, for example, a bath-robe of blanket

cloth as a lounging robe. One's own sense of fitness must be brought into play in the selection.

43. Construction of Robes.—A robe of this kind is made in much the same manner as a house coat but it is much longer, of course, usually extending to a point half way between the knees and the ankles or to the ankles. For such a garment, a plain notched coat collar or a shawl collar may be used, as desired. The robe is usually double-breasted, in coat fashion, and a cord or a narrow strap sash of the material is placed around the waist. In order to hold the cord or the sash in position, it is necessary to place small strips at the under-arm seams through which the cord or the sash may be inserted.

A bath-robe usually has the pockets below the waist line and is a trifle larger than a robe that is used as a house coat.

TROUSERS

TYPES OF TROUSERS

44. Short, Straight Trousers.—There are three distinct types of trousers, which may be varied to suit the prevailing fashion. The first type is the short, straight trousers for little boys. This type may be finished to wear with separate blouses or to be buttoned to a blouse, making a suit, the trousers being finished straight or bloused at the lower edges, or having a long flare as in the sailor type.

45. Knickerbockers.—The next type is the knickerbocker style, the trousers that blouse at the knee. This type is generally chosen for young boys, but from time to time, as Fashion dictates, it may be varied to suit both men and women for sports wear. The finish at the knee may be varied according to individual taste, the fulness being gathered or plaited into a band that is worn below the knee.

Breeches may be considered a variation of this type of trousers. These are made roomy above the knee, but below are fitted and laced tight to be worn inside leggings or boots.

46. Long, Straight Trousers.—The third type is the long, straight type of trousers, the lower edges of which may be finished with a plain hem or a cuff. The side seam is sometimes finished with silk braid, depending upon fashion and the occasions upon which the trousers are to be worn.

<hr>

MATERIALS FOR TROUSERS

47. Outside Materials.—The materials suitable for trousers are many and should be selected according to the season of the year, the occasions for which they are to be worn, and the age of the person for whom they are made.

Such materials include galatea, duck, drilling, khaki, mohair, panama cloth, linen, denim, corduroy, serge, Poiret twill, broadcloth, tweeds, homespun, covert cloth, flannel, and gabardine. There are many other fabrics, however, such as pongee and velvet, that may be used for trousers for very small boys.

48. Linings.—Then, too, there is the problem of linings for trousers, since lining of some kind is necessary for all trousers. At times only a belt facing, a crotch reinforcement, and pocket linings are made; again, the trousers may be lined half way or entirely, depending on the material used. Corduroy trousers for men and boys and woolen trousers for boys are generally lined throughout. When this is the case, a light-weight fabric is used for the lining proper and the pockets are made of a more firmly woven material than is used for the trousers.

For linings, such materials as cambric, percaline, silesia, or sateen may be selected. For pockets, sateen, galatea, drilling, or firm unbleached muslin is suitable.

<hr>

CONSTRUCTING BOYS' TROUSERS

49. The making of trousers is usually looked upon as a very difficult undertaking, but when one is thoroughly familiar with the foundation principles of sewing and exercises unusual care in the tailoring of such garments, very satisfactory results should be obtained.

There is real economy in making trousers for boys because they can so often be cut down from larger garments. Also, trousers for summer wear can be made of good quality material at considerable saving.

50. Cutting Out the Trousers.—In cutting out the trousers shown in Fig. 16, the point of main importance is to place the pattern so that the center of both the front and the back sections will be on a lengthwise thread of the material.

51. Stitching the Back and Side Seams.—After the material is cut out, join the leg portions at the center back, using a plain seam. Then join the outside edges of the front and the back leg portions with the cord seam, stitching to within 5 inches of the waist line.

52. Stitching the Front Seam and Providing the Fly.—The center-front seam should then receive attention. As a rule, an

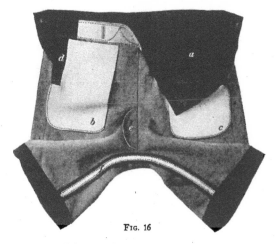

Fig. 16

inside flap, as at *e*, Fig. 16, is provided to cover an opening in the center-front seam of trousers for little boys. This opening is generally 1½ inches to 2½ inches long and comes to about 1 inch above the inside leg seam.

To make the flap or fly, proceed as follows: Cut a half circle from a piece of the material of which the trousers are made, having it a seam's width longer than the opening on either side; then cut a similar piece from lining material. Place the two together and stitch around the curved edge, leaving the straight side open. Turn the flap right side out and press.

Next, place the flap on the right front of the trousers at the place indicated for the opening, having the right side of the flap to the right side of the trousers, stitch it a seam's width from the edge, and fasten the threads securely.

Now place the right and the left fronts of the trousers together and stitch the center-front seam on each side of the fly, fastening the stitching above and below the opening with several back-stitches to prevent the seam from ripping.   The seam edges of the opening are finished when the lining is placed in the trousers.

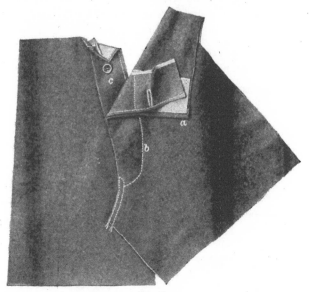

Fig. 17

In making wash trousers, it must be remembered that there is no lining and the seam edges at the opening in the center front are simply whipped back.

53.   Preparing a Blind-Fly Closing.—For trousers of a larger size, the finish of the center-front seam is somewhat different.   A closing with a fly-piece, such as the one shown in Fig. 17, is made. In cutting out trousers with this opening, the only difference is to supply the fly-pieces.

The pattern for the fly is laid on a double thickness of the material, either on a lengthwise or a crosswise thread.   After cutting this portion, place the same pattern piece on three thicknesses of lining material and cut the facings for the fly-pieces.

With one of the pieces of lining, face one portion of the fly for the left side of the opening and press the facing back ⅛ inch from the edge, as shown at *a*, Fig. 18.

Horizontal buttonholes may now be worked through the two thicknesses, as indicated by the chalk marks in Fig. 18, or if not convenient, they may be worked after the garment is finished.

The next step is to turn back the inside curved edge of a second lining piece about ¼ inch and crease along this line. Then open this fold, place the prepared fly-piece on it so that its finished edge is about ⅛ inch beyond the creased line, and baste securely. Stitch between the buttonholes, as at *b*, Fig. 18, sewing through the three thicknesses of material to secure the fly-piece to the facing of the trousers.

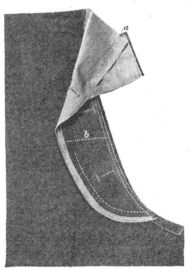

FIG. 18

54. Applying the Fly.—The fly-piece is now ready to be placed on the left front of the trousers. To do this, first crease the left front of the trouser section ⅜ inch from the edge, as at *a*, Fig. 17, and press. Now place the prepared fly-piece so that the side with the buttonholes is next to the right side of the trousers, and baste and stitch the underfacing to the trousers about ¼ inch from the outside edge. This will bring the fly-piece in from the edge of the trousers, thus preventing it from showing from the right side. Turn the fly portion to the wrong side, as shown in Fig. 18. Then baste and stitch the free edge of the fly portion to the trousers as shown at *b*, Fig. 17.

Next, finish the right front. To do this, face the remaining fly portion and place it on the right front of the trousers, as shown at *c*, Fig. 17. Then stitch around the outer edge of this portion to make it firm. The buttons are applied to this piece.

Finally finish the seam below the fly with a double stitching, turning both seam edges to one side.

55.   Lining Boys' Trousers.—The lining for little boys' trousers is cut and joined the same as the outside portion, but it is not basted in until the hip welt pocket is made.   Place the lining in the trousers with the seam lines in the same general position and having the raw edges of the seams next to the trousers.   Pin or baste the lining to the trousers along the seams to hold it in place until the trousers are finished.   The seam edges of the opening at the center front should be whipped to the seam edges of the outer portion of the trousers to make a neat finish for the opening.

56.   Placing the Hip Welt Pocket.—Place this pocket on the right side of the trousers, midway between the back and the side seams, as shown at *a*, Fig. 16, and apply according to the directions given in Arts. **32** to **39,** inclusive, Chapter III, only using a simple curve, as shown in the skirt at the lower right of the illustration in Fig. 35.

57.   Making the Side Pockets.—Next, proceed to make the side pockets.   Sew a lengthwise strip of material along the placket edges, turning the front edge over so that the cord seam of the lower side can be extended up to the waist line and arranging both sides alike.

In some patterns, allowance is made for these pieces; therefore, separate pieces will not have to be applied.   Then, for the pockets, cut two pieces of lining material 8 inches long by 10 inches wide, or smaller, depending, of course, on the size of the trousers.   Fold each of these pieces lengthwise through the center, so that the doubled piece measures 8 inches by 5 inches.   Round the corners at the lower edges, as shown at *b* and *c*, Fig. 16, and stitch the folded portions together along their lower edges and sides to within $4\frac{1}{2}$ inches of the top.   Bind one of the free edges of the sides of each pocket with a lengthwise strip of material that is $1\frac{1}{2}$ or 2 inches wide.

With the pockets made ready, sew them to the placket strips, as at *d*, so that the material of the pockets will be covered up at the side opening and will not show when the hands are put in the pockets.   The pocket must be caught across the top when the band is sewed in position, so that it will not pull down and cause the trousers to get out of shape.

58.   Joining the Inside Leg Portions.—After the pockets are in place, join the inside leg portions, making a plain seam to be pressed open.

If desired, additional strength may be given to the seams of the trousers by securing tape over them, as shown at f, Fig. 16. To do this, place the tape so that its center is directly over the seam line and stitch through to the right side on both sides of the pressed-open seam.

59. Making the Back Inside Belt.—The inside belt is the next portion to be considered. Such a belt may be purchased ready made, but if it is not convenient to procure one, a belt may be made, as shown in Fig. 19.

First, for the back waist line of the trousers, cut a facing 2 inches wide and as long as the measurement of the back waist of the

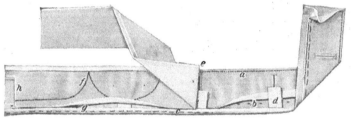

FIG. 19

trousers, plus 1 inch. Make a $\frac{3}{8}$-inch turn on one edge of this piece, and press the creased edge back.

For the inside-belt portion, which is shown in Fig. 19, cut a lengthwise strip of material 4 inches wide and the same length as the facing. Turn one lengthwise edge of this over $1\frac{1}{2}$ inches and baste and stitch this $\frac{1}{8}$ inch from the fold, as at a. Then, in the wider, or under, portion of this strip of material, baste a tuck $\frac{1}{4}$ inch deep, as at b, having the bottom of the tuck $1\frac{1}{2}$ inches from the top of the belt and even with the lower edge of the part that was turned back $1\frac{1}{2}$ inches, as shown. In basting this tuck, do not catch the stitches through the facing strip.

60. When the belt is thus prepared, work the buttonholes. As shown in Fig. 20, there are five vertical buttonholes in the back belt, one in the center back and the others spaced approximately 3 inches apart. Next, turn under the lower edge of the belt $\frac{1}{4}$ inch, or just to meet the other edge, as at c, Fig. 19. Over the fold, or tuck, b, and just opposite each of the three center buttonholes, place a piece of elastic about $\frac{1}{2}$ inch wide and 1 inch long,

4 W I—23

as shown at *d*, and pin in position at the lower edge.   This elastic serves to prevent any strain on the back of the trousers when the child is in motion and also to make it easier to button the belt.

Next, baste the belt portion to the facing strip, having the top of the strip about ⅛ inch above the folded edge of the belt, as shown at *e*.   The lower edge of the facing strip and the turned edge of the belt should be even, as at *c*.   With the basting done, stitch the belt to the facing strip, as at *f*, having the curved part of the stitching come just below the buttonholes and through the elastic, but taking care not to catch the top of the tuck in this stitching.   Then stitch the lower edge of the tuck in from each end and about 1 inch beyond

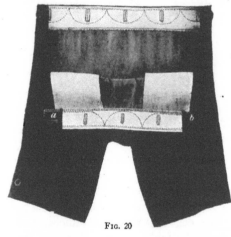

Fig. 20

the first buttonhole, as at *g*.   The rest of the tuck is left free.

61.   Making the Front Inside Belt.—The front belt is made and stitched to the facing in the same manner as the back belt, but, as elastic is used only in the back belt, no allowance is made for a tuck in the front.   Therefore, cut the belt portion only 3½ inches wide.   At each end of the front belt, stitch a piece of dark material about 2 inches long, as shown at *a* and *b*, Fig. 20, and cut the inside belt away under this piece.   This should be done so that the white lining will not show at the sides when the front is buttoned over the back. A buttonhole must be worked through the material and the lining, and this can be done more easily if the inside lining is cut away.

If it is desired to have the trousers fit snug around the waist, a dart about 2½ to 3½ inches long may be placed midway between the center back and the side.   A dart so located will reduce the fulness at the waist and give freedom through the hips.

62.   Applying the Belt.—In applying a belt to any pair of trousers, place the belt section against the right side of the trousers, having the facing strip toward you and its upper edge $\frac{1}{4}$ inch above the waist line. Open out the folded edge of the facing strip and baste and stitch along the creased line. Turn the belt over to the

FIG. 21

wrong side and baste through the two thicknesses of material at the waist line. Then cut away about $\frac{1}{2}$ inch of the inside part of the belt at each end, as at *h*, Fig. 19, and stitch through the belt and the trousers at the sides and the lower edge with two rows of stitching.

63. Finishing the Trousers.—When the band is on, fit the trousers so as to determine what the length should be. Turn a hem at the lower edge, making it $1\frac{1}{4}$ to $1\frac{5}{8}$ inches wide. As a finish for straight pants, three buttons are usually sewed near the lower edge, just in front of the cord seams.

64. Other Waist-Line Finishes for Trousers.—Besides the belt described in Arts. **59** to **61,** inclusive, there are other ways in which the waist line of trousers may be finished. If the trousers button on the outside of a blouse, as in the Oliver Twist type of suit, the waist line is faced back, as in Fig. 21, and buttonholes are worked through the two thicknesses of material.

FIG. 22

Another way is to apply a facing with an interlining, as at *a*, Fig. 22. Turn the lower edge of the facing *b* in a hem and stitch. Then catch this free edge to the seam with overhanding-stitches, as at *c*. You may catch it also to the pocket portion, if desired.   On the outside of the trousers, place straps of the material through which a belt may be drawn or place buttons on the inside of the belt for suspenders.

65.   Finishing Crotch Portion of Unlined Trousers.—The crotch portion of trousers, except those for small boys, is usually reinforced

by means of four pieces of lining material, as shown in Fig. 23.   Cut these pieces so that they fit smoothly and make the two pieces for the front section of the trousers smaller than those for the back.   In applying these pieces, stitch them in with the seams of the trousers, as shown.

The illustration shows these lining pieces notched,

Fɪɢ. 23

as this is the customary edge finish.   If, however, the lining material is likely to fray, the edges will have to be turned under once and stitched.

In the case of breeches, as for example, riding breeches, where not only the seams but the material must be reinforced, the lining pieces are stitched to the trousers.

<hr />

KNICKERBOCKERS

. **66.**   Knickerbockers are made in practically the same way as the straight trousers.   The only difference is in the length and the finish at the lower edge of the leg portions.   Knickerbockers are longer and the fulness is either gathered or plaited in to form a blouse at the knee.

There are two methods of finishing the leg portions; namely, by an elastic or a band of the material.

67.   Finishing With an Elastic.—The simplest method of finishing the leg portions of knickerbockers is with elastic and a casing, and this is especially suitable for very small boys.

Turn a hem or casing at the lower edge wide enough to accommodate the elastic.   Cut the elastic about 1 inch smaller than the leg measurement and insert in the casing. This will hold the fulness in and form the blouse for the trousers.

68. Finishing with a Band.—For knickerbockers with a band, examples of which are shown in Fig. 24, arrange an opening 2 inches deep at the side of the leg portion above the lower edge and finish the opening by facing or simply hemming it back. Then gather or plait the lower edge of each.

Next, prepare the band for each leg, by cutting a band of material ⅝ to 1 inch wide and long enough to fit around the leg above the knee, plus 1½ inches for finishing. Interline it with canvas or percaline, and then line it with a lining material of a color to match that of the knickerbockers. Place the bands so that the edges of the trousers are between the outer material and the lining of the band and so that the front section of the trousers laps over the back, having the end of the band extending 1½ inches beyond the front section of the trousers. Baste the band and stitch in position.

69. Fastening the Band. There are several methods of fastening the band. Perhaps the most popular way is to place a buttonhole in the band at the end that extends beyond the opening and to sew two buttons on the under portion of the band, spacing these so that one will permit the band to fit around the leg above the knee and the other below the knee.

Another method is to buckle the band. To do this, apply a small gun-metal or nickel buckle, putting it on the same way that a buckle would be applied to a belt, and work eyelets in the strap for the prongs

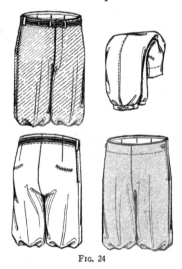

Fig. 24

of the buckles. Such buckles may be purchased or they may be taken from a worn pair of knickerbockers. If the buckles are for ornamentation only, they may be sewed to the straps directly below the side seam, and a large hook and eye placed underneath, so as to hold the strap in place.

70.   Men's pajamas, as shown in Fig. 25, consist of a short loose-fitting coat shirt and a pair of loose-fitting trousers. Such garments, which are frequently made in the home, are simple in the extreme; but, in order to be satisfactory, they must be accurately cut and neatly made.

71.   Materials.—As to materials, wash silk and soisette seem to be the most desirable for pajamas, but such materials as soft muslins and flannelettes, as well as soft madras, pongee, sateen, long cloth, and firm dimities in attractive stripes or crossbar effects,

Fig. 25

are frequently employed. Usually, 5½ or 6 yards of 36-inch material or 6½ or 7 yards of the 32-inch material is ample for pajamas to be worn by men of average size, especially if care is exercised in placing the pattern pieces on the material.

72. Constructing the Coat.—In constructing pajamas, the coat is seamed up in a way similar to a negligée shirt, but it is finished with a plain hem at the bottom of the sleeves and the coat. Or, as shown at the lower left in Fig. 25, pointed turned-back cuffs may be used.

As to the neck line, there are several appropriate finishes, perhaps the most popular being the fitted facing. This facing should be cut to form a yoke at the back and to extend all the way down the center front. The corners at the center front of the neck of the coat may be rounded, as shown in the illustration; or, if desired, they may be pointed.

Another way in which to finish the neck is to face the left-front section back to the center-front line and attach a military collar to the neck of the coat, as shown at the upper left.)

73. Constructing the Trousers.—The opening at the front of the trousers is finished in somewhat the same manner as the opening of a boy's trousers explained in Art. **54,** but with the lining omitted.

The waist line of the trousers is finished with a casing $1\frac{1}{4}$ inches wide, and through this casing is run a 1-inch tape, the ends of the tape extending sufficiently to tie at the center front, as shown. If it is not convenient to use tape for this purpose, a cord that is durable enough to bear considerable wear may be made by seaming up a lengthwise strip of the material and then turning it right side out. Such a cord may be neatly finished by sewing a tiny tassel on each end.

Often an elastic is preferred to a tape or a cord. This should be about 2 inches shorter than the waist measurement.

UNDERGARMENTS

TYPES AND MATERIALS

74. Styles of undergarments for men and boys vary considerably, but as the details of construction are all similar and as the construction of such garments is simple, they may be very easily made at home.

Types of such garments are shown in Figs. 26, 27, and 28. Figs. 26 and 27 show the one-piece garment with different styles of back closings, and Fig. 28 shows the two-piece suit. Any one of these types may have sleeves if desired. Also, they may have narrow facings around the neck or a reinforced back yoke, as in Fig. 26.

75. For such garments one may choose soisette, madras, or the soft cotton cross-bar generally referred to as pajama check. The one-piece type, of course, requires the least material and is the type usually preferred. From $2\frac{1}{2}$ to 4 yards of material is required for such garments, depending on the style of garment and the size of the person.

CONSTRUCTING ONE-PIECE UNDERGARMENTS

76. Cutting the Material.—In cutting these undergarments, the two points of greatest importance are: First, to place the pattern so that it is on a correct grain of the material, and second, to mark the joining points carefully.

77. Seam and Edge Finishes.—In making such undergarments, the same general construction details as given for shirts and trousers may be followed. The flat fell-seam is used throughout to give strength, and for the finish of the neck and armholes, bias facings are necessary, but for the legs and sleeves, if there are sleeves, narrow hems may be turned, as shown.

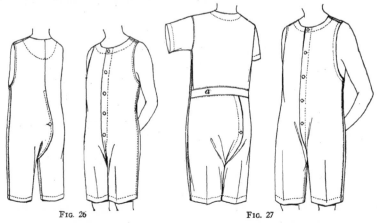

FIG. 26   FIG. 27

78. Front and Back Closings.—The *front closing* may be finished in the form of a plain hem, or a bias facing may be applied.

In the case of the *back closing*, the method depends on the style. For Fig. 26, simply seam the back and face the rounded section, providing, of course, the button-and-buttonhole joining as shown.

For the closing illustrated in Fig. 27, join the upper part of the drawers to the lower part of the shirt by means of a plain fell-seam. Or, if strength and ease in this part of the garment are desired, a bias piece of material 3 inches wide may be inserted, as at *a*, Fig. 27. Another method of preparing such a section is to place a $\frac{3}{4}$-inch tuck in the strip and baste but not stitch. The tuck is then secured only at the ends. When the basting is removed, the tuck is free to open, and this gives ease.

If a number of garments are being made, it will be advisable to purchase an inexpensive knitted shirt as such material is preferable for this inserted section. The upper back section is then brought down over this piece and basted and finished with a flat fell.

CONSTRUCTING TWO-PIECE UNDERGARMENTS

79. In constructing the two-piece undergarment, Fig. 28, the front, seams, arm-holes, and neck of the shirt are finished the same as in the one-piece suit, and a hem is turned at the lower edge.

80. The waist line of the drawers may be fitted slightly by taking a dart at each side. Then the waistband is

Fig. 28

applied and the yoke adjusted so that its upper edge is along the upper edge of the waistband. The yoke should be on the right side when finished. Such a yoke may be cut double and the drawers section placed between the two thicknesses of the yoke, if desired.

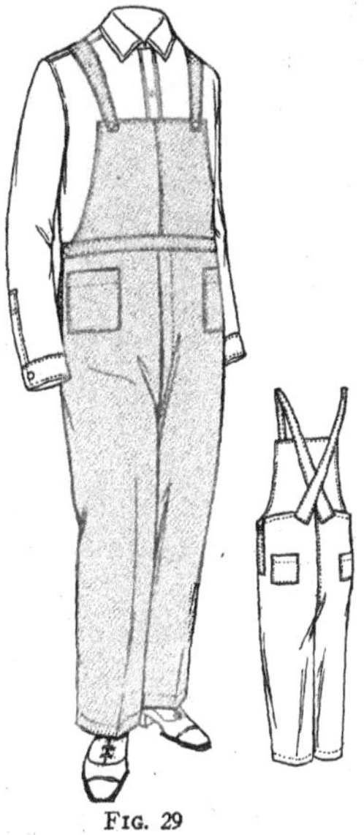

81. In Fig. 28 stay pieces are shown stitched in the crotch section. Such facings may be applied to any undergarment to give strength.

OVERALLS

TYPES AND MATERIALS

82. Under the term *overalls* are included the straight-pants style, the attached bib overall, the apron overall, which consists of the trousers and bib cut in one, and the one-piece combination overall suit consisting of an overall with a roomy work-shirt top. This last type is generally worn by dairymen and mechanics.

Fig. 29

83. For overalls, heavy, coarse materials that are not too firmly woven should be used, as such garments are subject to hard wear and require frequent laundering. Denim, khaki, drilling, and galatea meet these requirements and are very satisfactory.

CONSTRUCTING OVERALLS

84. Trousers and Bib.—The same method of procedure is followed for making overalls as for pajama trousers except that there is no fulness at the waist line.

First, finish the trousers with a placket facing at each side and turn a hem at the top across the back of the trousers. Next, finish the bib section by turning a hem at the upper edge and using a seam at the center front, if necessary.

Then finish the front by joining the trousers and the bib. To do this, place the outside-belt section with its right side to the right side of the trouser portion and baste. Then place the bib with its right side to the right side of the upper edge of the belt and baste. Next, turn all raw edges of the facing, or under section, to the wrong side of the material and place this on the belt section with their wrong sides together, covering the seams, and allowing the facing to extend slightly beyond the edges of the belt piece. Baste it flat and then stitch from the right side, catching all edges.

85. Straps.—To attach the straps, stitch them securely to the waist line at the back, cross them slightly above the waist line, and then stitch in position. To finish the straps in front, you may shape them in a pointed or a rounded end to draw through buckles fastened at the top of the bib, or you may provide them with buttonholes and button them in place.

86. Pockets.—The kind of pockets used in overalls depends upon the use of the garment. For boys' overalls, two medium-size patch pockets each side of the front will prove sufficient.

For work overalls, however, pockets should be both larger and more numerous. Patch pockets may be placed on the front- and back-trouser sections and even on the bib, some being made definite sizes for the purpose of carrying special tools. Straps stitched securely on the back of the trousers also prove convenient for tools. At the side near the placket openings, it is possible to insert long, narrow, inside pockets.

WORK COAT

TYPES AND MATERIALS

87. The work coat covers many uses and embraces many variations in style, including slightly fitted office coats, surgeons' coats, barbers' and mechanics' jackets, and the long type usually worn as dusters.

88. Materials for such garments cover a wide range because of the various uses of the coats. For office coats, light-weight homespun, mohair, and pongee are appropriate. For white coats, butcher's linen and duck or linen-finished suiting are generally preferred. For the typical work jacket, firm coarse fabrics in dark colors, such as denim, khaki, drilling, and galatea, should be chosen. All of these materials, you will notice, will stand frequent laundering, a most important requirement in coats of this kind.

CONSTRUCTING THE JACKET

89. The construction of a jacket like the one shown in Fig. 30 is similar to that of the pajama jacket in that seams are usually made in the form of a flat fell, and the pockets are patch pockets. There are several different features, however, such as the opening at the center front, the neck finish, and the cuff, and in some patterns the placing of the seams. Most patterns have just the seams under the arms, but in addition to these seams some provide a seam down the center back and others have a seam only in the back.

FIG. 30

Proceed as for making the pajama coat and finish the neck and sleeves according to the type of coat desired. If a notch collar is made, remember to place a soft interlining across the back to hold the collar in shape, as directed in Art. **34.**

BOYS' BLOUSES

MATERIALS AND TYPES

90. The same kinds of materials are used for boys' blouses as are employed for men's shirts, with possibly the exception that the quality is usually softer and lighter in weight. About $1\frac{1}{4}$ to $2\frac{1}{2}$ yards of material is generally sufficient for a boy's blouse. As will be seen on referring to the two styles shown in Fig. 31, a

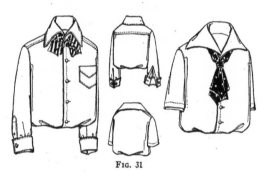

FIG. 31

blouse is finished in similar fashion to a man's shirt. The collar may be attached, as shown, or a Buster Brown or a stiff upright collar may be worn. The sleeves may be finished with cuffs, or they may be of a length that comes just to the elbow, when they should be finished with a plain 1-inch hem. Such a sleeve finish is very practical for blouses intended for summer wear.

METHODS OF CONSTRUCTION

91. To develop a boy's blouse, proceed just the same as in making a man's shirt. The pattern will contain practically the same lines as a shirt, and the method of finishing the seams, namely, with a flat fell, is the same.

Making the shirt into a blouse is the one feature that differentiates the blouse from the shirt, this requiring a casing for an elastic. Therefore, to provide for the blouse and a $\frac{5}{8}$- or $\frac{3}{4}$-inch casing through which elastic is run, allow $3\frac{1}{2}$ inches below the waist line.

BOYS' NORFOLK SUITS

NATURE OF SUITS

92. Although Fashion varies the style of boys' suits as in the case of other garments, the changes are less noticeable. In suits for boys, in fact, there is one type that may be considered almost as a standard, namely, the Norfolk, as shown in Fig. 32. This type of suit consists of knick-erbockers and an easy - fitting, straight, plaited jacket, used not only for boys but for girls, women, and men as well. The general lines of such suits vary slightly from time to time, but their construction details remain practically the same.

FIG. 32

93. Trousers.—Since the trousers for a Norfolk suit do not differ from separate trousers, the details of trouser making, already covered in this chapter, should be applied to the knickerbockers for a Norfolk suit. A point to be noted is that the trousers of even an unlined suit should have some lining, the inside band and fly facings always being lined.

94. Jacket.—It is the jacket that has special features, differentiating it from other short coats. Chief among these are the yoke, both back and front, and the box plaits at each side, both back and front. A belt, also, is a necessity in a Norfolk suit.

Jackets may be either lined or unlined, as desired, the unlined being generally the jackets of wash suits

MATERIALS

95. The material for a boy's Norfolk suit depends on the season of the year and the purpose for which the suit is required, a typical sports suit, such as this, requiring coarser fabric and reinforcements at points that will be subjected to hard wear.

In determining materials for suits, the same list suggested in Art. 47 as suitable for trousers may be followed. The lining and pocket materials also are the same as for trousers. In addition, for a heavy, lined suit that requires interlining, tailors' canvas is needed to give body and hold the suit in shape.

CONSTRUCTING AN UNLINED JACKET

96. Cutting Out the Material.—After adjusting the pattern pieces to make them correct in length and width to suit the measurements of the boy, place the pattern pieces on the material with especial care to have each piece on the proper grain of the cloth in order to insure its appearing well in the finished garment.

The pocket pieces for the jacket of an unlined suit are generally cut from the same material as the suit, at least in the case of the side of the pouch that shows inside the coat.

Occasionally, even in unlined suits, a slight firmness is required in the collar and lapels and sometimes in the fronts. Such firmness may be provided by using an interlining of cambric or unbleached muslin. The pieces for the interlining may be cut from the coat pattern and joined in the seams with the outer material.

97. Adjusting the Plaits.—The first step in making a Norfolk jacket is to form the plaits. Lay them in position and then baste, press, and stitch them.

98. Making Shoulder and Under-Arm Seams.—Lay out flat the fronts and the back, and place the yoke sections in position; then join by basting as directed in Art. 21 for the yoke in a man's shirt. Next, baste the shoulder and under-arm lines.

99. Sleeves.—The sleeves should now receive attention. Baste the seams, easing in, at the elbow, the slight fulness that is provided to give an easy fit. If the seam lines are straight, stitch the bottom, but if there are extensions on the pattern seams, leave these free and turn under the extension on the upper-sleeve piece and allow the other to extend under the lap. Baste these in position before stitching.

100. First Fitting.—The suit is now ready for the first fitting. Slip it on, adjusting it carefully, and note the fit of the neck line, the shoulders, the front, and the back, making any necessary altera-

tions in the seams. Mark the position of the pockets. Next, draw
on one sleeve to determine its length and width.

After removing the coat, baste the new lines, if changes were
made, and then stitch the seams, the kind of seam used depending
on the material and the purpose of the suit. Usually, the plain or
the welt seam provides a satisfactory finish, but a machine fell
may be used for a heavy cotton suit.

101. Taping and Facing.—It is now necessary to tape the edges
to make them firm and true. Tape is used whether the coat is
lined or unlined, except in the case of a suit of firm wash fabric for
a small boy, when taping may be omitted. Apply the tape as
explained in Art. **69**, Chapter VII, referring to Fig. 28 when
doing so.

If the coat is not to have outside stitching, whip the other edge
of the tape to the interlining, as shown, using stitches that will hold
well in place but that are not tight.

Fɪɢ. 33

If outside stitching is to be used, it is not necessary to secure the
inner edge of the tape, as the outside stitching serves this purpose.

102. Collar.—In preparation for the collar, first close the
center-back seam. Since, even in a suit of wash frabic, it is well
to have a firm collar, place over the collar a piece of canvas or firm
unbleached muslin cut a trifle smaller than the collar piece. Baste
this very flat and then, in the lower section indicated by the basting
or break line at *a*, Fig. 33, stitch through the two thicknesses of
material from *b* to *c* and then again below this several times to
give firmness to this section. Next, press the collar, drawing
the stitched piece around to shape it slightly.

Now, turn the neck edge of this prepared piece over the edge
of the interlining and stitch into place. Then apply the collar to the
coat and slip-stitch it along the neck edge.

103. Pockets.—The pockets may be simple patch pockets or flap pockets. For an unlined suit, patch pockets are advisable because they may be completed without cutting into the coat and are finished on the outside of the jacket.

104. Inserting the Sleeves.—After making the pockets, baste the sleeves into the armholes, turn a hem at the bottom, and whip it into position.

105. Second Fitting.—During the second fitting, adjust the closing properly and see that the collar and break line appear to the best advantage. If alterations are required, fit from the seams.

After fitting, make any necessary corrections and then stitch the sleeves in the coat.

The next step is to place a straight, seamless piece, cut the same as the collar, over the collar on the coat, placing the right side of the piece to the under side of the collar and stitching along the outer edge. Then turn to the right side and baste and press to give a true edge. Turn in the top of this upper-collar piece along the neck edge and baste and then slip-stitch into place.

106. Finishing.—To finish the seam edges in such a suit, the most satisfactory method is to bring the two edges together on each seam and cover them with seam binding. Next, work buttonholes and sew the buttons on the suit.

MAKING A LINED NORFOLK JACKET

107. The procedure in making a coat that requires a foundation, padding, and lining is similar to that in making a wash suit, but more care is required in handling woolen fabric and in cutting the suit.

108. Cutting the Sections.—When cutting out the coat, cut out the lining also. The same pattern may be used for the lining as for the suit, but the plaits should be laid in the pattern pieces and pinned before they are placed on the lining material, and the fronts should be cut to extend only 1 or 1½ inches beyond the front facings. Also, the lining should be cut without a yoke.

In cutting the back lining, place a ¾-inch lengthwise plait in the center of the material. This plait, when in the garment, is secured only at the top and the bottom and provides an easy-fitting lining.

If the coat is made of firm woolen material, in addition to the lining it is necessary to cut extra strips to be used as an interlining for the fronts of the coat and across the back of the neck. These may be cut from the coat pattern, if pattern pieces for them are not provided.

To do this, pin the yoke section to the lower-front section of the coat pattern. Place this front section on a piece of paper, and trace around the outer edge from the shoulder seam down the front and across the lower edge to a point that will make the section ½ inch narrower than the width of the coat facings. From this point, trace a curved line to a point on the armhole near the under-arm seam. This will give a pattern piece similar in shape to section *a*, Fig. 5 (*a*), Chapter VII. Then place the back of the yoke pattern on a piece of paper, having the center-back line on a fold, and trace the neck curve and along the shoulder line for about 2½ inches. Now measure down on the center-back line 2½ inches and join these two points by a curved line, following the neck line as a guide.

Interlinings of muslin or canvas must also be provided for the yoke, or, if there is no yoke pattern, a section may be traced from the coat pattern, as at *a* and *b*, Fig. 5 (*b*), Chapter VII. Such sections provide firmness. Pocket pieces also should be cut from firm lining.

109. Assembling the Sections.—In putting the interlinings in the coat, place them flat on the coat material under which they are used and baste thoroughly to prevent any possibility of drawing them out of place in working. More pressing is required in making a suit of woolen material than is necessary in the case of one of a washable fabric, but the general procedure in construction is the same.

Baste the seams of the coat and sleeves, fit the coat, and then stitch the seams that have been fitted. Join the facings by basting and stitching, and make the pockets. Next, make the collar and baste it to the coat; also, baste the sleeve into the armhole.

During the second fitting, it may be found necessary to put in padding at the shoulder and armholes to give a smooth fit. The padding may be joined to the armhole seam, as shown in Fig. 34, Chapter VII.   Cut the padding crescent shape of several thicknesses of sheet wadding, having each layer slightly smaller than the preceding one; arrange them so that the smallest is on top; and then fasten them together with diagonal basting.   After the second fitting, proceed to finish the coat as far as putting in the lining.

110.   Putting in the Lining.—Sew up the under-arm seams of the lining, but leave the shoulder seams free.   Next, slip the lining into the coat, turning the inside seams of the lining to the inside seams of the coat.   Smooth the lining and baste it carefully in place, bringing the back edge of the lining over the front at the shoulder and joining this seam with slip-stitching.   Turn under the outer raw edges of the lining, except at the bottom, bringing the lining over the edge of the facings and covering the joining line of the collar. Baste the lining in place and finish it with slip-stitching.

Finally, turn up the bottom about ½ inch from the edge and join to the lining by slip-stitching.

The sleeve lining should now be stitched and put into the sleeve. First, turn the lining up about ½ inch from the lower edge and slip-stitch this edge in place.   Then turn in the top edge over the coat lining at the armholes and whip the joining.

Fig. 34

BOYS' OVERCOATS

TYPES AND MATERIALS

111.   There is a place in every boy's wardrobe for at least one overcoat.   Such a coat should be made to give warmth, permit freedom of motion, and yet follow the lines of the prevailing fashion.

Boys' overcoats, like others, vary as to fashion features, but they may be divided into two distinct classes; single-breasted and double-breasted.   The double-breasted overcoats include the types referred to as reefers and mackinaws and are probably the more popular, especially for the older boys.   But for very small boys, the single-breasted overcoat proves very satisfactory. The one illustrated in Fig. 34 is the simplest style to make. This may be worn with or without a belt.

Coats for boys may be lined or unlined, as desired.

112. The materials used for boys' overcoats depend upon the season of the year, the age of the child, and the occasions on which the coat is to be worn. The following materials are all well adapted to such coats: serge, chinchilla, tricotine, Poiret twill, tweed, covert cloth, cheviot, Jersey cloth, kersey, homespun, camel's hair, polo cloth, Bolivia cloth, poplin, gabardine, velveteen, and broadcloth.

The materials used for lining purposes are the same as for the Norfolk suit.

_____

CONSTRUCTING A BOY'S SINGLE-BREASTED OVERCOAT

113. Cutting Out the Coat.—Before placing the pattern pieces on the material, test them to make sure that they correspond to the measurements of the child for whom the coat is intended. Then place the pattern on the material, following the instructions that accompany the pattern in order to have each piece on the proper grain of the material.

114. Cutting Out the Lining.—If the coat is to be lined, cut a lining over the coat pattern. Make the front sections just wide enough to extend a seam's width beyond the inner edge of the facing. This point is usually indicated by perforations on the pattern piece. In cutting the lining for the back of the coat, allow 2 inches at the center back for a plait. This gives ease to the lining and prevents the drawing of the coat across the back between the shoulders.

115. Actual Construction.—The first step in constructing a coat of this type is to baste the shoulder and under-arm seams. Next, baste the seams in the sleeves, easing in the slight fulness at the elbow. Now, try the coat on to see whether any alteration is necessary; then stitch the seams and apply the facings and tape. Next apply the collar and pockets as directed in making the Norfolk coat.

The method of finishing such a coat is the same as for the Norfolk jacket, except that in a coat for a small boy no padding is required.

CONSTRUCTING A BOY'S DOUBLE-BREASTED OVERCOAT

116. Practically the only point of difference between the single-
and the double-breasted overcoats is that the front sections of the
latter are wider, so that they overlap farther.   The instruction for
the cutting and constructing of this type of coat, therefore, is the
same as that given for the single-breasted overcoat.

The double-breasted coat is sometimes varied by adding a yoke,
as in the case of a mackinaw.   In that case, the instruction given in
regard to the yoke of the Norfolk coat is applicable.

EXAMINATION QUESTIONS

Your answers to the following list of questions, which is divided into three sections, constitute the work that you are required to send us on this Bound Volume. It will probably be of advantage to you to prepare the first section and send it to us, then the second, and finally the third. However, if you prefer and you feel that you understand the contents of the volume well enough, you may send your answers to all of these questions at one time.

PART I

1. (a) What features are to be avoided in press cloths? (b) How are the cloths prepared?

2. What are the uses of a ham cushion?

3. Why is an evenly moistened cloth essential for proper shrinkage?

4. How does the method used in shrinking glossy materials differ from the process employed for dull-surfaced wools?

5. What is the purpose of the eyelet in a tailored buttonhole?

6. Name the buttonholes that are generally classed as tailored buttonholes.

7. Why is an interlining necessary in garments in which tailored buttonholes are worked?

8. Submit a sampler of a tailored buttonhole.

9. Submit a sampler of the material-bound buttonhole.

10. Submit a sampler of a crowfoot.

PART II

1. What points are most important in making tailored pockets?

2. (a) Why is a reinforcing strip used under the opening of a pocket? (b) Of what material should it be cut?

3. (a) How is the position of flap pockets determined? (b) How are they marked?

4. What should be the size of a welt pocket when used as: (a) a breast pocket? (b) a side pocket?

5. Submit a sampler of a welt pocket, as shown in Fig. 25, Chapter III.

6. What are the four methods used in finishing the top of a skirt?

367

7. Submit a sampler of the plain hem in woolen material, using the finish recommended for materials that fray. Send in the sampler without removing the bastings.

8. At what point are plaits first arranged when plaiting a skirt by hand?

9. (a) Why must particular care be given when making a circular skirt? (b) What precaution should be taken to overcome sagging in a circular skirt?

10. Explain what is meant by the term *gored skirt.*

PART III

1. What are the two types of tailored blouses?

2. How are the various pattern pieces of the mannish blouse placed in relation to the grain of the material?

3. Tell in your own words how to insert the sleeves in a mannish blouse.

4. What precautions are necessary when buying a pattern for a tailored garment?

5. What four measurements are necessary when cutting the straight-line, one-piece dress?

6. How do you prepare and turn the belt for the straight-line, one-piece dress?

7. Why is the front of the blouse in the simplicity two-piece dress cut longer than the back?

8. Submit a sampler of center-stitched binding, as described in Art. **77,** Chapter VI.

9. When are darts particularly desirable in a tailored frock?

10. Why is it advisable to run a gathering thread across the back-neck line of a tailored dress?

11. Why is the neck line of the dress in Fig. 54, Chapter VI, finished separately?

12. Submit a sampler of machine couching.

13. How should the size of the hip line of the tailored frock with mannish yoke compare with the size of the hip measure?

14. Why is the tailored satin dress practical?

15. What is the chief recommendation of the tailored suit?

16. What are the first of the essential features to consider when planning a tailored suit?

17. Why is it wise to use a muslin model in making a tailored coat?

18. Why is the lining cut larger than the coat itself?

19. What is the mission of a coat foundation?

20. What sort of foundation is most in use at the present time?

21. Submit a sampler of the stitch used for quilting, known also as the padding-stitch.

22. If there is a slight fulness in the upper part of the sleeve in the back, how should it be handled?

23. Cut a picture of a tailored suit from a fashion publication and tell briefly the kind of material you would use in developing it, how much material would be required, and the coat makings that would be needed. Send the picture with your answer.

24. What is the advantage of fastening the seams of the sleeve lining and the sleeve together?

25. What are the advantages of a suit dress?

26. Name three practical features that are a part of the cape shown in Fig. 49, Chapter VII.

27. Why is a back yoke used in a man's shirt?

28. What measurements must be considered in purchasing a pattern for a shirt?

29. What is the most popular finish for the neck line of pajamas?

30. What features are necessary in a boy's overcoat?

INDEX

INDEX

INDEX

INDEX